This study by Dr Qaiser Julius represents an important contribution to research into the religious minority experience living under Islamic rule in Pakistan. The author's primary interest is in Pakistan's Christian community. However, his research is helpfully complemented by a consideration of the Pakistani Ahmadi community, who are effectively outcasts from Islam.

Dr Julius considers the history of both communities and their difficult experience of Pakistan's blasphemy laws. He also closely examines the differing responses of Christians and Ahmadis to blasphemy charges. His research is rigorous and his articulation of contemporary events is perceptive and original.

The study concludes with a set of powerful reflections on Christian responses to the blasphemy laws in Pakistan. The author thus provides a sense of hope to Pakistan's embattled Christian community. This book is essential reading for anyone interested in Pakistan and the march of blasphemy laws across the Muslim world.

Peter G. Riddell, PhD
Vice Principal (Academic), Melbourne School of Theology
Professorial Research Associate, Department of History, SOAS,
University of London

Other studies have described the predicament of Pakistan's Christian community. This book breaks new ground with its broad-ranging analysis and especially by comparing the experience of Christians with other religious minorities in Pakistan. It is a remarkable contribution by one of Pakistan's finest Christian theologians.

Rev Tim Green, PhD
General Secretary, Increase Association
Senior Consultant on church-based training, World Evangelical Alliance

This study of the effects of the blasphemy laws in Pakistan on two different communities, Christian and Ahmedi, is highly relevant and timely. The subject is not just extremely charged politically, but it has become an international issue. Qaiser Julius's scholarly and thorough treatment of this sensitive issue lays out the matter in an engaging and thorough manner, while at the same time offering a way forward for the Christian community of Pakistan. It is a must-read for anyone who wants to understand these laws, particularly as there has been so much misinformation about them.

James A. Tebbe, PhD
Rector, Forman Christian College, Lahore, Pakistan

Ahmadi and Christian Socio-Political Responses to Pakistan's Blasphemy Laws

A Comparison, Contrast and Critique with Special Reference to the Christian Church in Pakistan

Qaiser Julius

© 2017 by Qaiser Julius

Published 2017 by Langham Monographs
An imprint of Langham Publishing
www.langhampublishing.org

Langham Publishing and its imprints are a ministry of Langham Partnership

Langham Partnership
PO Box 296, Carlisle, Cumbria CA3 9WZ, UK
www.langham.org

ISBNs:
978-1-78368-301-7 Print
978-1-78368-330-7 Mobi
978-1-78368-329-1 ePub
978-1-78368-331-4 PDF

Qaiser Julius has asserted his right under the Copyright, Designs and Patents Act, 1988 to be identified as the Author of this work.

All rights reserved. No part of this publication may be reproduced, stored in a retrieval system or transmitted, in any form or by any means, electronic, mechanical, photocopying, recording or otherwise, without the prior written permission of the publisher or the Copyright Licensing Agency.

All Scripture quotations, unless otherwise indicated, are taken from the Holy Bible, New International Version®, NIV®. Copyright ©1973, 1978, 1984, 2011 by Biblica, Inc.™ Used by permission of Zondervan.

British Library Cataloguing in Publication Data
A catalogue record for this book is available from the British Library

ISBN: 978-1-78368-301-7

Cover & Book Design: projectluz.com

Langham Partnership actively supports theological dialogue and an author's right to publish but does not necessarily endorse the views and opinions set forth here or in works referenced within this publication, nor can we guarantee technical and grammatical correctness. Langham Partnership does not accept any responsibility or liability to persons or property as a consequence of the reading, use or interpretation of its published content.

Contents

List of Tables ix

Abstract xi

Acknowledgements xiii

Transliteration Scheme from Urdu/Arabic into English xv

Abbreviations xvii

Introduction 1
   The Research Issue, Methodology and Structure
      Research Issue 1
      Research Methodology 2
      Research Structure 3

Part I 5
   Backround

Chapter 1 7
   The Development of Pakistan's Blasphemy Laws
      Introduction 7
      First Period: 1947–1977 8
         The Genesis of Pakistan 8
         The Struggle for an Islamic Constitution 14
      Second Period: 1977–1992 26
         A New Wave of Islamization 26
         Blasphemy Laws 32
      Third Period: 1993–2011 42
         Efforts to Amend Blasphemy Laws 42
      Concluding Summary 48

Chapter 2 51
   A Theological Analysis of Pakistan's Blasphemy Laws in the Light of Islamic Shari'a
      Introduction 51
      Blasphemy in Islam: Definition and Scope 53
      Pakistan's Blasphemy Laws in the Light of the Qur'an 56
         Source Text #1: Surah An-Nisa (Women) 58
         Source Text #2: Surah At-Taubah (Repentance) 61

  Source Text #3: Surah Al-Maida (The Table) 63
 Pakistan Blasphemy Laws in the Light of the Sunna 66
 Pakistan's Blasphemy Laws in the Light of Islamic *Fiqh*
 (Jurisprudence) 71
  The Muslim Blasphemer: Apostate 72
  The Non-Muslim Blasphemer: An Unprotected Person 76
  The Right of God and the Right of Man 78
 Pakistan's Blasphemy Laws in the Light of Muslim Scholarship
 in the Modern Period 80
  Traditionalists 80
  Modernists 84
  The Reformers 88
 Concluding Summary 90

Chapter 3 93
*The Design Flaws in Pakistan's Blasphemy Laws
from a Legal Perspective*

 Introduction 93
 From All Religions to One Religion 95
 Requirement of Intent 100
 Absence of Definitional Specificity 109
 Cognizable Offences 114
 Disproportionate Penalties 119
 No Exceptions for Mentally Disturbed 121
 No Protection for Minorities 124
 Incompatibility with International Covenants 126
 Concluding Summary 128

Part II 131
Experience

Chapter 4 133
Ahmadis and Christians in the Minority Context of Pakistan

 Introduction 133
 Ahmadiyya Movement 133
  Historical Overview of Ahmadiyya Movement 133
  Doctrinal Issues 138
  Pakistan Experience 145
 Christianity in Pakistan 158
  Historical Overview of Christianity in Pakistan 158
  Pakistan Experience 162
 Concluding Summary 173

Chapter 5 175
*The Experience of Christians and Ahmadis under
Pakistan's Blasphemy Laws*
    Introduction 175
    Argument # 1 176
    Argument # 2 183
    Argument # 3 191
    Argument # 4 197
        Case Study of Gojra Incident.....................................200
    Argument # 5 202
        Judiciary 203
        Civil Society 207
        Media 208
    Concluding Summary...211

Part III 213
Response

Chapter 6 215
*An Exploration and Comparative Analysis of Christian
and Ahmadi Responses to Pakistan's Blasphemy Laws*
    Introduction 215
    Similarities..216
        A Sense of Fear and Insecurity 216
        A Trend of Exodus 221
        An Exclusive Approach 226
        A Sense of Disillusionment 229
        A Dependent Approach 231
    Dissimilarities...235
        Sociological Reasons 240
        Religious Reasons 246
        Political Reasons 252
    Concluding Summary...256

Chapter 7 259
*Theological and Contextual Reflections on the Christian Response
to Pakistan's Blasphemy Laws*
    Introduction 259
    Reflection: Sense of Fear and Insecurity 259
        Abandoning the Faith 261
        Fleeing the Country..268

  Question of Christian Ethics 271
  Question of Church's Survival 275
 Reflection: Social Stigma..278
  Theological Perspective 278
  Social Perspective 282
  Political Perspective...284
 Reflection: A Sense of Disillusionment......................................285
  Contextual Sensitivity...286
 Concluding Summary..292

Chapter 8 295
Conclusion: A Way Forward for the Christian Church in Pakistan
 Theological Front..303
 Sociological Front 305
 Political Front 307
 Educational Front 309
 Contextual Front 310

Glossary 313

Bibliography... 319
 Main Sources 319
 Court Cases 346
 (The All) Pakistan Legal Decisions 347

List of Tables

Table 1.1 A Summary of Pakistan's Blasphemy Laws 41

Table 3.1 Changes in the Criminal Procedure Code 97

Table 3.2 Comparison between British and Zia-framed Clauses 99

Table 3.3 Comparison between 298C with Original Clause 298 111

Table 3.4 Statistics of the Cases Registered against Ahmadis in Pakistan (1984 to 2010) 114

Table 3.5 Comparison of Penalties between British and Zia-framed Clauses 119

Table 4.1 Major Differences between Ahmadiyya Factions 136

Table 4.2 Doctrinal Differences between Mainline Islam and the Ahmadiyya Sect 145

List of Charts

Chart 5.1. Blasphemy Cases in Pakistan 1986–2012 177

Chart 5.2. Blasphemy Cases in Pakistan in 2012, with Shia/Sunni Distinction 180

Chart 5.3. Percentage of Blasphemy Cases in Pakistan 1986–2012, with Proportion of Population 181

Chart 5.4. Blasphemy Cases in Pakistan 1986–2012, by Province 182

Chart 5.5. Blasphemy Cases in the Eras before and after the Establishment of Pakistan's Blasphemy Laws 183

Chart 5.6. Blasphemy Cases 1981–2012, by Decade (last column covers only two years). 185

Chart 5.7. Extrajudicial Killings after Blasphemy Allegations Cases 1991–2012 185

Chart 5.8. Extrajudicial Killings of Those Alleged to Have Committed Blasphemy 1990–2012 188

Abstract

The roots of Pakistan's blasphemy laws can be traced back to the British colonial rule in India, but their harsher clauses were added to the Pakistan Penal Code (PPC) during a wave of intense Islamization in the 1980s. Since then, the way the blasphemy laws have been applied has become a serious issue for the minorities in Pakistan. Although no group in Pakistan – not even Muslims – is safe from the misuse of these laws, a disproportionate number of victims have come from two minority groups: Ahmadis and Christians. This study focuses on the ways in which these two minority groups have been affected by Pakistan's blasphemy laws, their different reactions to these laws and, more specifically, why they are responding differently despite living under the same circumstances. Due to the nature of the research subject, the author has employed a hybrid approach in methodology, which is a combination of ethnographic qualitative methods and text-based research, relying heavily on primary sources.

This dissertation begins by examining Pakistan's blasphemy laws on both theological and legal grounds and argues that these laws cannot be justified, either on the grounds of Islamic Sharīa or on the legal grounds of British law, which formed the basis of Pakistan's founding legal system. Therefore, it argues that these laws are contrary to the prevailing law of Pakistan, which is a combination of Islamic and British laws. Further, in the light of the experience of Ahmadis and Christians in Pakistan, the dissertation argues that there is a pressing need to repeal or drastically change these laws in order to stop their misuse. Finally, using an analytical framework, this dissertation examines how Ahmadis and Christians are reacting in different ways to the persecution they suffer and, more specifically, why they are responding differently despite living under the same circumstances. A theological and contextual reflection focuses on the Christian community's response, leading to suggestions for a way forward for the Christian church in Pakistan to understand the sensitive nature of its context and to deal with its circumstances in such a way that the church can survive in its existing circumstances in Pakistan.

Acknowledgements

It is entirely appropriate to acknowledge those who have been a great source of encouragement to me throughout my research journey and especially in writing this dissertation.

First, I want to extend my thanks to Langham Partnership Australia, Church Mission Society Australia, Melbourne School of Theology and Open Theological Seminary (OTS) for supporting my studies in Australia.

Second, I would especially like to thank my supervisors James A. Tebbe and Bernie Power for their encouragement along with their valuable critique on my work which kept me on the track which enabled me to finish my thesis successfully. I am also grateful to Isabel Dale who provided guidance especially in managing qualitative research.

Third, I would also like to name few of my sincere friends especially Fiona Maclean and Christa Cloete who have been a constant support and encouragement to me in my writing. I also like to thank my colleagues at OTS in Lahore: Nadeem Masih, Sajid Imdad and Shakeel Samuel who provided a great assistance to me in conducting the interviews in Pakistan.

Finally, I owe much to my lovely wife Rahila Julius together with my beautiful children Homilia and Hanan who have been an exceptional support during my studies. There are number of other friends in Melbourne and Lahore whose names have not been mentioned here, however they have been a great support to us in many ways during our time in Australia.

Transliteration Scheme from Urdu/Arabic into English[1]

CONSONANTS		INITIAL		NON-INITIAL	
Urdu/Arabic	Roman	Urdu/Arabic	Roman	Urdu/Arabic	Roman
ب	B	د	D	ظ	ẓ
بھ	Bh	دھ	Dh	ع	ʼ
پ	P	ڈ	ḍ	غ	G
پھ	Ph	ڈھ	ḍh	ف	F
ت	T	ذ	z	ق	Q
تھ	Th	ر	R	ک	K
ٹ	ṭ	ڑ	ṛ	کھ	Kh
ٹھ	ṭh	ڑھ	ṛh	گ	G
ث	s̱	ز	Z	گھ	Gh
ج	J	ژ	Zh	ل	L
جھ	Jh	س	S	م	M
چ	cʼ	ش	ś or śh	ن	N
چھ	Ch	ص	ṣ	و	w or v
ح	ḥ	ض	ẓ	ه	H
خ	kh	ط	ṭ	ي	Y

---

1. Tables adopted from John T. Platts, "Transliteration Scheme," in *A Dictionary of Urdu, Classical Hindi and English* (Lahore: Sang-e-Meel Publications, 2003).

VOWELS		INITIAL		NON-INITIAL	
Urdu/Arabic	Roman	Urdu/Arabic	Roman	Urdu/Arabic	Roman
ا	A	اب	Ab	بَد	Bad
اِ	I	اِس	Is	دِن	Din
اُ	U	اُس	Us	بُت	But
آ	Á	آس	Ás	بات	Bát
أو	Ú	أود	Úd	ثُو	Tú
او	O	اوک	Ok	سو	So
أَو	Au	أَور	Aur	نَو	Nau
اِي	I	ایکھ	Ikh	سِي	Si
أي	E	ایک	Ek	بے	Be
أَي	Ai	ایسا	aisá	ہِي	Hai

Abbreviations

Abbreviations of Law Reports

AIR	All-India (Law) Reporter
MLD	Monthly Law Digest
PCr.LJ	Pakistan Criminal Law Journal
PLD	(The All) Pakistan Legal Decisions
PPC	Pakistan Penal Code
PPrC	Pakistan Procedure Code
SCMR	Supreme Court Monthly Review
YLR	Yearly Law Reporter

Abbreviations of Journals, Reference Works and News Papers

AER	*The American Economic Review*
AFR	*The Australian Financial Review*
BECNT	Baker Exegetical Commentary on the New Testament
BST	*The Bible Speaks Today*
CAJ	*Central Asiatic Journal*
FJIL	*Florida Journal of International Law*
HRQ	*Human Rights Quarterly*
IBMR	*International Bulletin of Missionary Research*
IJMES	*International Journal of Middle Eastern Studies*
IJPS	*The Indian Journal of Political Science*
IRM	*International Review of Mission*
JAAR	*Journal of the American Academy of Religion*

JAH	*Journal of Asian History*
JIMH	*Journal of Immigrant Minority Health*
JPMA	*Journal of Pakistan Medical Association*
JPS	*Journal of Pakistan Studies*
JQS	*Journal of Qur'anic Studies*
JRAI	*The Journal of the Royal Anthropological Institute*
JRD	*The Journal of Race Development*
JSS	*Journal of Semitic Studies*
MAS	*Modern Asian Studies*
MJIL	*Minnesota Journal of International Law*
NICNT	The New International Commentary on the New Testament
OEIW	The Oxford Encyclopaedia of Islamic World
OJLR	*Oxford Journal of Law and Religion*
PNTC	The Pillar New Testament Commentary
RJGLB	*Richmond Journal of Global Law & Business*
SFM	*St. Francis Magazine*
TNTC	Tyndale New Testament Commentaries
TNS	*The News on Sunday*
UNDALR	*The University of Notre Dame Australia Law Review*
WTJ	*Westminster Theological Journal*
WUGSLR	*Washington University Global Studies Law Review*

Abbreviations of Publishers

AAII	Ahmadiyya Anjuman-i-Ishaat-i-Islam
AFP	Agence France-Presse
AIRP	Academy of Islamic Research and Publications
CCA	Christian Conference of Asia
CEIP	Carnegie Endowment for International Peace
CFP	Christian Focus Publications
CIPG	The Continuum International Publishing Group

CLAAS	Centre for Legal Aid and Assistance
CLS	The Christian Literature Society
CRSS	Centre for Research & Security Studies
CSC	Christian Study Centre
HRUCS	Human Right Unit, Commonwealth Secretariat
IACCA	International Affairs Christian Conference of Asia
IBS	Islamic Book Service
ICG	International Crises Group
IIC	Institute of Islamic Culture
IIP	Islam International Publications
ISI	Inter-Services Intelligence
IPS	Institute of Policy Studies
ISPCK	Indian Society for Promoting Christian Knowledge
LPH	Lucknow Publishing House
LTP	Law Times Publications
NCCP	National Council of Churches in Pakistan
NCJP	National Commission for Justice and Peace
NPH	National Publishing House
NPRC	Norwegian Peacebuilding Resource Centre
OTS	Open Theological Seminary
RSP	Research Society of Pakistan
SCM	Student Christian Movement
SMA	Shaikh Muhammad Ashraf
YPMM	Young People's Missionary Movement

Abbreviations of Christian Scriptures Quoted

Genesis	Gen
Exodus	Exod
Leviticus	Lev
Numbers	Num
Joshua	Josh

Judges	Judg
1 Samuel	1 Sam
2 Samuel	2 Sam
1 Kings	1 Kgs
2 Kings	2 Kgs
Esther	Esth
Psalm	Ps
Isaiah	Isa
Jeremiah	Jer
Matthew	Matt
Mark	Mark
Luke	Luke
John	John
Acts	Acts
Romans	Rom
Galatians	Gal
1 Corinthians	1 Cor
2 Corinthians	2 Cor
Ephesians	Eph
Philippians	Phil
1 Thessalonians	1 Thess
2 Thessalonians	2 Thess
Philemon	Phlm
James	Jas

Abbreviations of Islamic Scriptures

Qur'an	Q.

INTRODUCTION

The Research Issue, Methodology and Structure

Research Issue

The roots of the blasphemy laws can be traced back to the British colonial rule in India. However, five harsher clauses were added to the Pakistan Penal Code (PPC) during a wave of intense Islamization in the 1980s, under military dictator General Zia-ul-Haq (1977–1988). Under Clauses 295-B and C, anyone who speaks ill of the Qur'an faces a life sentence and anyone who defames the name of the Prophet of Islam faces the death penalty. Since the introduction of these harsher clauses in the blasphemy laws, the way these laws have been applied has become a serious issue for minorities in Pakistan.

Although no group in Pakistan, "not even Muslims," is safe from the misuse of these laws, a disproportionate number of victims have come from two minority groups: Ahmadis and Christians. Both communities in Pakistan feel that the blasphemy laws are like a sword hanging over their necks. This contributes substantially to a deeply imparting atmosphere of intimidation. The sensitive nature of the researched subject made some aspects of gathering information difficult.

This research will investigate the ways in which these two minority groups have been affected by Pakistan's blasphemy laws, the researcher will deal with their different reactions to the persecution they suffer under these laws and, more specifically, why they are responding differently despite living under the same circumstances. This study will help the church in Pakistan to understand the sensitive nature of the context in which it now exists and to respond to its circumstances appropriately, both socially and theologically, in order for it to survive and thrive in the repressive religio- and socio-political context of Pakistan.

Research Methodology

Due to the nature of the research subject, the author has employed a hybrid approach in methodology, which is a combination of ethnographic qualitative methods and text-based research, relying heavily on primary sources.

For the text-based research, the author has primarily relied on law reports, court judgments, newspaper reports, human rights organizations' reports and journal articles.

In order to explore the response of both Ahmadis and Christians to Pakistan's blasphemy laws, the author has employed a mix of strategies. First, semi-structured interviews with Pakistanis, including academics, intellectuals, religious leaders, politicians, legal technocrats, activists and people affected by blasphemy laws, both Ahmadi and Christian Pakistanis, 25 percent of whom were women. In November and December 2013, forty-two interviews were conducted by the author with interviewees, mentioned above. For the purpose of fair analysis, both communities have been given equal weight in data collection: that is, 50 percent of interviews were held with members of each community. Second, other keys have also been used to elucidate this delicate issue, such as the discussion of concrete examples, analogies, case studies, and, more importantly, the key of personal experience and observation.

The interviews were conducted trilingually. Liberty was given to interviewees to speak in Urdu or Punjabi or English so that they could express their views without language barriers. The interviews were audio recorded and notes were also taken alongside the recordings. All interviews have been transcribed into English. In this activity three colleagues of the author from the Open Theological Seminary in Lahore assisted him in recording, taking notes and transcribing the data into English. The data has been analyzed by the researcher.

Why were only 25 percent of the interviewee women when they represent 50 percent of the population in Pakistan? In the case of the Ahmadi community it was almost impossible to get access to the Ahmadi women because they strictly observe *pardah* (i.e. they avoid talking to strangers). The researcher gained permission from some Ahmadi women to interview them through the contacts of Dr James A. Tebbe (supervisor). However, throughout the interviews, no significant differences were found in the overall views expressed by male and female interviewees regarding the impact of blasphemy laws on their communities in Pakistan.[1]

Due to the sensitive socio-political and religious context, the majority of interview participants wanted to remain anonymous, so their identity has been concealed. The Christians are identified by the letter "C" and Ahmadis by the letter "A" in the footnotes.

Research Structure

This study is structured into three major parts:

Part I comprises three chapters. The first chapter explores the historical development of Pakistan's blasphemy laws as background to this research issue. In chapter 2, there is a theological analysis of Pakistan's blasphemy laws in order to assess the extent to which these laws are consistent with Islamic Sharia. Chapter 3 presents a legal analysis of these laws. The purpose of Part I is to assess in what ways these laws might be contrary to Islamic law as well as to the British law which formed the basis of Pakistan's founding legal system.

Part II of our study comprises chapters 4 and 5, which explore the experience of both Ahmadi and Christian communities of living as minority groups in Pakistan and specifically how they have been affected by Pakistan's blasphemy laws. Chapter 4 explores the nature of oppression for Ahmadis and Christians in Pakistan. After surveying the overall situation of Christians and Ahmadis in Pakistan, our study moves to a specific analysis of the experience of both communities under Pakistan's blasphemy laws. In the light of their experience, chapter 5 examines and responds to five arguments put forward by supporters of the blasphemy laws.

---

1. As part of the study various Christians involved in interfaith dialogue initiatives were interviewed. However little or no evidence was found of these initiatives having any impact on the blasphemy laws or on helping to avert violence associated with blasphemy accusations.

After exploring the experience of Ahmadis and Christians under these laws, our study moves to Part III, which examines how Ahmadis and Christians are reacting in different ways to the persecution they suffer and, more specifically, why they are responding differently despite living under the same circumstances. Chapter 6 explores both similarities and dissimilarities in Ahmadi and Christian responses to Pakistan's blasphemy laws. The section on similarities focuses on the ways in which the communities are similar in their responses to Pakistan's blasphemy laws. Our analysis of dissimilarities focuses more specifically on the reasons why each community is responding differently. As the focus of this thesis is the Christian community, chapter 7 provides a theological and contextual reflection on the Christian community's response. Finally, in chapter 8, we offer a way forward for the Christian church in Pakistan to understand the sensitive nature of its context and to deal with its circumstances in such a way that the church can survive in its existing circumstances in Pakistan.

PART I

BACKGROUND

CHAPTER 1

The Development of Pakistan's Blasphemy Laws

Introduction

The Islamic Republic of Pakistan, with a population of over 200 million,[1] is the second largest Muslim country in the world. More than 96 percent of Pakistanis are Muslims and fewer than 4 percent are minorities.[2] In this opening chapter, our aim is to trace the historical development of Pakistan's blasphemy laws. This phenomenon is integrally related to the process of Islamization in Pakistan. We will examine how Pakistan moved towards Islamization and what factors led her in this direction. For the purpose of our enquiry, this chapter's study of historical exploration is divided mainly into three chronological periods.

- First Period: 1947–1976
- Second Period: 1977–1992
- Third Period: 1993–2011

The first period covers the genesis of Pakistan as an independent nation up to the formation of its third constitution. In this period we will examine the Objectives Resolution (OR) followed by three major redrafts of the constitution of Pakistan. The second period will cover the eleven years during which General Zia ul-Haq was in power and the post-Zia years up to 1992.

---

1. Estimated population of 2017 according to Pakistan Bureau of Statistics (PBS), http://www.pbscensus.gov.pk, (accessed 28 August 2017).
2. 96.37% Muslims, 1.59% Christians, 1.60% Hindus, 0.22% Ahmadis, 0.25% Schedule Castes and 0.07% others.

This period is important for our study because it was during this era that Islam re-emerged in a more traditional way, and the harsher clauses of the blasphemy laws were introduced and then incorporated into the Pakistan Penal Code (PPC). Our study of the third period will be confined to mainly looking at the attempts made by different governments to introduce procedural amendments to Pakistan's blasphemy laws.

First Period: 1947–1977

The Genesis of Pakistan

For almost the first millennium after Islam arrived on the subcontinent, it steadily grew, partly through immigration, but much more through conversion.[3] By the time British rule arrived, Muslims had become the second largest community in the subcontinent after Hindus. In a context where religious identity is as important, if not more important, than national identity, there was always tension between these two religious groups. The solution proposed to the ongoing conflict was to separate Muslims and Hindus into two distinct nations. The genesis of the two-nation idea is generally attributed to Sir Sayyid Ahmed Khan.[4] However, the first authenticated clear reference to the demand of a separate homeland for the Muslims in the subcontinent is credited to the great poet and philosopher Allama Muhammad Iqbāl.[5] Initially, Muhammad Ali Jinnah, the man who became the founder of Pakistan, was not convinced by Iqbāl's idea to partition India. However, Jinnah was "looking for the safeguards in a system that would protect the minorities from the majority's arbitrary use of power."[6]

---

3. Kemal A. Faruki, "Pakistan Government and Society," in *Islam in Asia: Religion, Politics, and Society*, ed. John L. Esposito (Oxford: Oxford University Press, 1987), 53.

4. Ayesha Jalal, "Conjuring Pakistan: History as Official Imagining," *IJMES* 27, no. 1 (1995): 75. Some ideologues claim that Pakistan was born on that day when the first Muslim set foot on Indian soil.

5. In his presidential address to the twenty-first session of the All-India Muslim League (AIML) held at Allahabad on 29–30 December 1930, Iqbāl said that "the formation of a consolidated North-West Indian Muslim State appears to me to be the final destiny of the Muslims, at least of North-West India." Syed S. Pirzada, ed. *Foundations of Pakistan: All-India Muslim League documents, 1906–1947*, vol. 2 (Karachi: NPH, 1970), 159.

6. Lawrence Ziring, *Pakistan: At the Crosscurrent of History* (Oxford: Oneworld, 2003), 25.

A few years later, Liaquat Ali Khan (who became the first Prime Minister of Pakistan), convinced Jinnah to support the idea of a separate Muslim nation on the subcontinent. Khan argued that "Gandhi had aroused the Hindu masses and had virtually no opposition in pressing his campaign. Muslims, he noted, had a greater sense of danger than ever before."[7] Muslims felt intimidated because the Hindus outnumbered the Muslims by more than three to one. And "the arithmetic of democracy would assure the Hindus a commanding position from which to ensure that their distinctive tradition dominated that of the Muslims."[8]

The India Act of 1935 finally gave British India a large degree of autonomy in the provinces. But this degree of independence also reinforced the dominance of Hindus in the nation. In accordance with the Act, elections were held in eleven provinces in 1937. The Indian National Congress (INC), a Hindu political party, won with an overwhelming majority in nine provinces.[9] In contrast, in these elections the All-India Muslim League (AIML), was almost eliminated from the political scene.

Given this scenario, Jinnah insisted that the Congress include Muslim members in the government, but his demand was completely overlooked. For example, the Congress party provincial government of Bombay refused to include a Muslim minister in its cabinet.[10] From Congress's attitude, Jinnah and his colleagues perceived a mortal danger for the Muslims from the Hindu hegemony.[11] The bells of future dangers started ringing in the circles of the League's leadership. They felt that "we of the Muslim League who represent the Muslims are to have no further say in the government . . . where the Congress are in a majority."[12] Such feelings of the dangers of Hindu dominance had been expressed by Jinnah clearly in his presidential

---

7. Ibid., 15.

8. Wayne A. Wilcox, "The Wellsprings of Pakistan," in *Pakistan: The Long View*, eds. Lawrence Ziring, Ralph Braibanti, and W. Howard Wriggins (Durham: Duke University Press, 1977), 28.

9. Iftikhar H. Malik, *The History of Pakistan* (London: Greenwood Press, 2008), 105.

10. K. K. Aziz, *History of Partition of India: Origin and Development of the Idea of Pakistan*, 3 vols., vol. 3 (New Delhi: Atlantic, 1988), 627.

11. Ziring, *Pakistan*, 19.

12. Aziz, *History of Partition*, 627.

address to the twenty-fifth session of AIML held at Lucknow on 15–18 October 1937 where he said:

> The present leadership of the Congress, especially during the last 10 years, has been responsible for alienating the Musalmans [Muslims] of India more and more, by pursuing a policy which is exclusively Hindu; and since they have formed governments . . . they have by their words, deeds and programme shown, more and more, that the Musalmans cannot expect any justice or fair play at their hands.[13]

While Congress was enjoying power in the provinces, World War II broke out in 1939, and the Viceroy of India, Lord Linlithgow, declared the Indian Army's support to the British without consulting the Congress, despite the fact that it had control over nine provinces.[14] The Viceroy's declaration was bluntly rescinded by both Gandhi and Nehru, who ordered all the members of Congress to resign from provincial governments in protest against the viceroy having made a decision about India's participation in the war without seeking Congress's formal approval.[15] This act of Congress was a cause of great jubilation for Jinnah, who "called for celebration and declared a 'Day of Deliverance' from Hindu tyranny."[16]

During the war years, Gandhi led a non-cooperation movement to exert more pressure on the British in order to force them to leave India.[17] However, Jinnah and his colleagues in the AIML sensed that independence of India from the British Raj would not mean the independence of Indian Muslims. They foresaw that the consequence of independence from the Colonial Raj would be to bring Muslims under Hindu rule, just as they had experienced as the result of the 1937 elections. As a result, Muslims "would eventually lose their identity."[18] This led the AIML, under the leadership of Jinnah, to

---

13. Pirzada, *Foundations of Pakistan*, 267. See also Jaswant Singh, *Jinnah: India – Partition – Independence* (New York: Oxford University Press, 2010), 240–241.

14. Malik, *History of Pakistan*, 105.

15. Ziring, *Pakistan*, 20.

16. Ibid.

17. In contrary to Gandhi's view, another faction of the INC led by Subhas Chandra Bose sought independence through an armed struggle.

18. Abdullah Ahsan, "Pakistan since Independence: An Historical Analysis," *The Muslim World* 93, no. 3/4 (2003): 253.

put forward the "Pakistan Resolution" on 23 March 1940. This called for the secession of the Muslim-majority provinces from the rest of India to become the independent nation of Pakistan.[19]

During the movement towards the formation of Pakistan, minority Muslim groups raised concerns about their position in the new state where Sunni Muslims would form the overwhelming majority. Their concerns were very similar to those expressed by non-Muslim minority groups, including Christians. The Shia minority was hesitant to support the idea of Pakistan out of a fear that a majority Sunni Muslim state might be based upon Sunni principles and that therefore Shia Muslims would suffer discrimination.[20] In response to this fear, the council for Action of All-Parties Shia Conference passed a resolution on 25 December 1945 rejecting the idea of Pakistan.[21] The Ahmadis (who are generally considered heretical by both Sunni and Shia Muslims) were also reluctant to support the demand for a separate Muslim state.[22] To all these doubters, "Jinnah gave assurances that Pakistan will be a modern state, neutral on sectarian matters."[23] After Jinnah's assurance, Ahmadiyya leadership and many liberal-minded Shias started supporting the demand for Pakistan.[24] There is also strong evidence that many Christian leaders supported the notion of Pakistan as well.[25]

Jinnah was able to gain the support of religious minorities because they were assured of fair treatment in Pakistan.[26] This assurance of fair treatment and equality is clearly evident from the speeches of the founders of Pakistan.

---

19. H. V. Hodson, *The Great Divide: Britain – India – Pakistan* (London: Hutchinson, 1969), 42.

20. Syed A. Zaheer, "Letter to Quaid-e-Azam by Syed Ali Zaheer July 1944 and Quaid's Reply," in *Pakistan Movement: Historic Documents,* ed. G. Allana (Lahore: IBS, 1977), 375–379.

21. S. R. Bakshi, *The Making of India and Pakistan, Select Documents* (New Delhi: Deep Publications, 1997), 848–849.

22. M. Munir and M. R. Kayani, *Report of the Court of Inquiry Constituted under Punjab Act II of 1954 to Enquire into the Punjab Disturbances of 1953* (Lahore: Government of Punjab, 1954), 196.

23. Ishtiaq Ahmed, "Pakistan, Democracy, Islam and Secularism: A Phantasmagoria of Conflicting Muslim Aspirations," *Oriente Moderno* 84, no. 1 (2004): 17.

24. Ibid.

25. Ishtiaq Ahmed, "The 1947 Partition of Punjab," in *Region and Partition: Bengal, Punjab and the Partition of the Subcontinent,* eds. Ian Talbot and Gurharpal Singh (Oxford: Oxford University Press, 1999), 147.

26. Ahmed, "Pakistan, Democracy, Islam and Secularism," 17.

For example, Muhammad Iqbāl in his presidential address to the AIML at Allahabad in 1930 stated, "Nor should the Hindus fear that the creation of autonomous Muslim states will mean the introduction of a kind of religious rule in such States."[27] Jinnah affirmed this in his address to the twenty-eighth session of AIML held at Madras on 12–15 April 1941, where he said, "I am confident when the issue comes up, the minorities in our homeland will find that with our traditions and our heritage, with our teachings of Islam . . . not only shall we be fair and just to them but generous, too."[28]

Following the speech of Jinnah, the AIML passed a unanimous resolution that "adequate, effective and mandatory safeguards shall be specially provided in the Constitution for minorities in the above-mentioned units and regions for the protection of their religious, cultural, economic, political, administrative and other rights and interests in consultation with them."[29] Liaquat Ali Khan's comment on the resolution is notable: "the safeguards for non-Muslims in Pakistan would be framed in consultation with the minorities and would not be imposed on them."[30]

In 1946 Jinnah described what Pakistan would be like in an interview with Reuters correspondent Don Campbell in New Delhi: "The new state would be a modern democratic state with sovereignty resting in the people and the members of the new nation having equal rights of citizenship regardless of their religion, caste or creed."[31] On 22 July 1947, only three weeks before the partition of the subcontinent, the Partition Council, which included the top leadership of both the INC and the AIML, issued a formal statement affirming:

> Both the Congress and the Muslim League have given assurances of fair and equitable treatment to the minorities after the transfer of power. The two future governments re-affirm these assurances. It is their intention to safeguard the legitimate interests of all citizens irrespective of religion, caste or sex. In the

---

27. Pirzada, *Foundations of Pakistan*, 160.
28. Ibid., 362.
29. Ibid., 372.
30. Ibid., 376.
31. Cited in Muhammad Munir, *From Jinnah to Zia*, 2nd ed. (Lahore: Vanguard Books, 1980), 29; Kayani, *Report of the Court of Inquiry*, 210.

exercise of their normal civic rights all citizens will be regarded as equal and both the governments will assure to all people within their territories the exercise of liberties such as freedom of speech, the right to form associations, the right to worship in their own way and the protection of their language and culture.[32]

Moreover, Jinnah's first presidential address to the Constituent Assembly of Pakistan on 11 August 1947 is quoted as one of the clearest expositions of the covenant made with the minorities for fair treatment in a secular democracy which he envisioned for Pakistan:

> You are free; you are free to go to your temples, you are free to go to your mosques or to any other places of worship in this State of Pakistan. You may belong to any religion or caste or creed – that has nothing to do with the business of the State . . . We are starting with this fundamental principle that we are all citizens and equal citizens of one State . . . Hindus would cease to be Hindus and Muslims will cease to be Muslims, not in the religious sense because that is the personal faith of each individual, but in the political sense as citizens of the State."[33]

There was considerable confusion caused by Jinnah's speech and, in particular, his reference to the minorities and his statement that Hindus would cease to be Hindus and Muslims would cease to be Muslims. The traditionalists in Pakistan wanted to know what Jinnah meant by saying this. Several influential leaders argued that Jinnah had not really meant what he said. Abul A'ala Maududi (1903–1973), perhaps the most influential Muslim thinker and writer of the twentieth century, and the man responsible for the Islamic resurgence in modern times, especially in Pakistan, argued some years afterwards that Jinnah had expressed merely a personal opinion:

> It was however difficult for the nation to believe that this statement really meant what its words apparently indicated . . . from a great man of stature and standing of Quaid-i-Azam it could

---

32. Jamil-ud-Din Ahmad, ed. *Speeches and Writings of Mr. Jinnah*, 6th ed., 2 vols., vol. 1 (Lahore: SMA, 1960), 43.
33. Mahomed Ali Jinnah, *Quaid-i-Azam Mahomed Ali Jinnah: Speeches as Governor-General of Pakistan 1947–48* (Karachi: Pakistan Publications, 1962), 8–9.

not be expected that all the principles on the basis of which he had waged the struggle for Pakistan for ten years would be thrown over-board and discarded as soon as Pakistan was established . . . It was after all a personal opinion . . .[34]

Further, Khwāja Nazimuddin, who became the second Prime Minister of Pakistan, stated that "a single nation, consisting of Muslims and non-Muslims with equal rights of citizenship was not his [Jinnah's] view of an Islamic State."[35]

By contrast, Jinnah vividly denied the idea of a theocracy in which the 'ulamā (Islamic clerics) would have a final say in politics, and that he stood for the separation of religion and politics. Justice Munir, a very close associate of Jinnah from 1936 until his death in 1948, strengthens this view by saying:

I swear he [Jinnah] did not at any time envisage the creation of backward theocratic state, Islamic in name and un-Islamic otherwise. He did not create Pakistan to put on the map a state which should live in the clouds of pre-medievalism sliding backward instead of marching forward, and in indecent haste to slide in the nether depths of degradation and theocracy equaling Tibet.[36]

Unfortunately, Jinnah died in September 1948, before the basic lines of the first constitution had been laid, and his dream for Pakistan to become a "secular, modern-nation state was buried with him."[37] Thus his influence on the formation of the constitution was greatly reduced.

The Struggle for an Islamic Constitution

With the establishment of Pakistan as an independent nation, debate started around the question of the place of Islam in the political life of

---

34. Maududi's written statement before the Court of Inquiry with reference to the statment of Quaid-i-Azam. Kayani, *Report of the Court of Inquiry*; Also reproduced in Masudul Hasan, *Sayyid Abul A'ala Maududi and His Thought*, 1st ed., 2 vols., vol. 1 (Lahore: Islamic Publications, 1984), 454–456.

35. Kayani, *Report of the Court of Inquiry*, 259.

36. Munir, *From Jinnah to Zia*: 43.

37. Lawrence Ziring, "The Phases of Pakistan's Political History," in *Iqbal, Jinnah, and Pakistan: The Vision and the Reality*, ed. C. M. Naim (New York: Syracuse University, 1979), 148.

Pakistan.³⁸ In a nutshell, the debate revolved around the question of whether Pakistan would be:
- a secular democracy founded on the Western model;
- a modern Islamic democracy; or
- an Islamic state based on Shari'a.

Although Jinnah had favoured a secular democracy, this first model was completely set aside after his death and "his secular propensities were virtually ignored."³⁹ Some argue that "the [later] constitutional changes, the blasphemy laws and the laws declaring Ahmediyyas [Ahmadis] to be non-Muslims are stains on the Jinnah-of-Pakistan model."⁴⁰

The debate, therefore, revolved around the last two models. The leadership of the Muslim League following Jinnah's death tended to favour the second model, while Islamic clerics pursued with great zeal the introduction of the third model. One of the main advocates for the third model was Maulana Maududi and his party Jamā'at-ē-Islami.⁴¹

This debate over the formulation of the new constitution of Pakistan exposed a vivid distinction between two camps, the modernists and the traditionalists, both of whom were involved in the legislature process of Pakistan. The traditionalists vigorously demanded an Islamic constitution in which Shari'a would be supreme, whereas modernists put an emphasis on the reinterpretation of Islamic laws according to the needs of the modern society.⁴²

---

38. Faruki, "Pakistan Government and Society," 55; John L. Esposito, "Islamization: Religion and Politics in Pakistan," *The Muslim World* 72, no. 3–4 (1982): 197–223; Leonard Binder, *Religion and Politics in Pakistan* (Los Angeles: University of California, 1961), 4–9.

39. Ziring, *Pakistan*, 53.

40. Stephen P. Cohen, *The Idea of Pakistan* (Washington: Brookings Institution, 2004), 44.

41. See Irfan Ahmad, "Genealogy of the Islamic State: Reflections on Maududi's Political Thought and Islamism," *The Journal of the Royal Anthropological Institute* 15 (2009): 152–156; Seyyed V. R. Nasr, *Mawdudi and the Making of Islamic Revivalism* (New York: Oxford University Press, 1996); Hasan, *Sayyid Abul A'ala Maududi*, 336–338; Warren F. Larson, *Islamic Ideology and Fundamentalism in Pakistan: Climate for Conversion to Christianity* (New York: University Press of America, 1998), 53–55.

42. Rizwan Hussain, "Pakistan," in *The Oxford Encyclopedia of the Islamic World*, ed. John L. Esposito (New York: Oxford University Press, 2009), 314.

The Objectives Resolution

The legislative history of Pakistan begins with the Objectives Resolution (OR) adopted on 7 March 1949. The first Constituent Assembly failed to formulate a new constitution for Pakistan, because it was dissolved by the Governor-General on 24 October 1954 on the charges of its non-functionary role and inability to frame the constitution, which was its prime responsibility.[43] However, this Constituent Assembly succeeded in laying, through the OR, fundamental principles on which the new constitution would be based. The importance of the OR is evident, as noted by S. M. Zafar: "The Objectives Resolution was always there as the centre-piece to serve either as the preamble of a new constitution or as a constitutional *Grundnorm*, and in 1985 it was incorporated as an operative part of the constitution."[44]

The purpose of the OR was to fill the constitution vacuum until the formulation of a new constitution. Its main Islamic features were as follows:

> Whereas sovereignty over the entire Universe belongs to God Almighty alone and the authority which he has delegated to the State of Pakistan through its people to be exercised within the limit prescribed by Him is a sacred trust . . . Wherein the Muslims shall be enabled to order their lives in the individual and collective spheres in accord with the teachings and requirements of Islam as set out in the Holy Quran and the Sunnah.[45]

The first salient feature of the resolution was that it declared Allah as the source of all authority and power. This echoes a distinctive religious philosophy rather than a democratic political system where the sovereignty rests with the people of the state. The message given to the world and to minorities was ambiguous: although Jinnah had stated that sovereignty

---

43. The Act of the Governor-General was challenged in the Chief Court of Sindh by the President of the Assembly, Moulvi Tamizuddin Khan. The provincial court disapproved of the Governor-General's action and declared that it was unconstitutional. *Moulvi Tamizuddin Khan v. Federation of Pakistan*, 7 PLD 96, 178 (1955). But the Federal Court reversed the orders of the Chief Court of Sindh and validated the Governor-General's action as constitutional. *Federation of Pakistan v. Moulvi Tamizuddin Khan*, 7 PLD 240, 378 (1955).

44. S. M. Zafar, "Constitutional Development " in *Pakistan: Founder's Aspirations and Today's Realities*, ed. Hafeez Malik (Karachi: Oxford University Press, 2001), 31–32.

45. "The Objectives Resolution," *Islamic Studies* 48, no. 1 (2009): 91.

would rest with the people, the OR stated that the new political framework of Pakistan would be based on the ideology of Islam.

Some regard the OR as the first step of the traditionalists towards establishing an Islamic constitution. In this move, "Jinnah's successors [the modernists] allowed themselves to be led into a trap on the question of sovereignty."[46] Maulana Maududi regarded the passing of the OR as his personal triumph. In this regard he expressed his views:

> The passing of the Objectives Resolution was a great victory for Jamā'at-ē-Islami . . . It was an important turning point for the Islamic movement. In view of this Resolution the nature of the State has been completely transformed. The ideal of the Muslim nation and the State of Pakistan has now been defined in specific terms. As a matter of principle the State of Pakistan has now been transformed into an Islamic State . . . which has opened for us new avenues.[47]

The Jamā'at-ē-Islami was of the view that the Jinnah's "conception of a secular state became obsolete with the passing of the Objectives Resolution."[48] This was considered a great achievement by the traditionalists. On the other hand, others argue that the OR was not simply a defeat of the modernists but rather a compromise between traditionalists and modernists.[49]

The OR was a very important document with regard to the ideology of Pakistan, as it provided the basic framework for the formation of the new constitution of Pakistan. Because of its Islamic orientation, the OR provided a solid foundation for the future justification of Islamization in Pakistan. It can be argued that the process of Islamization actually started with the adoption of this resolution, which effectively set aside the covenant made with the minorities by Jinnah some years earlier.

---

46. Munir D. Ahmed and Khalid Duran, "Pakistan," in *Islam in the World Today: A Handbook of Politics, Religion, Culture and Society*, ed. Werner Ende and Udo Steinbach (London: Cornell University Press, 2010), 345.

47. Hasan, *Sayyid Abul A'ala Maududi*, 367–368.

48. Kayani, *Report of the Court of Inquiry*, 203.

49. Fazlur Rahman, "Islam and the Consitutional Problem of Pakistan," *Studia Islamica* 32, no. 2 (1970): 277–278.

The Constitution of 1956

India and Pakistan began their political history together as Independent States in 1947. India was able to frame its constitution within one year but the same process was such a dilemma for Pakistan that it took about nine years to frame its first constitution. Haqqani made this assessment of the early political exigencies of Pakistan: "It is an unfortunate reality that those who came to rule the country from the outset were not particularly fond of or trained in democratic traditions."[50] Haqqani's assessment held Jinnah's political successors in the Muslim League accountable for their inability to frame the new constitution and to set the direction for the nation on the lines given by Jinnah.

Although Haqqani's assessment is partly true, he overlooked one of the major factors which delayed the framing of the constitution, that is, the demands for an Islamic constitution by the traditionalists who wanted to base the new setup on their theocratic ideology. In this regard Feldman says "the most intractable obstacles have arisen [out of] two circumstances . . . the first is that the country is divided into two parts . . . the second is involved in the difference of view as to the place which Islam should occupy in the constitution."[51]

In 1950, when the first interim report of the Basic Principle Committee (BPC)[52] came out, the *ulamā* (Islamic clerics) strongly criticized the committee's report and insisted on an Islamic constitution. They "dubbed the report as secular and an abject insult to Islam, smacking of a fascist approach, and subversive of the ideology of Pakistan."[53] Maududi argued that "it is evident that . . . they are nothing short of the draft constitution of a purely secular state and are absolutely devoid of Islamic ingredients . . . The Objectives Resolution passed by the Constituent Assembly to appease you, has been

---

50. Irshad Ahmad Haqqani, "Failure of Democracy in Pakistan," *The Muslim World* 96, no. 2 (2006): 222–223.

51. Herbert Feldman, *A Constitution for Pakistan* (Karachi: Oxford University Press, undated), 10; See also Mohammad Jahangir Bader, *The Constitutional History of Pakistan*, 2nd rev. ed. (Lahore: Mansoor Book House, undated), 42–43; Binder, *Religion and Politics*, 201–203.

52. The Basic Principles Committee was formed on 12 March 1948 to make proposals and other guidelines for the new constitution of Pakistan.

53. Zulfikar K. Maluka, *The Myth of Constitutionalism in Pakistan* (Karachi: Oxford University Press, 1995), 128.

totally replaced by a totally un-Islamic document."[54] BPC published three reports, one after another, but every time its report was criticized.[55] Finally they agreed on the famous 22-point formula in which the Qur'an and Sunnah would have the first and the last say.[56]

One of the recommendations of this committee relating to the Islamic character of the proposed constitution was the formation of an advisory Board of Islamic Teachings. It was comprised of five religious scholars, who would review legislation so that nothing against the teachings of Islam was enacted. This is what the *ʿulamā* had been demanding: they saw their role as watchdogs to ensure the conformity of the laws to the Sharīʿa. From the view point of the modernists, the *ʿulamā* were being given power outside the Parliament which could veto any legislation.[57]

The first constitution of Pakistan was adopted on 23 March 1956, the same date on which the Pakistan Resolution had been passed sixteen years previously. The Objective Resolution was put as the preamble of the constitution and Pakistan became an "Islamic Republic" under its first constitution. A number of opposition leaders as well as the representatives of minorities walked out in protest.[58] They argued that, though the constitution speaks about democracy, its content was in conflict with the vision of Jinnah for a democratic state. In Munir's view "the constitution spoke about safeguarding the minorities which is contrary to Jinnah's commitment that there was to be no distinction between minorities and majorities which had been affirmed by the Liaqat-Nehru Pact in 1950."[59]

---

54. Abul Ala Maududi, *Selected Speeches and Writings of Maulana Maududi*, trans. S. Zakir Aijaz (Karachi: IIP, 1981), 155.

55. Bader, *Constitutional History*, 45.

56. Afzal Iqbal, *Islamization of Pakistan* (Lahore: Vanguard Books, 1986), 51–53.

57. Ahsan, "Pakistan since Independence," 358.

58. Callard states that "The highest 'opposition' vote at the period came on the decision to adopt the title of 'Islamic Republic.'" Keith B. Callard, *Pakistan, a Political Study* (New York: Macmillan, 1957), 121. See also Ahmed Salim, "Religious Fundamentalism and Its Impact on Non-Muslims" (Rawalpindi: Christian Study Centre, 2008), 93–97.

59. Munir, *From Jinnah to Zia*, 76. The pact between Prime Ministers Liaquat Ali Khan and Jawhar Lal Nehru, according to which minorities in both countries were declared to have equal rights with the majority, including all offices in governments, civil and military was made on 8 April 1950. Pakistan violated this pact by adding discriminatory clauses in her first constitution, e.g. "The Head of the State is to be a Muslim."

Generally, the constitution was framed on the pattern of the government of India Act of 1935 and the Indian Independence Act of 1947, a legacy of the British. However, the new constitution of Pakistan was distinguished from both of these by its Islamic character. This is apparent from one of the Directive Principles of the State Policy, which said, "Steps shall be taken to enable the Muslims . . . to order their lives in accordance with the Holy Quran and Sunnah. The State shall endeavour . . . to make the teachings of the Holy Quran compulsory; [to observe] Islamic moral standards; to secure proper organization of Zak[ā]t, Auqāf and Mosques."[60] The president was directed to set up an organization for Islamic research and instruction to assist in the construction of a Muslim society on a truly Islamic basis.[61] The constitution further provided in Article 198 that "no law shall be enacted which is repugnant to the Injunctions of Islam . . . and existing laws shall be brought into conformity with such injunctions."[62] (Later this article became a foundation for the process of Islamization in Pakistan.)

Sheikh Mujib-ur-Rehman, the leader of Awami League reacted with concern about Islamic provisions inducted to the constitution, by saying, "It were the poor masses of India who died and made sacrifices for Pakistan. Now you are playing with the poor masses of Pakistan in the name of Islam. Sir, let Pakistan be a pure and simple Pakistan of the people. Do not try to hoodwink the people of Pakistan in the name of Islam."[63]

Due to its Islamic features, Maulana Maududi gave qualified approval to this constitution.[64] Nonetheless, not all the members of the traditionalist camp were fully pleased with the Islamic identity of the constitution. Similarly, modernists had strong reservations.[65] In Usama's words: "Islamists felt betrayed on the [lesser] role of the religion involved in the running of

---

60. G. W. Choudhury, "The Constitution of Pakistan," *Pacific Affairs* 29, no. 3 (1956): 245. This section was important because the future policy of the state would be framed in the light of these principles.
61. Ibid.
62. Ibid.
63. Constituent Assembly of Pakistan Debates, vol. 1, no. 76 (1956): 3376–3377.
64. James A. Tebbe, "Freedom Movement Revisited," *Al-Mushir* 28, no. 1 (1986): 9.
65. Iqbal, *Islamization of Pakistan*, 65.

the state, and the secularists similarly became annoyed at the inclusion of a part-Islamic ideology . . ."66

Pakistan now finally had its first constitution (which, incidentally, was one of the lengthiest written constitutions in the world). However, the country was politically unstable and, as a result, the first constitution proved to be short lived. A tragedy of Pakistan's political life was that its first constitution, which had taken nine years to be framed due to the controversy of the question of Islamic identity, survived for barely two and half years. It was abrogated on 7 October 1958, with the imposition of martial law in Pakistan.

The Constitution of 1962

In 1958, a major shift occurred in the political structure of Pakistan: power shifted from the civil bureaucracy to the military which then remained dominant in the following years.

General Ayub Khan, a military leader, was a Muslim with modern views, and his era is described as the modernization of Pakistan.67 He launched an intellectual assault on the *ulamā* and challenged them on number of doctrinal and jurisprudence issues, particularly with regard to the status of women.68 Under his leadership a second constitution was developed in 1962. While this constitution was being framed, the *ulamā* were as active in their demands for an Islamic constitution as they had been for the previous one: however, Ayub Khan did not heed their demands. Ayub notes in his autobiography:

> The demand for the Islamic Constitution was so ardently advocated by the *Ulama*. Since no one had defined the fundamental elements of an Islamic Constitution, no Constitution could be called Islamic unless it received the blessings of the *Ulama* . . . A

---

66. Usama Butt, "Pakistan's Salvation: Islam or Western Inspired Secular-Liberal Democracy," in *Pakistan's Quagmire: Security, Strategy, and the Future of the Islamic-Nuclear Nation*, eds. Usama Butt and N. Elahi (New York: CIPG, 2010), 27.

67. He viewed himself as a reformer and followed Turkey's Kemal Ataturk as his role model to promote a moderate form of Islam. Surjit Mansingh, "Historical Setting," in *Pakistan, a Country Study*, ed. Richard F. Nyrop (Washington: US Government Printing Office, 1984), 44. Despite his dictatorial tendencies, Ayub envisioned a modern Pakistan. See Malik, *History of Pakistan*, 148–150.

68. Hussain, "Pakistan," 315.

Constitution could be regarded as Islamic only if it were drafted by the *Ulama* and conceded them the authority to judge and govern the people. This was a position which neither the people nor I was prepared to accept . . .[69]

On 17 February 1960, Ayub Khan established an eleven member Constitution Commission, comprised of eminent judges, lawyers and technocrats.[70] After a stormy genesis, a new constitution was promulgated on the 1 March 1962. It created a form of government that was presidential, federal and unicameral and it allotted enormous power to the president.[71]

The general perception about the Constitution of 1962 was that it was quite liberal in its spirit. This is evident from the fact that it changed the name of the country from "Islamic Republic of Pakistan" to the "Republic of Pakistan" and that it dropped the Objectives Resolution from the constitution. When the National Assembly met in 1962, there was a great demand that the word "Islamic" should be reintroduced.[72] There was also intense pressure from the masses outside the assembly who had been mobilized by the traditionalists. Consequently, Ayub was compelled to restore both the Islamic name of the country as well as the Objectives Resolution into the constitution in 1964.[73]

There were other striking contrasts between 1956 and 1962. The preamble to the Constitution of 1956 included the words "authority to be exercised by the people within the limits prescribed by Allah."[74] In contrast, in the preamble to the Constitution of 1962, there was no such reference to the fact that people would exercise authority "within the limits prescribed

---

69. Muhmmad Ayub Khan, *Friends Not Masters: A Political Autobiography* (London: Oxford University Press, 1967), 203–204.

70. One of the terms of reference was to examine the causes of failure of the parliamentary system and identify reasons for the short survival of the first constitution in Pakistan.

71. See Hamid Khan, *Constitutional and Political History of Pakistan* (Karachi: Oxford University Press, 2001), 257–266.

72. Ibid., 278.

73. Khurshid Ahmad, "Pakistan: Vision and Reality, Past and Future," *The Muslim World* 96, no. 2 (2006): 371–372.; ibid., 315.

74. Choudhury, "Constitution of Pakistan," 245.

by Allah."[75] Another example is that the most significant Islamic provision in the Constitution of 1956 was Article 198 (That no law should be enacted which would be repugnant to the Injunctions of Islam and existing laws should be brought in conformity with such injunctions).[76] In contrast, the 1962 constitution substituted this sentence with a simple clause that stated merely that "no law should be repugnant to Islam."[77]

In the late sixties, the *ulamā*, along with other religious and political parties, launched a campaign to dislodge Ayub, with the slogan *Islam khaṭery meṅ hai* (Islam is in danger), in which mosques were frequently used to organize anti-Ayub demonstrations.[78] This slogan worked well and created such opposition to Ayub's regime throughout the country that he was forced to step down. Ayub handed over power to the army Commander in Chief, General Yahya Khan, on 25 March 1969. General Yahya immediately abrogated the constitution of 1962 and declared martial law and, a week later, he assumed the office of the president.[79]

Our brief examination of the Islamic character of the Constitution of 1962 demonstrates that it was making a significant effort to turn Pakistan into a liberal, democratic and non-theocratic state. However, these values were viewed by the traditionalists as antagonistic to Islam, and thus were fiercely opposed.

The Constitution of 1973

Following Pakistan's split into two nations in 1971 (the East wing of Pakistan became Bangladesh), there was again a shift from a military to a civil regime. Zulfikar Ali Bhutto, a charismatic leader, came into power with the slogan "*Roṭi, Kaprā, aur Makān*" (food, clothing, and shelter).[80] After the episode

---

75. Its preamble says that "the authority exercisable by the people is a sacred trust." *The Constitution of the Republic of Pakistan* (Karachi: Government of Pakistan Press, 1962), 1.

76. Choudhury, "Constitution of Pakistan," 245.

77. *Constitution of the Republic of Pakistan*, 4.

78. Lawrence Ziring, "Government and Politics," in *Pakistan, a Country Study*, ed. Richard F. Nyrop (Washington: US Government Printing Office, 1984), 233.

79. The first constitution of 1956 hardly survived for two and half years, and fortunately the second constitution of 1962 was able to survive for seven years (1 March 1962 to 25 March 1969).

80. Stanley Wolpert, *Zulfi Bhutto of Pakistan: His Life and Times* (New York: Oxford University Press, 1993), 139.

of Bangladesh, it was strongly felt that Pakistan should have had a stronger emphasis on Islam to maintain unity. Consequently, there was a renewed emphasis on the Islamic identity of Pakistan.

The constitution of 1973, framed under Bhutto, is considered one of his key achievements. It is still in effect, although several amendments have been made to it by successive regimes. The Constitution of 1973 was much more Islamic than the previous constitutions of 1956 and 1962, as is apparent from the following features:

- Pakistan continued to be described as an "Islamic Republic."[81]
- For the first time, Islam was declared the state religion.[82]
- Although the previous constitutions had required that the office of the president be held by a Muslim, the 1973 constitution extended that requirement to the prime minister's office as well.[83]
- Government officials were required to strive to preserve the Islamic ideology on which Pakistan was based.
- Muslims of Pakistan would be facilitated to shape their lives in accordance with the fundamental principles and basic concepts of Islam.[84]
- The constitution stated that the State would endeavour, as respects the Muslims of Pakistan:
  a) to make the teaching of the Holy Qur'an and Islamic studies in schools mandatory, to facilitate the learning of the Arabic language and to secure the correct and exact printing and publishing of the Holy Qur'an;
  b) to promote unity and the observance of the Islamic moral standards;
  c) to secure the proper organization of zakāt, auqāf and mosques.[85]

---

81. Muhammad Naseem Chaudhri, *Constitution of Islamic Republic of Pakistan of 1973 with Commentary* (Lahore: LTP, 2005), Article 1(1): 31. On this issue, see Wolpert, *Zulfi Bhutto*, 206.
82. Chaudhri, *Constitution of Islamic Republic*, Article 2: 32.
83. Ibid., Articles 41(2) & 91(2): 94, 176.
84. Ibid., Article 3: 191.
85. Ibid., Article 31(2) (a), (b) and (c).

- Existing laws had to be in conformity with the Qur'an and Sunnah, and no future law could be framed if it were repugnant to the Qur'an or the Sunnah.[86]
- The Islamic Ideology Council was formed with a role to make recommendations to the legislature for bringing existing laws into conformity with the Injunctions of Islam.[87]

In 1974, under pressure from the 'ulamā, the Bhutto regime amended the constitution to declare Ahmadis as non-Muslims.[88] Despite this, Bhutto was considered by the traditionalists as a socialist rather than pro-Islamic due to his emphasis on socialism (albeit an Islamic version of socialism).[89] In 1977, the traditionalists launched a huge campaign and rallied people around the desirability of making Pakistan into a truly Islamic state by instituting *niẓam-ē-muṣṭafā* (system of the prophet).

As a result, Bhutto was made to enforce another set of Islamic reforms that included bans on alcoholic drinks, gambling, horse-racing, and dance and night clubs.[90] In order to appease the traditionalists, and to reduce the pressure of the situation, he promised that Islamic Shari'a would be enforced in Pakistan within six months.[91] Bhutto was willing to accommodate the traditionalists' demands in order to maintain power. Nonetheless, he failed to hold onto power, but his extensive Islamic provisions in the constitution of 1973 raised high expectations for the traditionalists and softened the soil for intensified Islamization under the military regime of Zia-ul-Haq, who succeeded him.

---

86. Ibid., Article 227: 701–702.
87. Ibid., Articles 228, 229, 230: 702–704.
88. *Act 49 of 1974: Constitution (Second Amendment) Act*, (17 September 1974), 26 PLD Central Statutes (1974), 425.
89. Faruki, "Pakistan Government and Society," 57; Wolpert, *Zulfi Bhutto*, 213.
90. *Act 24 of 1977: Prohibition Act* (17 May 1977), 29 PLD Central Statutes (1977), 312–317; *Act 28 of 1977: Prevention of Gambling Act* (21 May 1977), 29 PLD Central Statutes (1977), 305–308.
91. M. Geijbels, "Pakistan, Islamization and the Christian Community," *Al-Mushir* 21, no. 2 (1979): 42.

Second Period: 1977–1992

A New Wave of Islamization

Islamic sentiments have been present in Pakistan since its inception and the process of Islamization has continued over the years. However, the Zia era is significantly different from the previous eras. During this time, Islam re-emerged with a wave of extreme Islamization which has not been seen before or since in Pakistan's politics. The slogan *niẓām-ē-muṣṭafā* was largely used to topple the Bhutto government and legitimize the military coup of General Zia-ul-Haq.

General Zia was a fervent supporter of *niẓam-ē-muṣṭafā*. This is evident from the fact that when he became the chief of army staff, he changed the army's motto to "Faith, Piety and Jihād" in lieu of "Unity, Faith and Discipline," a motto which had been coined by Jinnah, the founder of Pakistan.[92] Zia went on to introduce the "beard allowance" in the army to reward those who keep beards because this gesture was considered a sign of religious obedience.[93] General Zia changed the secular fabric of Pakistan's army by incorporating Islam into its organizational structure.[94]

In his first address to the nation of Pakistan on 5 July 1977 (the day of the army coup), Zia declared, "Pakistan, which was created in the name of Islam, will continue to survive only if it sticks to Islam. That is why I consider the introduction of the Islamic system as an essential prerequisite for the

---

92. Ayesha Jalal, "The Past as Present," in *Pakistan: Beyond the Crises State*, ed. Maleeha Lodhi (New York: Columbia University Press, 2011), 15.

93. Benazir Bhutto, *Reconciliation: Islam, Democracy and the West*, 1st ed. (New York: Simon & Schuster, 2008), 117.

94. Zahid Hussain notes: "For the first time Islamic teachings were introduced into Pakistan Military Academy. Islamic training and philosophy were made a part of the curriculum at the Command and Staff College. A Directorate of Religious Instruction was instituted to educate the officer corps on Islam. Islamic education became a part of the promotion exams. The officers were required to read the *Qur'anic Concept of War* . . . To gain promotion an officer was required to be a devout Muslim. Scores of highly professional and secular officers were sidelined for not meeting the criterion of a 'good Muslim.' As a consequence of this policy, many conservative officers reached the senior command level . . . Mullahs [Islamic clerics] belonging to the Deobandi sect were appointed to work among the troops . . . Soldiers were encouraged to attend 'Tablighi' [Islamic propagation] gatherings. The purpose was to indoctrinate cadets and young officers with an obscurantist interpretation of Islam." Zahid Hussain, *Frontline Pakistan: The Path to Catastrophe and the Killing of Benazir Bhutto* (London: I. B. Tauris, 2008), 19–20.

country."⁹⁵ In an interview with Brian Barron of BBC in April 1978, Zia affirmed that "he had a mission to purify and to cleanse Pakistan."⁹⁶ Here Zia echoed Maulana Maududi's ideas. Zia's Islamic initiatives had been enthusiastically endorsed by Maududi and his party Jamā'at-ē-Islami.⁹⁷ Nasr strengthens this view by saying that Maududi and his party became "a pillar of the Zia's regime and ardent supporters of the general's Islamic state."⁹⁸

The Supreme Court of Pakistan validated Zia's martial law by appealing to the doctrine of State necessity and the welfare of the people.⁹⁹ This judgment of the Supreme Court gave Zia extraordinary legislative power which led him to make constitutional amendments through many ordinances and orders. Zia always used this judgment as shield, claiming, "I am empowered by the Supreme Court of the country."¹⁰⁰

US support for Zia's regime (in the form of money and arms to resist Soviet intervention in Afghanistan) also greatly bolstered his confidence in domestic matters.¹⁰¹ The US made no attempt to resist Zia's policy of Islamization: "The Reagan White House turned a blind eye to both human rights and non-proliferation violations on the grounds of the Soviet threat."¹⁰² In the absence of internal and external checks and balances, Zia got a free hand to initiate the process of Islamization on all fronts in Pakistan. For brevity, focus and relevance, we will stick to the judicial system.

The Effects on the Judicial System

Soon after assuming power, Zia declared that the judiciary would be empowered to strike down all laws of the country that are repugnant to the Holy Qur'an and Sunnah and to declare them null and void. To achieve

---

95. Geijbels, "Pakistan, Islamization," 43.
96. Zia-ul-Haq, *President of Pakistan, General Muhmmad Zia-ul-Haq, Interviews to Foreign Media*, vol. 1 (Islamabad: Government of Pakistan, 1980), 29.
97. Ahsan, "Pakistan Since Independence," 364.
98. Seyyed V. R. Nasr, "Islamic Opposition to the Islamic State," *IJMES* 25, no. 2 (1993): 261–262.
99. *Begum Nusrat Bhutto v. Chief of Army Staff and Federation of Pakistan*, 29 PLD 657 (1977): 660.
100. Maluka, *Myth of Constitutionalism*, 262.
101. Husain Ḥaqqani, *Pakistan: Between Mosque and Military* (Washington: CEIP, 2005), 140.
102. Ian Talbot, *Pakistan: A Modern History* (London: Hurst, 1998), 250.

this objective, a "Shariat Benches of Superior Courts Order" was issued on 2 December 1978,[103] coming into effect on 10 February 1979.[104] This order constituted four Sharīat Benches, one in each high court (Lahore, Peshawar, Karachi and Quetta), comprising of three Muslim judges, and one Sharīat Appellate Bench in the Supreme Court.[105] Their function was to be watchdogs to make sure that any law or provision of law should not be legislated in Pakistan if not in conformity with the Injunctions of Islam.[106] This arrangement was "applauded by the traditionalists as a landmark in the enforcement of *Nizam-i-Mustafa.*"[107]

Through this initiative, the civil judicial system was altered, operating alongside a parallel Islamic judicial system which was strengthened in an unprecedented way. The Sharīat Benches were empowered to declare to what extent the law was un-Islamic and how it could be reshaped to make it consistent with Islam, and the government was bound to implement their orders.[108] On 9 February 1979, Zia amended the Pakistan Penal Code by introducing *ḥudụd* Laws[109] through a series of four Presidential Ordinances and one Presidential Order.[110] These laws were not seen only as harsh in their nature but also discriminatory against women and non-Muslims. One example of this is that to prove *zinā* (either adultery or rape) there must be "at least four Muslim adult males . . . [to] give evidence as eyewitness of

---

103. *President's Order 22 of 1978: Shariat Benches of Superior Courts Order* (2 December 1978), 31 PLD Central Statutes (1979): 6–10.

104. *President's Order 3 of 1979: Constitution (Amendment) Order* (7 February 1979), 31 PLD Central Statutes (1979), 31–33.

105. *President's Order 22 of 1978*, 6–7.

106. *President's Order 3 of 1979*, 31.

107. Munir, *From Jinnah to Zia*: 141–142.

108. *President's Order 3 of 1979*, 32.

109. In Muslim criminal law *hadd* the singular of *hudud* means punishment ordained by the Holy Qur'an and Sunnah. These punishments are stoning or scourging for "Zinā" (adultery) and drinking of liquor, and cutting off the hands for theft, etc. See H.A. R. Gibb and J. H. Kramers, "Hudud Laws," in *Concise Encyclopedia of Islam* (Leiden: Brill Academic, 2001), 116.

110. *Ordinance 6 of 1979: Offences against Property (Enforcement of Hudood) Ordinance* (9 February 1979) 31 PLD (1979), 44–51; *Ordinance 7 of 1979: Offence of Zina (Enforcement of Hudood) Ordinance* (9 February 1979) 31 PLD Central Statutes (1979), 51–56; *Ordinance 8 of 1979: Offence of Qazf (Enforcement of Hudood) Ordinance* (9 February 1979) 31 PLD (1979), 56–60; *Ordinance 9 of 1979: Execution of the Punishment of Whipping (Enforcement of Hudood) Ordinance* (9 February 1979) 31 PLD (1979), 60–61; *President Order No. 4 of 1979: Prohibition (Enforcement of Hadd) Order* (9 February 1979) 31 PLD (1979), 33–41.

the act of penetration necessary to the offence."[111] Apart from the absurdity of this requirement, there was a major flaw in the offence of *zinā*, in that it made no distinction between *zinā* (adultery) and *zinā bi'l-jabr* (rape). Further, cruel and unusual punishments were introduced, such as stoning to death, amputation of hands and whipping.[112] "In stressing the punitive provisions of Islam, General Zia's government appeared to seek a return to seventh century Arabia."[113] It was suggested that a Saudi Arabian expert had dictated the drafting of these laws.[114]

Zia was transforming the judicial system of Pakistan with quick Islamic changes. After little more than one year, the Shariʿat Benches were replaced with the Federal Shariʿat Court (FSC) under Article 203-C, a constitutional amendment made by the president's order in 1980.[115] The FSC was empowered under Article 203-D "to examine and decide the question whether or not any law or provision of law is repugnant to the Injunctions of Islam."[116] Any citizen of Pakistan could approach the FSC to protest against any law which was considered not according to the teachings of Islam.[117]

In 1982, the powers of the FSC under Article 203-DD were further enhanced to become authorized *suo motu* to take up examination of any law on its own.[118] Nasim Hasan Shah, the former Chief Justice of the Supreme Court of Pakistan, said, "The conferment of such power of judicial review,

---

111. *Ordinance 7 of 1979*, Section 8, 53.

112. The women's lobby in Pakistan protested the implementation of the *Hudud* Ordinance, when a woman Lal Mai was sentenced by a session judge in Khanpur with three year's rigorous imprisonment and 15 lashes for *zinā*, she was flogged by a man in public before a large crowd. In another case, a blind girl, Safia Bibi, was given similar sentence by lower court in Sahiwal for *zinā*. She was declared guilty on giving a birth to a illegitimate child, even though, she had been raped. P. Lewis, "News from the Country: The Women's Lobby," *Al-Mushir* 26, no. 1 (1984): 43.

113. M. Rafi Raza, "The Continuous Process of Re-writing the Constitution," in *Pakistan in the 80s*, eds. Wolfgang P. Zingel and Stephanie Z. Lallemant (Lahore: Vanguard Books, 1985), 28.

114. Waqar Gillani, "Hudood Laws Not Based on Reason or Religion," *Daily Times*, 25 June 2004, online.

115. *President's Order 1 of 1980: Constitution (Amendment) Order* (26 May 1980), 32 PLD Central Statutes (1980), 90–91.

116. Ibid., 91–92.

117. Ibid., Section 203-D, 91.

118. *President's Order 5 of 1982: Constitution (Second Amendment) Order* (22 March 1982), 34 PLD Central Statutes (1982), 155.

with a view to Islamising the existing laws, has no parallel in judicial history. No such power was conferred on Courts during the Muslim Rule when Islamic *fiqh* [Jurisprudence] was the governing law."[119] Subsequently, appellate powers against the conviction and sentences under the *ḥudūd* laws were also conferred on the FSC with the insertion of Article 203-DD into the constitution.[120] This was done to curtail the appellate powers of the high courts,[121] and was considered another blow to the independence of the judiciary in Pakistan, which had been brought under the heavy weight of Zia's Islamization process.

Further evidence of this is seen in changes to the FSC. When the FSC was introduced, it was said that the court would comprise five judges from the High Court or Supreme Court of Pakistan.[122] However, in 1981, "stoning to death" for *zinā* was challenged in the FSC and the court gave a ruling that this punishment was repugnant to the Injunctions of Islam.[123] As a result of this judgment, there was an outcry from the *'ulamā*, who claimed that they should be included in the FSC because judges trained in secular law lacked Islamic knowledge. Zia heeded the *'ulamā* and, with another Presidential order, a panel of three Islamic *'ulamā* was added to the FSC "to attend the sittings of the Court as *'ulamā* members and they shall have the same powers and jurisdictions" as the member judges of the FSC.[124] General Zia went further, giving more Islamic influence to the FSC ordering that "the court shall consist of eight 'Muslim member' judges."[125]

Similarly, in the Federal Shariʿat Appellate Bench (SAB) of the Supreme Court, the number of judges was extended from three to five: three Muslim

---

119. Nasim H. Shah, *Essays & Addresses on Constitution, Law and Pakistan Legal System* (Lahore: University of the Punjab, 1999), 64.
120. *President's Order 5 of 1982*, 155.
121. Khan, *Constitutional and Political History*, 641.
122. *President's Order 1 of 1980*, Sections 203-C (2–5), 91.
123. *Hazoor Bakhsh v. Federation of Pakistan*, 33 PLD 145, 244 (1981).
124. *President's Order 5 of 1981: Constitution (Amendment) Order* (13 April 1981), 33 PLD Central Statutes (1981), 251. The earlier judgment of the FSC in the case of Hazoor Bakhsh was reviewed by the FSC after the new arrangement of Ulema sitting in the FSC. The earlier judgment was set aside and the punishment of "stoning to death" in the offence of Zina was validated by the FSC as in line with the Injunctions of Islam. *Federation of Pakistan v. Hazoor Bakhsh*, 35 PLD 255, 479–480 (1983).
125. *President's Order No. 7 of 1981*, 276.

judges and two *ʻulamā* to sit on the bench.[126] Thus Islamic clerics who had already been appointed to the FSC, now were able to have an influence on the Supreme Court, the top judicial body in Pakistan.

The bias towards the supremacy of Islam is also evident from the fact that Shariʻa laws are applied to non-Muslims, but non-Muslim solicitors are not entitled to appear before the FSC.[127] This discrimination can also be seen in the *Qānūn-ē-Shahādat* (Law of Evidence) decreed by a presidential order in October 1984. It laid down that the testimony of one Muslim man is equal to that of two Muslim women (in financial matters) or two non-Muslim men; and that the testimony of four non-Muslim women is equal to one Muslim man.[128] The FSC was further empowered to have the power to revise the judgments of the criminal courts in *ḥudūd* offences. The decisions of the FSC under Article 203-GG were also binding on the high courts, which curtailed their powers and brought them under the FSC.[129]

With regard to the judiciary, the last move of Zia was on 31 May 1988, when he passed the Shariʻa Ordinance, which was designed to enforce Shariʻa in Pakistan.[130] It declared that "Shariʻa shall be the supreme source of law in Pakistan and *Grund Norm* for guidance for policy making by the State . . ."[131] It also declared that "experienced and qualified *ʻulamā* shall be eligible to be appointed as judges, and *amicus curiae* in the court."[132] Provision was also made for appointment of *muftis* for assistance to the Supreme Court, the High Court, and the Federal Shariʻat Court in matters involving the interpretation of Shariʻa.[133] With this move, Zia wanted to create a class of supporters within the judiciary.[134] Zia's Shariʻa Ordinance laid a foundation

---

126. *President's Order No. 12 of 1982: Constitution (Third Amendment) Order* (15 August 1982) 34 PLD Central Statutes (1982), 344.

127. Section 203-E (4) states that "A party to any proceedings before the court . . . may be represented by a legal practitioner who is a Muslim." *President's Order 1 of 1980*, 92.

128. *President's Order 10 of 1984: Qanun-e-Shahadat (Law of Evidence)*, (26 October 1984), 37 PLD Central Statutes (1985), 14.

129. *President's Order 5 of 1982*, 156.

130. *Ordinance 1 of 1988: Enforcement of Shariah Ordinace* (15 June 1988), 40 PLD Central Statutes (1988), 29–36.

131. Ibid., 30–31.

132. Ibid., 33.

133. Ibid.

134. Khan, *Constitutional and Political History*, 696–697.

for the Sharīʿa Act, which was passed by the National Assembly on 16 May 1991. It declared that "the Sharīʿa . . . shall be the supreme law of Pakistan."[135]

The above discussion demonstrates that Zia altered the judicial system of Pakistan significantly to make it more Islamic. The blasphemy laws are part of the process of Islamization under Zia, and will now be considered in detail.

Blasphemy Laws

British-Framed Clauses

The blasphemy laws in the Penal Code of Pakistan (PPC) are based on the Indian Penal Code (IPC), which was formulated by the British in 1860. These laws are part of chapter 15 – "Offences Relating to Religion" in the IPC. With regard to this chapter the framers of the Code said:

> The principle on which this chapter has been framed is a principle on which it would be desirable that all governments should act, but from which the British Government in India cannot depart without risking the dissolution of society; it is this, that every man should be suffered to profess his own religion, and that no man should be suffered to insult the religion of another.[136]

This preface shows the intention of the framers to introduce laws designed to curb religious violence and to maintain peace and order among the multi-faith communities living in India under the British. The object of the legislature in framing this chapter was to promote religious tolerance in a pluralistic society. Originally this chapter comprised four clauses (295, 296, 297 and 298).[137]

---

[135]. *Act 10 of 1991: Enforcement of Shariah Act* (5 June 1991), 43 PLD Central Statutes (1991), 373–378. For good discussion on Sharīʿa Act, see Christine and Charles Amjad-Ali, *The Legislative History of the Shariah Act* (Rawalpindi: CSC, 1992).

[136]. S. K. Sarvaria, *R A Nelson's Indian Penal Code*, 9th ed., 4 vols., vol. 2 (New Delhi: LexisNexis Butterworths, 2003), 2565.

[137]. **"295: Injuring or defiling a place of worship with intent to insult the religion or any class.** – Whoever destroys, damages or defiles any place of worship, or any object held sacred by any class of persons with the intention of thereby insulting the religion of any class of persons or with the knowledge that any class of persons is likely to consider such destruction, damage or defilement as an insult to their religion, shall be punished with imprisonment of either description for a term which may extend to two years, or with fine, or with both.

In 1927, the British government inserted a further clause to Section 295 of the IPC in response to a controversial article with the title *Rangīlā Rasūl* ("colourful prophet"), which had been produced by a Hindu author, Paṇḍit Chamupati, and published by Raj Pal. This article contained objectionable material about the Prophet's life which infuriated the Muslims in the Punjab in India. They agitated with anger and demanded that the British government take legal action against the culprits. Raj Pal was tried under Section 153-A of the IPC, which made the publication of material with "a conscious intention of promoting, causing or exciting enmity and hatred against another community a crime."[138]

The magistrate dismissed the case and acquitted Raj Pal on 13 November 1924. Keeping in view the religious feelings of the Muslim community, the British government filed a criminal revision in the High Court, where the court upheld the previous decision of the lower court and, on 13 November 1925, dismissed the case on the basis of a lack of deliberate intention.[139] The defeat in the Lahore High Court caused a lot of anguish among the Muslims

---

296: Disturbing religious assembly. – Whoever voluntarily causes disturbances to any assembly lawfully engaged in the performance of religious worship, or religious ceremonies, shall be punished with imprisonment of either description for a term which may extend to one year or with fine, or with both.

297: Trespassing on burial places, etc. – Whoever, with the intention of wounding the feelings of any person, or of insulting the religion of any person, or with the knowledge that the feelings of any person are likely to be wounded, or that the religion of any person is likely to be insulted thereby, commits any trespass in any place of worship or on any place of sepulchre, or any place set apart for the performance of funeral rites or as a depository for the remains of dead, or offers any indignity to any human corpse, or causes disturbance to any persons assembled for the performance of funeral ceremonies, shall be punished with imprisonment of either description for a term which may extend to one year, or with fine, or with both.

298: Uttering words, etc., with deliberate intent to wound religious feelings. – Whoever, with the deliberate intention of wounding the religious feelings of any person, utters any word or makes any sound in the hearing of that person or makes any gesture in the sight of that person, or places any object in the sight of that person, shall be punished with imprisonment of either description for a term which may extend to one year or with fine, or with both."

Pakistan, *The Pakistan Code with Chronological Table and Index*, 3rd ed., vol. 1 from 1836–1871 (Karachi: Government of Pakistan, 1982), 172.

138. Sarvaria, *R A Nelson's Indian Penal Code*, 1413.

139. *Emperor v. Raj Pal*, AIR 195, 196 (1926). The High Court relied on the judgment of one of the learned judges, Sir William Clark, who held the view that intention was an element in the offence, and said that unless he was satisfied that the accused has a conscious

in the Punjab, which led to Hindu-Muslim conflict. Several people from both sides were killed. Raj Pal was assassinated by a 19-year-old Muslim zealot, Ilam Din, who was subsequently charged under Section 302 of the IPC and sentenced to death for murder.[140]

In 1927, in another case, Devi Sharan Sharma was tried under Section 153-A on the charges of writing an article called *Sair-ē-Dozakh* (Trip to Hell), which created considerable annoyance to Muslims in the Amritsar region.[141] The court held the view that the article had been written by Sharma "with a deliberate intention of promoting hatred between Muslims and Hindus. Sharma was punished under section 153-A."[142] Nevertheless, the Court also held the view that "any criticism of a religious leader, whether dead or alive, may not fall within the ambit of Section.153-A."[143]

In another contemporary case in 1927, the book *Bic'itra Jiwan* ("Strange or Wonderful life"), which negatively depicted the life of the Prophet of Islam, caused lot of tension between Muslims and Hindus. Consequently the book was confiscated by the government and its writer Kali Sharma was also tried under Section 153-A of the IPC. In this case a special bench, consisting of three judges of the Allahabad High Court, held the view that the book "promoted feelings of enmity between Hindus and Mohammadans [Muslims]."[144] On this ground, Kali Sharma was found guilty. But the special bench also ruled that criticism of religious leaders does not come under section 153-A.[145]

The above cases reveal that there was no law in chapter 15 (Offences Relating to Religion) designed to deal with malicious writings against religious leaders, therefore they were "dealt with only [under Section] 153-A as attempts to promote feelings of enmity or hatred between different classes of citizens."[146] In order to deal with such a situation, the British framed an ad-

---

intention of promoting, causing, or exciting enmity and hatred he would not maintain the conviction. *Jaswant Rai v. King*, 10 P.R (1907).

140. *Ilam Din v. Emperor*, AIR 157, 158 (1930).
141. *Devi Sharan Sharma and Another v. Emperor*, AIR 594, 594 (1927).
142. Ibid., 602.
143. Ibid., 594, 601.
144. *Kali Charan Sharma v. King-Emperor*, AIR 649, 652-53 (1927).
145. Ibid., 649.
146. Sarvaria, *R A Nelson's Indian Penal Code*, 2: 2581.

ditional clause in chapter 15, which could "make malicious acts insulting the religion, or outraging the religious feelings, of any class of citizens, punishable as offences relating to religion, whether or not they amount to attempts to promote feelings of enmity or hatred between classes."[147] Thus, Section 295-A was enacted through the Criminal Law (Amendment) Act of 1927:

> 295-A: **Deliberate and malicious acts intended to outrage religious feelings of any class, by insulting its religion or religious beliefs**. Whoever, with deliberate and malicious intention of outraging the religious feelings of any class of his [Majesty's subjects][148], by words either spoken or written, or by visible representations insult the religion or religious beliefs of that class, shall be punished with imprisonment of either description for a term which may extended to [two years][149], or with fine, or with both.[150]

It is important to note here that when this section of 295-A was proposed to be inserted in the IPC, it drew a well-reasoned response from Muhammad Ali Jinnah in the Central Legislative Assembly on 5 September 1927, where he warned the legislators by stating:

> I thoroughly endorse the principle that while this measure should aim at those undesirable persons who indulge in wanton vilification or attack upon the religion of any particular class or upon the founders and prophets of a religion, we must also secure this important and fundamental principle that those who are engaged in historical works, those who are engaged in *bona fide* and honest criticism of a religion, shall be protected.[151]

---

147. Ibid.

148. Substituted for "the Citizens of Pakistan" by President Order No. 1 of 1961: Central Laws (Adoption) Order (21 January 1961), 13 PLD (1961), 108. It was further amended that it shall be deemed to have taken effect from 23 March 1956.

149. Substituted for "Ten years" by *Act 16 of 1991: Criminal Law (Second Amendment) Act* (25 November 1991), 44 PLD Central Statutes (1992), 31.

150. "Act No. 25 of 1927: Criminal Law (Amendment) Act, (22 September 1927)," in *The Current Indian Statutes* (Lahore: Law Times, 1927), 139.

151. A. G. Noorani, "Forbidden Pages," *Dawn*, 12 July 2014, online.

Zia-Framed Clauses

When Pakistan became an independent country in 1947, the Indian Penal Code (IPC) was adopted as the Pakistan Penal Code (PPC). During the military regime of Zia, five additional clauses, 295-B and C, and 298-A, B and C, were enacted to chapter 15, "Offences Relating to Religion," of the PPC through a series of Ordinances and Acts. We have seen above Zia's zeal for Islamization and these additional clauses of the blasphemy laws were largely motivated by his Islamic ideology and political convictions. We will look at these amendments in chronological order.

Since the inception of Pakistan, one of the demands of the traditionalists was to declare Ahmadis non-Muslims. This was finally achieved in 1974, when Ahmadis were declared non-Muslims and included in the list of minorities in Pakistan.[152] During Zia's Islamization process, the anti-Ahmadi forces found a conducive environment for their agendas to be fulfilled regarding more restrictions on Ahmadis. In 1980, they were able to persuade General Zia-ul-Haq to ban the Ahmadis from using titles reserved for members of the family and companion of the Holy Prophet, and the first four caliphs of Islam, for the family and companions of Mirza Ghulam Ahmad Qadaini (whom Ahmadis revere as Prophet and Messiah). Consequently, the first additional clause, 298-A, was enacted on 17 September 1980, and is as follows:

> **298-A: Use of derogatory remarks, etc., in respect of holy personages.** Whoever by words either spoken or written, or by visible representation, or by any imputation, innuendo, or insinuation, directly or indirectly defiles the sacred names of any wife *(Ummu'l Mūminin)*, or members of the family *(Ahl-ē-bait)* of the Holy Prophet (peace be upon him) or any of the righteous caliphs *(Khulafā-ē-Rāshidin)* or companions *(Ṣiḥāba)* of the Holy Prophet (peace be upon him) shall be punished with imprisonment of either description for a term which may extend to three years or with fine, or with both.[153]

---

152. *Act 49 of 1974*, 425.

153. *Ordinance 44 of 1980: Pakistan Penal Code (Second Amendment) Ordinance* (17 September 1980), 33 PLD Central Statutes (1981), 84.

After less than two years, another clause, 295-B, was introduced on 17 March 1982:

> 295-B: **Defiling etc, of Holy Qur'an.** Whoever willfully defiles, damages or desecrates a copy of the Holy Quran or of an extract therefrom or uses it in any derogatory manner or for any lawful purpose shall be punishable with imprisonment for life.[154]

In 1981, definitions of Muslim and non-Muslim had been framed. Ahmadis were named in the list of non-Muslims in Pakistan.[155] The Ahmadiyya movement had been generally missionary oriented and very active in propagating their faith by claiming themselves as the ambassadors of true Islam. Their missionary activities had therefore been of great concern to the Sunni Muslims in Pakistan. In response, on 26 April 1984, Clauses 298-B and C were enacted to prohibit the activities of Ahmadis, which were regarded as anti-Islamic.[156]

---

154. *Ordinance 1 of 1982: Pakistan Penal Code (Amendment) Ordinance* (17 March 1982), 34 PLD Central Statutes (1982), 147.

155. *C.M.L.A Order 2 of 1981: Provisional Constitution (Amendment) Order* (7 April 1981), 33 PLD Central Statutes (1981), 310–311.

156. 298-B **Misuse of epithets, descriptions and titles reserved for certain holy personages and places of Islam.** "(1) Any person of the Quaidiani group or Lahori group (who call themselves 'Ahmadis' or by any other name) who by words, either spoken or written, or by visible representation, - refers to, or addresses, any person, other than a Caliph or companion of the Holy Prophet Muhammad (peace be upon him), as 'Ameer-ul-Mumineen,' 'Khalifat-ul-Muslimeen,' 'Sahaabi' or 'Razi Allah Anho';
- refers to, or addresses, any person, other than a wife of the Holy Prophet Muhammad (peace be upon him), as 'Ummul-ul-Mumineen';
- refers to, or addresses, any person, other than a member of the family (Ahle-bait) of the Holy Prophet Muhammad (peace be upon him), as 'Ahle-bait'; or
- refers to, or names, or calls, his place of worship as 'Masjid'; shall be punished with imprisonment of either description for a term which may extend to three years and shall also be liable to fine."

(2) "Any person of the Quadiani group or Lahori group (who call themselves 'Ahmadis' or by any other name), who by words, either spoken or written, or by visible representation, refers to the mode or form of call to prayers followed by his faith as 'Azan,' or recites Azan as used by the Muslims, shall be punished with imprisonment of either description for a term which may extend to three years and shall also be liable to fine"

298-C "Any person of the Quaidiani group or Lahori group (who call themselves 'Ahmadis' or by any other name) who, directly or indirectly, poses himself as a Muslim, or calls, or refers to his faith as Islam, or preaches or propagates his faith, or invites others to accept his faith, by words, either spoken or written, or by visible representation or any manner whatsoever outrages the religious feelings of Muslims, shall be punished with imprisonment of either description for a term which may extend to three years and shall also be liable to fine." *Ordinance 20 of 1984: Anti-Islamic Activities of Quadiani Group, Lahori Group and*

In 1983 a book with the title *Heavenly Communism* was published in Pakistan, containing criticism of all religions and their leaders, including the Prophet of Islam. A blasphemy case was registered against the author Mushtaq Raj under Section 295-A, because there was yet no clause specifically dealing with offence against the prophet of Islam.[157] Consequently, in 1984, Muhammad Ismail Qureshi, a lawyer and active member of Jamā'at-ē-Islami, moved a petition in the Federal Shariʿat Court (FSC) to direct the Parliament to legislate a separate clause, specifically dealing with offences against the Holy Prophet. He further advocated in his petition that Shariʿa should prescribe the death penalty for the offender.[158]

His petition did not go unchallenged: the defence council for the government raised the objection that "since legislation fell under the jurisdiction of parliament, [the FSC could] issue a direction to the federation?"[159] The FSC reserved the judgment and meanwhile a bill was moved in the Majlis-ē-Shuʿra (Parliament) seeking the insertion of 295-C in the PPC, drafted by Ismail Qureshi and presented in Parliament by Ms Nisar Fatima of Jamā'at-ē-Islami.[160] According to Ismail Qureshi, the law minister and many other Islamic-minded members of the assembly did not support the death penalty because "they thought the imprisonment for life was sufficient punishment for blasphemy."[161] The bill was not properly discussed in the Parliament because its supporters insisted that it related to the Holy Prophet therefore the issue was not debatable.[162] Consequently, 295-C was passed, with the addition of life imprisonment as an alternative punishment to the death sentence. The final clause was:

> 295-C "Whoever by words either spoken or written, or by visible representation, or by any imputation, innuendo, or insinuation, directly or indirectly defiles the sacred name of

---

Ahmadis (Prohibition and Punishment) Ordinance (26 April 1984), 36 PLD Central Statutes (1984), 103.

157. Muhammad Ismail Qureshi, *Nāmūs-ē-Rasūl Aur Qānūn Tauhin-ē-Risālat* [Dignity of the Prophet and the Law of Blasphemy] (Lahore: Al-Faisal Kutab, 1994), 42–43.

158. Ibid., 44.

159. I. A. Rehman, "The Blasphemy Law," *Dawn*, 25 November 2010, online.

160. Qureshi, *Nāmūs-ē-Rasūl*, 45.

161. Ibid., 45–46.

162. Rehman, "Blasphemy Law."

the Holy Prophet Muhammad (peace be upon him) shall be punished with death, or imprisonment for life, and shall also be liable to fine."[163]

However, Ismail Qureshi was not happy with this outcome, and took advantage of Article 203-D, previously established by Zia. Under this law, Zia had constituted the FSC and empowered it to strike down or amend any law that was not in line with the Injunctions of Islam.[164] The FSC used its prerogative to conform Pakistani laws to the letter and spirit of Islam. Accordingly, Ismail Qureshi filed a further constitutional petition to the FSC in 1987, challenging the alternative of life imprisonment for contempt of the Holy Prophet. The original draft of the bill had proposed only the death penalty but the Ministry of Law had amended this by adding the alternative of a life sentence, which was passed by the Parliament. Qureshi challenged this change with the FSC. He argued that, according to the *hudud* punishments, the penalty for contempt of the Holy Prophet is death and nothing else.[165] This meant that the option of life imprisonment should be nullified and mandatory punishment of death be retained. The FSC was persuaded by the *hudud* argument and passed judgment as:

> . . . we are of the view that the alternate punishment of life imprisonment as provided in Section 295-C, P.P.C. is repugnant to the Injunctions of Islam as given in Holy Qur'an and Sunnah and therefore, the said words to be deleted therefrom. A copy of this order shall be sent to the President of Pakistan under Article 203-D(3) of the Constitution to take steps to amend the law so as to bring the same in conformity with the Injunctions of Islam. In case, this is not done by 30th April, 1991 the words "or imprisonment for life" in Section 295-C, P.P.C. shall cease to have effect on that date.[166]

---

163. *Act 3 of 1986: Criminal Law (Amendment) Act* (5 October 1986), 38 PLD Central Statutes (1986), 71.

164. Article 203-D (1) inserted to the constitution of Pakistan states: "The court [FSC] may, on the petition of a citizen of Pakistan or the Federal Government or a Provincial Government) examine and decide the question whether or not any law or provision of law is repugnant to the Injunctions of Islam . . ." *President's Order 1 of 1980*, 91.

165. *Muhammad Ismail Qureshi v. Pakistan* 43 PLD 10(1991).

166. Ibid., 35.

Khalid Saifullah, an Islamic law expert, points out that the judgment "rested on two basic ideas: first, that blasphemy is practically the same as apostasy, and second, the idea that whoever insulted the Holy Prophet is, in effect, waging a war with him."[167]

The above ruling of the FSC came into effect in 1991 during the democratic government of Muhammad Nawaz Sharif. This judgment of the FSC made the death penalty mandatory and left no room for the previous option of life imprisonment. Benazir Bhutto, then the opposition leader, criticized the FSC's judgment for making the law harsher.[168] The government of Nawaz Sharif filed a review petition against the FSC's decision in the Shariʿat Appellate Bench of the Supreme Court, but later withdrew it. Qureshi claimed that:

> I warned the then Prime Minister of Pakistan Mian Muhammad Nawaz Sharif of its implications and thank God, he took notice of it in time and government's appeal was dismissed as withdrawn in the year 1990. Thereafter penalty of death for blasphemer has been settled as irrevocable law of Pakistan.[169]

To give effect to the FSC's verdict, the Sharif government moved the Criminal Law (Third Amendment) Bill 1991 in the Parliament.[170]

---

167. Khalid S. Khan, "What Is the Punishment for Blasphemy in Islam" (accessed 22 August 2012), online.

168. Maulana Abdul Sitar Niazi, a Muslim cleric holding the office of Federal Minister for Religious Affairs gave a "fatwā" (verdict) to declare Benazir "Kafir" (infidel), deserving death sentence. Patrick Sookhdeo, *A People Betrayed: The Impact of Islamization on the Christian Community in Pakistan* (England: CFP, 2002), 253.

169. Muhammad Ismail Qureshi, *Muhammad: The Messenger of God and the Law of Blasphemy in Islam and the West* (Lahore: Nuqoosh Press, 2008), 60–61.

170. The Standing Committee on Law and Justice after detailed deliberations decided to recommend the proposed deletion of "or imprisonment of life" from Section 295-C of PPC. Nonetheless the committee was "of the considered opinion that the law is very generalized" and a more specific definition needs to be defined by the Council of Islamic Ideology. Rehman, "Blasphemy Law."

The Development of Pakistan's Blasphemy Laws

Table 1.1 A Summary of Pakistan's Blasphemy Laws

PPC	Description	Sentence	Enacted/ Changed
295	Damaging or defiling places of worship of any class.	Imprisonment for two years, or a fine, or both.	1860 for IPC and adopted for PPC in 1947.
295-A	Deliberate and malicious acts intended to outrage religious feelings of any class.	Imprisonment for two years, or a fine, or both.	1927 for IPC and adopted for PPC in 1947.
295-A	*The words "his Majesty's subjects" were changed to "the citizens of Pakistan."*	*A two year sentence was extended to ten years.*	*1961 and 1991.*
295-B	Defiling a copy of the Holy Qur'an.	Imprisonment for life.	1982
295-C	Use of derogatory remarks in respect of the Holy Prophet.	Life imprisonment or death sentence.	1986
295-C	*Option of life sentence was deleted and death sentence became mandatory.*	*Death sentence.*	*1991*
296	Disturbing religious assembly.	Imprisonment for one year, or a fine, or both.	1860 for IPC and adopted for PPC in 1947.
297	Trespassing on burial places, etc.	Imprisonment for one year, or a fine, or both.	1927 for IPC and adopted for PPC in 1947.
298	Uttering words with deliberate intent to wound religious feelings.	Imprisonment for one year, or a fine, or both.	1860 for IPC and adopted for PPC in 1947.
298-A	Use of derogatory remarks in respect of holy personages of Islam.	Imprisonment for three years, or a fine, or both.	1980
298-B	Misuse of epithets, descriptions and titles reserved for certain holy personages or places of Islam.	Imprisonment for three years, and additional possibility of a fine.	1984

| 298-C | Person of Quadiani/Ahmadi group calling himself a Muslim or preaching or propagating his faith. | Imprisonment for three years, and additional possibility of a fine. | 1984 |

Third Period: 1993–2011

Efforts to Amend Blasphemy Laws

There has been an outcry from the minorities, human rights activists and moderate sections of Pakistani society, calling for the pressing need to review these laws and to make appropriate changes to stop their misuse. This concluding part of the chapter will look at the post-Zia era, in which some efforts were made to bring procedural changes to the blasphemy laws.

First Effort

In 1994, Farooq Sajjad, a Muslim and also a *Ḥāfiẓ-ē-Qur'an* (Memorizer or Preserver of the Qur'an) was dragged onto the streets in Gujranwala and stoned to death after a Qur'an in his house accidentally caught fire. The cleric of a local mosque announced that a Christian had burned the Qur'an and the mob grabbed Sajjad out of police custody and pelted him with stones, eventually setting him on fire.[171] Benazir Bhutto, the then prime minister (1993–1996), took note of this incident and showed her intent to amend the laws. She gave this task to the Ministry of Law. Iqbāl Haider, the then Minister of Law. He soon declared that he had won the agreement of other parties, including the hardline religious parties, for making amendments.[172] However, when this statement was published in the newspapers, mass demonstrations started by the hardline religious groups made the government retreat from its position. The religious groups mounted such a campaign against the government that Prime Minister Benazir Bhutto declared that her government had only envisaged procedural changes and added: "we will not amend the law." Iqbāl Haider quickly negated his previous statement and

---

171. Staff Reporter, "Timeline: Accused under the Blasphemy Law," *Dawn*, 19 September 2012, online.

172. Farieha Aziz, "Interview: Iqbal Haider," *Newsline*, December 2010, 37.

declared that the blasphemy law would not be repealed, as the government believed that there should be a deterrent for defiling the name of the Prophet.

Second Effort

A second effort was made to moderate the blasphemy laws under General Pervez Musharraf. He had come to power by overthrowing the civilian government of Nawaz Sharif with a bloodless coup in 1999. General Musharraf portrayed himself as a reformist, like the first military ruler Ayub Khan, promising to deal with political and economic problems.[173] When he took office, Musharraf announced a seven-point agenda of which the foremost was the eradication of Islamic extremism. He showed a determination to undo General Zia's legacy of Islamic extremism by putting Pakistan on the path to becoming a moderate Muslim state.

The liberal image of Musharraf and his government brought high hopes to minorities, particularly when he announced his intention to make procedural changes to the blasphemy laws in Pakistan. Under the proposed amendment, blasphemy cases could be registered after investigation by the local administration.[174] This was his first battle with the Islamic extremists: it took place in the beginning of his rule in April 2000. Islamic fundamentalists fought back, using Musharraf's proposed minor procedural changes as a tool to launch a vehement campaign against his intentions to change the blasphemy laws. Thousands of Islamic activists filled the streets of the big cities of Pakistan, demanding that there be no change to the existing blasphemy laws. Some said "it was the first major test for Musharraf as he tried to move the country away from General Zia's orthodox Islamic ideology."[175] However, due to the pressure of the Islamic extremists, Musharraf withdrew his proposal to reform the procedural aspects of the blasphemy laws.[176]

Zahid Hussain points out that "the blasphemy issue also exposed division within the military leadership. Some members of junta, who were often

---

173. There is a striking resemblance between Ayub and Musharraf: both were admirers of Mustafa Kemal Ataturk, who emphasized the promotion of a moderate Islam. See Hussain, "Pakistan," 318; Anatol Lieven, *Pakistan: A Hard Country*, 1st ed. (New York: Public Affairs, 2011), 63–70.
174. Hussain, *Frontline Pakistan*.
175. Ibid., 8.
176. Hussain, "Pakistan," 319.

described as 'jihadist generals' were openly sympathetic to hardline Islamic groups. They were opposed to any move to change Islamic laws."[177] It was not only the Islamic activists on the street but also the Islamic-oriented wing within the Pakistan army that made Musharraf step back. Ahmed Rashid strengthens this view, saying that "[a]fter Musharraf reneged on his promise to reform the unjust blasphemy law, liberal civilians who had joined began to resign."[178] In May 2000, Musharraf went back on his promise to reform the blasphemy law. Musharraf's "promised reform had been relatively mild – merely a procedural change – but General Aziz advised Musharraf to back down because it would annoy the fundamentalists."[179]

Musharraf was finally able to introduce a mild procedural change in 2004 that only a superintendent of police (SP) could investigate a charge of blasphemy before a First Investigation Report (FIR) was filed. Unfortunately, this change has not been followed by the police and seems impractical. Nonetheless, Mufti Muneebur Rehman, Chairman of the Central Rūyat-ē-Ḥalal Committee in Pakistan, expressed his views that this change, introduced by Musharraf, must be done away with because it made registration of blasphemy cases difficult, and it would result in unrest among Muslims.[180] In the end, Musharraf came to the opinion that "blasphemy was deeply sensitive in the country and doing away with it was not possible."[181] He further said that "rather than amend the legislation . . . Pakistan needed to ensure the laws were not misused."[182]

Third Effort

The third effort to change the blasphemy laws was the result of the courageous and dangerous actions of three main advocates, Mr Salman Taseer, Mr Shahbaz Bhatti and Ms Sherry Rehman, who raised their voices louder

---

177. Hussain, *Frontline Pakistan*, 9.

178. Ahmed Rashid, *Descent into Chaos: The US and the Failure of Nation Building in Pakistan, Afghanistan, and Central Asia* (New York: Viking, 2008), 54.

179. Ibid., 414.

180. Staff Reporter, "Muneeb Says Blasphemy Accused Should Be Tried by FSC," *Dawn*, 18 March 2013, online.

181. Ben Farmer, "Blasphemy Laws Must Not Be Scrapped, Says Musharraf," *The Telegraph*, 11 January 2011, online.

182. Ibid.

than any other political figures in Pakistan about the need to amend the blasphemy laws.

Salman Taseer was governor of Punjab when he was assassinated for criticizing the blasphemy laws. In 2010, Asia Bibi, a Christian woman, drew attention once again to the stringent blasphemy laws when she was convicted under 295-C by the Session Court in Sheikhupura and sentenced to death. Salman Taseer went with his wife to jail to sympathize with Asia. He addressed the media and pledged that Asia would receive a presidential pardon. In reaction to his announcement, the provincial judiciary became involved into the matter and K͟hwāja Sharif, the Chief Justice of the Lahore High Court, ruled that the president had no right to grant a presidential pardon until the appeals process had been exhausted.[183]

During his press conference, Taseer pointed out that the blasphemy law was a man-made law and not a God-made law and that many, like Asia, were victims of this law. In this context, he used the words "black law" to describe the blasphemy laws as a miscarriage of justice. In response, the Islamic religious parties called for a countrywide demonstration against the governor. His effigy was burned in almost every big city of Pakistan. Muslim clerics passed *fatwās* (verdicts), declaring him a blasphemer who deserved the death penalty.

On 4 January 2011, one of Taseer's security guards, named Mumtaz Qadri, assassinated him in Islamabad, the capital of Pakistan. Mumtaz Qadri admitted that he killed the governor but he denied that "it was murder saying he had acted on the directives of the Koran (sic) and the teachings of the Prophet Muhammad regarding an apostate."[184] Qari Hanif Qureshi, a fiery speaker who was the apparent inspiration for Qadri to assassinate the governor, said that "Islam rewarded the killers of apostates."[185] Similarly, Fazul-ur-Rehman, the leader of the Jamait-e-Ulamā Islam party, said that the "Assassin of the Governor has fulfilled his obligation as a Muslim and we

---

183. Rana Tanveer, "Lahore High Court Stalls Pardon Moves for Aasia Bibi," *The Express Tribune*, 30 November 2010, online.

184. AFP, "Qadri Indicted in Salman Taseer Murder Case," *Dawn*, 14 February 2011, online.

185. Ibid.

will defend him in the court."[186] Governor Taseer, along with Ms Rehman, have been the only leaders from the ruling Pakistan People Party to openly oppose the controversial blasphemy laws and seek to repeal or amend them.[187]

The second key political figure to speak out against the blasphemy law was a Christian politician named Shahbaz Bhatti. Bhatti became the Federal Minister for Minorities in 2003. He was a staunch advocate for amending the blasphemy laws because of their misuse, especially against minorities. Bhatti said:

> I want to send a message of hope to the people living a life of disappointment, disillusionment and despair. Jesus is the nucleus of my life and I want to be his true follower through my actions by sharing the love of God with the poor, oppressed, victimized, needy and suffering people of Pakistan.[188]

He was appointed by the President Asif Ali-Zardari to head a committee to look into the possibilities for amending the blasphemy laws. Soon after that he began to receive death threats from the hard liners. In an interview with the BBC, Shahbaz Bhatti said, "I was told that if I was to continue the campaign against the blasphemy law, I will be assassinated. I will be beheaded. But forces of violence, forces of extremism cannot harass me, cannot threaten me"[189] About two months after Taseer's assassination, on 2 March 2011, Bhatti was also shot dead in the capital of Pakistan. A pamphlet found at the site of the killing, attributed to the Taliban, gave a "warning of the same fate for anyone opposing the blasphemy laws."[190]

The third advocate to speak up against the injustice of the blasphemy laws was Sherry Rehman, former Information Minister, who introduced a private bill to the National Assembly with proposed amendments to the

---

186. Zahid Hussain, "World News: Asia: Islamists Rally in Pakistan for Blasphemy Laws," *The Wall Street Journal Asia* 2011, 5.

187. Murtaza Razvi, "Murder Most Foul," *Dawn*, 4 January 2011, online.

188. Amir Wasim, "Shahbaz Bhatti, a Fearless Rights Crusader," *Dawn*, 3 March 2011, online.

189. Orla Guerin, "Pakistan Blasphemy Law Reformers' Death Threats," *BBC News*, 11 January 2011, online.

190. Staff Reporter, "Pakistan's Only Christian Minister Assassinated over Blasphemy Row," *The Telegraph*, 2 March 2011, online.

blasphemy laws. Some of the key amendments proposed by Rehman are highlighted here.

- First, she proposed to replace the harsh penalties with lesser punishments, for example, to replace the death penalty in 295-C with ten years' imprisonment. Sherry argued in the defence of her proposal that when the harsher penalties were introduced "the curve of the blasphemy-related abuses went up."[191]
- Second, she proposed to make *mens rea* mandatory, which is a central requirement of the criminal law. With this amendment, the accuser must provide the basis that "the accused acted with malicious and premeditated intent . . . This shifts the burden of proving intent back on the accuser."[192]
- Third, she proposed that trials should be removed from the jurisdiction of the Session Courts and that, instead, blasphemy cases should be tried directly in the high courts, because judges of the trials courts are easily pressurized by mobs.[193] Rehman argued that the higher judiciary is relatively resistant to such pressure and is under greater public scrutiny.[194]
- Fourth, she proposed that a false accuser should be penalized with the penalty that would have applied to the person whom they were accusing, had they been guilty.[195]

In reaction to her proposal to amend the blasphemy laws, the hardliners launched a campaign against any move to amend the blasphemy laws. They warned the government that they would not tolerate any type of amendment of the blasphemy laws.[196] The *imām* (cleric) of Sultan Mosque in Karachi in his Friday sermon called Ms Rehman a *kafir* (infidel) and *wājibu'l-qatl* (fit to be killed) for suggesting changes in the blasphemy laws.[197] *Fatwās* (verdicts) were issued by several clerics, declaring Rehman to be a non-Muslim

---

191. Maheen B. Adamjee, "Interview: Sherry Rehman," *Newsline*, December 2010, 33.
192. Ibid.
193. Ibid., 34.
194. Ibid., 33–34.
195. Ibid., 34.
196. Staff Reporter, "Clerics to Launch Campaign If Blasphemy Laws Amended," *Daily Times*, 13 December 2010, online.
197. Hussain, "World News: Asia," 5.

and demanding the death sentence for her.[198] Yousaf Raza Gilani, the then prime minister, announced that "Sherry Rehman agreed to withdraw her bill according to party policy."[199] In response Ms Rehman said that "she had no option but abide by the decision after the prime minister ruled out any discussion."[200]

In this way, the third effort also withered under pressure from hardliners, who had sent a clear and violent message that any change in Pakistan's blasphemy laws would not be tolerated. It seems that, for Christians, Ahmadis and other minorities in Pakistan, any amendments to the blasphemy laws in the near future are out of the question.

Concluding Summary

The main objective of this opening chapter has been to explore the historical development of Pakistan's blasphemy laws, and how this phenomenon has been integrally related to the process of Islamization in Pakistan. For this purpose, our study of historical exploration was divided into three periods spanning the period from 1947 up until 2011.

Our enquiry into the first period demonstrated that, soon after its establishment, Pakistan drifted away from its founder's vision, which had been for a secular democracy, and started to move towards Islamization. Right after the death of Jinnah, a debate began about the place of Islam in Pakistan, which moved towards achieving this goal, to making Pakistan a purely Islamic country run by an Islamic constitution in which Sharīa would be supreme.

The process of Islamization continued over the years as the constitution of Pakistan was developed. Although some meager efforts have been made, especially by Ayub Khan, to slow down this process of Islamization, he and others ultimately surrendered to extremist forces. The extremists have proven hard to please, even though Ayub Khan's successor, Zulfikar Ali Bhutto tried

---

198. Asad Farooq, "Fatwa Demands Death for Sherry," *Daily Times*, 9 January 2011, online.

199. Mubashar Nizam, "Government Has No Intention to Amend Blasphemy Law: PM," *Pakistan Times*, 31 January 2011, online.

200. AFP, "'No Option' but to Abide by PM's Decision on Blasphemy: Sherry," *Dawn*, 3 February 2011, online.

to appease the Islamists by taking drastic steps towards the Islamization of Pakistan. However, he, like Ayub Khan, was thrown out of power because the hardliners did not believe he was committed enough to the implementation of *niẓam-ē-muṣṭafā* (System of the Prophet) in Pakistan. This has been the major demand of the traditionalists. Therefore General Zia-ul-Haq's military coup was strongly supported by them.

Our study of the second period, which covers the rule of General Zia, demonstrated that Islam re-emerged in Pakistan in a more traditional way than any in era before or since. It was evident from this period's study that Zia used Islam for his own political ambitions and took every step to make Pakistan more Islamic. Our examination of Zia's era demonstrated that his Islamic policies unprecedentedly affected the judicial system of Pakistan. Moreover, Zia's Islamic orientation coupled with his political motives, led him to introduce five additional clauses to the blasphemy laws in the Penal Code of Pakistan. We have also seen that the changes that Zia made to the Islamic judicial system and, in particular, the creation of the Federal Shariat Court (FSC), made the blasphemy laws significantly harsher. Most notably, in 1991 the FSC ruled that the death penalty was the mandatory penalty for violating Section 295-C. Since then, this law has been misused largely for settling personal scores.

Our study of the third period showed that some efforts were made by courageous moderates to bring procedural changes to the blasphemy laws in order to reduce their misuse. In this regard, major efforts were made by three post-Zia governments. However, this study has indicated that all their efforts had been conclusively defeated, leaving a big question mark over any possibility of change in Pakistan's blasphemy laws in the near future.

CHAPTER 2

A Theological Analysis of Pakistan's Blasphemy Laws in the Light of Islamic Shari'a

Introduction

Muslims have shown a range of attitudes to criticism of and insults towards their religion. At one extreme are people such as Ayatollah Majilis, a ninth-century cleric, who said that he would prefer to die before he saw Islam insulted.[1] Likewise, this attitude is reflected in the Arab proverb which says "kill me but do not mock my faith."[2] On the other hand, Mustafa Bisri, a revered Muslim intellectual, wrote, "If all of the 6 billion human inhabitants of this earth, which is no greater than a speck of dust, were blasphemous . . . or pious . . . it would not have the slightest effect upon His [Allah's] greatness."[3]

Muslims' responses to critique of their religion and especially of their Prophet Muhammad can be profoundly theological. The traditional view is that the blasphemy laws in Pakistan are divine in their origins and therefore theologically justified: for this they claim ample support from the Qur'an and, more specifically, from *sira* and *hadith* literature.[4] On the basis of the

---

1. Richard Webster, *A Brief History of Blasphemy – Liberalism, Censorship and the Satanic Verses* (Southwold, UK: Orwell Press, 1990), 30–31.
2. Ibid.
3. Abdurrahman Wahid, "God Needs No Defence," in *Silence: How Apostasy and Blasphemy Codes Are Choking Freedom Worldwide*, eds. Paul Marshall and Nina Shea (Oxford: Oxford University Press, 2011), xvii.
4. Qureshi, *Muhammad*.

traditional view, the harsher clauses of the blasphemy laws were introduced by Zia-ul-Haq in passim response to the demand of *niẓām-ē-muṣṭafa* (system of the Prophet) in Pakistan, as the study in chapter 1 showed.

In contrast, the progressive Muslim view holds that the blasphemy laws are not divine, but the creation of the classical medieval jurists of Islamic *fiqh* (jurisprudence) and a product of their *ijtihad* (interpretation) in the context of the Islamic empire.[5] Moreover, the advocates of this view argue that the interpretation by the medieval jurists was entirely dependent on their circumstances, and therefore inapplicable to modern times. According to the progressive view, Pakistan's blasphemy laws cannot be justified on theological grounds because Shari'a law needs to be continuously reviewed in accordance with ever-changing circumstances.

This chapter's main objective is to examine the traditional view, which underpins Pakistan's blasphemy laws and which argues for the theological justification of Pakistan's blasphemy laws in the light of Islamic. The term "Shari'a" is generally used in reference to the entire system of law and jurisprudence in Islam. The Qur'an and *sunna* (sayings and deeds of the Prophet Muhammad) are the two fundamental sources of Islamic Shari'a. They have been, in the course of time, supplemented by a body of interpretation largely agreed upon by *ijma* (the consensus of majority of jurists) to form the basis of Islamic jurisprudence called *fiqh* in Arabic.[6] In order to analyze our subject matter, we will examine these sources in this order: (1) Qur'an, (2) *sunna*, (3) *fiqh*, and (4) the final section of this chapter will look at Muslim scholarship in the modern period. However, before we move to our analysis, it would be appropriate to have a brief glance at the concept of blasphemy in Islam. We begin with its definition and scope.

---

5. Abdullah Saeed and Hassan Saeed, *Freedom of Religion, Apostasy and Islam* (Burlington: Ashgate, 2004), 66–68; Shemeem B. Abbas, *Pakistan's Blasphemy Laws: From Islamic Empires to the Taliban*, 1st ed. (Texas: University of Texas Press, 2013), 47–50.

6. Irshad Abdal-Haqq, "Islamic Law: An Overview of Its Origin and Elements," in *Understanding Islamic Law: From Classical to Contemporary*, ed. Hisham M. Ramadan (Oxford: AltaMira Press, 2006), 3.

Blasphemy in Islam: Definition and Scope

According to the *Encyclopedia of Religion* the concept of *sabb* (blasphemy) in Islam is quite broad: "In describing Islamic concept of blasphemy, it is necessary to include not only insulting language directed at God, the Prophet, and the revelation, but also theological positions and even mystical aphorisms that have come under suspicion."[7] From the point of view of Islamic law, blasphemy, whether against Allah or the Prophet Muhammad or the Qur'anic revelation, is regarded as part of the offence of either *riddah* (apostasy), *kufr* (infidelity) or *zandaqah* (heresy).[8] Accordingly, the majority of the jurists of Islamic *fiqh* dealt with the crime of blasphemy under apostasy. Thus, blasphemy overlaps with apostasy in the classical literature of *fiqh* (as we will see in detail under the *fiqh* section).

Some suggest that the reason that Islamic jurists, specifically in the medieval period, made no distinction between blasphemy and apostasy is, perhaps, due to the fact that during the life of the Prophet of Islam, "almost all instances of apostasy were accompanied by hostility [towards] and abuse [of] the Prophet."[9] Because of this, they believe the concept of blasphemy in the Islamic *fiqh* is very much correlated with apostasy. However, others object to this view by arguing that "these laws [about apostasy and blasphemy] grew out of political rivalry and not out of Muhammad's *sunna* or the Qur'an."[10] They claim that these laws were the product of the post-Muhammad Islamic state which used them to exercise political and social control.[11]

The trend of classifying blasphemy with apostasy exists even among modern scholars, as can be seen from Yahaya Bambale's description of acts, deeds or words that result in *riddah*. These include: "(b) Throwing the Holy Qur'an in a filth. (c) Abuse or say Holy Prophet Muhammad is not the last

---

7. Carl W. Ernst, "Blasphemy: Islamic Concept," in *The Enclyclopedia of Religion*, ed. Mircea Eliade (New York: Macmillan, 1987), 243.

8. Mohammad H. Kamali, *Freedom of Expression in Islam* (Kualalumpur: Berita, 1994), 208; Bernard Lewis, "Behind the Rushdie Affair," *American Scholar* 60 (1991): 187; Ernst, "Blasphemy: Islamic Concept," 242–243.

9. Kamali, *Freedom of Expression*, 208.

10. Abbas, *Pakistan's Blasphemy Laws*, 46.

11. Ibid., 47–48.

prophet or abuse other prophets of Allah . . ."[12] Likewise, Ibn Warraq notes, "A Muslim becomes an apostate if he defames the Prophet's character, morals, or virtues, and denies Muhammad's prophethood and that he was the seal of the prophets."[13] It is important to note here that if the offence of blasphemy is committed by a Muslim it is classified as apostasy. However, if a non-Muslim commits blasphemy, he cannot be accused of apostasy, as apostasy involves renouncing the faith of Islam. Hashim Kamali, Professor of Islamic law, argues that "it is on this basis that blasphemy can be distinguished from apostasy."[14] Kamali defines blasphemy thus: "The hallmark of blasphemy is, of course, a contemptuous and hostile attack on the fundamentals of religion, which offends the sensibilities of its believers."[15]

As we turn the pages of Islamic history, some examples can be found when insults against Allah and against holy personalities, like the Prophet's wives and his companions, were considered as blasphemy by jurists of Islamic *fiqh*. However, blasphemy came to be associated primarily with perceived insults to the Holy Prophet of Islam. The Islamic law books reveal that jurists took a comparatively strict view towards the reviling of the Prophet of Islam. This is evident from a legal source of the eighth century, the *Muwatta'* of 'Abdallah b. Wahb (d. 812), which proposes the death penalty for anyone who insults the Prophet Muhammad.[16] This trend of identifying blasphemy primarily with insults against the Prophet can also be traced from the words of al-Ghazali, a great religious thinker of the twelfth century, who wrote that "calling a Prophet [of Islam] a liar in any respect; this is to equate infidelity with blasphemy."[17] One of the earliest reports that the charge of blasphemy in Islam became focused on the Prophet Muhammad is related to Abu Bakr, the first rightly guided caliph, who believed that blasphemy was mainly

---

12. Yahaya Y. Bambale, *Crimes and Punishments under Islamic Law*, 2nd ed. (Nigeria: Malthouse, 2003), 75.

13. Warraq Ibn, ed. *Leaving Islam: Apostates Speak Out* (New York: Prometheus Books, 2003), 16.

14. Kamali, *Freedom of Expression*, 206.

15. Ibid.

16. Lutz Wiederhold, "Blasphemy against the Prophet Muhammad and His Companions," *JSS* 42, no. 1 (1997): 43.

17. Ernst, "Blasphemy: Islamic Concept," 244.

insulting the Prophet and formulated the principle that a response to this offence was the prerogative of the Prophet alone.[18]

This focus on the Prophet Muhammad is also evident from Allama Qurtubi's assertion: "The glorification and exaltation of Prophet is the base of the religion and [thus] depriving it is depriving the religion."[19] This can be further seen from Asrar Madani's definition of blasphemy. It comes, perhaps, from the verdict of the Pakistan Federal Shari'at Court, given on 30 October 1990, in the famous case of *Ismail Qureshi vs. Pakistan*, where blasphemy was described as:

> Reviling or insulting the Prophet in writing or speech; speaking profanely or contemptuously about him or his family; attacking the Prophet's dignity and honour in an abusive manner; vilifying him or making an ugly face when his name is mentioned; showing enmity or hatred towards him, his family, his companions and the Muslims; accusing or slandering the Prophet; refusing the Prophet's jurisdiction or judgment in any matter . . ."[20]

The central status of the Prophet Muhammad is also evident from Pakistan's blasphemy laws, where blasphemy against the Prophet is considered a much more heinous crime than blasphemy against Allah or the Qur'an or other holy personalities of Islam. Clause 295-C of the PPC makes capital punishment the mandatory penalty for blasphemy against the Prophet of Islam.[21] The primacy of the Prophet Muhammad is further evident from the fact that the Parliament of Pakistan gave no attention to the suggestion of the Federal Shari'at Court (FSC) that insults against other prophets should attract the same penalty as blasphemy against the Holy Prophet.[22]

---

18. Once Abu Baker was insulted by a man in an open meeting. In reaction, Abu Barzah, sought permission from the Caliph to cut off the neck of the contemner. In response "Abu Baker said: I swear by Allah, this is not allowed for any man after Muhammad." Abu Dawud, *Sunan Abudawud*, trans. Ahmad Hasan, 8th ed., 3 vols., vol. 3 (New Delhi: Kitab Bhavan, 2008), 1215.

19. Cited in *Muhammad Ismail Qureshi v. Pakistan* 21.

20. Mohammad A. Madani, *Verdict of Islamic Law on Blasphemy and Apostasy* (Lahore: Idra-e-Islamiat, 1994), 19–20.

21. *Act 3 of 1986*, 71; *Muhammad Ismail Qureshi v. Pakistan*, 35.

22. *Muhammad Ismail Qureshi v. Pakistan*, 35.

The sensitivity of the issue of blasphemy against the Prophet becomes apparent from how the blasphemy law is applied, as witnessed in the following newspaper reports:

> Even more curiously, mockery of God – what one would expect to see as the most outrageous blasphemy – seems to have escaped their attention as well. Satirical magazines such as Charlie Hebdo have run cartoons ridiculing God (in the Jewish, Christian and Muslim contexts), but they were targeted with violence only when they ridiculed the Prophet Muhammad.[23]

In another example, a mere misplaced dot led to accusations of blasphemy against a Christian eighth-grade student in Abbottabad, who "erroneously misspelt a word in an Urdu exam while answering a question on a poem written in praise of the Holy Prophet (PBUH). The word in [answer] was 'laanat'[curse] instead of 'naat'[praise] – an easy error for a child to make, as the written versions of the words are similar."[24]

Having briefly surveyed the concept of blasphemy in Islam, now we turn to examine our main subject matter – that is, whether Pakistan's blasphemy laws are consistent or inconsistent with Islamic Sharīa.

Pakistan's Blasphemy Laws in the Light of the Qur'an

In Arabic, two common verbs for blasphemy, *sabba* (to abuse, insult) and *shatama* (to vilify) are used. There is no example of the verb *shatma* or any derivation from the root *sh-t-m* (in the sense of vilification) in the Qur'an. Furthermore, the word *sabb* is only used twice in one verse of the Qur'an as a part of commandment to Muslims to refrain from insulting other people's gods.[25] "Do not abuse [*sabba*] those to whom they pray, apart from God, or they will abuse God in revenge without knowledge" (Q.6:108). When the

---

23. Mustafa Akyol, "Islam's Problem with Blasphemy," *The New York Times*, 14 January 2015, A25.

24. Muhammad Sadaqat, "Girl Accused of Blasphemy for a Spelling Error," *The Express Tribune*, 25 September 2011, online.

25. For the background of this commandment see Ibn Ishaq, *The Life of Muhammad: A Translation of Ibn Ishaq's Sirat Rasul Allah*, trans. A. Guillaume (Karachi: Oxford University Press, 2007), 162.

subject of blasphemy in the light of the Qur'an comes under discussion, the following issue is the most debated among scholars:

Does the Qur'an speak about capital punishment for blasphemy?

There are two positions held among scholars about what the Qur'an specifies regarding the fate of the blasphemer. One side argues that the Qur'an specifies the death penalty,[26] while the other side argues that the punishment for blasphemy will be the wrath of Allah on judgment day, in the after-life, thus after a natural death.[27]

For the sake of analysis we will call those who argue that the punishment for blasphemy is not mentioned in the Qur'an, modernists, while we will call those who argue that the penalty for blasphemy is death and that this penalty is found in the Qur'an, traditionalists. The interesting fact of this debate is that both sides appeal to the same Qur'anic text but, because of different hermeneutical approaches, come to opposite conclusions. The modernists make their argument by citing several references in the Qur'an[28] relating to the abuses of the Holy Prophet, none of which mention a punishment.[29] In contrast, the traditionalists argue that a person who abuses the Prophet becomes an apostate, and that the punishment for apostasy is death. In this regard Iqbāl Siddiqi (a traditionalist) notes, "Islam has looked down upon it [apostasy] as a very grave offence and has recommended

---

26. Maulana Ahmad Saeed Kazmi writes, "Looking into the Book [Qur'an] . . . we have no doubt and we are sure that death is the only penalty for one who blasphemes the Prophet." Cited in Qureshi, *Muhammad*, 173. Abdul Aziz bin Baz, former grand Mufti of Saudi Arabia, issued a *fatwā* (verdict) with reference to the Holy Qur'an, *hadith* and the consensus of jurists of Islamic *fiqh* that the only punishment prescribed for the blasphemer is death. Ibid., 172.

27. Khalid Zaheer, an eminent Islamic scholar in Pakistan, argued that "if there was a punishment for blasphemy in Islam, it should have been mentioned clearly in the Qur'an, especially in the passages where occurrences of it during the Prophet's lifetime are mentioned." Khalid Zaheer, "The Real Blasphemers," *The Express Tribune*, 2 January 2011, online.

28. It is stated in the Qur'an: Disbelievers made a jest of the Holy Prophet (Q.21:37); he was called a mad man (Q.15:7); they said: there is madness in him (Q.23:71); he was called a victim of deception (Q.17:48); he was treated as a liar (35:26); they called the Qur'anic revelation as 'mere stories of the past' (Q.16:25); the Qur'an was called 'confused dreams' and the Holy Prophet a 'poet' (Q.21:6); he was called 'a fabricator' (Q.16:102); they said: It is only a man who teaches him'(Q.16:104); they urged the people 'not to listen Qur'an but make noise during its recitation' (Q.41:27); they 'tore the Qur'an into pieces (Q.15:92).

29. Khan, "What Is the Punishment?"

capital punishment for it."³⁰ However, the modernist camp refutes this logic, pointing out that no punishment for apostasy is mentioned in the Qur'an. In this regard, Hashim Kamali, a professor of Islamic law, notes that "there are 20 references [to] apostasy in the Qur'an but none of them represent that apostate should be killed."³¹ Likewise, Abu-Zayd notes that, while "the Qur'an prescribes no earthly punishment for either blasphemy or apostasy, the historical development of Islamic law has . . . prescribed the death penalty as punishment for both."³²

Although there are several verses in the Qur'an which have become a point of debate between traditionalists and modernists,³³ our space does not allow us to review all of these. We will instead examine the main Qur'anic passages presented by the traditionalists as source texts for the punishment of apostasy/blasphemy.

Source Text #1: Surah An-Nisa (Women)

The first Qur'anic passage presented by the traditionalist camp as a source text in support of their view is from *Surah An-Nisa:*

> "But if they turn back (from Islam) take (hold of) them and kill them and kill them wherever you find them . . . If they withdraw not from you, nor offer you peace, nor restrain their hands, take (hold of) them and kill them wherever ye find them. In their case, we have provided you with a clear warrant against them." (Q.4:89; 91)³⁴

---

30. Muhammad I. Siddiqi, *The Penal Law of Islam* (Delhi: International Islamic Publications, 1991), 96.

31. Mohammad H. Kamali, "Punishment in Islamic Law: A Critique of the Hudud Bill of Kelantan, Malaysia," *Arab Law Quarterly* 13, no. 3 (1998).

32. Nasr Hamid Abu-Zayd, "Renewing Qur'anic Studies in the Contemporary World," in *Silenced: How Apostasy and Blasphemy Codes Are Choking Freedom Worldwide*, eds. Paul Marshall and Nina Shea (Oxford: Oxford University Press, 2011), 294. Zwemer is also of the view that there is no mention in the Qur'an that an apostate or blasphemer will receive the capital punishment. Samuel M. Zwemer, *The Law of Apostasy in Islam* (New York: Marshall Brothers, 1924), 9.

33. For good analysis of both positions, see Declan O'Sullivan, "The Interpretation of Qur'anic Text to Promote or Negate the Death Penalty for Apostates and Blasphemers," *JQS* 3, no. 2 (2001).

34. Text of the Qur'an in English published by King Fahd Complex, Madinah.

The main point of debate between modernists and traditionalists concerns the significance of the political background of the prophetic and post-prophetic period in which the classical Islamic law of apostasy was formulated. The modernists argue that this passage must be exegeted in the light of its socio-political context. During the time of the Prophet, Muslims were engaged in defensive wars and those who became apostate joined the enemy and were therefore treated as a part of the enemy force. In this political context, apostates were deemed a serious social and political threat to the Muslim community and their killing was justified as a punishment for committing a political crime. Thus Abdullah Saeed, professor of Islamic Studies at the University of Melbourne, argues, "In the early Muslim reasoning, apostasy was more akin to treason, rather than a matter of simply changing one's belief. The death sentence therefore was a punishment for committing a serious political crime."[35] Likewise, Abdurrahman Wahid, former president of Indonesia and head of *Nahdlatul Ulama*, the world's largest Muslim organization, stated that the "punishment for apostasy is merely the legacy of historical circumstances . . . when apostasy generally coincided with desertion . . . and thus constituted treason or rebellion."[36] In summary, according to the modern view, apostasy was conflated with treason, and this is why it incurred the death penalty.

Traditionalists disagree with this view and do not conflate apostasy with treason. Their hermeneutical approach is more literal and gives no importance to the socio-political context of the text. In this regard, Muhammad Asad, in his commentary note, argues that the Arabic script of the Qur'an should be literally translated.[37] This is, perhaps, due to the belief that the Qur'an was dictated to the Prophet and that there is no human element involved in the transmission of the Qur'an.

The modernists' view is largely supported by renowned commentators of the Qur'an. For example, Ibn Kathir's view is that this command to impose the death penalty is for those hypocrites who sympathized with

---

35. Abdullah Saeed, "Rethinking Classical Muslim Law of Apostasy and the Death Penalty," in *Silenced: How Apostasy & Blasphemy Codes Are Choking Freedom Worldwide*, eds. Paul Marshall and Nina Shea (Oxford: Oxford University Press, 2011), 296.

36. Wahid, "God Needs No Defence," xviii.

37. Muhammad Asad, *The Message of the Qur'an* (Lahore: Kazi Publications, 1980), 155.

the idolaters: "They pretend to be Muslims . . . However, they support the idolaters in secret and worship what they worship . . . These people have secretly sided with the idolaters."[38] Undoubtedly, these idolaters were the enemies of the Muslims because they showed no allegiance to the Prophet of Islam and thus undermined the Prophet as ruler of the new Islamic state. Although Abu Ala Maududi represents the traditionalist camp, he classifies the offenders in this verse as hypocrites who are against the Muslim state: "This is the verdict on those hypocritical confessors of faith who belong to a belligerent, non-Muslim nation and actually participate in acts of hostility against the Islamic state."[39]

Some commentators on the Qur'an leave room for both views. For example, Anwer Ali, in his commentary on the Qur'an, points out that the commandment refers to two groups of apostates who are to be seized and slain. The first group includes apostates who did not migrate with the believers to Madinah and also those who, after migration, returned to their home (Mecca); and the second group of apostates includes "those who merely pretend to be believers and made fraudulent offer of peace, but when occasion arose, they came forward for fighting against the believers. They were also seized and slain like the first one."[40] Anwer Ali is clear that the second group of apostates joined the enemy forces (thus becoming guilty of treason, as the modernists point out). But Ali does not specify whether the first group of apostates simply returned to their previous beliefs or whether they joined the enemy forces. This interpretation leaves room for the traditional view: the first group can be labeled simply as apostates who turned away from Muslim beliefs but did not raise their swords against the Islamic state established by the Prophet.

It is apparent from the above commentators that some of those mentioned in these texts did not just turn away from Muslim beliefs but joined the enemies of the Muslim state. So their offence of apostasy was combined with treason, and it was treason, not apostasy, that attracted the death penalty.

---

38. Ibn Kathir, *Tafsir Ibn Kathir*, 2nd ed., 10 vols., vol. 2 (Riyadh: Darussalam, 2003), 540.

39. Abul Ala Mawdudi, *Tafhim al-Qur'an: Towards Understanding the Qur'an*, trans. Zafar I. Ansari, 8 vols., vol. 2 (Leicester: Islamic Foundation, 2001), 67.

40. Syed Anwer Ali, *Qur'an: The Fundamental Law of Human Life*, 16 vols., vol. 5 (Karachi: Hamdard Foundation, 1989), 142.

This view is strengthened by Ibn Hashim, one of the early biographers of the Prophet Muhammad. He records that the Prophet allowed those from among his followers who wanted to return to Mecca and their previous beliefs to do so, without penalty.[41] If this view is correct, then any punishment for apostasy and blasphemy is unjustifiable in the light of Qur'anic teaching.

Source Text #2: Surah At-Taubah (Repentance)

The second Qur'anic passage cited by the traditionalists as a support text for the death penalty for apostasy/blasphemy is the following:

> But if they repent, perform As-Salat, (Iqamat-as-Salat) and give *Zakat,* then they are your brethren in religion . . . But if they violate their oaths after their covenant, and attack your religion with disapproval and criticism, then fight (you) the leaders of disbelief – for surely their oaths are nothing to them – so that they may stop (evil actions). (Q.9:11–12)

The Arabic word *ahd* (covenant/pledge/oath) in verse 12 is a subject of debate between traditionalists and modernists. Maulana Maududi, one of the advocates of the traditionalist view, argued that covenant breaking refers to a breach of faith in the Prophet. He argued that "covenant breaking" can in no way be construed to mean "breaking of political covenants." Rather "the context clearly determines that it refers to confessing Islam and then renouncing it."[42] Therefore, he argues, apostasy incurs the death penalty ("fight the heads of disbelief").

In contrast, others like Mohammad Ali, Tahir Ahmad and Justice S. A. Rahman, contend that the word *ahd* was used "as equivalent to a political pact."[43] Tahir Ahmad notes that "these verses [Q.9:11–12] refer to idolaters who have broken their pledges and ridicule religion; there is no mention of

---

41. Ishaq, *Life of Muhammad,* 504.
42. Abul Ala Maududi, *The Punishment of the Apostate according to Islamic Law,* trans. Silas Husain and Ernest Hahn (Lahore: Islamic Publication, 1994), 14; Abul Ala Mawdudi, *Tafhim al-Qur'an: Towards Understanding the Qur'an,* trans. Zafar I. Ansari, 8 vols., vol. 3 (Leicester: Islamic Foundation, 2001), 193.
43. Mohammad Ali, *The Holy Qur'an: Containing the Arabic Text with English Translation and Commentary* (Lahore: Ahmadiyya Anjuman-I-Ishaat-I-Islam, 1920), 399; S. A. Rahman, *Punishment of Apostasy in Islam* (Lahore: IIC, 1972), 12.

people renouncing their faith."⁴⁴ They support their argument by appealing to the historical background of this passage (Surah al-Tawbah).

The passage is set in the context of the "Peace Treaty of Hudaybiyah" between the Muslims of Madina and the *mushrikin* (polytheists) of Mecca, who initially made a covenant with Muslims but later deliberately broke it. Consequently, Rahman and Tahir argue that these verses indicate nothing about the apostasy of individual persons but instead describe the breach of a political treaty. Rahman cites the support of classical authorities, including Baidawi, Zamarkhshari, al-Jassas, Fakhr-ud-din al-Razi and al-Alusi.[45]

This view is also supported by Ibn Kathir who describes the covenant breakers in verse 12 as the idolaters of Quraysh.[46] We know that when the Prophet Muhammad started preaching the message of Islam, his major opponents were the Quraysh tribes, who were his own people, and their influential members. They remained in conflict with the Prophet and his followers until they were subdued in the conquest of Mecca. Most commentators think that those referred to in these verses are those who broke this Peace Treaty.

However, other commentators seem undecided about the identification of the people mentioned in the text. For example, in this passage, Yusuf Ali simply mentions that "the enemies break their oaths shamelessly."[47] Here Yusuf Ali does not state whether the enemies were Muslim apostates (as Maududi argued) or polytheists (as Rahman and Tahir insisted).

It is significant that traditionalists equate blasphemy with apostasy in both of these Qur'anic passages, and thus argue for the death penalty for blasphemy by equating it with apostasy. However, illogically, the Pakistan Penal Code (PPC) includes punishment for blasphemy but not for apostasy.[48] The

---

44. Mirza Tahir Ahmad, "Punishment for Apostasy: A Scrutiny of the Qur'anic Teachings on Apostasy and How this Conflicts with Maududi's Analysis.," *The Review of Religions* 101, no. 6 (2006): 55.

45. S. A. Rahman, *Punishment of Apostasy in Islam*, 2nd ed. (Lahore: Institute of Islamic Culture, 1978), 12.

46. Ibn Kathir, *Tafsir Ibn Kathir*, 2nd ed., 10 vols., vol. 4 (Riyadh: Darussalam, 2003), 383–384.

47. Abdullah Yusuf Ali, *The Meaning of the Glorious Qur'an: Text, Translation and Commentary*, 2 vols., vol. 1 (Cairo: Dar Al-Kitab Al-Masri, 1934), 441.

48. The National Assembly of Pakistan sent a bill (called Apostasy Act 2006), tabled by six party Islamic alliance known as *Muttahida Majlis-e-Amal* (MMA), to the standing

crime of apostasy has never been considered by the Parliament of Pakistan, perhaps due to this fact which was highlighted by the *Report of the Court of Inquiry to Enquire into the Punjab Disturbances of 1953* in Pakistan, known as the Munir report: "Keeping in view the several definitions given by *ulama* . . . And if we adopt the definition given by any one of the *ulama*, we remain Muslims according to the view of the *ālim* [scholar] but *kafirs* [apostates] according to the definition of everyone else."[49] This, perhaps, made the Parliament of Pakistan worry that everyone could be guilty of apostasy in Pakistan because of the existing diversity among the Muslims which would result in many Muslims needing to be killed. It is pertinent to note here that even Zia-ul-Haq did not include apostasy as a *ḥadd* crime in his infamous *ḥudūd* ordinances.

In the light of the traditionalists' view, does this render the PPC invalid because the lawmakers have not taken seriously the crime of apostasy by enshrining it in their legal code? It is hard to justify the blasphemy laws in the absence of apostasy laws, especially given that the punishment for blasphemy in Clause 295-C of the PPC relies heavily on the punishment for apostasy in the Qur'an.

The earlier point leads us to argue that it is an apparent inconsistency in the PPC to have blasphemy laws in the absence of apostasy laws.

Source Text #3: Surah Al-Maida (The Table)

The third Qur'anic passage cited in support of capital punishment for blasphemy reads as follows:

> The recompense of those *who wage war against Allah and His Messenger*, and do mischief in the land is only that they shall be killed or crucified or their hands and their feet be cut off from opposite sides, or *be exiled from the land*. That is their disgrace in this world, and a great torment is theirs in the Hereafter. Except for those *who came back* (as Muslims) with repentance

---

committee for deliberations in 2006. Since then this bill has never been presented for a vote by the Parliament of Pakistan. Text of Apostasy Act 2006 (Proposed) is available at www.thepersecution.org/50years/apostasybill.html.

49. Kayani, *Report of the Court of Inquiry*, 218.

before they fall into your power; in that case, know that *Allah is Oft-Forgiving, Most Merciful.* (Q.5:33–34) (Emphasis mine)

Massignon reports that this Qur'anic text has been used by political authorities to punish *zindiq* (a freethinker) like Mansur al-Hallaj (858–922) and their other opponents.[50] In the case of *Ismail Qureshi vs. Pakistan*, the FSC relied heavily on Ibn Taymiyya's argument that denouncing Islam and its Prophet should be considered as real war.[51] To support Taymiyya's view, Islamic scholars, invited by the FSC as jurist consults, used the above passage to argue that contemnors of the Holy Prophet fall into the category of people who wage war against Allah and His Messenger and for whom the punishment of death is prescribed. This argument convinced the FSC as is evident from the remarks made by the court: "So these verses clearly prescribe the severe punishment of death for the opponents of Allah and his Prophet, who include contemnors of the Prophet."[52]

Commentators such as Al-Bukhari, who support this interpretation, state that "to wage war against Allah means to reject faith in Him."[53] Ibn Kathir explains that the phrase "waging war" means "oppose and contradict, and it includes disbelief…"[54] By this logic, the traditionalists propose that whoever speaks a word against Prophet Muhammad, or confesses disbelief in his prophethood, could be regarded as being at war with Allah and his Prophet and by implication with Muslims.[55]

However, there is significant disagreement between Muslim scholars on the identity of the subjects of this passage. There are three main views regarding the subjects: first, that they are polytheists; second, they are apostates who wage war against Muslims; and third, they are Muslims who commit highway robbery. Maududi argued in support of the second position: "The

---

50. Louis Massignon, *The Passion of Al-Hallaj: Mystic and Martyr of Islam*, trans. Herbert Mason, Bollingen series (Princeton: Princeton University Press, 1994), 205.

51. Ibn Taymiyyah, *Al-Sarim al-Maslul Ala Shatim al-Rasul* [The Isssue of Blasphemy against the Prophet], trans. Ghulam Ahmed Harari (Lahore: Maktaba Qadusia, 2011), 206–207.

52. *Muhammad Ismail Qureshi v. Pakistan*, 19–20.

53. Muhammad Ibn Ismaiel Al-Bukhari, *Sahih Al-Bukhari*, trans. Muhammad Muhsin Khan, 9 vols., vol. 6 (Riyadh: Darussalam, 1997), 109.

54. Ibn Kathir, *Tafsir Ibn Kathir*, 2nd ed., vol. 3 (Riyadh: Darussalam, 2003), 161.

55. Mark Durie, *The Third Choice: Islam, Dhimmitude and Freedom* (China: Deror Books, 2010), 103.

expression 'to wage war against Allah and His Messenger' denotes war against the righteous order established by the Islamic state."[56]

In contrast, Khaled Abou El Fadl, who produced a scholarly work on this subject, argued in support of the third position: "The punishment of execution, amputation from opposite ends, or banishment, as the verse specifies, are reserved for brigands or highway robbers."[57] Fadl claimed that this position was eventually adopted by the vast majority of Muslim jurists.[58] Fadl argued in the light of the historical political context of early Islam, while Maududi focused narrowly on the content of these verses, which refer specifically to one who literally takes up arms against the Islamic state and its order. It is notable, however, that even Maududi's view does not support the death penalty for apostasy alone unless it is accompanied by rebellion against the Islamic state.

Our discussion above demonstrates that the punishment prescribed in these verses is for the offences of *muhraba* (rebellion), committed by those who take arms against the Islamic state, and for *fasād* (disorder), committed by those who create disorder in the society. The supporters of the death penalty for blasphemy ignore the fact that this passage prescribes a range of punishments from severe to lenient. Javed Ghamidi, a moderate Pakistani scholar, argued that "the capital punishment is not obligatory and the recommendation of banishment in the verse is for such offenders who deserve leniency."[59] In contrast, according to Clause 295-C of Pakistan's blasphemy law, capital punishment for blasphemy is obligatory and there is no option of a lesser punishment.

Moreover, this Qur'anic passage explicitly speaks of repentance. Ghamidi argues that verse 33 makes it clear that the punishments proposed will not be applicable to those who submit and repent before the law. There is provision for repentance and reformation in this Qur'anic passage. However, Pakistan's blasphemy laws allow no provision for confession and repentance, and the

---

56. Mawdudi, *Tafhim al-Qur'an*, vol. 2, 156.
57. Khaled Abou El Fadl, *Rebellion and Violence in Islamic Law* (Cambridge: Cambridge University Press, 2001), 52.
58. Ibid.
59. Javed Ahmad Ghamidi, "Punishment for Blasphemy against the Prophet (sws)," online.

blasphemy cases are decided solely on the basis of the accusers' testimony. No importance is given to the testimony of the accused, regardless of whether this is a confession or denial. There is no mention in the laws that if the offender repents then he should be forgiven, despite the fact that there is an obvious provision for this according to this passage of the Qur'an. The advocates of the death penalty focus single-mindedly on the idea of capital punishment and overlook the mention of repentance and transformation which is quite explicit in this Qur'anic passage. The lack of Qur'anic teaching supporting the death a penalty for blasphemy coupled with the Muslim interpretation both present and in history lead us to conclude that there must be another driving force that brought these laws into existence. Part of our thesis is to explore what that is.

Pakistan Blasphemy Laws in the Light of the Sunna

There are divergent views within orthodox Islam. In the case of capital punishment for blasphemy, particularly against the Prophet of Islam, it is largely the *hadith* and the *sira* literature that informs any Qur'anic interpretation. However, it is interesting to note that there are references to pardoning as well as punishing blasphemers in the *hadith* and *sira* literature. Although there are some examples of punishing vilifiers in the *hadith* and *sira*, advocates of the modern view argue that there are more incidents recorded in the same sources where the Prophet tolerated insults against himself and left the matter of punishment to God.[60] Moreover, they argue that the examples of the Prophet pardoning offenders are more in line with Qur'anic teaching because "there is no mention in the Qur'an of any kind of penalty [for apostasy/blasphemy], neither death nor any other."[61]

The traditionalists object to this view by appealing to the opinion of Ibn Taimiyyah,[62] a great historical ideologist, who argued that the Prophet

---

60. Q.51:66; 43:83; 73:11–14. Al-Bukhari 4:158, 278, 760; 5:507; 6:89; 8:226, 271, 777, 836

61. Mohamed Talbi, "Religious Liberty: A Muslim Perspective," in *The New Voices of Islam*, ed. Mehran Kamrava (London: I. B. Tauris, 2006), 116.

62. "He became famous through his campaign for the execution of a Christian who insulted the Prophet . . . [He] was against all 'innovation.' For him, 'innovation' was apostasy from the 'right mean': heresy and unbelief which was to be fought with every possible

himself had the right to pardon his vilifiers but Muslims have no right to pardon the contemnors of the Prophet.[63] Scholars from the traditionalist camp argue that this role of pardoning the blasphemers of the Prophet cannot be transferred to others, as it was not even given to the Prophet's *sahaba* (companions). As the Prophet is no longer alive, this right cannot be exercised by anyone on his behalf.[64] This argument played a pivotal role in convincing the Federal Shariʿat Court to make the death penalty mandatory for the offence of blasphemy against the Prophet in Clause 295-C of the PPC. "We have also noted that no one after the Holy Prophet (PBUH) exercised or was authorized the right of reprieve or pardon."[65]

Moreover, the traditionalists cite several incidents from *sira* and *hadith* related stories where the Prophet of Islam ordered or condoned the killing of those who mocked him. For example, when the Prophet conquered Mecca he ordered the execution of two singing girls belonging to Abd Allah b. Khatal who had ridiculed him in their songs.[66] In another episode, recorded by Abu Dawud, a blind man killed a slave girl, who had borne him children, on the charges of repeatedly slandering the Prophet. When this man's action was reported to the Prophet he said, "Oh, be witness, no retaliation is payable for her blood."[67] Another Jewish woman was killed on the same charges. This report is related by Ali, who said, "A Jewess used to abuse the Prophet (PBUH) and disparage him. A man strangled her till she died. The Apostle of Allah (PBUH) declared that no recompense was payable for her blood."[68] Ibn Ishaq, the main biographer of the Prophet, reports the case of Uqba, a man who had thrown camel dung and intestines on the Prophet. Uqba was captured at Badr and pleaded for his life saying, "But who will look after my children, O Muhammad? 'Hell,' he said, and Asim b. Thabit . . . killed

---

mean." Hans Küng, *Islam: Past, Present and Future*, trans. John Bowden (Oxford: Oneworld, 2007), 385.

63. Taymiyyah, *Al-Sarim al-Maslul Ala Shatim al-Rasul*, 222–223.
64. Madani, *Verdict of Islamic Law*, 109, 26.
65. *Muhammad Ismail Qureshi v. Pakistan*, 26.
66. Taymiyyah, *Al-Sarim al-Maslul Ala Shatim al-Rasul*, 404.
67. Dawud, *Sunan Abudawud*, 1214–1215.
68. Ibid., 1215. This shows that if even a non-Muslim abuses the Prophet he will be killed

him."⁶⁹ Another report often cited by the traditionalists relates to Umar Ibn Khttab who struck off the head of a man who refused to accept the Prophet's legal verdict on a certain occasion. This episode is most cited often by the traditionalist *'ulamā* in Pakistan who encourage people to show the same attitude towards blasphemers of the Prophet as reflected in the narrative. This is reinforced by the interpretation of Ibn Taymiyya, who suggested that denouncing Islam and its Prophet should be considered as real war.⁷⁰ There are several other traditions like those mentioned above which convey the idea that "denouncing Islam and vilifying the Prophet is as harmful as an attack with the force of arms."⁷¹

Some modern scholars argue that these reports are not credible enough in terms of the historical authenticity of the *sanad* (chain of narrators).⁷² Critics of the *hadith* literature say that, for this reason, Umar al-Khattab, the second pious caliph, "used [his] own judgment in legal verdicts rather than depending on *hadith* attributed to the Prophet."⁷³ With regard to the report about Umar, Javed Ghamidi notes: "This narrative comes from a *gharib* (with an isolated chain of narrators) and *mursal* (with omissions in the chain)."⁷⁴ This suggests that it is not a very trustworthy account.

In support of his view he argued that Ibn Jarir Tabari, who often related all categories of narratives, did not regard it as worthy of consideration.⁷⁵ Ghamidi goes on to cite the incident of a water dispute between the Prophet's paternal cousin, Zubayr, and a man belonging to *Ansar*, recorded by Al-Bukhari and Muslim ibn al-Hajjaj, both regarded as the most authentic narrators. When the dispute was brought before the Prophet for ruling, he gave Zubayr the right to irrigate his fields first but leave the remaining water for the man from *Ansar*. The *Ansari* immediately accused the Prophet of being unjust and nepotistic: "O Prophet of Allah, is this because Zubayr is your cousin." (Al-Bukhari 6:109)

---

69. Ishaq, *Life of Muhammad*, 308.
70. Taymiyyah, *Al-Sarim al-Maslul Ala Shatim al-Rasul*, 206–207.
71. Yohanan Friedmann, *Tolerance and Coercion in Islam: Interfaith Relations in the Muslim Tradition* (New York: Cambridge University Press, 2003), 150.
72. Rahman, *Punishment of Apostasy*, 79; Saeed and Saeed, *Freedom of Religion*, 64, 68.
73. Abbas, *Pakistan's Blasphemy Laws*, 49.
74. Ghamidi, "Punishment for Blasphemy."
75. Ibid.

It is recorded that the Prophet's face changed colour but he did not say anything in response to this blasphemous statement. Ghamidi argued that it is hard to believe the stance of the traditionalists who ignore "this highly credible narrative reported by Bukhari and Muslim that reflects the Prophet's forbearance, forgiveness, compassion and kindness and instead . . . relate everywhere a weak and improbable narrative related to how Umar struck off someone's neck."[76]

Ghamidi and Zaheer further argue that, even supposing the weak traditions are accepted as reliable, capital punishment for blasphemy still cannot be justified because "such punishments were meant to be applicable to [a] certain group of people living in a particular era . . ."[77] In other words, these punishments were applicable to the direct addressees of the Prophet only and they have nothing to do with the generations afterwards.[78] According to Zaheer, a general principle cannot be drawn from these specific incidents, because the general rule is already mentioned in the Qur'an which states that "blasphemers are meant to be ignored – this was meant to continue to remain applicable for all times to come."[79] What Ghamidi and Zaheer imply, Mahmoud Taha, one of Sudan's leading Islamic scholars and an advocate for reform, says explicitly: "Many aspects of the present Islamic shari'a are not the original principles or objectives of Islam. They merely reflect . . . time and the limitations of human ability."[80] Taha goes on to argue that Madinan teachings were never intended to be permanent. In line with Taha, Abdullah Nai'm, a renowned Islamic scholar, argues that the Madina parts of the Qur'an mostly refer to the particular situation of the first Muslim community and cannot be applied to modern circumstances.[81]

Ghamidi made another notable point: that the Prophet executed and condoned punishments as a ruler, not as a law giver, and that therefore these

---

76. Ibid.

77. Zaheer, "Real Blasphemers."

78. Farieha Aziz, "Interview: Dr Khalid Zaheer, Religious Scholar," *Newsline*, December 2010, 29; Ghamidi, "Punishment for Blasphemy."

79. Zaheer, "The Real Blasphemers"; Aziz, "Interview: Dr Khalid Zaheer," 29.

80. Maḥmoud M. Ṭaha, *The Second Message of Islam*, trans. Abdullahi Ahmed An-Na'im, 1st ed. (New York: Syracuse University Press, 1987), 137.

81. Abdullahi A. An-Na'im, *Islam and the Secular State: Negotiating the Future of Sharia* (Cambridge: Harvard University Press, 2008), 61–62.

punishments were not part of the Sharia.[82] This argument is strengthened from these examples that there is no reference to any penalty for blasphemy in the constitution of Madina or in the Treaty of Hudybia, both of which originally came from the Prophet. Moreover, the Prophet himself did not execute anyone for the offence of blasphemy and apostasy.[83]

In the light of our discussion above two observations are worth mentioning with regard to Pakistan's blasphemy laws.

First, during the proceedings of the FSC in the case of *Ismail Qureshi v. Pakistan*, the court did not give any space to the view advocated by Ghamidi and Zaheer above. The recorded proceedings of the case demonstrate that the FSC invited only traditionalist Islamic scholars as consultant jurists. Six out of the seven religious scholars who were invited to assist the FSC as consultant jurists supported the death sentence for the offence of blasphemy against the Prophet, as prescribed in 295-C.[84] In the light of those traditions cited above, they concluded that the only appropriate punishment for blasphemy against the Prophet is death. On the basis on their opinion, the FSC made the death penalty mandatory in 295-C and deleted the option of a life sentence. It can be argued that this decision of the FSC was one-sided, as the court did not look into other positions which have been advocated by Pakistani scholars like Javed Ghamidi and Khalid Zaheer.

Second, as we have seen in the first chapter, Zia was a conservative ruler who gave much heed to the traditionalists' view and largely ignored other viewpoints in the formation of Pakistan's blasphemy laws. He introduced five new clauses of the blasphemy laws, including 295-B and C, which imposed harsher punishments. This echoes what has happened previously in Islamic history. During the time of Abbasid caliphs al-Ma'mun (d.218/833), and later al-Mu'tasim (d.227/842) and al-Wathiq (d.232/847), the Mu'tazilite movement was patronized and it took shape as a theological school. Al-Ma'mun supported the Mu'tazili position on the "createdness" of the Qur'an as a state policy. Furthermore, the non-Mu'tazili position that the Qur'an

---

82. Javed Ahmad Ghamidi, "Islamic Punishments: Some Misconceptions," online.

83. Muhammad ordered that the men of Ukl and Uraina be killed. They had reverted to heathenism after embracing Islam, but they had also killed the Prophet's shepherds and stole his camels, so the law of brigandry may have been the cause of their death sentence. (Al-Bukhari 5:505; 7:623; 8:794, 797; 9:37)

84. *Muhammad Ismail Qureshi v. Pakistan*, 16–18.

was "eternal" was discouraged. However, both views were commonly continued until the time of the Abbasid Caliph al-Mutawakkil (d.247/861), who turned against the Mu'tazilites and persecuted them. As a result, he adopted the traditionalists' position that the Qur'an is eternal, not created, and sought to ensure the dominance of this theological position by enshrining it in state policy.[85]

In the same manner in Pakistan, during the eleven years in which General Zia-ul-Haq (1977–1988) was military dictator, the traditionalists' view of Islam was adopted as state policy and the modernists' view was discouraged. In this regard, Abbas notes that "General Zia enforced a Wahabi-dictated Shari'a and . . . Maruf al-Dawalibi, the Saudi adviser on Zia's Shari'a project, personally supervised the insertion of Shari'a laws."[86] As a result of this state policy, the harsher clauses of the blasphemy law were enacted.

Pakistan's Blasphemy Laws in the Light of Islamic *Fiqh* (Jurisprudence)

The Shari'a, the sacred law of Islam, literally means "drinking place" or "path to the water hole." It is "God given and prescription for the right life in this world and for salvation in the world to come."[87] It is often expressed in scholarly Muslim circles that the Shari'a is an ocean and *fiqh* is the human attempt to understand it.[88] The Shari'a has never been a fixed document, but has evolved over the centuries, as jurists and jurist consultants interpreted the Qur'an and Sunna in particular contexts. In other words, it was not legislated but discovered by Islamic jurists.[89] In classical Sunni Islam (to which Pakistan belongs) there are four major schools of interpretation of Shari'a law: Hanafi , Maliki, Shafi'i and Hanbali. They evolved differently in different regions (Shiites follow still another school of interpretation.) It is beyond the scope of this research to discuss the historical development of

---

85. Abdullah Saeed, *Islamic Thought: An Introduction* (New York: Routledge, 2006), 64–65.
86. Abbas, *Pakistan's Blasphemy Laws*, 136.
87. L. W. Adamec, *Islam: A Historical Companion* (Gloucestershire: Tempus, 2007), 139.
88. Laleh Bakhtiar, *Encyclopedia of Islamic Law: A Compendium of the Views of the Major Schools* (Chicago: ABC International Group, 1996), xxxii–xxxiv.
89. Ibid., xxxiv.

these schools of Islamic *fiqh*. Instead, we will focus on the rulings of these Sunni schools with regard to the punishment for blasphemy.

The Muslim Blasphemer: Apostate

In the *fiqh*, vilifying the Prophet has generally been dealt with under the topic of apostasy. This is evident from the apostasy lists prescribed by classical jurists. For example, Ahmad b. Naqib al-Misri (d.769/1368), a Shafi'i jurist, lists twenty "acts that entail leaving Islam [including]: (4) to revile Allah or His messenger . . .; (6) to be sarcastic about Allah's name . . .; (16) to revile the religion of Islam."[90] Another medieval jurist, Abu Baker al-Jaz'iri says that someone who does the following becomes an apostate "(1) Slandering God or a prophet or an angel . . . (7) Throwing a copy of the Qur'an into a dirty place or stepping on it."[91] Shaykh Abd al-Azeez ibn Baaz, Saudi Arabia's Grand Mufti, stated, "If the one who reviles the Lord [Prophet Muhammad] . . . or reviles the Deen [Religion of Islam] is a Muslim, then he becomes an apostate from Islam."[92]

The manuals of the Islamic *fiqh* reveal that there is general consensus among the jurists of the *fiqh* that vilification of the Prophet is a capital offence. *However, jurists differ on the question of whether the culprit should be given the opportunity to repent or not.*

The Hanafi and Shafii schools are relatively lenient, providing the opportunity for repentance, whereas the Maliki and Hanabali schools allow no chance for repentance. According to the Hanafi school, the apostate must be given an opportunity to repent. Shaybani, one of the disciples of Abu Hanifa, reports his ruling that a male apostate must be given three days to repent, after which, if he does not repent, he is liable to be killed.[93] Similarly, according to al-Misri, a Shafi'i jurist, "it is obligatory for the caliph to ask

---

90. Ahmad ibn Naqīb al-Misri, *Reliance of the Traveller: The Classic Manual of Islamic Sacred Law*, trans. Nuh Ha Mim Keller, rev. ed. (Maryland: Amana Publications, 1994), 596–598.

91. Abu Bakr al-Jaza'iri, *Min Kitab al-Fiqh ala al-Madhahib al-Arba'ah* (Beirut: Dar al-Fikr), 535–536.

92. English Translation of Majmoo Fatawa al-Shaykh Ibn Baz available at: http://www.islamland.com/uploads/books/en_01_Majmoo_alFatawa_IbnBaz.pdf (accessed 14 March 2014).

93. Muḥammad al-Shaybānī and Majid Khadduri, *Shaybānī's Siyar: The Islamic Law of Nations:* (Baltimore: Johns Hopkins Press, 1966), 195.

the [apostate] to repent and return to Islam. If he does, it is accepted from him, but if he refuses, he is immediately killed."[94]

Some jurists of the Maliki school are of the opinion that a blasphemer should be treated like an apostate and given the opportunity to repent. However, Imam Malik, the founder of the Maliki school, was of the view that there is no chance for repentance. Qazi Iyaz writes that Haroonur Rashid asked Imam Malik which punishment was appropriate for contemnors of the Prophet. The former noted that some jurists of Iraq had the view that whipping could be an appropriate punishment. It is recorded that Imam Malik became furious and said, "O Amir ul-Muminin! How the Ummah has the right to exist when her Prophet is abused? So kill the person who abused the Prophet and whip the one who abuses the companions of the Prophet."[95]

Some jurists of the Hanbali school are of the view that repentance is acceptable on the condition that the apostate completely rejects his former position by citing the two *al-shahadatayn* (testimonials of the faith).[96] The pardon is accompanied by a stern punishment in order to deter the apostate from this act in the future. However, Ibn Tammiyyah, a Hanbilite jurist who has discussed the transgression of vilification more extensively than any other medieval jurist, took quite a hard position on this subject and classified apostasy into two distinct types: (a) *ridda mujarrada or mahda* (common apostasy) and (b) *ridda mughallaza* (aggravated apostasy). Aggravated apostasy occurs when the vilifier has set out to deliberately impugn the Prophet's honour. For this reason, Ibn Taymiyyah considers the offence of vilifying the Prophet (aggravated apostasy) as more heinous than that of common apostasy. He argues that, in this case, repentance is neither necessary nor acceptable and execution must be performed without delay.[97] He goes on to argue that the crime of vilifying the Prophet is like transgressions such as murder or rebellion, for which there is no option to repent.[98]

---

94. al-Misri, *Reliance of the Traveller*, 596.
95. Qazi Ayaz, *Al-Shifa*, vol 2, 215.
96. "There is only one God and Muhammad is the Prophet of God."
97. Taymiyyah, *Al-Sarim al-Maslul Ala Shatim al-Rasul*, 117–118. For a good discussion on Taymiyya's position, see Friedmann, *Tolerance and Coercion*, 151–152.
98. Taymiyyah, *Al-Sarim al-Maslul Ala Shatim al-Rasul*, 363–367.

The positions of these four schools were a subject of debate among the Islamic scholars in the highly significant case of *Ismail Quereshi vs. Pakistan*. As mentioned above, the FSC invited seven Islamic scholars as jurist consultants to assist the court to decide what punishment Islamic Sharia prescribes for those who vilify the Prophet. Ismail Qureshi, the petitioner, claimed that there is no punishment for the vilifier of the Prophet other than death. Out of the seven jurist consultants, three (Maulana Subhan Mahmood, Mufti Ghulam Sarwar and Hafiz Salahuddin Yousaf) referred to the preferred view of the Hanafi jurists that repentance of the vilifier is acceptable and that, in the case of repentance, no sentence should be imposed. Another scholar, Maulana Saeed-ud-din Sherkoti, expressed the view that a lesser punishment could be imposed.[99]

This shows that four out of seven Islamic scholars supported the view that repentance should be taken into account when the penalty for blasphemy be applied in 295-C of the PPC. However, the FSC gave more attention to the punishment endorsed by the other three scholars (Maulana Muhammad Abdo-hu Al-Falah, Maulana Syed Abdul Shakoor and Maulana Fazle Hadi) and overlooked the provision for pardon which was vigorously supported by the majority (four), of the jurist consultants. The FSC's ruling says, "In view of our above discussion we are of the view that [the] alternative punishment of life imprisonment as provided in Section 295-C, PPC is repugnant to the Injunctions of Islam . . ."[100] and the death penalty was made the mandatory punishment for the offence of blasphemy against the Prophet of Islam.[101] The FSC ruling did not mention the possibility of pardon highlighted by four of the scholars.

In case of a female offender, the Hanafi position is that she is not subject to capital punishment but she is to be kept in prison until she recants.[102] This is based on Q.4:15. Hanafis, in support of their view, argue that the Prophet laid down a general principle for Muslims that they must not kill women.[103] In contrast, Malikis, Shafi'is and Hanbalis hold the position that

---

99. *Muhammad Ismail Qureshi v. Pakistan*, 16–17.
100. Ibid., 35.
101. Ibid.
102. Shaybānī and Khadduri, *Shaybānī's Siyar*, 205.
103. Saeed and Saeed, *Freedom of Religion*, 52.

a female offender must repent within three days, otherwise she faces death. (However, Malikis also suggest that execution may be delayed in the case of breast-feeding.[104])

Justice Munir, former Chief Justice of Pakistan, pointed out: "In the common law, the later the decision, the better it is and the earlier decision has no value for the case. Whereas in Islamic law the earlier the opinion the better it is."[105] From this perspective, the views of the founding jurist of Islamic *fiqh*, Abu Hanifa (d.702–767) should carry more weight than others: Malik Ibn Anas (d.717–801), Muhammad Idris ash-Shafii (d.769–820), and Ahmad ibn Hanbal (d.778–855).

Shabani, Abu Hanifa's disciple, records the ruling of his teacher that a woman offender should not be killed. (In the proposed Act of Apostasy 2006, this position of the Hanafi school was endorsed by the presenters, and it was proposed that women apostates should be imprisoned instead of being executed.) However, the framers of Clause 295-C of Pakistan's blasphemy laws completely overlooked the position of the Hanafi school, as this clause makes no distinction between males and females. In support of the Hanafi position, Maulana Subhan Mahmood, a juris consultant, argued before the FSC that there should be a distinction between males and females with regard to punishment. He argued that a women offender should be given life imprisonment instead of the death penalty.[106] But the FSC did not pay any attention to the Hanafi position, but made the death penalty mandatory for both men and women. In fact, Asia Bibi, a Christian woman, who was sentenced under 295-C by the lower court in Pakistan in 2010 with her sentence upheld by the Lahore High Court in 2014, was the first woman to be sentenced with the death penalty.

In the light of the discussion above, two points of concern can be argued, as follows:

---

104. Ibid.

105. Muhammad Munir, "Precedent in Islamic Law with Special Reference to the Federal Shariat Court and the Legal System in Pakistan," *Islamic Studies* 47, no. 4 (2008): 469.

106. See paragraph 4 of *Muhammad Ismail Qureshi v. Pakistan,* 17. It is also notable that the proposed "Apostasy Act 2006" makes a clear distinction between male and female apostates and offers an alternate punishment for female apostates, which is imprisonment till penitence, instead of capital punishment.

- First, the framers of the blasphemy laws in Pakistan and later the FSC did not acknowledge the principle of Islamic law which (as Justice Munir pointed out) states that more weight should be given to the earlier opinion (in this case, the Hanafi school).
- Second, despite the fact that the majority of Sunni Muslims in Pakistan, even the majority of Muslims in the world,[107] follow the Hanafi school, the position of this school has been largely ignored by the framers of blasphemy laws and later by the FSC in favour of other schools. In other words, the minority view has been imposed on the majority.
- Third, the constitution of Pakistan declares that the country is the *Islami Jumhūria Pakistan* (Islamic Republic of Pakistan), the word *Jumhūr* means people which affirms that Pakistan is an Islamic as well as democratic. In the light of two earlier observations, it can be argued that Pakistan's legislature and judiciary have violated a norm of Islamic law, where early legal opinion has more weight than later opinions, as well as a norm of democracy, where the view of the majority should be given precedence.

The Non-Muslim Blasphemer: An Unprotected Person

Traditionally, non-Muslims were divided into two categories. The first were the *ahl al-kitab* (adherents of revealed scripture). They could remain within the Muslim state by paying *jizya* (poll tax). According to Bassiouni, these *dhimmis* were "equal before the law in every respect." However, Khadduri asserts that they were second-class citizens, while Al-Ghunaimi calls them non-citizens.[108] The second category was non-*kitabis* who were not adherents of the revealed scriptures. Islamic law deals with them differently.

When *ahl al-kitab* are accused of blasphemy, the Islamic law does not regard this as apostasy, because apostasy applies only to Muslims. Imam Shafi'i, in his *Kitab al-Umm*, has given some draft agreements that may be made with non-Muslims. In these draft agreements, treaties, rights and privileges

---

107. Küng, *Islam*, 271.

108. Cited in Donna E. Arzt, "The Application of International Human Rights Law in Islamic States," *Human Rights Quarterly* 12, no. 2 (1990): 209.

guaranteed to non-Muslims in an Islamic state should stand withdrawn where a person insults the Prophet of Islam.[109] Another Shafi'i law manual, *The Reliance of the Traveller,* states that "The agreement [the covenant of protection] is also violated . . . if one of the subject people . . . mentions something impermissible about Allah, the Prophet (Allah bless him and give him peace) or Islam."[110]

There is a variation of opinion among the schools of law with regard to the appropriate punishment for blasphemy committed by a *dhimmi*. According to the Maliki school, the punishment for a *dhimmi* blasphemer is capital punishment, but execution may be avoided if the transgressor converts to Islam.[111] Ibn Taymiyya, a Hanabali jurist, differs by asserting that execution cannot be avoided by the blasphemer converting to Islam.[112] There is also a difference of opinion among the Shafi'i jurists: al-Misri prescribes that the caliph is authorized to decide between a range of punishments, including "death, slavery, release without paying anything, or ransoming himself in exchange for money or for a Muslim captive held by the enemy."[113] On the other hand, another view within the Shafi'i school is that no discrimination should be made in the punishment for the offence whether committed by a Muslim or a non-Muslim.[114] By contrast, the Hanafi position is comparatively lenient, saying that "If a Zimmee [sic] . . . blaspheme the prophet . . . yet his contract of subjection is not dissolved . . ."[115] From this Hanafi position, it can be read that there should be no consequences for a non-Muslim

---

109. Mahmud A. Ghazi, "The Law of Tawhin-i-Risalat: A Social, Political and Historical Perspective," in *Pakistan between Secularism and Islam*, ed. Tarik Jan (Islamabad: Institute of Policy Studies, 1998), 221.

110. al-Misri, *Reliance of the Traveller*, 609.

111. Abdullah ibn Abi Zayd Al-Qayrawani, *The Risala: A Treatise on Maliki Fiqh*, 359, online.

112. Asrar Madani cites Ibn Taymiyya's fatwa, "In the case of non-Muslim who embraces Islam after committing the crime, his conversion cannot save him from punishment." Madani, *Verdict of Islamic Law*, 124.

113. al-Misri, *Reliance of the Traveller*, 604.

114. Marghinani, Hanafi jurist, quotes: "Shafei has said that the contract of subjection is dissolved by a Zimmee's blaspheming the prophet; because if he were a believer, by such blasphemy his faith would be broken; and hence in the same manner, his protection is thereby broken, since the contract of subjection is merely a substitute for a belief." 'Alī ibn Abī Bak Marghīnāni, *The Hedaya: A Commentary On the Islamic Laws*, trans. Charles Hamilton, 2 vols., vol. 2 (New Delhi: Kitab Bhavan, 1985), 221.

115. Ibid.

who blasphemes the Prophet. Abu Hanifa taught that Muslims must not be too severe with *dhimmis* who insult the Prophet. Maulana Sawar Qadri, applying Abu Hanifa's position, suggested to the FSC that the penalty for non-Muslim contemner of the Prophet should be life imprisonment.[116] In summary, Sookhdeo says that "according to Hanafi law, a Christian or Jew who blasphemes against the Prophet Muhammad is only acting as a non-Muslim naturally would act, and therefore should not be penalized."[117] The views of the Hanafi school have traditionally been followed by the Muslim rulers in India, especially by the Moghals,[118] and the majority of Muslims in Pakistan still follow the Hanafi school. Despite this, the position of this school was completely neglected by the FSC when they made capital punishment the mandatory punishment for the offence of abusing the prophet in 295-C, without any distinction between Muslims and non-Muslims.

The Right of God and the Right of Man

There are diverse views in the *fiqh* on the question of whether *sabb al-rasūl* (blasphemy against the Prophet) is a violation of the *hāq Allah* (right of God) or the *hāq al-adami* (right of man). The Hanabali and Maliki schools consider that insulting the Prophet is a violation of the "Right of Man," for which pardon can be granted only by the injured party. The jurists of both these schools ruled that "blaspheming the Prophet consists of a violation of his personal right and that only the Prophet himself could pardon such conduct."[119] They argued that the right to pardon only existed till the demise of the Prophet, as only he could pardon the offender. If the Prophet is no longer alive, then pardon cannot be granted, as no Muslim is ever entitled or authorized to pardon on the Prophet's behalf. Hence the punishment of death becomes mandatory even if the offender repents.

On the other hand, the Hanafi and Shafi'i schools base their arguments on different grounds. The Hanafis and Shafi'is hold that "after the demise of the Prophet, the offence of *sabb al-rasul* should be no different to *sabb*

---

116. *Muhammad Ismail Qureshi v. Pakistan*, 17.

117. Sookhdeo, *People Betrayed*, 249.

118. This is evident from al-Fatawa al-Alamigriyyah, the most exhaustive and authoritative book of the Hanafi jurisprudence written on the order of Awrangzeb by a group of scholars. Munir, "Precedent in Islamic Law," 470.

119. Kamali, *Freedom of Expression*, 224.

Allah as both of these violates the Right of God."[120] Hashim Kamali fully endorses the view of the Hanafi and Shafii schools that:

> ... blasphemy, in both of its varieties ... consists of a violation of public rights. Therefore ... the head of state and competent judicial authorities, in their capacities as defenders and representatives of the Right of God should act in the same role, not only with regard to *sabb Allah,* but also with regard to *sabb al-rasul.*[121]

He further argued that the Prophet Muhammad has a central place in Islam as a transmitter of Allah's revelation, and the one who has set down the creed and dogma of Islam, and that therefore blasphemy against the Prophet is considered equal to reviling God: ". . . both of these are first and foremost violations of the religious beliefs of Islam and of the rights of the community of believers. Blasphemy in either of these two forms is, therefore, a blatant violation of the Right of God."[122] Likewise, Shemeem Abbas argued that the Qur'an in "*Sura-e-Lahab,* explicitly prescribes the punishment for blasphemy is right of God (*haq Allah).*" Abbas goes on to say that the state should not impose any penalty for blasphemy, as this is something that Allah alone can do.[123]

Some argue that offences against the "Right of God" are pardonable, but that blasphemy against the Prophet is an offence that breaches the "Right of Man" and it is not pardonable because the Prophet is no longer alive. To counter this argument, it has been pointed out that Islamic law prescribes *tazir* (not fixed but discretionary) punishments for the offences that violate the "Right of Man" and *hadd* punishments are prescribed for violating "Right of Allah." Muhammad Salim al-Awa argues that the punishment for the offences of apostasy and blasphemy is not the prescribed punishment therefore it comes under *tazir.* He goes on to argue that *tazir* punishments can be changed from time to time, as recognized in the Islamic law.[124] It is

---

120. Ibid.
121. Ibid., 225.
122. Ibid.
123. Abbas, *Pakistan's Blasphemy Laws,* 64.
124. Muhammad S. al-Awa, *Punishment in Islamic Law: A Comparative Study* (Indianapolis: American Trust Publications, 1982), 50.

up to the judge to adjudicate the punishment according to the nature of the offence.

In contrast, Clauses 295-B and C of the PPC prescribe mandatory punishments: life imprisonment for defiling the Qur'an (in 295 B) and the death penalty for insulting the Prophet (295-C). There is no option for the judge to give a lesser punishment, even if he or she considers that the offence is not serious. Thus, it could be argued that Pakistan's blasphemy laws are a breach of Sharia because they do not allow the *qazi* (judge/court) to take into account the motives of offenders, nor to determine the type and severity of the penalty, as specified under *tazir*.

Pakistan's Blasphemy Laws in the Light of Muslim Scholarship in the Modern Period

There is considerable diversity among contemporary Muslim scholars on the issue of Islamic Sharia and its applicability to modern times. As we have seen above, the offence of blasphemy and the penalty of death related to it were part of the Islamic Sharia established by the medieval jurists. It is beyond the scope of our study here to cover all aspects of Sharia and their applicability in the modern times, therefore this section will firstly examine three main positions with respect to Sharia and secondly the question: *Are blasphemy laws man made or divine in origin?*

In this regard, three main positions have emerged in modern times. Abdullah Saeed has called them: Pre-modern position restated; pre-modern position challenged; and pre-modern position restricted.[125] We will classify the advocates of these positions respectively as (1) Traditionalists; (2) Modernists and (3) Reformers.

Traditionalists

Generally traditionalists are those whose understanding is based largely on a literal interpretation of the Qur'an and *sunna*. Moreover, they believe that the consensus of the Islamic *fiqh* is infallible. Historically speaking, this view emerged after the fall of Baghdad in 1258 (to the Mongols), when Muslim

---

125. Saeed and Saeed, *Freedom of Religion*, 88–98.

leaders started "to elevate and regard the schools of *fiqh* as divinely ordained manifestations of Islam."[126]

According to this view, specifically in Sunni Islam, *ijtihād* (reasoned interpretation) was permitted for a certain period of time after the Prophet's death, during which different schools of orthodox jurisprudence (specifically Hanafi, Maliki, Shafii and Hanbali) were developed. Eventually, however, the *bab ul-ijtihād* (gate of interpretation) was formally closed with the death of Ahmad ibn Hanbal, the founder of the Hanbali school, (241/855).[127] Bernard Lewis eloquently describes the conviction of traditionalists that, "[j]ust as there is only one God in heaven, so there can be only one sovereign and one law on earth," and that is the law of Shariʻa.[128] They regard Shariʻa as the final and ultimate formulation of the law of God. Consequently, they do not leave room for any change in it, as the process of *ijtihad* is now closed. This view demands only *taqlid* (imitation or emulation) of Shariʻa. No aspect of the Shariʻa is open for revision and any further employment of *ijtihad* is considered *bidah* (sinful innovation).[129] This is, perhaps, due to their conviction that "to do so is to allow human beings to correct what God has decreed."[130] A defence of *taqlid* is evident from a legal opinion issued in the twentieth century in Tunisia:

> It is generally admitted that, ever since the codification of the doctrine of Islam by the four great orthodox imams, this door of *ijtihad* is closed and that Muslims must conform their opinion strictly to the opinions enumerated by these imams, without seeking to arrive by means of their own reasoning at a personal opinion about the tenets of Islam.[131]

The traditionalists, in Sunni Islam, believe that exegetical work is closed in the same way as the Canon has been closed, and that therefore no addition

---

126. Abdal-Haqq, "Islamic Law," 6.
127. Arzt, "Application," 204.
128. Bernard Lewis, *Discovery of Europe* (New York: Norton & Co., 1982), 61.
129. Adamec, *Islam: A Historical Companion*, 132.
130. Abdullahi A. An-Na'im, "Religious Minorities under Islamic Law and the Limits of Cultural Relativism," *Human Rights Quarterly* 9, no. 1 (1987): 10.
131. This translation appears in John O. Voll, "Renewal and Reform in Islamic History: *Tajdid and Islah*," in *Voices of Resurgent Islam*, ed. John L. Esposito (New York: Oxford University Press, 1983), 38.

or extraction is lawful. (In contrast, Shia Muslims believe that *ijtihad* can still be continued, though it is restricted to special teachers in every age.) By implication, Sharīʿa is perceived, by traditionalists, not as a methodology of Islamic jurisprudence but as a divine law which is perfect and unchangeable.

On the basis of this view, traditionalists believe that the blasphemy laws "are indeed derived from Islamic law, and hence are immune to any suggestion of repeal or abolition."[132] This notion is evident from Ansar Abassi, one of the columnists representing the traditionalists in Pakistan, who wrote in an editorial in the Urdu daily newspaper, the Jang:

> Certain westernized sections of Pakistani society have used Salman Taseer's assassination for their own personal agenda of abolition of laws regarding Blasphemy against the Holy Prophet. These "enlightened classes" have tried to portray this law as "man made." By doing so, they have tried to stifle the proper implementation of Islamic laws in this country.[133]

In line with this view, traditionalist *ʿulamā* in Pakistan assert that blasphemy laws have not been made by any dictator, but are the laws of Islam and it is un-Islamic to question their rationale or endeavour to modify them. On 9 January 2011, Qari Ahsaan, one of the leaders of *Jammat ud Dawa*, led a rally of 40,000 people in Karachi against proposed changes to the blasphemy laws, stating that "we can't compromise on the blasphemy law. It's a divine law and nobody can change it."[134]

This can also be seen from the recent debate over procedural changes in Pakistan's blasphemy laws, held in the Council of Islamic Ideology (CII), a constitutional body that advises the legislature whether or not a certain law is repugnant to Islam. This Council ruled that "there is no need to amend the blasphemy law,"[135] despite the fact that it had previously agreed with the claim of one of its prominent members, Maulana Tahir Ashrafi, who stated,

---

132. Anqa Dehlvi, "Pakistan's Blasphemy Law: The Great Untouchables," *Ahmadiyya Times*, 22 February 2013, online.

133. Cited in ibid.

134. AFP, "More than 40,000 Protest Blasphemy Law Change," *Dawn*, 9 January 2011, online.

135. Correspondent, "Advice to Legislature: No Need to Amend Blasphemy Law, says CII," *The Express Tribune*, 20 September 2013.

"All the religious scholars agreed to put an end to the misuse of blasphemy laws."[136] In order to stop the misuse of the blasphemy law in Pakistan, Ashrafi had put forward a proposal to impose the death penalty on those who make false accusations under the blasphemy law. He argued that "[those] making a false accusation [should] face death penalty because the words attributed to the accused were actually uttered by the accuser."[137] A serious ideological difference surfaced over this proposal and the traditionalists in the CII, who were in the overwhelming majority, opposed this amendment by saying that "they did not want to discourage people from coming forward [to] lodge complaints against blasphemers."[138]

This shows that the traditionalists do not want to allow the legislature to touch the law, which they believe is divine, even for the purposes of making procedural changes. Maulana Muhammad Khan Sherani (the CII chairman), in a press conference, declared that the position of the CII was that "there is no need to change the blasphemy law."[139] This position is further evidenced by the comments of Muhammad Ammar Khan Nasir, a leading traditional scholar in Pakistan, who commented that "such moves to repeal the blasphemy laws were a conspiracy conducted by the enemies of Islam."[140]

This shows that traditionalists view the blasphemy laws as part of the divine Shariʿa. They believe that they represent the mind of God and, as fallible humans cannot understand the mind of God, if any aspect of his law appears unjust, that is simply because the human has an infantile or incomplete understanding of Shariʿa.[141] They suggest that critics, instead of criticizing, should study Shariʿa more deeply in order to comprehend the mind of God.[142]

---

136. Asif Aqeel, "A Renewed Debate over Blasphemy Laws," *WorldWatch Monitor*, 2 October 2013, online.

137. Kalbe Ali, "CII Debate on Blasphemy Law," *Dawn*, 20 September 2013, online.

138. Ibid.

139. Aqeel, "Renewed Debate."

140. M. A. Khan Nasir, "Comment on Blasphemy by Leading Traditional Scholar," online.

141. Neville Cox, "The Clash of Unprovable Universalisms – International Human Rights and Islamic Law," *OJLR* (2013): 12.

142. Ibid.

In summary, the traditionalists have reproduced these laws as they exist in the medieval Islamic legal manuals and apply them without giving any consideration to the changed conditions of the modern period. The traditionalists want to implement the pre-modern position of Islamic *fiqh*, according to which blasphemy is punishable by death. This line of reasoning is evident from Maulana Maududi who argued that "jurists have different opinion with regard to execution but . . . they have unanimously declared that one who blasphemes the Prophet must be put to death . . . and no one can be allowed to change this established law."[143]

Modernists

The second group of Muslim scholars are the Modernists, who dispute the traditionalists' point of view. The Sharia, by the tenth century, was cast into an orthodox mould. It remained in it for another millennium, and did not break out until, in the twentieth century, modern scholarship emerged. The modernists claimed that the reason that Sharia remained unchanged for so long was because of the state policy of the Abbasids who closed the door of *ijtihad*. As Hans Küng pointed out, "it was in the interest of the Abbasids that the development of religious law should come to an end in the eighth century. After the ninth century, the interpretation of Qur'an and *sunna* was allowed only within the four law schools."[144]

The modern Muslim scholars claim that the Islamic jurists developed Sharia in a specific context under the umbrella of the Islamic state, and that it is therefore appropriate to revise Sharia due to different contexts. Shemeem Abbas, through her scholarly study of the Muslim empires, argued that blasphemy laws were created by the Islamic empires that "arose outside Arabia, such as the Abbasids in Iraq, the Ommayads in al-Andalus (Spain), and the Ottomans in Turkey . . . these earlier empires validated their laws through Muhammad's Islam."[145] The modernists claim that the punishments for blasphemy, apostasy and heresy have no grounds in the Qur'an, nor are they derivable from the Prophet's life and practice. They argue, for example,

---

143. Cited in Qureshi, *Messenger of God*, 172.

144. Küng, *Islam*, 276. Although there is no documentary proof available that "after the tenth century, at least in Sunni Islam, the 'door of independent judgment' (*bab al-ijtihad*) was regarded as closed, as has often been claimed" by the traditionalists. Ibid.

145. Abbas, *Pakistan's Blasphemy Laws*, 29.

that there is no reference to blasphemy in the constitution of Madinah or in the Treaty of Hudybia, both of which originally came from the Prophet of Islam. Moreover, the Prophet himself did not execute anyone exclusively for the offence of blasphemy and apostasy. Abbas goes on to argue that the blasphemy laws are the creation of the Islamic state which "evolved in a political domain" and that the political authorities manipulated these laws in order to subdue their opponents and maintain their authority.[146]

The jurists were used by the state to suppress its political opponents by charging them with blasphemy and heresy. For example, the Abbasids implemented a legal system with jurists and jurisconsults who gave a strict interpretation of Islamic law. This can be seen, for instance, in the trial of Husayn ibn Mansur Hallaj (858–922), who was condemned as a heretic and executed by the Abbasid state on the charge of blasphemy. Abbas argues that Hallaj was a threat to the Abbasid state because of his egalitarian views. Hallaj had criticized the autocratic policy of the state and showed sympathy with the working classes.[147]

Another substantial example of how Sharīa was shaped by political interests can be found in the time of the great Islamic Mughal Empire in India. Aurangzeb Alamgir, in his quest for the throne, tried his elder brother Dara Shikoh (1659), the rightful heir of his father Shahjehan, for the offence of apostasy and blasphemy. The state jurists, who were loyal to Aurangzeb, declared Dara guilty of apostasy/blasphemy and sentenced him to death. When Dara's severed head was brought before Aurangzeb, he exclaimed, "As I did not look at this infidel's face during his life time, I have no wish to do so now."[148] These two examples demonstrate and strengthen the view of modernists that the jurists interpreted Sharīa in ways which suited the

---

146. Ibid.

147. Ibid., 90. A few centuries later Ibn Taymiya (1263–1328), a conservative reformist, gave fatwās against Hallaj which are often cited by the traditionalists. According to Taymiya, Hallaj's offence was unpardonable "what Hallaj said is only falsehood [*hajj* could be performed fully outside Mecca] and that those like him deserve death." See Herbert Mason, *Al-Hallaj* (Surrey: Curzon Press, 1995), 52.

148. Akbar S. Ahmed, *Journey into Islam: The Crisis of Globalization* (Washington: Brookings Institution Press, 2007), 49. Some argued that the religious clerics went against Dara because he opposed all these state-backed clerics: "Paradise is there where there is no mullah." In the end these state-backed clerics decided his fate by declaring him apostate and blasphemer. Ibid., 50–51.

rulers, in order to maintain the authority of the rulers. In this regard Abbas argues that,

> blasphemy and its related offences such as heresy, heterodoxy, and apostasy are justifications, under an Islamic cover, for the state to repress independent thinking – disagreement, dissenting political opinion, or *ijtihad-e ra'y*. The state establishes authority through faith, as did states like England through the divine right of kings until the Reformation changed the politics of faith.[149]

In the same manner, the harsher clauses of Pakistan's blasphemy laws were a product of the regime of Zia-ul-Haq, who used religion for his political purposes (as the study of chapter 1 showed). The idea that Zia had used religion for political purposes was echoed recently by Makhdoom Javed Hashmi, the president of Pakistan Tehreek-e-Insaf (PTI) and a senior politician in Pakistan. Hashmi expressed his views in the National Assembly of Pakistan over the massacre of Christians in Peshawar. He said that the blasphemy laws were a product of those who used religion to attain power, therefore "he had first opposed the blasphemy laws when they [were] introduced by President Zia in the 1980s."[150] He further said, "This blasphemy law was wrong . . . and contrary to Islam . . . [Therefore] he had voted against it in violation of his then Pakistan Muslim League Party's discipline when it was brought to the house for approval."[151]

The main critique of the modernists is that early jurists of Islamic *fiqh* played a significant role in developing Sharia in the specific context of the early Muslim experience, and within the worldview of an Islamic state, and that therefore Sharia does not represent the whole of Islam but rather just the early Muslims' understanding of the sources of Islam in the context of an Islamic state.[152] Al-Sadiq al-Nayhoun from Libya, a specialist in comparative

---

149. Abbas, *Pakistan's Blasphemy Laws*, 112.
150. Aqeel, "Renewed Debate."
151. Raja Asghar, "Javed Hashmi Assails Blasphemy Law in NA," *Dawn*, 25 September 2013, online.
152. An-Na'im, "Religious Minorities," 10.

religion, argues that the Islam inherited from the *salaf* (pious ancestors) is not the Islam of Qur'an but a distorted Islam.[153]

Therefore, Said Ramadan suggested that the term "Muslims jurisprudence" rather than "Islamic jurisprudence" should be used in referring to *fiqh*, so that the incorrect legal conclusions of the Muslim jurists may not be classified as Islamic.[154] Likewise, Joseph Schacht also suggested that "Islamic law represent[s] an extreme case of 'jurists' law," [as] it was created and developed by private specialists . . ."[155] The modernists' main critique is that, because religion was used by the state to achieve its purposes, we need to understand the political context in which the blasphemy laws were first established and understand that they were used to subdue political opponents. Modernists are of the view that religion must be kept separate from the state, and that state matters must be run in a secular manner, where belief is considered a private matter. This idea of the separation of state and religion was advocated by Muhammad Ali Jinnah, the founder of Pakistan, who stressed many times in his speeches that Pakistan would not be a theocracy. In his presidential address to the Pakistan Constituent Assembly on 11 August 1947, he said:

> You are free to go your temples, you are free to go to your mosques or to any other places of worship in this State of Pakistan. You may belong to any religion or caste or creed – that has got nothing to do with the business of the State . . . We are starting this fundamental principle that we are all citizens of one State.[156]

Justices Muhammad Munir and R. M. Kyani, in their report known as the Munir Commission report, explicitly stated that it was not the business of the state to declare a person Muslim or non-Muslim. Religion was thus considered a largely private affair, and subject to one's personal faith and belief.[157]

---

153. Nayhoum cited in Saeed and Saeed, *Freedom of Religion*, 94.
154. Said Ramadan, *Islamic Law: Its Scope and Equity* (London: P. R. Macmillan, 1961), 62.
155. Joseph Schacht, *An Introduction to Islamic Law* (Oxford: Clarendon Press, 1964), 5.
156. Jinnah, *Quaid-i-Azam*, 8–9.
157. Kayani, *Report of the Court of Inquiry*, 241.

The above demonstrates that modernists challenged the Sharīʿa of medieval jurists, arguing that their interpretation and implementation is inapplicable to modern times. They are in favour, more or less, of the western secular democratic models of the state where religion should be confined to private affairs and has no place in state matters.

The Reformers

Our above analysis demonstrates that the traditionalists are on one extreme and the modernists on the other extreme: they are completely opposite and resistant to each other. The reformers lean towards the modernists' camp while trying to find a way between these two extremes. On the one hand, the reformers, like the modernists, believe that the Sharīʿa is not the whole of Islam but represents the early Muslims' understanding of the sources of Islam. They are of the opinion that pre-modern Islamic law cannot be applied directly to modern circumstances. However, unlike the modernists, they are comparatively sympathetic to the early jurists of Islamic *fiqh*. This can be seen from Abdullah Saeed's comment:

> How they [early jurists] read early Islamic history as well as Qurʾanic and prophetic texts perceived to be in support of capital punishment can therefore be understood as natural, logical and relevant for their day. Had they lived in the late twentieth century, in which capital punishment became out of step with the ethos of the time, their responses to the punishment of blasphemy/apostasy may have been very different.[158]

On the other hand, the reformers are not in favour, unlike the modernists, of keeping the state separate from religion. They argue for the rationale of their approach:

> The non-Muslims living in Muslim states prefer the western model of secular state over the model of historical Sharīʿa state because they believe that they will be discriminated under the Sharīʿa law. On the other side, the vast majority of Muslims reject the idea of secular state on the ground that they have a

---

158. Saeed and Saeed, *Freedom of Religion*, 67–68.

religious duty to conduct their affairs in accordance with the tenets of Islam.[159]

The reformers, like the modernists, are of the view that the door of *ijtihad* is not closed and that there is always room for exploring the meaning of the Qur'an and Sunnah according to the need and situation of the people and time (context). They argue that the early commentators expounded the text according to their own time and situation, and now the circumstances have completely changed, so that the understanding and exposition of the early commentators cannot be directly applied to the present situation. The questions of the present age cannot be addressed with the historical answers of the early jurists: instead, new answers must be developed out of the Qur'an and *sunna*.[160] In other words, Islamic Shari'a for today needs to be developed through the exercise of *ijtihad* just as the early jurists did in their own situation.

An example of prominent advocates and international scholars for developing "Modern Shari'a" are Mahmoud Taha, from Sudan, followed by his student Abdullahi An-Na'im. Na'im argued that Muslims can develop a new Shari'a from the fundamental source of the Qur'an, in accordance with the spirit of Islam in order to meet the needs and aspiration of the modern times and in full consistency with the demands of human rights.[161] Na'im endorses the view of his teacher Mahmoud Taha that the

> Qur'an was designed to provide the Muslims with a comprehensive source of guidance and instruction. The Muslims should apply themselves to that source in order to derive their law, the modern shari'a, in the same way the Muslims of 7th century Arabia and the Middle East applied themselves to that fundamental source and developed the law which has been handed down to us as historical shari'a.[162]

---

159. An-Na'im, "Religious Minorities," 10.
160. Ibid.
161. Abdullahi A. An-Na'im, "Constitutionalism and Islamization in the Sudan," *Africa Today* 36, no. 3/4 (1989): 27–28; Abdullahi A. An-Na'im, "The Islamic Law of Apostasy and Its Modern Applicability: A Case from Sudan," *Religion* 16 (1986): 205; see also Taha, *Second Message of Islam*.
162. An-Na'im, "The Islamic Law of Apostasy," 216.

Their argument is based on the rationale that since both the social and physical environment has changed enormously from the time historical Sharīʿa was developed, the law must also change in response to the new circumstances. They claim that this approach of modern Sharīʿa has the ability to reconcile conflicts between the Muslim majority and the non-Muslim minority and also to meet the demands of human rights in the modern age.[163] Such thinking should be an important part of the Pakistan's public discourse in its current discussion on blasphemy laws.

Concluding Summary

The main objective of this chapter was to assess the extent to which Pakistan's blasphemy laws are consistent or inconsistent with the sources of Islamic Sharīʿa. For this purpose, we divided this chapter into four sections. In the first section, we specifically analyzed this question: Does the Qur'an speak about capital punishment for blasphemy? Our study showed that modernists and traditionalists employed different hermeneutical approaches towards interpreting the text of the Qur'an, through which they came up with opposite conclusions. The modernists argue that the offence of blasphemy will be dealt with by Allah on judgment day and that the Qur'an is silent on the question of how to deal with the offence of blasphemy in this world. In contrast, the traditionalists insist that the Qur'an specifies that the punishment for blasphemy is death (in this world). Our analysis argues that there is no explicit evidence or clear Qur'anic mandate for capital punishment for blasphemy.

In the second section, the case for capital punishment for blasphemy was analyzed in the light of *sunna*, which is the second fundamental source of Islamic Sharīʿa. Interestingly, both traditionalists and modernists argue for their own positions using the same sources to validate their position. The traditionalists argue that there is clear evidence in the *sira* and *hadith* literature that the Prophet authorized the execution of his vilifiers. In contrast, modernists argued that the sources cited by the traditionalists, with regard to execution of blasphemers, are not authentic enough to be relied on. Moreover, modernists argued that we need to recognize the dual role

---

163. An-Naʿim, "Constitutionalism and Islamization," 28.

of Muhammad as prophet and ruler. The modernists claimed that in those incidents of the death penalty for blasphemy, cited by the traditionalists, the sentence was carried out by Muhammad as the ruler (rather than as Prophet), therefore those actions and rulings were related to the original context of the Prophet and cannot be applied to succeeding generations.

We have seen in the third section, where we examined the *fiqh* of four Sunni schools, that there is general consensus among the jurists that vilification of the Prophet requires capital punishment. However, there is considerable difference of opinion among the jurists on the question of whether or not the culprit should be given the opportunity to repent. Our analysis demonstrated that the Hanafi and Shafi'i schools are comparatively lenient, compared to the Maliki and Hanabali schools. The majority of the Hanafi and Shafi'i jurists are of the opinion that the offender should be given the opportunity to repent and that, if he repents, he should be forgiven. However, the Malaiki and Hanabali jurists are much stricter, arguing that repentance is neither necessary nor acceptable and that therefore execution must be performed without delay. We have also noted that the Hanafis have a lenient position with regard to women and non-Muslim offenders. In the light of our analysis, we raised three points of concern:

First, the framers of the blasphemy laws in Pakistan and later the FSC did not acknowledge the principle of Islamic law which demands that more weight should be given to the earlier opinion (in this case, the Hanafi School).

Second, the majority of Muslims in Pakistan, even most Muslims worldwide, follow the Hanafi School. Despite this fact, the position of this school has been largely ignored by the framers of blasphemy laws and later by the FSC, in favour of other schools whose followers are in the minority. This shows that a minority view has been imposed on the majority.

Third, the constitution of Pakistan declares that the country is the *Islami Jamhuria Pakistan* (Islamic Republic of Pakistan), the word *Jamhur* meaning "people" affirming that Pakistan is Islamic as well as democratic. We argued that Pakistan's legislature and judiciary have violated the norms of Islamic law, where early legal opinion has more weight than later opinions, as well as the norms of democracy, where the view of the majority should be implemented.

In the final section, we focused on Muslim scholarship in the modern period generally with regard to the applicability of Sharia and blasphemy laws and specifically to opinions about whether these laws are man made or divine in origin. We divided the modern Muslim scholarship into three groups. In the first group are traditionalists, who hold to the pre-modern position that Sharia is divine and that the blasphemy laws, being a part of Sharia, are also divine in origin and therefore must be implemented according to the letter and the spirit of the historical Sharia. In contrast, modernists challenge this view by arguing that historical Sharia is not divine, but evolved through the hermeneutical exercise of the medieval jurists in the context of the Islamic state.

Modernists insist that the blasphemy laws were the creation of the Islamic political regimes that used these laws to subdue their political opponents. These laws were therefore man made. A more recent example of this is the harsher blasphemy laws that Zia-ul-Haq introduced for his own political purposes. The traditionalists and modernists form two extremes: the former argued that religion cannot be separated from the state whereas the latter argued that religion should be restricted to private affairs. The reformers lie between these two extremes: they propose that modern Sharia needs to be developed with the process of *ijtihad* according to the needs of the modern context.

The tension between these three views is due to Pakistan's identity as being both Islamic and a republic. Pakistan faces a big challenge in trying to reconcile these two aspects particularly as it pertains to the blasphemy laws.

CHAPTER 3

The Design Flaws in Pakistan's Blasphemy Laws from a Legal Perspective

Introduction

Very few blasphemy cases surfaced before the introduction of the harsher clauses 295-B, C, and 298-A, B and C into the Pakistan Penal Code (PPC) in the 1980s.[1] But hundreds have since faced blasphemy charges following their introduction and arbitrary enforcement.[2] The data of the reported cases shows that false allegations mushroomed after the verdict of the Federal Shariat Court (FSC) in 1991, which made the death penalty the mandatory sentence for breaking Clause 295-C. Additionally, there are actually many more cases which were registered with the police and went up to the trial courts but never made it to the appellate courts and are therefore not counted in the official data. The Lahore High Court Division Bench, while acquitting a person accused of blasphemy under 295-C, stated in one of its judgments

---

1. According to the Dawn report prior to 1986, only 14 cases pertaining to blasphemy were reported. Staff Reporter, "Timeline: Accused under the Blasphemy Law," online. Prior to the 1980s only 9 blasphemy cases surfaced, according to CLAAS Pakistan. Joseph Francis, "Claas Pakistan: Annual Report 2010" (Lahore: CLAAS, 2010), 102.

2. The data collected by the National Commission for Justice and Peace in Pakistan shows that among the total of 1244, 608 Muslims, 457 Ahmadis, 159 Christians, 20 Hindus had been accused until 2012. Peter Jacob, "Human Rights Monitor 2012-13: A Report on the Religious Minorities in Pakistan " (Lahore: NCJP, 2013), 203–204.

in 2002 that "it appears that ever since the law became more stringent, there has been an increase in the number of registration[s] of blasphemy cases."[3]

The misuse of the blasphemy laws continues to be a cause of concern to the international community as well as to the minorities within the country.[4] Various human rights organizations have been pointing out that these laws are being misused.[5] One of the key elements of the blasphemy laws which makes them open to misuse is the vagueness of the clauses introduced by General Zia-ul-Haq in the 1980s. Due to this, these laws have become an easy tool for settling personal scores. Tahir Ashrafi, the Chairman of the Ulamā Council in Pakistan (who had been a strong opponent of any amendments to the blasphemy laws) admitted that "the law of the jungle is taking over now and anybody can be accused of anything."[6] In 2010, the Council of Islamic Ideology (CII,) Pakistan's top constitutional advisory body on Islamic injunctions, recommended procedural amendments to the government "to ensure that laws are not misused against any individual irrespective of his religion."[7] However, the majority of those in Islamic academia in Pakistan rule out any possibility of amending the Pakistan Penal Code (known as substantive law) because they perceive this as divine law.[8] In consequence, discussions have generally been confined to procedural amendments in the Criminal Procedure Code (known as adjective law).

Due to this popular misconception about their divine origins, little or no attention is being paid to the design defects in the laws. This makes them open to abuse. In this regard, Osama and Zahra note that "apart from procedural inadequacies of the Pakistani legal system and its special social

---

3. *Muhammad Mahboob v. State*, 54 PLD 587, 589 (2002).

4. David Pinault, "Losers' Vengeance," *America* 194, no. 13 (2006): 10.

5. See Najam U Din, "State of Human Rights in 2010" (Lahore: HRCP, 2010), 13135; "Use and Abuse of the Blasphemy Laws" (Amnesty International, 1994), online.

6. Tahir Ashrafi, "He Died in Defence of Humanity," *Daily Times*, 4 January 2013, online. It seems a new development that, with Rimsha's case, even Muslim clerics with extremist views are admitting that the law is being misused – something that minorities and human rights activists have been persistently pointing out.

7. Qaiser Butt, "Top Islamic Body Proposes Changes in Blasphemy Law," *The Express Tribune*, 19 December 2010, online; Manzoor Qadir, "No Amendments in Blasphemy Law Despite Recommendations," *Daily Times*, 28 August 2012, online.

8. On 10 January 2011, Qari Ahsaan from Jamaat ud Dawa, addressed a rally in Karachi: "We can't compromise on the blasphemy laws. It's a divine law and nobody can change it." "Pakistan Rally Backs Blasphemy Law" (Al Jazeera (Qatar), 2011).

political circumstances, the very form and design of the blasphemy laws invite abuse."[9] In order to fully understand this phenomenon, this chapter will explore the design flaws of Pakistan's blasphemy laws which lead to miscarriages of justice.

From All Religions to One Religion

The British-enacted clauses of the blasphemy law in chapter 15, *Offences Relating to Religion* (Clauses 295, 296, 297 and 298 of the Indian Penal Code) were passed by Act 45 of 1860. Clause 295-A was introduced by the Criminal Law Amendment Act 25 in 1927. For the purpose of our analysis, they are reproduced (emphasis mine) here:

1. 295: Whoever destroys, damages or defiles *any place of worship*, or any object held sacred by *any class of persons* with the intention of thereby insulting the *religion of any class of persons* or with the knowledge that *any class of persons* is likely to consider such destruction, damage or defilement as an *insult to their religion*,
2. 295: Whoever with deliberate and malicious intention of outraging the religious feelings of *any class* of the citizens of Pakistan.
3. 296: Whoever voluntarily causes disturbances to *any assembly* lawfully engaged in the performance of religious worship, or religious ceremonies, . . .
4. 297: Whoever, with the intention of wounding the feelings of *any person, or of insulting the religion of any person*, or . . . commits any trespass in *any place of worship* or on *any place of sepulture*, or *any place* set apart for the performance of funeral rites or as a depository for the remains of dead, or offers *any indignity to any human corpse*, or causes disturbance to *any persons* assembled for the performance of funeral ceremonies, . . .

---

9. Osama Siddique and Zahra Hayat, "Unholy Speech and Holy Laws: Blasphemy Laws in Pakistan – Controversial Origins, Design Defects, and Free Speech Implications," *MJIL* 17, no. 2 (2008): 305.

5. 298: Whoever, with the deliberate intention of wounding the <u>religious feelings of any person,</u> utters any word or makes any sound in the hearing of that person . . .

The Indian Penal Code (IPC) was drafted by the British for the new judicial system introduced to the subcontinent to replace the "Mahomedan criminal law" by which the courts were principally guided before the enactment of the IPC in 1860. On the attaining of independence in 1947, the IPC was inherited by both India and Pakistan and later by Bangladesh in 1971. In Pakistan, it was adopted as the Pakistan Penal Code (PPC).

The British IPC was clearly intended to provide protection to all religions. The underlined words ("any class," "any person," and "any place of worship") in all clauses of Chapter 15 which relate to religious offences clearly provide cover to all religions. The Commentary in the IPC applies "any class of persons" to mean that "this expression may include any religious sect however small in number. The application of this section is not limited only between those who follow different religions. It applies to different sects or classes . . ."[10]

In contrast, the Zia-framed blasphemy clauses seek specifically to protect one religion, that of Islam, in Pakistan. For example, Clause 295-B deals with an offence regarding the defilement of the Qur'an, the holy book of Islam. Clause 295-C pertains to using derogatory remarks in respect to the Holy Prophet of Islam and Clause 298-A pertains to derogatory remarks in respect to holy personages of Islam. Further sections, Clauses 298-B and C, deal specifically with the Ahmadis, who were excommunicated from the mainstream Islam by the Parliament of Pakistan in 1974 and since then have been considered as non-Muslims. In Clause 298-B, they were restricted from using descriptions and titles which are reserved for certain holy personages and places of Islam. Clause 298-C forbids anyone from the Ahamdi sect calling himself a Muslim or preaching or propagating his faith as Islam. The wording and design of the Zia-framed clauses demonstrate that they are extremely exclusive in their design.

---

10. Ranchhoddas Ratanlal et al., *Ratanlal & Dhirajlal's Law of Crimes: A Commentary on the Indian Penal Code, 1860*, 24th ed., 2 vols., vol. 1 (New Delhi: Bharat Law House, 1997), 1148.

This reveals that the motives behind Zia's regime were none other than to "Islamize" Pakistan's judicial system. This bias is also evident from the Criminal Law Amendment Act of 1986, through which Clause 295-C was introduced. This Act further amended the Code of Criminal Procedure, 1898 (Act V of 1898). It stated that, after the entries relating to 295-A in Section 99-B of the Code of Criminal Procedure, the following new entries shall be inserted:[11]

Table 3.1 Changes in the Criminal Procedure Code

1	2	3	4–6	7	8
295-A (1927)	Deliberate and malicious acts intended to outrage religious feelings on any class	May not arrest without warrant	Ditto	Two years imprisonment or with fine or with both	Trial Court
295-B (1982)	Defiling, etc., of copy of Holy Qur'an	May arrest without warrant	Ditto	Imprisonment for life	Court of Session
295-C (1986)	Use of derogatory remarks, etc., in respect of the Holy Prophet	Ditto	Ditto	Death or imprisonment for life, and fine	Court of Session which shall be presided over by a Muslim

As can be seen from column 8 in the above table, offences under Clause 295-C would now be tried under the jurisdiction of a "Court of Session which shall be presided over by a Muslim."[12] This demonstrates that the underlying intention and purpose of those who framed these laws is to protect only one religion – Islam. Clearly the clauses pertain only to offences against Islam, the religion of the overwhelming majority in Pakistan, whereas the

---

11. *Act 3 of 1986*, 71.
12. Ibid.

British-framed clauses were inclusive in their nature, providing protection to all religions, and even to all sects within religions.

The intention of privileging only one religion is further evident from the fact that no corresponding clause was framed "to provide a remedy to the non-Muslims from any act of other citizens that may hurt their religious feelings."[13] Some within the Pakistani legal system have acknowledged and objected to the exclusivity of the laws. In its judgment on making the death penalty mandatory in section 295-C of the PPC in 1991, the Federal Shariat Court suggested: "A clause may further be added to this section so as to make the same acts or things when said about other prophets, also an offence with the same punishment [death penalty]."[14] In April 1994, the Lahore High Court (LHC) suggested in its ruling to "make blasphemy qua other Prophets including the Holy Christ, punishable with the same sentence of death . . . it is hoped that the needful would be done in the near future."[15] However, neither of these rulings were heeded by the government or judiciary of Pakistan. By contrast, the FSC's ruling to make death penalty mandatory in Clause 295-C, was implemented without any hindrance.[16] Further changes to the law which also discriminate in favour of Islam can be seen in the introduction of Clauses 295-B and C, as shown in the table below.

---

13. "Blasphemy Laws in Pakistan: Historical Overview" (Islamabad: CRSS, 2012).

14. *Muhammad Ismail Qureshi v. Pakistan,* 35.

15. *Riaz Ahmad and 3 Others v. State,* 46 PLD 485, 502 (1994). In this case two Christian parties expressed their view that the ambit of this law should include Jesus and other prophets. See ibid., at 494. However, a large number of Christians in Pakistan do not support this view because it could open the door for further litigation and abuse of laws. Former bishop of Lahore Alexander Malik expressed his view in a TV program that most Christians are not in favour of any such law for securing the honour of Jesus Christ for two reasons: first, who are we to secure his honour? And second, if such law is passed in Pakistan, half of Pakistan will come under this law. Alexander J. Malik, interview by Kamran Shahid, *Front Line,* Duniya TV, 29 November 2010.

16. The FSC directed the government of Pakistan to effect the necessary legal changes and added, "in case this is not done by 30 April 1991 the words 'or punishment for life' in Section 295-C, PPC, shall cease to have effect on that date." *Muhammad Ismail Qureshi v. Pakistan,* 35.

The Design Flaws in Pakistan's Blasphemy Laws from a Legal Perspective

Table 3.2 Comparison between British and Zia-framed Clauses

British-framed	Zia-framed
295-A "Whoever, with deliberate and malicious intention of outraging the religious feelings of any class of the citizens of Pakistan, by words, either spoken or written, or by visible representations insults or attempts to insult the religion or the religious beliefs of that class, shall be punished with imprisonment of either description for a term which may extend to two years or with a fine, or with both."	295-B "Whoever wilfully defiles, damages or desecrates a copy of the Holy Qur'an or of an extract there from or uses it in any derogatory manner or for any unlawful purpose shall be punishable with imprisonment for life." 295-C "Whoever by words either spoken or written, or by visible representation, or by any imputation, innuendo, or insinuation, directly or indirectly defiles the sacred name of the Holy Prophet Muhammad (peace be upon him) shall be punished with death, or imprisonment for life, and shall also be liable to [a] fine."

When these are read in parallel, it is hard to see what has been introduced as new in 295-B and C which was not covered by 295-A, except for two elements. First, the latter clauses are designed to protect only the religion of Islam. Second, the penalties for offending against Islam are much harsher than those imposed in Clause 295-A for offending against other religions. This implicitly shows the belief of the framers in the superiority of Islam over other religions. The Indian Law Commission which drafted the IPC made some interesting comments about the previous judicial systems implemented in India:

> It appears to us that none of the systems of penal law established in British India has any claim to our attention except what it may derive from its own intrinsic excellence. All those systems are foreign. All were introduced by the conquerors differing in race, manner, language and religion from the great mass of people. The criminal law of the Hindus was long ago superseded, throughout the greater part of the territories now subject to the Company, by that of the Muhammedans, which

is certainly the last system of criminal law which an enlightened and human government would be disposed to receive.[17]

We can read between the lines of the Law Commission's statement the opinion that judicial systems should not be biased towards any religion, but that everyone should be considered equal before the law. This is what the UN treaties depict[18] and this is even what is mandated by the constitution of Pakistan.[19] However, the government of Pakistan has refused to rule in accordance with these sections of the constitution. In 1993, Ahmadis challenged the constitutionality of Ordinance 20 of 1984 in the Supreme Court of Pakistan (SCP) on the grounds that it violates Articles 20, and also 19 and 25, of the constitution of Pakistan. The SCP dismissed all eight petitions and upheld Ordinance 20 of 1984, arguing that "every man-made law must now conform to the Injunctions of Islam as contained in the Qur'an and Sunnah . . . Therefore even the fundamental rights given in the constitution must not violate the norms of Islam."[20] Our analysis above demonstrates that the law (specifically, the Zia-framed clauses of the blasphemy law) has given Islam superiority over all other religions. These laws are thus discriminatory in terms of their protective ambit.

Requirement of Intent

A visible and fundamental difference between the British and the Zia-framed clauses of the blasphemy laws is the requirement of intent. The British laws made it clear that a statement or action is legally liable only if it is done

---

17. Nand Lal, *The Indian Penal Code, Act 45 of 1860 with an Exhaustive, Explanatory, and Critical Commentary*, 2 vols., vol. 2 (Lahore: Krishen Lal & Co., 1929).

18. UN Declaration of Human Rights article 18.

19. Article 19 guarantees that "Every citizen shall have the right to freedom of speech and expression . . ."; art. 20 says that "Every citizen shall have the right to profess, practice and propagate his religion; and . . . shall have the right to establish, maintain and manage its religious institutions"; and art. 25 states that "All citizens are equal before law and are entitled to equal protection of law . . ."

20. *Zaheeruddin v. State*, 26 SCMR 1718, 1773 (1993). The SCP took this position on the ground that the Objectives Resolution had been made a substantive part of the constitution in 1985 through the 8th Amendment. It says that "Muslims shall be enabled to organize their lives in accordance with the teachings and requirements of Islam as set out in the Qur'an and the Sunnah" and "Therefore the injunction of Islam as contained in the Qur'an and Sunnah are adopted as the real and effective law." See ibid., at 1774.

with the intention of causing offence. There is a repeated emphasis on the requirement of intent in all the British-framed clauses dealing with offences to religion. Section 295 says (emphasis mine) "*with the intention* of thereby insulting the religion of any class persons . . ."; Section 295-A says "*with the deliberate and malicious intention* of outraging the religious feelings of any class"; Section 297 states "*with the intention* of wounding the feelings of any person or of insulting the religion of any person"; and Section 298 states "*with the deliberate intention* of wounding the religious feelings of any person." The underlined words above in all four sections of the blasphemy law indicate vividly that an act will only be considered blasphemous if it is done with deliberate intention.

The law commentaries on the Indian Penal Code provide a detailed interpretation of the meaning of intent. The commentary on Section 295 states: "In the first place, then, there must be the intention to insult, or at least the knowledge of the likelihood of the act being taken as an insult."[21] In reference to 295-A, the commentary states, "An act may be deliberate without being malicious and it may be malicious without being deliberate, since it may be reckless without being intentional. What is required to constitute the offence is the presence of both."[22] It is notable here that the expression "wounding religious feelings" was used in Section 298, while in Section 295-A (framed later, in 1927) the expression used was "outraging the religious feelings." The latter phrase was explained by the Select Committee in its report:

> We think that to penalize even with intentional outrage or attempted outrage upon the religious feelings of any class would be casting the net too wide for the cases with particular reference to which the Bill has been introduced. At the time we realize that the reference to the outraging of religious feelings was inserted to provide for the case of an insult to the founder of the religion . . . where such an outrage does not amount to an insult of religion. It has in one instance been held that an

---

21. Hari Singh Gour, *The Penal Law of India: Being a Commentary – Analytical, Critical and Expository on the Indian Penal Code*, 11th ed., 4 vols., vol. 3 (Allahabad: Law Publishers 2000), 2327.

22. Ibid., 2335–2336.

insult to the founder of a religion is not necessarily an insult to the religion although it may outrage the religious feelings of the followers of that religion. We have therefore provided that the new section shall only apply in cases where a religion is insulted with the deliberate intention of outraging the religious feelings of its followers.[23]

This makes it clear that a significant emphasis had been placed on deliberate intention in the offences relating to blasphemy clauses framed by the British. It is evident from our above discussion that deliberate intention is a vital factor in establishing guilt in Clauses 295, 295-A, 297 and 298. There can be no offence without deliberate intention. It is apparent from the above that it is necessary to show concrete evidence of "deliberate and malicious" intent before someone is charged under these laws. In other words, the burden for proving deliberate intent is laid on the complainant, rather than it being the responsibility of the defender to disprove it. Accordingly, the law commentaries of the IPC expressed the strong opinion that the police and court were required not to take accusations seriously unless malicious and deliberate intent could be shown.[24]

This emphasis is also apparent from the judgments of the superior courts in Pakistan prior to the Zia-framed clauses, in which the courts gave careful attention to whether or not an act was done with "deliberate intent." For example, in 1952, Khawaja Nazir Ahmad wrote a book called *Jesus in Heaven on Earth* in which he claimed that the Roaza Bal, shrine of the holy man Yuz Asaf in Srinagars Kashmir, had been visited by Jesus of Nazareth.[25] The book contained the view that Jesus journeyed to Kashmir, preached to the lost tribes of Israel, died and was buried in Srinagar. Although the book was published in England in 1952, it was widely circulated in Pakistan by the Ahmadis. This book was confiscated by the government of Punjab in April 1953 on the grounds that the book contained insulting remarks to Christian belief. However, the Lahore High Court could not determine

---

23. Ratanlal et al., *Ratanlal & Dhirajlal's Law of Crimes*, 1153.
24. Gour, *Penal Law of India*, 2335–2336.
25. Khwaja Nazir Ahmad, *Jesus in Heaven on Earth* (Woking, UK: Literary Trust, 1952), 362.

the malicious intent of the accused under 295-A of the PPC, so the court quashed the case.[26]

In 1960, another vital case, that of the Punjab Religious Book Society Lahore vs. State, provides a fine exposition of the "deliberate intent" required in Section 295-A.[27] The Lahore Court made its ruling with the following interesting observations:

> The author did not deny that his object was to show the superiority of Christianity over Islam, but he has said [in] more places than one that he had no intention of injuring the feelings of Muslims whom at places he called his brethren . . . The intention contemplated by Section 295-A of the PPC is not just the ordinary intention . . . but a deliberate and malicious intention . . . Things may be said or written which will outrage the religious feelings of followers of other religions . . . But even though the ingredients of section 295-A of the PPC will not have been satisfied because they can be satisfied only if it is established that the intention to insult the religious beliefs was deliberate and malicious.[28]

In 1962, another book entitled *Development of Muslim Theology, Jurisprudence and Constitutional Theory* was confiscated by the government of Pakistan on the basis that it tended to outrage the religious feelings of some sects of Muslims in Pakistan.[29] The full bench of the Lahore High Court headed by Justice M. R. Kayani examined the case and stated:

> Here it will be noticed that there must be an intention to outrage the religious feelings of a class of people and that intention should not only be deliberate but also malicious . . . we should have to find, before we can uphold the order of the government,

---

26. *Khawaja Nazir Ahmad v. State*, PLD 724 (1954).

27. The Home Department declared that the book with a title "Mizan-ul-Haq" published by the Punjab Religious Book Society Lahore contained religious material which outrages the religious feelings of the Muslims because it presents the superiority of Christianity over Islam in a comparative mood. Therefore the publication is punishable under Section 295-A of PPC. *The Punjab Religious Book Society v. State*, 12 PLD 629 (1960).

28. Ibid., at 631–638.

29. *Muhammad Khalil v. State*, 14 PLD 850, 850 (1962).

> that the primary purpose of the book was to outrage religious feelings of Muslims, and to do so maliciously. In the surface, however, we find a different purpose . . . we are therefore, of the opinion that his book does not within the mischief of sections 153-A and 295-A of the Penal Code . . . Since, however it does contain some offending passages . . . the publisher has offered to delete such of passages appear to us to be offensive. In doing so we are taking into consideration the fact that the research value of the book has to be preserved and that certain passages, even though somewhat offensive, should be left intact in order to give an idea to the research students of the personal opinion which the author held about Muslims' theology . . . we set aside the order of forfeiture and direct all forfeited copies be restored . . .[30]

These judgments reveal that the superior courts made decisions according to the letter and spirit of 295-A, and so in line with the expectations of the original law makers. The Select Committee responsible for drafting Clause 295-A in 1927 noted:

> We were impressed by an argument to the effect that an insult to a religion or to the religious beliefs of the followers of a religion might be inflicted in a good faith by a writer . . . we have therefore amplified the words "with deliberate intention" by inserting reference to malice and we think that the section which we have now evolved will be both comprehensive and at the same time of not too wide an application.[31]

In contrast, the clauses which Zia framed, especially Clause 295-C, crucially omitted the word "intent" in defining the crime of blasphemy. The new clause thus removes the prosecution's burden to prove that the accused had committed blasphemy with deliberate intent.[32] We have noted above that, in the original clauses, the Penal Code laid responsibility on the prosecution to prove deliberate intent. However in Clause 295-C, "the burden of proving

---

30. Ibid., at 851, 52, 55.
31. Ratanlal et al., *Ratanlal & Dhirajlal's Law of Crimes*, 1152–1153.
32. Beena Sarwar, "Malicious Intent – Pakistan's blasphemy laws " online.

that an offence was unintended was to be on the accused."[33] When it comes to criminal law, intent becomes central. But it is surprising that, despite the severity of the penalty (death), there is no distinction between intended and unintended offences under Clause 295-C, such that even unintended offence is liable to death.[34] It can be argued that this law was enacted in a hurry without any serious debate in a parliament whose function was to be no more than the rubber stamp of a dictator. This rush factor is evident from all the President's Ordinances and Acts between 1980–1986 relating to blasphemy clauses; they were all declared with this order: "It shall come into force at once."[35]

Careful analysis of the wording of Clause 295-C shows that it is too vague. It stipulates "derogatory remarks in respect of the Holy Prophet . . . either spoken or written or by visible representation or by an imputation, innuendo or insinuation directly or indirectly." According to legal experts, "direct and indirect imputation and insinuation" can be misread and therefore "convictions under the law regulating blasphemy against the Prophet of Islam are easier to obtain because it does not establish a link between an offence and the intention, so that even an unintentional act can also be treated as a wilful offence."[36] This is one of the major flaws in their design that invites serious abuse, particularly against the minorities. To obtain a legal conviction for blasphemy, it is not required to prove the intent. In an extreme example in Karachi a person from an Ismaili community was accused of blasphemy under Clause 295-C after throwing away the business card of a man named Muhammad, because it is also the name of the prophet of Islam.[37]

The former Federal Information Minister of Pakistan, Sherry Rehman, submitted a private member's bill to the Parliament in November 2010. It was intended to clarify the vagueness of the blasphemy laws in order to avoid the miscarriages of justice that had been occurring. Rehman said that

---

33. I. A. Rehman, "Blasphemy Law Revisted," online.
34. Ibid.
35. See Ordinance 1 of 1982, 147; Ordinance 20 of 1984, 102; Act 3 of 1986, 71.
36. "Q&A: Pakistan's Controversial Blasphemy Laws," *BBC News – South Asia*, 20 November 2012, online.
37. Rabia Mehmood, "Pakistan Blasphemy Laws Retake Center Stage," online.

the "blasphemy laws as set out in the PPC . . . had in their present form become a source of victimization and persecution of the minorities in the country."[38] She proposed amendments to both the PPC (substantive law) and the Cr.PC (adjective law) in a private bill to the National Assembly of Pakistan.[39] One of the essential amendments included the requirement for the complainant to demonstrate premeditation or malicious intent by the accused. The bill redrafted Sections 295-C and 298-C of the PPC to include acts done "maliciously, deliberately and intentionally," thus codifying this essential aspect of intentionality in criminal law. Thus the proposed Section 295-C reads:

> Whoever maliciously, deliberately and intentionally, by words, either by spoken or written, or by visible representation, or by any imputation, directly or indirectly, defiles the sacred name of the Holy Prophet Muhammad (peace be upon him) shall be punished with imprisonment of either description for 10 years, or with fine, or with both.[40]

Asad Jamal's opinion on the proposed bill is worth noting:

> The existing provision had rendered the offence under these sections a strict liability in which showing criminal intent seemed to have been ignored. As a result, it was easier for the courts to pronounce death sentences. The addition of [the] words maliciously, deliberately and intentionally, takes care of this particular lapse in the existing laws.[41]

A report by Freedom House entitled "Policing Belief" highlights the fact that "Pakistan's blasphemy laws fail to consistently distinguish between

---

38. Amir Waseem, "Sherry Submits Bill for Amending Blasphemy Laws," *Dawn*, 30 November 2010, online.

39. The bill was strongly opposed by leaders from the religious rightwing who have been threatening the government with dire consequences if the proposed amendment was not withdrawn. Thousands of people (an estimated 40,000) rallied in Lahore and Karachi against the bill. Then the Prime Minister, Yousa Raza Gilani, reiterated his government's earlier stance in the National Assembly, stating that the government would not support any move to amend the law. Nizam, "Government Has No Intention."

40. Beena Sarwar, "Sherry Rehman Proposed Bill to Amend Offences Relating to Relgion," online.

41. Asad Jamal, "Some Called for Changes," *The News*, 12-19 December 2010, online.

malicious, deliberate acts of blasphemy and unintended ones – a distinction normally provided for in criminal law."[42] There are a number of cases and court judgments which reveal that this aspect has been largely ignored by the courts, especially in the lower judiciary. (Courts in the superior judiciary have given considerable attention to this important factor.)

The failure to distinguish between intentional and unintentional offence is also evident from the Ranjah Masih's case. Masih was part of a crowd mourning the death of Faisalabad Bishop Dr John Joseph in 1998. (The bishop had shot himself in the head in protest against the judgment of a Sahiwal court, which had sentenced Ayub Masih to death in a blasphemy case on 27 April 1998.) According to the First Information Report (FIR) registered on 5 May 1998, the complainant was present, along with some friends, in the main bazaar of Faisalabad when a procession of Christians, who were protesting, passed by shouting out slogans. The complainant stated that the Christians started hitting plates affixed around the Gumti bearing *Durūd Sharif*[43] and a board on the Heera Paan Shop with *Kalama Ṭaiyiba*[44] inscribed thereon, with their shoes, and also started abusing Muslims. On 26 April 2003, Ranjah Masih was convicted of an offence under Section 295-C and was sentenced to life imprisonment and a fine of Rs. 50,000.[45] However, Masih appealed this decision, and his appeal was heard in April 2006 by the Lahore High Court. The Superior court observed that

> The record of this case shows that all eyewitnesses produced by the prosecution had leveled only a *generalized and collective allegation* [italics for emphasis] against the appellant and other members of the procession and no particular individual utterance or action of the appellant had even been specified by them . . . there is nothing available on the record of this case to suggest why the appellant would commit such [a] grave offence . . . the appellant had been arrested in connection with

---

42. Jo-Anne Prud'homme, "Policing Belief: The Impact of Blasphemy Laws on Human Rights" (Freedom House, 2010), 73–74.
43. Praises bestowed upon the Prophet Muhammad. See Q.33:56.
44. The Muslim Creed: "There is no God but Allah and Muhammad is the Prophet of Allah."
45. *Ranjah Masih v. State*, 9 YLR 336 (2007).

this case way back [in] 19.05.1998 and for the last about eight and half years he is rotting and languishing behind the bars in a case which been found by me to be replete with serious doubts and infirmities. An offence under Section 295-C [of] PPC is indeed a very grave offence but not grave enough to brutalize justice in its name . . . a conclusion is irresistible and inescapable . . . the conviction and sentence of the appellant recorded by the learned trial court are set aside and he is acquitted of the charge.[46]

The above noted judgment of the Lahore High Court reveals that evidence produced by the complainant was not specific enough to prove the conviction and that the trial court had found Masih guilty on the inadequate grounds of a "generalized and collective allegation."

Another important and famous blasphemy case is that of Asia Bibi. At her trial, Asia stated that,

On the alleged day of occurrence, I, along with a number of ladies, was working in the fields. Both the ladies Mafia Bibi and Asma Bibi quarreled with me over fetching water. I had offered to bring water for them but they refused saying that I was a Christian, and they never took water from the hand of a Christian. Because of this, a quarrel ensued and some hot [words] were exchanged between us.[47]

The law commentaries on the Indian Penal Code of 1860 make it clear that "the intention to wound must be deliberate, that is, not conceived on the sudden in the course of discussion."[48] In Asia's case, the trial court concluded that "the hot [words]" must have included blasphemy:

So the phenomena was ultimately switched into religious matter and Hot Words could had not been other than the blasphemy . . . Hence, I convict the accused Mst. Asia Bibi wife of Ashiq u/s [under Section] 295-C [of] PPC and sentence

---

46. Ibid., at 340.
47. The State v. Asia Bibi, (2009).
48. Ratanlal et al., *Ratanlal & Dhirajlal's Law of Crimes*, 1165.

[her] to death penalty. The accused [to] be hanged from the neck till her death.[49]

Asia has been in jail since 2009 and, although she has appealed to the High Court against her conviction, her appeal is still waiting to be heard.

From the above two cases, it is evident that trial courts in Pakistan have completely neglected the element of deliberate intent, reflecting the newer laws, in which intent is not considered relevant, despite having been very much an integral part of the British-framed blasphemy clauses.

Absence of Definitional Specificity

Another fundamental factor causing the misuse of these laws is that they are "written in broad language and include severe punishments."[50] The absence of specificity, especially in Clauses 295-C and 298-C, makes their scope of application limitless. The phrase in Clause 295-C "defiles the sacred name of the Holy Prophet Muhammad (PBUH)" can be interpreted in many ways as it "offers no elucidation on the types of behaviour that can constitute defilement."[51]

Moreover, the wording "imputation, innuendo, or insinuation either direct or indirect" creates complications for judicial proceedings because the interpretation of what constitutes defilement is entirely subjective. Shakir, a defence lawyer, notes that the words in this section are "so wide in their connotation, including 'innuendo' or 'insinuation,' that to allege blasphemy against any one has been made so easy. The import of these provisions is quite vague in nature."[52]

The recent visible example of this ambiguity is the fact that Pakistan's Supreme Court bench, headed by Justice Zaheer Jamali, approved a petition on 17 January 2013 seeking a case to be registered against Sherry Rahman, the former Federal Minister, under section 295-C of the PPC, for allegedly

---

49. The State v. Asia Bibi, (2009).
50. Jeremy Patrick, "The Curious Persistence of Blasphemy," *FJIL* 23, no. 2 (2011): 201.
51. Hayat, "Unholy Speech," 351.
52. Naeem Shakir, *The Blasphemy Law in Pakistan and Its Impact*, ed. Mathews G. Chunakara (Hong Kong: CCA, 1998), 18.

committing blasphemy.⁵³ The two-judge apex bench directed the police head in Multan to take action within the law. Feisal Naqvi, the senior advocate of the Supreme Court of Pakistan (SCP), gave his legal opinion with regard to the prospects of the Supreme Court's judgment:

> As a consequence of the Supreme Court's order, our current jurisprudential situation is that any person with access to a television can now impose a virtual death sentence on any person with an opinion. Even if one disregards the term "death sentence" as mere hyperbole, the fact remains that any person watching a television talk show can now initiate criminal proceedings against a talk show participant merely because the person watching is aggrieved by something the participant said. In order to avoid arrest, the accused will most likely have to appear in criminal investigative proceedings in the place of residence of the aggrieved person.⁵⁴

This is a clear example of the vagueness of the blasphemy laws, which means that they can be very loosely interpreted. Sherry Rehman has been accused of blasphemy because of what she said in a television interview about her private bill, suggesting amendments to the blasphemy laws. In this case, even the superior court overlooked the norm that the "legislative proceedings are exempt from judicial interference, even though their final result is not."⁵⁵

Clause 298-C, which deals mainly with the Ahmadis, states that anyone who, "in any manner whatsoever outrages the religious feelings of Muslims,"

---

53. The petitioner, Faheem Akhtar Gull, submitted a constitutional petition accusing Sherry Rehman of committing blasphemy on *Dunya TV's* program *"Dunya Meray Aagay"* broadcast from Islamabad on 19 January 2011. During that program Rehman expressed her opinion that the blasphemy laws needed to be amended. The Petitioner alleged in his application that she outraged the religious feelings of Muslims with deliberate intent. This was rejected by the Multan Police on the grounds that the program was telecasted from Islamabad therefore it was outside of their territorial jurisdiction. He applied to the Session Court and High Court Multan both courts refused his petition and supported the Police stance. Then the petitioner took his grievances to the Supreme Court of Pakistan. Azam Khan, "Blaphemy Petition against Sherry Rehman Accepted," *The Express Tribune*, 18 January 2013, online.

54. Feisal Naqvi, "Discretion and Valour," *The Express Tribune*, 4 February 2013, online.

55. Yasser L. Hamdani, "One Man's Qadri Is Another Man's Kafir," *Daily Times*, 21 January 2013, online. Pakistan's politicians are already too scared to say much about the law and this judgment poses a real threat to the legislature.

is liable to conviction. It is instructive to compare 298-C with the original clause 298.

Table 3.3 Comparison between 298C with Original Clause 298

298	"utters any words or makes any sound in the hearing of that person or makes any gesture in the sight of that person"	298-C	"in any manner whatsoever outrages the religious feelings of Muslims"

The original clause specifies how a person's religious feelings may be offended. It is obvious that the offence must take place where the two people can see and/or hear one another. It clearly specifies the manner of wounding the religious feelings of any person, and thus helps the judiciary to make the distinction between unintentional and intentional acts. In contrast, 298-C is so vague in its definitional specificity that it depends entirely on interpretation. As one commentator has argued, "interpreting what falls under Pakistan's anti-blasphemy laws is essentially a theological question and, since there is no black-letter definition of the crime in the Qur'an or other authoritative Islamic sources, it is one that remains unsettled."[56] Another noticeable phrase in 298-C – "directly or indirectly, poses himself as a Muslim" – is also very vague because it can be interpreted in numerous ways. The implication that can be drawn from it is that if Ahmadis even look like Muslims this is considered to be offensive to Muslims, which makes the Ahmadis liable to be punished under this law. In this regard Sadiq noted:

> The Prophet Muhammad kept a beard . . . If an Ahmadi follows the Sunna and keeps a beard, he is criminally liable because he looks like a Muslim. Islam prohibits Muslims from eating pork. If an Ahmadi refrains from pork consumption, he or she is assuming the attitude of a Muslim and is thus criminally liable. Muslim women observe purdah (the practice of wearing veils to cover their heads and bodies). If an Ahmadi woman wears

---

56. Nina Shea, "Testimony before the Tom Lantos Human Rights Commission of the Committee on Foreign Affairs of the US House of Representatives: Pakistan's Anti-Blasphemy Laws," Hudson Institute, online.

a veil she is taking on the appearance of a Muslim and is thus posing as a Muslim (?). Any resemblance of an Ahmadi action to a tradition of the Prophet Muhammad or an Islamic teaching exposes that person to criminal penalties . . . [298 B-C] makes Ahmadi daily life a penal offense . . .[57]

This issue of "posing as a Muslim" was raised before the SCP in the case of Zaheeruddin vs. State. During the proceeding, Fakhruddin G. Ebrahim, senior advocate and learned council for the appellants, pointed out before the court that "the word 'posing' is abominably vague and incapable of judicial enforcement."[58] He argued that "spacious meaning can be given to the expression 'posing as a Muslim.'"[59] Nonetheless, the court rejected the point of learned council by saying that, "We are not inclined to agree with him because already in the language of law the words like 'fraud,' 'misrepresentation,' 'deception,' 'cheating' which have a wide undefined connotation are in use and have meaning similar to that of 'posing.'"[60] It is notable that the court simply gave a lexical meaning of the word pose, which means to "claim" or "propound."[61] However, English dictionaries provide a range of meanings for the word "pose." For example, the Oxford Dictionary of English defines "pose" as follows:

> An attitude or posture of the body or of a part of the body, especially one deliberately assumed, or in which figure is placed for effect, or for artistic purpose; an attitude of mind; to suppose for argument's sake; to lay down; put forth (an assertion, claim, instance); to propose (a question, problem); to place an attitude (as an artist's model, etc.); to assume a certain attitude; to set up as, give oneself out as; to attitudinizes; . . .[62]

---

57. Nadeem Ahmad Saddiq, "Enforced Apostasy: Zaheeruddin v. State and the Official Persecution of the Ahmadiyya Community in Pakistan," *Law and Inequility* 14 (1995).

58. *Zaheeruddin v. State*.

59. Ibid.

60. Ibid.

61. Ibid., at 1771.

62. William Little et al., *The Oxford English Dictionary on Historical Principles*, 3rd ed., 2 vols (Oxford: Clarendon Press, 1973), 1634.

Surprisingly, the Supreme Court simply relied on two lexical words for explaining a quite complex phrase, causing trouble for the judiciary. However, the superior court was unable to provide a concrete interpretation of the word "pose" which could help the lower judiciary deal with cases under this section.

Our above discussion demonstrates that these expressions and phrases have not been clearly defined by the law makers or by the superior judiciary in Pakistan. Consequently, they remain vague and open to abuse. Ahmadis have been charged with putting Qur'anic inscriptions on wedding and invitation cards.[63] They have been charged with adopting Islamic poses for prayer, and for simply saying greetings like Muslims and for reciting the Qur'an. Ahmadis are often charged with offering the blessing "Peace be upon him" for Mirza Ghulam Ahmad, which Muslims believe should be strictly reserved only for the prophet of Islam.[64] Under these laws Ahmadis cannot figure out "what conduct is lawful for them because every aspect of their lives can be considered a criminal offense."[65] The Ahmadis' sources provide statistical data for the registered cases against Ahmadis since the introduction of these laws up to 2010.[66]

---

63. See *Nasir Ahmad v. State*, 26 SCMR 153 (1993).
64. See *Mirza Mubarak Ahmad v. State*, 7 MLD 896 (1989).
65. Saddiq, "Enforced Apostasy."
66. "Persecution of Ahmadis in Pakistan" (2010), 135, online.

Table 3.4 Statistics of the Cases Registered against Ahmadis in Pakistan (1984 to 2010)

Ahmadis booked for:		Ahmadis booked for:	
displaying Kalima Tayyaba;	764	calling "*Azan*"(call to prayer)	38
"posing" as Muslims	434	using Islamic epithets	161
offering prayers	93	Preaching	724
burning the Holy Qur'an under 295-B	27	charged under 295-C	298

The above table shows that a large number of cases have been registered against Ahmadis as a direct result of the vague expressions used in these laws so dependent on interpretation that they are easily twisted.

Our above analysis demonstrates that these laws are wider in their ambit than the previous laws: as noted by Sidque and Hayat, "such phrases are open to diverse interpretations and potential abuse and lend themselves to a high degree of subjectivity on the part of the complainants, the police, magistrates and judges involved in blasphemy cases."[67]

Cognizable Offences

The English common law introduced by the British in the subcontinent comprised of two documents: the Penal Code (PC), which describes crimes and their penalties (known as substantive law), and the Criminal Procedure Code (CrPC), which prescribes steps for enforcing criminal law (known as adjective law). The procedural laws are further divided into two categories: cognizable and non-cognizable, defined in sections 4(f) and 4(n) of the

---

67. Siddique, "Unholy Speech," 352.

CrPC.⁶⁸ In a nutshell, with cognizable offences, the police acquire substantial authority to investigate and make arrests; however, with non-cognizable offences, police action against the accused is much more restricted.

Chapter 15 of the PPC originally consists of five sections. Sections 295 (relating to injuring or defiling a place of worship), 296 (relating to the disturbing of religious assemblies, including worship) and 297 (relating to trespassing on any burial/funeral place or humiliation of a dead body) are cognizable, bailable and non-compoundable. However, Sections 295-A and 298 had been declared non-cognizable.

When Section 295-A was enacted in the Penal Code in 1927, Sections 99A and 196 of the CrPC were also amended for procedures relating to offences under Section 295-A. In Section 196, Section 295-A was inserted with a note that "the provision requiring the sanction of the government to the institution of a prosecution has been made to avoid factious or vindictive proceedings . . ."⁶⁹ It further stated that the words "shall not arrest without warrant" should be inserted following the entry.

There is only one example in Indian judicial history where a process was issued by the trial court against the petitioner for commitment of an offence under Section 295-A on the basis of a private complaint. The criminal proceedings were initiated without previously obtaining the sanction of the concerned government under Section 196(1) of CrPC. Accordingly, the High Court held the view that "obtaining a sanction is a *sine qua non* and no magistrate can take cognizance of the complaint unless the order granting sanction is produced."⁷⁰

It is notable that from 1947 until 1980, the superior courts in Pakistan have held almost the same position relating to offences under Section 295-A. This is demonstrated clearly from the case of Major-General Fazal-I-Raziq, who was then the Chairman of Water and Power Development Authority

---

68. "'Cognizable case' means a case in which a police officer, may arrest without warrant [A written order issued by a magistrate] . . . 'Non-cognizable case' means a case in which a police officer, may not arrest without warrant." Sections 4(f) and 4(n) of PCrP are available at: Pakistan, "The Code of Criminal Procedure."

69. Act No 25 of 1927, received the assent of the Governor-General on 22 September 1927. "Act No. 25 of 1927," 140.

70. *Shalibhadra Shah v. Swami Krishna Bharati* PCr.LJ 113 (1981), cited in Ratanlal et al., *Ratanlal & Dhirajlal's Law of Crimes*, 1156.

(Wapada) Lahore. On 18 June 1977, he addressed the officers of Wapada.[71] Riaz Ahmad, with some other officers, felt that the speech of the Chairman was objectionable, as it injured their religious sentiments.[72] Riaz Ahmad filed a complaint against the chairman before the magistrate under section 295-A of the PPC.[73] Then Raziq filed a petition in the Lahore High Court against the complaint. The court examined the case and gave the following ruling:

> For the offences mentioned in Section 196 of Cr.P.C, it is for the appropriate government alone to decide whether a particular person should be prosecuted or not. In the instant case admittedly the appropriate government (Central Government) has neither passed any order to file such complaint against the petitioner nor the said government has authorized Riaz Ahmad . . . The result is that the present complaint against the petitioner under Section 295-A, PPC not having been filed by an appropriate government as required by law but by an unauthorized person, the trial magistrate will have no power to record preliminary evidence . . . Accordingly I quash the proceedings pending before the trial magistrate against the petitioner under section 295-A.[74]

Significantly between 1947 and 1980 only eight blasphemy cases were reported in the superior courts.[75] A careful reading of all eight cases reveals that most of the cases were dismissed by the worthy courts on the basis that 295-A requiring the authorization of the government. This demonstrates that the law was clearly laid down in the Penal Code and appropriate measures were taken into account in the Criminal Procedure Code to avoid its misapplication and abuse.

---

71. *Fazal-I-Raziq v. Riaz Ahmad* 30 PLD 1082, 1083 (1978).
72. Ibid.
73. Ibid., at 1085.
74. Ibid., at 1086–1087.
75. *Khawaja Nazir Ahmad v. State*; *The Punjab Religious Book Society v. State*; *Okil Ali and Others v. Behari Lal Paul*, 14 PLD 487(1962); *Muhammad Khalil v. State*; *Abdul Karim v. State*, 15 PLD 669(1963); *Shafiqur Rehman v. State*, PCr.LJ 1456(1976); *Fazal-I-Raziq v. Riaz Ahmad*; *Qaiser Raza v. State*, PCr.LJ 758(1979).

In contrast, when 295-C was introduced in the PPC in 1986, no such measures were taken into account. For example, one of the amendments was that the police "may arrest without warrant."[76] In other words 295-B and C were declared cognizable offences, allowing the police to take action under these sections without requiring the warrant of the court.[77] Therefore any person can register a complaint with the police and the police can arrest the accused immediately without having to verify the accusations.

In Pakistan, the police department is not well equipped with modern techniques of investigation, and the Pakistani police force is notorious for being inefficient, corrupt and brutal. The track record of incompetency on the part of Pakistani police is disastrous for persons accused of blasphemy.[78] The judgments of the appellate courts reveal that innocent persons have been found guilty in police investigations. One of the most highly publicized blasphemy cases in Pakistan is that of Salmat Masih vs. State in 1995.[79] The High Court heard the case for seven consecutive days and during the case several senior advocates were requested to assist the court as *amicus curiae*. One of the *amicus curiae*, Khawaja Sultan Ahmad, advocate, submitted his findings:

> There is not an iota of evidence against the appellants. He referred to the negligent attitude of the investigating agency . . . They failed to perform their respective duties in a case based on a serious charge. The police did not take remand of the accused and not tried to take their samples of hand writing to compare the same with the writing.[80]

The police often fail to do their professional and moral duty in ordinary cases, but when it comes to blasphemy cases the police behave even more irresponsibly. On a number of occasions, they have even been guilty of taking the law into their own hands and putting the accused to death without

---

76. See table 3.1.
77. Asad Jamal, "Herald Exclusive: What the Law Says," *Dawn*, 15 February 2011, online.
78. See *Jagdesh Kumar v. State*, 61 PLD 1 (2009).
79. *Salamat Masih v. State*, 28 PCr.LJ 811 (1995).
80. Ibid., 823.

giving them the benefit of a formal investigation or trial. The US State Department's International Religious Report 2010 states that:

> [Pakistani] Police reportedly tortured and mistreated those in custody on religious charges and were accused of at least one extrajudicial killing in a blasphemy case. For example, on September 16, 2009, a young Christian man, Robert Fanish, who had been accused of blasphemy, died while in police custody. The case prompted widespread media attention, and several human rights groups asserted that he had been killed extrajudicially. Christian and Ahmadiyya communities claimed their members were more likely to be abused. Non-Muslim prisoners generally were accorded poorer facilities than Muslim inmates.[81]

In 2002, the Division Bench of the Lahore High Court, commenting on a case brought under Clause 295-C, noted the increase in accusations of blasphemy against people who were innocent, and the failure, inefficiency and incompetence on the part of police investigations.[82] The court directed the Inspector General of Police of the Punjab province:

> To ensure that whenever such a case is registered, the same may be entrusted for the purposes of investigation to a team of at least two Gazetted Investigating Officers . . . and the team should then investigate as to whether an offence is committed or not and if the team comes to the conclusion that the offence is committed, the police may only then proceed further in the matter.[83]

Reading between the lines, the court was suggesting that these blasphemy laws be made non-cognizable. Even the Islamic Council of Ideology accepted that these laws should become non-cognizable, in view of their misuse.[84]

---

81. "International Religious Freedom Report 2010" (US Department of State 2010), 15.

82. The Court observed that "this is because the police would readily register such a case without checking the veracity of the facts . . ., would proceed to arrest an accused. That an Assistant Sub-Inspector or a Moharrir was academically not competent to [judge] whether or not the circumstances constitute an act of blasphemy." *Muhammad Mahboob v. State*, at 589.

83. Ibid., at 588–589.

84. Butt, "Top Islamic Body Proposes Changes."

Our above discussion demonstrates that one of the drawbacks of the Zia-framed clauses is that they are cognizable, which means that the police are authorized to take action on their own before the case comes to the knowledge of the court. Furthermore, there is no requirement to obtain government permission to proceed with the cases. Amer Nadeem, an attorney-at-law in Pakistan, is of the opinion that "in non-cognizable offences the possibility of booking persons in the [fabricated] cases is dim."[85] In other words there is less chance of fabrications in non-cognizable offences.

Disproportionate Penalties

Another factor that distinguishes the earlier British-framed blasphemy laws from the later Pakistani blasphemy laws is the severity of the penalties. The comparative chart in table 3.5 below reveals that the British-framed sections 295 and 295-A provide for a maximum of "two years imprisonment or fine or both." In contrast, the penalty in Clause 295-B is "life imprisonment" and, for Clause 295-C, a "mandatory death penalty."

Table 3.5 Comparison of Penalties between British and Zia-framed Clauses

	British-framed clauses		*Zia-framed clauses*
295	Two years, or fine or both		
295-A	Two years, or fine or both	295-A	Ten years, or fine or both
		255-B	Imprisonment for life
		295-C	Death sentence
296	One year, or fine or both		
297	One year, or fine or both		
298	One year, or fine or both	298-A	Three years, or fine or both
		298-B	Three years and shall also be liable to fine
		298-C	Three years and shall also be liable to fine

---

85. Amer Nadeem, "Blasphemy Laws in Pakistan: Make Them Better If Not Change," online.

It is significant that originally Clause 295-A carried a penalty of "two years imprisonment" but later, through an Act 16 of 1991, the punishment was extended to "ten years imprisonment."[86] Similarly, Clause 295-C previously carried options of life imprisonment or the death sentence, but in 1991, the Federal Shariʿat Court (FSC) made the death penalty mandatory for breaches of Section 295-C of the PPC.[87]

Although the death penalty has not been completely abolished by international law, the United Nations has outlined clear guidelines for this penalty, reserving it only for the most serious crimes.[88] The UN Human Rights Council has routinely interpreted "the most serious crimes" to mean those offences that result in loss of life.[89] Despite being a signatory to various international treaties Pakistan had introduced harsher penalties for blasphemy offences. In 1982, Clause 295-B was enacted with life imprisonment; in 1986, Clause 295-C was enacted with a life sentence or the death penalty; and, in 1991, the death penalty was made mandatory under Clause 295-C.

Afghanistan, Iran, Pakistan, Saudi Arabia and Yemen are the only countries where blasphemy is punishable by death. However, Pakistan is the only country to have used legislation to introduce the death penalty for blasphemy, while the other four countries have used Shariʿa law and religious decrees to implement the death penalty. In the United Arab Emirates, the penalty for Muslims accused of breaking blasphemy laws is death under the Shariʿa, whereas non-Muslims are dealt with under civil law. Most Muslim-majority countries such as Algeria, Bangladesh, Egypt, Kuwait, Jordan, Indonesia and Sudan, use modern laws, in which the punishment for blasphemy is no more than for a minor crime. In the light of our brief survey of the Muslim countries, it can be said that Pakistan is the only example in the entire Islamic world where blasphemy laws have been enacted with harsher penalties.

---

86. *Act 16 of 1991*, 31.

87. See *Muhammad Ismail Qureshi v. Pakistan* at 35. The ruling of the FSC poses a big question mark in Pakistan's judicial history. Some viewed that the FSC has exceeded its boundaries because the purpose of judiciary is to interpret the law rather than formulate the law. It is the predominant view that "the legislature alone possess the competence to enact legislative amendments." Siddique, "Unholy Speech," 380.

88. Article 6(2) of ICCPR states: "In countries which have not abolished the death penalty, sentence of death may be imposed only for the most serious crimes . . ."

89. Cited in Prud'homme, "Policing Belief," 76.

No Exceptions for Mentally Disturbed

In 1912, the mental health law was introduced in the subcontinent by the British as the Lunacy Act 1912. In 2001, the Lunacy Act of 1912 was replaced by the Mental Health Ordinance (MHO 2001) in Pakistan. It used comparatively humane and relatively up-to-date psychiatric terminology, such as "mental illnesses" and "psychiatric facility care in the community."[90] (The Pakistani law drew heavily on the Indian Mental Health Act 1987). So far as the legislature was concerned, it was an excellent piece of law which reflects the conditions in a more enlightened society. However, there has been a big question mark over the implementation of this law in Pakistan,[91] especially in blasphemy cases. There have been cases where mentally ill persons have been charged and imprisoned without trial for years.[92] Under the 1912 Act, a person could be held for only ten to thirty days before an inquiry began. The conditions of the Mental Health Ordinance 2001 were even more strict: the law states that a mentally unstable person cannot be detained for more than seventy-two hours and that it is mandatory to conduct a psychiatric evaluation within that period.[93] However, these laws have not been applied in practice. For example, Zaibunnisa, a Muslim woman, was detained in 1996 on blasphemy charges outside Islamabad after a Muslims Cleric registered a complaint about the desecration of Qur'an.[94] Despite the fact that the report of the medical board confirmed that she was mentally ill, she was held in jail for fourteen years under blasphemy charges.[95] In July 2010, after she had spent fourteen years behind bars, the Lahore High Court declared her innocent, not on medical grounds but due to serious

---

90. *Ordinance 8 of 2001: Mental Health Ordinance* (20 February 2001) 54 PLD Central Statutes (2002).

91. For good discussion on this issue, see Yasir Abbasi, "Mental Health Ordinance 2001 – Is it really being used?" *JPMA* 58, no. 10 (2008): 578–579.

92. Mubasher Bukhari, "Mentally Ill Persons Have Been Charged and Imprisoned without Trial for Years," *Reuters*, 22 July 2010, online. Claas Special Report on Jail Visits in 2011 affirms this fact. This special report produced in Francis, "Claas Pakistan: Annual Report 2011," 115–142.

93. *Ordinance 8 of 2001.*

94. Bukhari, "Mentally Ill Persons."

95. Asad Jamal, "The Law of Diminishing Utility," *Herald Exclusive*, February 2011, online.

lack of evidence against her.[96] Moreover the Court, commenting on her mental illness, stated that the "treatment meted out to the woman was an insult to humanity and the government and the civil organizations should be vigilant enough to help such people."[97] Abid Minto, an Advocate of the SCP, says that her case is not an exception: "many blasphemy cases go on for years. Sometimes even bail applications are not taken up because judges and prosecution lawyers are using delaying tactics to keep the accused in jail as long as they possibly can without his or her trial reaching a conclusion."[98]

The High Court of Islamabad has noted that "no man can be tried or imprisoned for any act which is committed du[e] to any delusion or misconception of mind."[99] However this aspect has been largely ignored by the trial courts in some cases, such as that of Zaibunnisa. Another example where the Mental Health Ordinance seems to have been ignored is that of Arshad Javed, a mentally handicapped young Muslim man who was convicted of blasphemy by the trial court in Bhawalpur and sentenced to death under 295-C.[100] Javed's brother pleaded before the court that Javed was mentally ill. Further, multiple medical examinations showed that "he was suffering from Hypomania and [was] not yet fit to stand trial," and he had "totally lost his mental balance."[101] Moreover it was clearly stated in the First Information Report (FIR) that the accused was mentally deranged.[102] The High Court was astonished to see the conviction of a mentally deranged man by the trial court.[103] Consequently, on the basis of his medical reports, the High

---

96. Ibid. "The cleric informed the court that he had registered his complaint with police against "unknown people" and had never accused Zaibunnisa of blasphemy in his complaint by name." Bukhari, "Mentally Ill Persons."

97. Nasim Zehra, "Time to Repeal the Blasphemy Law," *The Express Tribune*, 16 November 2010, online.

98. Jamal, " Law of Diminishing Utility."

99. *Rimsha Masih v. Police Station Ramna*, APP (2012).

100. *State v. Muhammad Arshad Javed*, 13 MLD 667, 669 (1993). The charges against the accused stated that he claimed that "I am Hazrat Isa (Jesus) and I have no father. The day of judgment would fall on 21-02-1989."

101. Ibid., at 171, 75.

102. Ibid., at 175.

103. A similar situation occurred in the Peshawar High Court (PHC) in the blasphemy case of the mentally ill man Saifullah who was convicted under 295-A by the magistrate. His conviction was upheld by the session court, despite the declaration of the Medical Board that he "is suffering from bipolar disorder with psychotic feature." The PHC noted that "it is shocking to note that trial court had been carried away by emotional/religious sentiments

Court set aside the conviction by the trial court and exempted him from criminal liability.[104]

A special report on the state of those confined under blasphemy charges in thirteen jails in the province of Punjab was conducted by the Centre for Legal Aid Assistance & Settlement (CLASS) in 2011. According to the report, there were ninety-four prisoners confined under blasphemy charges in Punjab. Of these, twenty-nine were mentally ill and their cases were under proceedings in different courts.[105] The report further noted:

> Mostly accused of blasphemy were in the solitary confinement for their protection from other inmates and guards . . . the blasphemy prisoners are suffering from the unfair and prejudicious practices of the judicial system and the misuse of the blasphemy laws. The blasphemy accused have been harassed and implicated in false blasphemy cases and most of the prisoners have lost their memory . . .[106]

The report also pointed out that many of these mentally ill prisoners have been confined in jail for years. Some have been sentenced by the trial courts and are waiting to have their appeals heard by the superior courts.[107] This is despite the fact that the 2001 Act and the superior courts' decisions have made it clear that mentally ill persons cannot be charged. However the vague language of the blasphemy laws "makes no reference to a potential offender's state of mind or intention [thus] exacerbating its impact and inviting widespread abuse."[108]

As shown above, the fact that the lower judiciary has largely ignored the presence of mental disability in blasphemy cases is another significant flaw in the blasphemy laws. Due to this, people with mental illnesses accused of blasphemy often suffer for years in jail under miserable conditions before their appeals are taken up by the superior courts.

---

and had gone away with the winds . . . Such an approach is against the universal principle of justice." *Saifullah Khan v. State*, 54 PLD 140, 142–143 (2006).

104. *State v. Muhammad Arshad Javed*, at 676.
105. Francis, "Annual Report 2011," 115–142.
106. Ibid., 117.
107. Ibid.
108. "Reforming the Judiciary in Pakistan: Asia Report No. 160" (ICG, 2008), 6.

The effects of this shortcoming in the law are further apparent in the case of Anwar Kenneth who was arrested and charged with blasphemy in 2001 for distributing a Christian pamphlet and declaring that Muhammad was a false prophet. Kenneth also claimed that he was a reincarnation of Christ.[109] It was confirmed by a number of sources that he suffered from severe psychiatric problems.[110] His lawyer, Saadia Khalid, persistently requested a medical examination to determine whether his client was mentally fit to stand trial, but the request was denied. The judge argued that Kenneth's mental status was irrelevant as he had already admitted to declaring that Muhammad was a false prophet. Consequently, in July 2002, Kenneth was sentenced to death. His death sentence was contrary to the Ordinance 2001 as well as to international law, which, since 1999, has stipulated that the death penalty should not be applied to persons suffering from mental retardation, mental disorder, or limited mental competence.

No Protection for Minorities

Although Muslims ruled India for over seven hundred years, the fact is that prior to partition, they had been the minority in a predominantly Hindu subcontinent. It is apparent that the British government's main intention was to establish its writ over a multi-religious society by establishing order and maintaining peace within it by stopping religious-based violence. Osama and Zahra read between the lines of the preface of the chapter 15: Offences related religion of the Indian Penal Code that "it is plausible that part of the motivation for the inclusion of this chapter was the protection of the religious rights of the minorities [in India]."[111] Justice Ali Nawaz Chohan of the Lahore High Court noted in one of his judgments that "[h]istorically speaking, the Blasphemy Law was enacted by the British to protect the religious sentiments of the Muslim minorities in the subcontinent before partition against the Hindu majority."[112]

---

109. Paul Watson, "A Deadly Place for Blasphemy," *Los Angeles Times*, 5 August 2002, online.
110. "Pakistani Christian Sentenced to Death," *BBC*, 18 July 2002, online.
111. Siddique, "Unholy Speech," 337.
112. *Muhammad Mahboob v. State*, 597.

However, the Zia-framed clauses 295-B and C and 298-A, B, and C are completely antithetical to the above motivation.[113] Although Muslims form a majority of about 96 percent in Pakistan, the clauses mentioned above protect only Islam – the religion of the overwhelming majority in Pakistan. As mentioned above, between 1947 and 1980 only about eight blasphemy cases were reported. These cases were all registered against Muslims by either Muslims or by non-Muslims: no blasphemy case was registered against non-Muslims. However, since the introduction of the later clauses of the blasphemy law, statistical analysis of blasphemy cases demonstrates that minorities are being victimized. Rather than protecting minorities, the blasphemy laws have made them more vulnerable. This is clearly indicated by the Human Rights Commission of Pakistan in its annual report of 2007:

> Affiliation of a state to a religion has always led to institutionalizing discrimination against those who profess a different faith – and that is exactly what has happened in Pakistan. Discrimination by the state, duly enshrined in the constitution and the laws of the land, encourages additional social discrimination, virtually reducing religious minorities to second-class citizens whose rights and welfare are easily ignored and violated both by the majority community and the state.[114]

The report recommends to the government of Pakistan that all laws that allow discrimination on grounds of belief be repealed or reformed.[115] I. A. Rahim claims, "These laws are retrogressive, because they discriminate against minorities, impinge on their rights to freedom of belief and pose a serious threat to their right of liberty. So these laws are in conflict with their constitutional and fundamental rights."[116]

---

113. Siddique, "Unholy Speech," 338.

114. Najam U Din and Saira Ansari, "State of Human Rights in 2007" (Lahore: HRCP, 2007), 109.

115. Ibid., 110.

116. I. A. Rahim, "A Critique of Pakistan's Blasphemy Laws," in *Pakistan between Secularism and Islam*, ed. Tarik Jan (Islamabad: IPS, 1998), 199.

Incompatibility with International Covenants

Pakistan's blasphemy laws are incompatible with international covenants. The Universal Declaration of Human Rights (UDHR) of the United Nations is the fundamental document which acknowledges and guarantees religious freedom, including in Article 7, which prescribes equality before the law and protection against discrimination, and Article 19, which relates to freedom of expression. However, the most prominent example is Article 18, which guarantees that "everyone has the right to freedom of thought, conscience and religion . . . to manifest his religion or belief in teaching, practice, worship and observance."[117] It is a notable fact that Pakistan is a signatory to this Declaration.[118] Justice Rehman, the former Chief Justice of Pakistan, opined that "although the UN declaration may not be legally binding for signatory nations, it is the common aspirations of the entire world community and places on member nations of the United Nations at least the moral obligation not to disregard the provisions of the declaration."[119] A cursory glance reveals that the blasphemy clauses 295-B, C and 298-B, C of the PPC are in conflict with Articles 7, 19 and 18 of the UDHR.

Another significant UN treaty, known as the International Covenant on Civil and Political Rights (ICCPR), was put into effect on 23 March 1973: "The ICCPR was intended to serve as a source for legal obligations and to more fully specify the human rights outlined in the Universal Declaration."[120] It was in line with the UDHR and was ratified by almost 160 nations. Pakistan, however, did not ratify this covenant until 2010 (with reservations), and until July 2011 (completely). Nonetheless, Pakistani jurists are of the opinion that the ICCPR is an affirmed international norm and that Pakistan should respect it. In 1988, Muhammad Haleem, then Chief Justice

---

117. United Nations, "Universal Declaration of Human Rights, 10 December 1948," online.

118. When the draft of the UN Declaration was under discussion in 1947, the delegates from some Muslim countries (mainly Arab) objected to the wording of Article 18 ("this right includes the freedom to change his religion or faith") and abstained from voting. In contrast, Pakistan strongly endorsed the UN declaration on theological grounds and signed it without any reservations. M. Geijbels, "Pakistan, Islamization and the Christian Community. Part 2: The Status and Calling of Christians," *Al-Mushir* 22, no. 3 (1980): 106.

119. Rahman, *Punishment of Apostasy*, 135–137.

120. Brian J. Grim and Roger Finke, *The Price of Freedom Denied: Religious Persecution and Conflict in the 21st Century* (New York: Cambridge University Press, 2011), 26.

of Pakistan, gave his opinion that "the international human rights norms are in fact part of the constitutional expression of the liberties guaranteed at the national level."[121] The Zia-framed clauses of the blasphemy laws violate Articles #18 (freedom of thought, conscience and religion), #19 (the freedom of opinion and expression), #20 (prohibition of racial or religious hatred), and #27 (the right for religious minorities to enjoy their culture and practice their religion) of the ICCPR.[122]

The United Nation's support for religious freedom was further strengthened on 25 November 1981, when the General Assembly of the United Nations passed the Declaration on the Elimination of All Forms of Intolerance and of Discrimination Based on Religion or Belief.[123] It is notable that right after this declaration, Pakistan, under General Zia-ul-Haq, successively incorporated the blasphemy clauses into the Pakistan Penal Code (PPC): Clause 295-B in 1982, Clause 298-B and C in 1984, and Clause 295-C in 1986. It is clearly evident that these changes to the PPC were an apparent breach of the UN Declaration of 1981.

In 1996, Pakistan ratified the Conventions for the Elimination of Racial Discrimination and Discrimination against Women (CEDAW) and on the Rights of Children (CRC).[124] In 2008, Pakistan ratified the International Covenant on Economic, Social and Cultural Rights and the Convention on the Rights of Persons with Disabilities (CRPD). In 2009, Pakistan further ratified the 1966 Covenant on Economic, Social and Cultural Rights and the Covenant on Civil and Political Rights.[125] In June 2010, Pakistan formally ratified the International Covenant on Civil and Political Rights (ICCPR) and the Convention against Torture.[126] In August 2011, Pakistan ratified the CRPD and the Option Protocol to the Convention on the Rights of the

---

121. Muhammad Haleem, "The Domestic Application of International Human Rights Norms," in *Developing Human Rights Jurisprudence* (London: HRUCS, 1988).

122. "International Covenant of Civil and Political Rights (ICCPR)," online.

123. "Implementation of the Declaration on the Elimination of All Forms of Intolerance and of Discrimination Based on Religion or Belief," online.

124. I. A. Rehman, "New Threats to Rights," *Dawn*, 9 December 2010.

125. Ibid.

126. Correspondent, "President Signs Convention on Civil, Political Rights," *Daily Times*, 4 June 2010, online.

Child on the Sale of Children, Child Prostitution and Child Pornography.[127] Altogether Pakistan has now ratified seven out of nine core international human rights treaties. The President of Pakistan, Asif Zardari, said that "the government would accomplish its international obligations and was committed to protect and promote human rights in the country."[128] Nonetheless, Pakistan's record of "implementing these treaties has been, on the whole, dismal."[129] The French government's spokesman called on Pakistan "to respect its international commitments in this respect," stating that "the very existence of a crime of blasphemy is in breach of fundamental liberties, the freedom of religion or of conviction as well as the freedom of speech."[130] The death penalty in Clause 295-C is in conflict with the first clause of the UN Economic Social Council that has provided safeguards for the rights of those facing capital punishment, stating that, "capital punishment may be imposed only for the most serious crimes, it being understood that their scope should not go beyond intentional crimes with lethal or other extremely grave consequences."[131] In contrast, as seen above, in Clause 295-C, the death penalty is mandatory but it is not obligatory to prove intent in the offence.

In summary, Pakistan's blasphemy laws are incompatible with international human rights standards not only because they impose undue restrictions on freedom of expression, freedom of religion, and other human rights, but also because they are discriminatory in their effect.[132]

Concluding Summary

In this chapter we have analyzed the defects of the Zia-framed laws, especially in comparison with the original clauses of the PPC inherited from

---

127. APP, "UN Periodic Review: Islamabad Reaffirms Pledge to Human Rights," *The Express Tribune*, 31 October 2012, online.

128. Staff Reporter, "International Human Rights Day " *Daily Times*, 10 December 2010, online.

129. I. A. Rehman, "Recognising the UN," online.

130. Cited in Malik Siraj Akbar, "Who Benefits from Pakistan's Blasphemy Law," in *Huffington Post* (2012).

131. Siddique, "Unholy Speech," 382.

132. Prud'homme, "Policing Belief," 73. For good discussion on Pakistan's obligations towards human rights and international treatise see, Bilal Hayee, "Blasphemy Laws and Pakistan's Human Rights Obligations," *UNDALR* 14, no. 3 (2013).

the British. Our analysis demonstrated that the Zia-framed clauses explicitly favour Islam, which is the religion of the majority in Pakistan. By contrast, the British-framed clauses provided protection to all religions and even to sects within religions. Furthermore, the Zia-framed clauses are seriously flawed as they lack the requirement of intent, which was a salient feature of the British-framed clauses and a key factor in the prevention of their misuse.

We have also seen that the Zia-framed clauses are so vague and depend so entirely upon interpretation that their ambit is dangerously wide. In consequence, these laws have become open to misuse, especially as a tool in the hands of people who wish to settle personal disputes. One of the drawbacks of Zia-framed clauses is that they are cognizable therefore any person can register a complaint with the police and police can arrest the accused without having to verify the accusations. Once the case is registered, it makes life of the accused hell.

We showed clearly that, contrary to international covenants and even Pakistan's own mental health laws, people with mental disorders are suffering under these laws because of their ambiguity. The laws are incompatible with the international human rights covenants signed by Pakistan over the years, particularly with regard to the use of the death penalty and the exercise of freedom of religion. Under these covenants, Pakistan pledged to amend these laws, but Pakistan's governments have repeatedly failed to fulfill their commitments, due to public pressure. A significant number of people in Pakistan believe that the laws are mandated by Islam.

PART II

EXPERIENCE

CHAPTER 4

Ahmadis and Christians in the Minority Context of Pakistan

Introduction

In the previous chapter, we examined the design flaws in Pakistan's blasphemy laws from a legal perspective. Our study indicated that, due to defects in the design of these laws, they have become open to misuse. Although no group in Pakistan – not even Muslims – is safe from the misuse of the blasphemy laws, the data from the reported cases shows that a significant number of victims of these laws have come from two minority groups: Ahmadis and Christians. This is one of the reasons why this thesis focuses on how these two minority groups have been affected by Pakistan's blasphemy laws.

It is appropriate to note here that the oppression of the Ahmadiyya and Christian communities stems not just from the blasphemy laws in Pakistan. Strong religious and social discrimination existed long before the tightening of the blasphemy laws under General Zia-ul-Haq in the 1980s, and even before the creation of the nation of Pakistan. This chapter will explore the nature of oppression for the Ahmadis and Christians in the minority context of Pakistan. We begin with the Ahmadi community.

Ahmadiyya Movement

Historical Overview of Ahmadiyya Movement

The Ahmadiyya movement was founded in 1889, during the British Raj, by Mirza Ghulam Ahmad at Qadian, a small town located in Punjab, India.

Ahmad's family earned great respect in the eyes of the British because of his father Mirza Ghulam Murtaza's loyalty to and support of the British during the Indian Mutiny in 1857. Some argue that "this was the main reason why the British gave constant encouragement and support to the Ahmadiyya sect."[1]

Ghulam Ahmad was born in Qadian in 1835,[2] and learned both Persian and Arabic through home tutoring. Ahmad's biographers say that he showed a great interest in religious literature from his early youth.[3] However, his father wanted him to earn respect for the family, so he secured employment for Ahmad as a reader in the district court of Sialkot in 1864. During his time in Sialkot (1864–1868), Ghulam Ahmad had religious debates with both Indian and foreign Christian missionaries like R. A. Butler and Elisha Swift.[4] Some commentators suggest that, due to his encounters with Christian missionaries, "some initial organizational ideas took shape in his mind for the cause of Islam."[5] These early encounters with Christians proved to be a turning point for Ghulam Ahmad to move towards a serious study of other religions, especially Christianity, in order to defend Islam.

Leaving his employment in Sialkot in 1868, Ghulam Ahmad returned to Qadian and devoted the rest of his life to the study of religion. He started writing in defence of Islam. As a result, he produced a monumental work, *Barāhin-ē-Ahmadiyya*, (Ahmadi proofs). They comprised four volumes on Islamic doctrines, which were published in 1880, 1881, 1882 and 1884 respectively.[6] Ahmad's work was well received by Muslims across India and

---

1. S. Nath Kaushik, *Ahmadiya Community in Pakistan: Discrimination, Travail, and Alienation* (New Delhi: South Asian Publishers, 1996), 3.

2. A. R. Dard, *Life of Ahmad: Founder of the Ahmadiyya Movement* (Tilford: IIP, 2008), 32. There is no consensus on the date of birth of Mirza Ahmad, some held the view that he was born in 1839. See F. K. Khan Durrani, *The Ahmadiyya Movement* (Lahore: AAII, 1927), 21.

3. Durrani, *Ahmadiyya Movement*, 22.

4. Dard, *Life of Ahmad*, 48–49.

5. Spencer Lavan, *The Ahmadiyyat Movement: A History and Perspective* (Delhi: Manohar Book Service, 1974), 31; H. A. Walter, *The Aḥmadiya Movement* (Calcutta: Association Press, 1918), 14.

6. Mirza Bashiruddin Mahmud Ahmad, *Hadhrat Ahmad* (Ohio: IIP, 1998), 24, online.

this made him hugely popular as a defender of Islam. Nevertheless, it did not go uncriticized because of his claim to several divine revelations:

> The reader also frequently encounters in Mirza's book references to his divinely inspired revelations, to miracles and to divine communication and prophecies, and last but not the least, his boastfulness . . . a work in which, again and again, the author stoops to self-advertisement and self-glorification.[7]

A turning point in his life came in 1889, when he claimed, through a divine revelation, the right to accept *bai't* (allegiance given to a religious leader).[8] Moreover, two years later in 1891, Ahmad claimed to be the promised Messiah expected by Christians and Jews as well as the *Imam Mehdi* expected by Muslims.[9] He further claimed that "the spiritual personality of the Messiah and the *Mehdi* is a combination of the spiritual personalities of the Holy Prophet [Muhammad] and Jesus . . ."[10] He also claimed, "I am Krishna for the Hindus and the Promised Messiah for the Muhammadans and the Christians . . . Thus spiritually Krishna and the Promised Messiah are one and the same person."[11] These claims made him a highly controversial figure and created a great stir among the Muslims all over India. Moreover, his claims caused a "sharp line of demarcation to be drawn between himself and the larger world of Islam."[12] This is evident from the fact that, before he died in May 1908, he was denounced as an imposter and his followers

---

7. Abul Easan Al Nadwi and Zafar Ishaq Ansari, *Qadianism: A Critical Study*, 6th ed. (Lucknow: AIRP, 1980), 29.

8. The first covenant ceremony took place at Ludhiana in 1889 where forty followers showed allegiance to him. See Ahmad, *Hadhrat Ahmad*, 27.

9. Mirza Ghulam Ahmad, *Fateh Islam* [Victory of Islam] (Tilford: IIP, 2002). He made this claim on the basis that he has received the revelation that Jesus of Nazreth had died natural death and he will not return to earth. What Christians and Muslims believed in, his second advent, meant that a person should appear in the power and spirit of Jesus and he himself was that person.

10. Mirza Ghulam Ahmad, "The Early Life and Mission of the Promised Messiah," *The Review of Religions* 2, no. 2 (1903): 67.

11. Mirza Ghulam Ahmad, "The Future of Islam," *The Review of Religions* 3, no. 11 (1904): 411.

12. Walter, *The Aḥmadiya Movement*, 16.

were labeled *kāfir* (infidel), *ṭāghut* (devil), *murtadd* (apostate) and *munāfiq* (hypocrite) by orthodox Islam.[13]

Split in Ahmadiyya Movement

After Ahmad's death, Maulana Nuruddin was appointed as the first *Khalifa* (Caliph) to lead the Ahmadiyya community. With the demise of Nuruddin in March 1914, a split occurred in the Ahmadiyya community over the election of Mirza Bashiruddin Mahmud Ahmad as the second *Khalifa*. Mirza Mahmud Ahmad was the son of Mirza Ghulam Ahmad. Although the majority at Qadian supported this move, a group within the Ahmadiyya community, led by Khwaja Kamaluddin and Muhammad Ali, both of Lahore, rejected the idea of succession and of the institution of *Khilafat* (caliphate). This group withdrew from Qadian and formed a separate entity called *Ahmadiyya Anjuman-ē-Ishāt-ē-Islam* (Ahmadiyya Society for the propagation of Islam), with Muhammad Ali as its leader.[14] Since then, both groups have existed as the Lahore and Qadian groups of the Ahmadiyya Movement. The salient differences between the groups are as follows:

Table 4.1 Major Differences between Ahmadiyya Factions

Ahmadiyya: Lahore Group	Ahmadiyya: Qadian Group
1. Prophet Muhammad is the greatest and last prophet.[15]	1. Prophet Muhammad is the greatest but not last of the prophets.
2. The office of prophethood is closed.[16]	2. The office of prophethood is continued.
3. Mirza Ghulam Ahmad was not a prophet but a *mujaddad* (reformer).[17]	3. Mirza Ghulam Ahmad was a prophet.[18]

---

13. Naveeda Khan, *Muslim Becoming: Aspiration and Skepticism in Pakistan* (Durham: Duke University Press, 2012), 109.

14. Muhammad Ali, *The Ahmadiyya Movement*, trans. S. Muhammad Tufail (Lahore: AAII, 1973), 6; Murray T. Titus, *Islam in India and Pakistan* (Madras: CLS, 1959), 267.

15. Muhammad Ali, *The Split in the Ahmadiyya Movement* (Lahore: AAII, 1994), 51–55.

16. Ibid., 57–60.

17. Muhammad Ali, *The Ahmadiyya Doctrines* (Lahore: AAII, 1932), 17–20.

18. Mirza Bashiruddin Mahmud Ahmad, *Truth about the Split*, new ed. (Tilford: IIP, 2007), 31–32. violates the company and trademark laws.

4. Anyone who professes a *kalama* (there is one God and Muhammad is His messenger) is Muslim and not a *kafir*, even if he does not believe in Mirza Ghulam.[19]	4. Anyone who does not believe Mirza Ghulam Ahmad is a prophet is a *kafir* (outside the pale of Islam).[20]
5. It is permitted to say *namāz* (prayer) behind a non-Ahmadi *imam* (cleric) and to attend the funeral services of Muslims.[21]	5. It is not permitted to say *namāz* behind a non-Ahmadi *imam* nor to attend non-Ahmadi funeral services.[22]
6. Marriages are permitted with non-Ahmadi Muslims.[23]	6. Females are not permitted to marry non-Ahmadi men, however males are permitted to marry non-Ahmadi women.
7. *Waḥi-ē-waliyāt* (saintly revelation) continues but *Waḥi-ē-Nubūvat* (prophetic revelation) is closed.	7. *Waḥi-ē- Nubūvat* (prophetic revelation) continues.
8. The *Anjuman* (organization) should have entire control of the Ahmadiyya community and there should be no *Khalifa* (Caliph).	8. Belief in the succession of *Khilafat* because it is a divine institution established by Mirza Ghulam Ahmad.
9. The Lahore group reserves the title Ahmadi for themselves and refer to the other group as *Qadiani or Mirzai*.	9. The Qadian group considers the Lahore group heretics.

---

19. Ali, *Split in the Ahmadiyya Movement*, 79–87.
20. Mirza Ahmad, *Truth about the Split*, 169–170. In 1954, Mirza Mahmud Ahmad denied before the Munir Commission that he had called the Muslims *Kafirs* in the sense that they are out of the pale of Islam. Kayani, *Report of the Court of Inquiry*, 199.
21. Ali, *Split in the Ahmadiyya Movement*, 90–93.
22. Ahmad, *Truth about the Split*, 156–162.
23. Ali, *Split in the Ahmadiyya Movement*, 88–89.

Doctrinal Issues

Having had a brief glance at the historical origins of the Ahmadiyya movement and its subsequent split, we now move to the doctrinal issues which have been a cause of huge controversy between Ahmadis and mainline Islam.

Finality of Prophethood

First and foremost, the theological issue which has been most divisive between the Ahmadis and mainline Muslims is the status of Ghulam Ahmad, who claimed that he was a messenger, apostle and prophet. The controversy revolves around the question of whether it is possible for another prophet to come after Prophet Muhammad, who was <u>Kh</u>*atamun Nabiyyin* (that is, the last prophet). In response to this objection, Ghulam Ahmad explained that he was a prophet by way of *Zill* (a shadow or reflected image) and *Buruz* (a re-appearance or reincarnation). Ahmad stated that " he will acquire nothing on his own but will acquire everything from [the] Holy Prophet and will lose himself in him as to reflect his very image . . . by way of *Zill* – his name character and knowledge . . .by the *Buruz* . . . it reflects the excellence and perfection of the original in every aspect."[24] He further said, "Since I am the *Buruz* of Muhammad that has been ordained since eternity, I have therefore [been] granted prophethood in the form of *Buruz,* and the entire world is powerless to stand against it."[25] This whole debate revolves round the following verse of the Qur'an: "Muhammad . . . is the Rasul Allah and the Khatam-un-Nabiyeen . . ." (Q.33:41).

The Arabic phrase *Khatam-un-Nabiyeen* has been the subject of controversy between the Ahmadis and mainline Muslims. This word can be read and interpreted in two ways: as *Khatim,* meaning one who finishes or ends; or *Khatam,* meaning the seal of the prophets. Mainline Islam teaches that the Prophet Muhammad was the last of the prophets; they also say that the word "seal" indicates the closing of a document. In contrast, Ahmadis interpret the word "seal" as a stamp, something that certifies genuineness and correctness.[26] They believe that the era of the prophets is not closed,

---

24. Mirza Ghulam Ahmad, *A Misconception Removed,* rev. ed. (Tilford: IIP, 2007), 15–16.

25. Ibid., 18.

26. Safiur-Rahman Al-Mubarakpuri, *The Sealed Nectar: Biography of the Noble Prophet,* rev. ed. (Riyadh: Darussalam, 2002), 92–93.

but that, after the Prophet Muhammad, whoever claims to be a prophet must bear the seal of the Prophet Muhammad.[27] According to the Ahmadis, some kind of prophethood is attainable under the seal of the prophethood of Muhammad. They argue that he was "an *Ummati Nabi* [a prophet from the (Muslim) community] [who] cannot bring a new *Shari'a* (law) nor could he operate outside the zone of the eternal Prophethood of the Holy Prophet."[28] Their opponents object that the ideas of *buruz* and *zill* are foreign to Islamic dogma.[29]

As we have seen above, the issue of Ahmad's prophethood also became a point of departure for the Lahore group of Ahmadis. They are of the view that "the words *Nabi* and *Rasūl* have been used . . . as metaphor or simile."[30] In this regard, Muhammad Ali says that "he [Ahmad] was a prophet in a certain sense – in the sense in which every *mujaddad* [reformer] was a prophet."[31] The scholars of the Lahore group argue that Ghulam Ahmad used such terms *Zill Nabi* or *Ummati Nabi* to explain the words *Nabi* and *Rasūl*.[32]

Whatever explanation is given by the Qadian or Lahore group for Ghulam Ahmad's prophethood, it is undeniable that orthodox Islam believes that Ahmad "did a grave offence to the Muslims' sensibilities by using the term *Nabi* (prophet) to describe himself."[33] Maududi writes that "Muslims have believed, and so they do today, that Prophet Muhammad (PBUH) is the last messenger of God and there can be no prophet after him."[34]

---

27. Sahibzada M. M. Ahmad, "Exalted Status of the Holy Prophet as the Khatamun Nabiyeen," online.

28. Saleem Nasir Malik, "Muhammad – The Holder of the Seal," *The Review of Religions* 80, no. 5 (1985): 29.

29. Kayani, *Report of the Court of Inquiry*, 188.

30. Masud Akhtar, "The Finality of Prophethood," *The Islamic Review* 6, no. 5 (1986): 10–11.

31. Muhammad Ali, "Two Sections of the Ahmadiyya Movement," *The Islamic Review* 7, no. 4 (1987): 6; Ali, *Ahmadiyya Doctrines*, 18–20.

32. These terms have been coined by the Sufis centuries before Ghulam Ahmad in order "to indicate *Wallayat* or *Muhdaddathiyat*, that is a non-prophet who has attained communion with Allah and receives Revelation from Allah due to perfectly following the Holy prophet Muhammad." Akhtar, "Finality of Prophethood," 11.

33. Lavan, *Ahmadiyyat Movement*, 58.

34. Abul Ala Maududi, *The Qadiani Problem* (Lahore: Islamic Publications, 1953), 2, online.

Christology

The second key theological issue between mainline Islam and the Ahmadis is Christology. First, Ghulam Ahmad made numerous claims of superiority over Jesus, in order to counter Christian missionaries: "The son of Mary has slightest superiority over other men . . . the writer of these pages has been sent to convince people that he enjoys a greater grace and favour in the sight of God than Jesus Christ."[35] And, "I have seen him many a time, but he has always expressed his humbleness and submissiveness . . . Jesus is from me and I am from God; blessed is he who recognizes me, and undone is the person from whose eyes I am hidden."[36] Moreover, he said that "Ye Christian missionaries: say no more that Christ is your God for there is among you who is greater than Christ."[37]

This was, of course, offensive to Christians as well as, in some regards, to Muslims. However, the real point of concern for Muslims came up when Ahmad refuted the Islamic belief that someone else resembling Christ was crucified, while Christ himself ascended to heaven in bodily form, by claiming instead that Jesus had been removed from the cross in a swoon and that his body had been laid in the grave, where he was resuscitated. Ahmad claimed that his wounds had been healed by the application of *marham-ē-īsa* (ointment of Jesus).[38] Then, he said, after remaining forty days with his disciples, Jesus traveled from Jerusalem through Iran and Afghanistan to Kashmir, in order to evangelize the lost tribes of Israel. Ahmad sought to prove that Jesus got married and also had children and died in Kashmir at the age of 120 years. In support of his view, he claimed that he had discovered Jesus's grave at Khan Yar Street in Srinagar, Kashmir in India.[39]

---

35. Mirza Ghulam Ahmad, "An Answer to Dr. Dowies Prediction of General Destructions of all Muhmmadans," *The Review of Religions* 1, no. 9 (1902): 340.

36. Ibid., 348–349.

37. Mirza Ghulam Ahmad, "The Plague," *The Review of Religions* 1, no. 6 (1902): 251. See for further evidence of his claim of superiority over Christ. Mirza Ghulam Ahmad, "The Appearance of Promised Messiah," *The Review of Religions* 1, no. 5 (1902): 205–207.

38. In 1898, Ghulam Ahmad announced that the same medicine which healed Jesus from his wounds is available for sale by him "as miraculous remedy for the plague, prepared solely under the influence of divine inspiration." Walter, *Ahmadiya Movement*, 42. This medicine was confiscated and removed from the market by the government on the orders of the Chief Court of Punjab on 8 June 1900.

39. See Mirza Ghulam Ahmad, *Masih Hindustan Mein* [Jesus in India], trans. Qazi Abdul Hamid and Muhammad Ali, new ed. (Tilford, Surrey: Islam International Publications, 2007).

It is beyond the scope of our study here to examine in detail the motivation behind this theory. However, a careful reading of Ghulam Ahmad's writings reveals that his main purpose behind this theory was to prove that Islam was a superior religion to Christianity. This led him to refute Christian apologists' argument that Christianity is superior because its founder is alive. As Walter observed, "Ahmad saw that a live Jesus, whose tomb nowhere existed, and a dead Muhammad, whose tomb at Medina was an object of pilgrimage for Muslims, gave Jesus an advantage of which Christian missionaries might have made far more use than they had."[40] This is evident from Ahmad's statement: "I tell you a secret . . . you may upset all the arguments which the Christians put forward. Prove to them that in reality Christ, the son of Mary, is forever dead . . . you will be able to wipe out the Christian religion off from the face of earth."[41] In this regard, Jones' observation is worth noting: Ahmad wanted "Islam to be the superior religion which could only be gained by proving Jesus' death because what Prophet of Islam cannot be, Christ shall not be."[42]

We may draw the conclusion that Ahmad assumed that he served Islam by negating Christian Christology, even if this was at the cost of undermining orthodox Islamic belief. The Qur'an denies the crucifixion of Jesus (Q.4:157), but affirms that Jesus was taken up in his earthly body to one of the heavens (Q.4:158). By contrast, Ghulam Ahmad accepted the crucifixion of Jesus, but sought to prove that Jesus eventually died like all ordinary mortals.

Jihād (Holy War)

Another key doctrinal issue on which Ahmadis and the majority of Muslims diverge is *jihād* or holy war. There is an abundance of evidence in the Qur'an (9:5, 6, 29; 4:74, 76; 2:214, 215, 216; 8:39, 41) and the early history of Islam to support the doctrine of *jihād*.[43] Nevertheless, Ghulam Ahmad

---

40. Walter, *Ahmadiya Movement*, 132.

41. Mirza Ghulam Ahmad, *Izāla-ē-Auham* [The Removal of Misconceptions] (Amritsar: Riād-ē-Hind Publisher, 1891).

42. L. Bevan Jones, *The People of the Mosque: An Introduction to the Study of Islam with Special Reference to India* (Calcutta: Association Press, 1932), 289.

43. Reuven Firestone, *Jihād: The Origin of Holy War in Islam* (New York: Oxford University Press, 1999), 51–65.

said in 1900: "I have come to you with an order: *jihād* with a sword has ended from this time forward, but the *jihād* for purifying your souls must continue."[44] He abrogated *jihād* with the argument that the Messiah had come, therefore now *"jihād* is strictly prohibited and that the person who takes up the sword for the propagation of religion is a sinner before God."[45] The orthodox Islamic *'ulamā* accused Ahmad of instituting this doctrine in order to show his loyalty to the British and to please them. In this regard the remarks of the Federal Sharīat Court are notable:

> Ahmadiyya Movement had the blessings of the [British] government and was started on their instructions and under their blessed protection. The interest of the government after the war of independence 1857 was to cause disintegration and disharmony in the Muslim Ummah and carving out a new religion out of Islam served that purpose.[46]

It becomes difficult for the Ahmadis to refute this assertion in the light of Ahmad's statements, where, for example, he argued, "Moreover [a] half century has passed since the advent of the British in the Punjab and from this long experience we can say that the British government is an invaluable blessing to the people of this country in general, and to the Muhammadans [Muslims] in particular."[47] Therefore, he argued, it is un-Islamic to wage *jihād* against a government which eminently supports the cause of Islam.[48] (Note that other Islamic *'ulamā* issued *fatwās* [religious verdicts] that *jihād* was not permissible against the British on two grounds: that there was no *imam* to lead; and that they had no weapons with which to fight).[49] Although Ghulam Ahmad argued that he was not introducing a new law, his opponents objected that "he was not merely expounding a Qur'anic doctrine but

---

44. Mirza Ghulam Ahmad, *The British Government and Jihad* (Tilford: Islam International Publications 2006), 17.

45. Mirza Ghulam Ahmad, "Religious Controversies and Our Position in Them," *The Review of Religions* 1, no. 2 (1902): 45.

46. *Majibur Rehman and 3 Others v. Federal Government of Pakistan*, 37 PLD 8, 84 (1985).

47. Mirza Ghulam Ahmad, "A Proposal for the Utter Extinction of Jehad," *The Review of Religions* 1, no. 1 (1902): 2. See also Ahmad, "Religious Controvercies," 43, 47–50.

48. Ahmad, "Proposal for the Utter Extinction," 3.

49. *Majibur Rehman and 3 Others v. Federal Government of Pakistan*, 84.

was repealing an existing law of the Qur'an."⁵⁰ He was instituting a new law by abrogating one of the existing essential doctrines of Islam.

K͟hilafat (Caliphate)

After the death of Prophet Muhammad in AD 632, one of his companions, Abu Bakr, succeeded him (k͟halifa rasūl allah). Bernard Lewis, a prominent historian of Islam, observes: "Abu Bakr was given the title of k͟halifa or 'Deputy' (of the prophet) . . . and his election marks the inauguration of the great historic institution of the Caliphate . . . The sole condition of his appointment was the maintenance of the heritage of the Prophet."⁵¹ The first four k͟halifas, Abu Bakr, Umar, Uthman, and Ali, were close associates of the Prophet. They are regarded as the rashidun (rightly guided) because of their great integrity and devotion.⁵² The period of the "rightly guided" k͟halifas (632–661) constituted the golden age of pure Islam. After the assassination of Ali, the last "rightly guided" Caliph, a major schism occurred over the question of the right to the k͟hilafat in Islam. Consequently, Muslims split into the Sunni and Shia sects. The title of k͟halifa was borne by the fourteen Umayyad kings of Damascus (661–750) and subsequently by the thirty-eight Abbasid monarchs of Baghdad (750–1258). After the fall of the Umayyad dynasty, the title was also assumed by the Spanish branch of the family who ruled in Spain at Córdoba (755–1031) and by the Faṭimid rulers of Egypt (909–1171). The last titular Abbasid caliph of Cairo was captured in 1517 by the Ottomans, after which the Ottoman sultans claimed the title of k͟halifa and wielded it for four centuries until it was abolished in 1924 by Mustafa Kamal Ataturk, the founder of Turkish Republic.⁵³

Since then, there has been a voice in the Islamic world arguing for the restoration of the caliphate as a means of uniting Muslim nations. Maulana Abul Al-Kalam Azad, a prominent leader of "K͟hilafat Movement" in India

---

50. Kayani, *Report of the Court of Inquiry*, 192.

51. Bernard Lewis, *The Arabs in History*, 6th ed. (New York: Oxford University Press, 1993), 49.

52. Rafi Ahmad, "The Islamic Khilafat – Its Rise, Fall, and Re-emergence," online.

53. D. Sourdel, "The History of the Institution of the Caliphate," in *The Encyclopedia of Islam*, ed. Bernard Lewis (Leiden: E. J. Brill, 1990), 937–946.

said, "Without the Caliphate the existence of Islam is not possible . . ."[54] Some want to achieve this goal through peaceful political means (for example, Tarek Masoud of the Harvard Kennedy School, envisions the caliphate somewhat like the European Union for Muslims). However, others are in favour of using force (for example, Osama bin Laden called the 9/11 attacks "a great step towards the unity of Muslims and [the establishment of] the righteous caliphate"[55]).

In contrast, the Ahmadiyya movement is convinced that a political caliphate will never emerge because a spiritual *khilafat* has already been established in 1908 by Ghulam Ahmad, in the form of the "Ahmadiyya Khilafat," which is purely spiritual in nature.[56] On the basis of its spiritual nature, the "Ahmadiyya Khilafat" categorically rejects militancy in every form and instead wages an intellectual *jihād* of the pen. After the demise of the founder of the Ahmadiyya community in 1908, Nuruddin was elected the first *khalifa* (1908–1914), followed by Ghulam Ahmad's son Mirza Mahmud Ahmad as the second *khalifa* (1914–1965). Since then, the "Ahmadiyya Khilafat" has become dynastic and restricted to the family of Ghulam Ahmad. This is due to the fact that the Ahmadis draw a parallel between the Ahmadiyya Khilafat and the rightly guided Khilafat (*khulfa-ē-rāshdun*). See table 4.2.

This parallelism is very disturbing to mainstream Muslims, especially those from Sunni Islam. Ahmadis use titles such as "Razi Allah Anho" (Allah is pleased with him) for their khalifas, which has been a cause of great concern to Sunni Muslims. Since 1984, Ahmadis in Pakistan have been prohibited from using epithets like "Ameer-ul-Mumineen" (Chief of the believers), "Khalifa-tul-Mumineen" (Caliph of the believers), "Khalifa-tul-Muslimeen" (Caliph of the Muslims), and "Razi Allah Anho" for their khalifas.[57]

Our above discussion on doctrinal differences between the Ahmadiyya sect and mainline Islam sets the context for the following exploration of the experience of the Ahmadiyya community as a minority group in Pakistan.

---

54. Abu Al-Kalam Azad, *Masla-e-Khilafat* [The Issue of Caliphate] (Lahore: Maktabah Jamal, 2006), 195.

55. Mubasher Ahmad, "Khilafat and Caliphate," online.

56. Mirza Bashiruddin Mahmud Ahmad, *Khilafat-e-Rashidah* (Tilford: IIP, 2009), 5.

57. *Ordinance 20 of 1984*, 103.

Table 4.2 Doctrinal Differences between Mainline Islam and the Ahmadiyya Sect

The Guided Khilafat	The Ahmadiyya Khilafat
1. Hazrat Abu Baker (Razi Allah Anho) maintained the unity of the Muslim community after the death of the Holy Prophet.	1. Hazrat Nurrudin (Razi Allah Anho) established the unity of the Ahmadiyya community after the death of the Promised Messiah.
2. Hazrat Umar (Razi Allah Anho) established an effective system of Islamic administration and governances.	2. Hazrat Mahmud Ahmad (Razi Allah Anho) established the administrative structure of the Ahmadiyya community.[58]

Pakistan Experience

Before we discuss the Ahmadi experience in Pakistan, for the sake of continuity, it is appropriate to have a brief glance at their experience before partition.

Pre-partition Experience

We have seen above that anti-Ahmadi sentiments have existed since the inception of the Ahmadiyya movement. However, the seeds of the Ahmadi controversy in Pakistan had been sown by the *Majlis-ē-Aḥrār-ē-Islam* (Committee for the Freedom of Islam) which was a religio-political party. During the Kashmir agitations over the issue of Kashmiri Muslims who were being discriminated against by the Hindu Dogra Raj under Maharaja Hari Singh in 1931,[59] Aḥrār leaders refused to be part of the All-India Kashmir Committee because Mirza Mahmud Ahmad (*Khalifa* of the Ahmadiyya) was serving as the president of the committee. In this regard, Lavan argued that Aḥrār "entered Kashmir politics as much to oppose the Ahmadiyya as to aid the Muslims in Kashmir."[60] Justice Munir's Inquiry Report of 1954 into the Ahmadi issue in Punjab, Pakistan, strengthens this view: "If the demands be compared to a baby, the whole subject [Ahmadi controversy]

---

58. Khilafat the successorship of prophethood, http://www.alislam.org/topics/khilafat/, (accessed 10 June 2013).

59. Lavan, *Ahmadiyyat Movement*, 146.

60. Ibid., 149.

of responsibility can be put into a single sentence and that is that the Aḥrār gave birth to a baby and offered it to the *Ulamā* for adoption who agreed to father it."[61] The rejection of the Ahmadis is also evident from the hard stance taken by Aḥrār leadership against them: "Ahmadis licked the boots of British . . . Gandhi will free us where Ghulam [Ahmad] has made us slaves."[62]

The Aḥrār's anti-Ahmadi sentiments were evident when Zafrullah Khan, an Ahmadi, presided over the All-India Muslim League (AIML) meeting held at New Delhi on 10 December 1931. The Aḥrār demonstrated outside the meeting against AIML because they had allowed their meeting to be presided over by an Ahmadi, whom the Aḥrār considered "heretical."[63] The tensions between the Aḥrār and the Ahmadis continued until 1936. During these years the "Aḥrār were on the offensive, the Ahmadiyya on the defensive."[64]

First Wave of Anti-Ahmadi Campaign (1947-1950)

The *Majlis-ē-Aḥrār* and other religious parties, including *Jamait-ē-Islami* (founded by Maulana Maududi), had been explicitly opposed to the formation of Pakistan. This is evident from the fact that *Majlis-ē-Aḥrār* met at Delhi on 3rd March, 1940, disapproved of the Pakistan plan . . . Pakistan was dubbed as 'Palidistan'[filthy place]."[65] The Aḥrār regarded Jinnah, Pakistan's founder, as an "infidel" because of his liberal views and western lifestyle.[66] When Pakistan came into existence in 1947, the anti-Pakistan leaders of Islamic parties found no place for their politics in India, so, despite their opposition to the new nation, they were compelled to migrate to Pakistan. They brought with them their legacy, "the curse of *takfir* (calling one another infidel) . . . The leading part in this *takfir* was taken by the Aḥrār and their first target was the Ahmadis."[67]

---

61. Kayani, *Report of the Court of Inquiry*, 286.
62. Lavan, *Ahmadiyyat Movement*, 149.
63. Ibid., 152.
64. Ibid., 164.
65. Kayani, *Report of the Court of Inquiry*, 11.
66. Aḥrār's leader Maulana Mazhar Ali commented about Jinnah by using this couplet: "*Ik kafira ke waste Islam ko chhora yeh Quad-i-Azam, hai keh hai kafir-i-azam*" (For one infidel lady [The infidel lady was Jinnah's second wife Rattanbai Petit, a Parsi], he left Islam, is this a great leader? This is indeed a great infidel.) Ibid.
67. Munir, *From Jinnah to Zia*: 38.

On arrival in Pakistan, the Aḥrār changed its name from *Majlis-ē-Aḥrār-ē-Islam-ē-Hind* to *All Pakistan Majlis-ē-Aḥrār*.⁶⁸ After the Aḥrār had acquired a new identity, they started to campaign against the Ahmadis in their new homeland:

> On May 1, 1949, Aḥrār activists made their first public demand that Ahmadis be declared a non-Muslim minority. The Aḥrār insisted that all Ahmadis in public service be removed from their positions. They also accused members of the Ahmadiyya Muslim Community of conspiring with India . . .⁶⁹

In response to Aḥrār's anti-Ahmadi call, a young military officer, Major Mahmud, was stoned and stabbed to death by a violent mob in Quetta.⁷⁰ The central government of Pakistan took stern action against the Aḥrār, and a number of their leaders were arrested and tried in court. Thus, the Aḥrār's initial move against the Ahmadis was discouraged by the newly established government of Pakistan.

Second Wave of Anti-Ahmadi Campaign (1950–1953)

However, after a brief pause, the Aḥrār reactivated their campaign against the Ahmadis in 1950. The Aḥrār reproduced a pamphlet called *Ash-Shahab*, which had originally been written by Maulana Shabbir Usmani (a Deobandi scholar in India). The pamphlet contained a *fatwā* that Ahmadis were *murtadds* (apostates), and, under Islam, the penalty for apostasy is death.⁷¹ The pamphlet was widely circulated in Punjab and frequently cited by Aḥrār's leaders in their public speeches during the 1950s. Their speeches provoked a new wave of sectarian violence against the Ahmadis in the Punjab region resulting in killings, looting and burning the worship places of Ahmadis.⁷²

During these disturbances, a case known as the "Rawalpindi Conspiracy"⁷³ came to light in March 1951. This was used as a tool by the Aḥrār to dub

---

68. Kaushik, *Ahmadiya Community*, 24.
69. Mansoor Ahmed Shah, "1974: Anti-Ahmadi Hostilities," *The Review of Religions* 103, no. 3 (2008): 54.
70. Kayani, *Report of the Court of Inquiry*, 13–14.
71. Ibid., 18; Kaushik, *Ahmadiya Community*, 26.
72. Kayani, *Report of the Court of Inquiry*, 30.
73. A plot was discovered that high-ranking military officers wanted to overthrow the civilian government. One of the accused persons was Major-General Nazir Ahmad, who

Ahmadis as anti-Pakistan. The day the conspiracy was uncovered was celebrated as *yaum-ē-tashakkar* (thanksgiving day) by the Aḥrār, who demanded that "the Ahmadis be declared a minority or forced to leave this country and settle in India."[74] In Aḥrār agitation rallies, the following slogan became a popular way to stir up Muslim antagonism against Ahmadis: "*namak-ḥarām-ē-Pakistan murdabad, ghaddār-ē-Pakistan murdabad, . . .* and *mirzāiat murdabad* [Death on disloyalists of Pakistan, death on conspirators of Pakistan and death on Ahmadi religion]."[75] In May 1952, in order to counter the venomous campaign of the Aḥrār, the Ahmadiyya community held a conference in Karachi where one of their prominent figures, Zafruallah Khan, the first Foreign Minister of Pakistan, concluded his speech in the following manner:

> Ahmadiyyat was a plant, implanted by God himself, that this plant had taken root to provide a guarantee for the preservation of Islam in fulfillment of the promise contained in the Qur'an, and that if this plant were removed, Islam would no longer be a 'live religion' (*Zinda Mazhab*) but would be like a dried up tree having no demonstrable superiority over other religions.[76]

Unfortunately, this speech aggravated the situation and gave the Aḥrār more fuel for their anti-Ahmadiyya campaign. In retaliation, an All-Pakistan Muslims Parties Convention was held under the umbrella of *Majlis-ē-Amal* (Action Committee) in Karachi from 16–18 January 1953. An ultimatum was given to the government that "if within a month the Ahmadis were not declared a non-Muslim minority and Chaudhri Zafrullah Khan, the Foreign Minister who is an Ahmadi, and other Ahmadis occupying key posts in the State, [were] not removed from their offices, the *Majlis-ē-Amal* would resort to direct action (*rāst iqdam*)."[77]

In response, the government rejected their demands and arrested some of the key leaders of *Majlis-ē-Amal*. This government action mostly affected the Punjab, where disturbances commenced immediately on a massive level.

---

was an Ahmadi. Ibid., 28.
    74. Ibid., 29.
    75. Ibid.
    76. Ibid., 75.
    77. Ibid., 1.

This second wave of anti-Ahmadi hatred produced disastrous results: several Ahmadis were killed and their mosques and property burned and looted.[78] The violence increased to such a level that the government imposed martial law in the Punjab in order to restore law and order. On 19 June 1953, the governor of Punjab enacted an ordinance known as Punjab Act II of 1954.[79] Under this Act, a Court of Inquiry, comprising of two eminent judges, Muhammad Munir and R. M. Kayani, was set up to hold a public inquiry into the disturbances. The inquiry produced a thorough report, known as the Munir report, which included recommendations to the government of Punjab. It has been acknowledged as the most fair and unbiased document ever produced by the Judicial Commission in Pakistan.

The report concluded that it would not only be unconstitutional and illegal, but also religiously impossible to expel someone from Islam on the grounds of the *Ulamā's* definition of a Muslim:

> Keeping in view the several definitions given by the *ulama* . . . If we attempt our own definition as each learned divine has done and that definition differs from that given by all others, we unanimously go out of the fold of Islam. And if we adopt the definition given by any one of the *ulama*, we remain Muslims according to the view of that *alim* but *kafirs* according to the definition of everyone else.[80]

The strong recommendations of Munir's Report to the government for maintaining law and order succeeded in stopping anti-Ahmadi violence for at least twenty years. With regard to the Ahmadiyya issue in Pakistan, 1954 to 1973 was a period of relative calm and peace.

The Third Wave of the Anti-Ahmadi Campaign (1973–1974)
After twenty years, the anti-Ahmadiyya movement was again launched on the eve of the high-profile Islamic Summit of the heads of the Muslim world, convened in Lahore by Zulifikar Ali Bhutto in February 1974. Anti-Ahmadi

---

78. Munir, *From Jinnah to Zia*, 38.

79. *Ordinance 3 of 1953: Punjab Disturbances (Public Inquiry) Ordinance*, (19 June 1953) 5 PLD Central and Provincial Statutes (1953), 101–103.

80. Kayani, *Report of the Court of Inquiry*, 218.

literature was distributed freely even among the delegates of the Summit.[81] One month after this summit, in April 1974, the Rabita-e-Islam conference was held in Jidda, Saudi Arabia. It was attended by eminent scholars of the Muslim world including Maulana Maududi from Pakistan. At this summit, it was decided "to condemn Ahmadiyyas as agents of Israel and International Zionism, and to declare Ahmadiyyas as non-Muslims throughout the Islamic world . . ."[82] One of the leaders of Maududi's party (Jamait-e-Islami), Tufail Muhammad, sent a telegram to Saudi Arabia, requesting King Faisal to persuade Bhutto to resolve this long standing Ahmadi issue in Pakistan in the light of above-mentioned resolution.[83]

Dr Mubasher Hasan, a close friend of Bhutto, admitted that Bhutto was well aware that King Faisal was behind anti-Ahmadi forces in Pakistan.[84] The Saudi king's support enabled the internal forces, like Jamait-ē-Islami and Majlis-ē-Aḥrār, to launch an anti-Ahmadi movement again.[85] In Maududi's words, Ahmadis "should be proclaimed heretics and that this finding of heresy against them includes also their expulsion from the pale of Islam . . . In the presence of the Qadiani religion, we cannot live with them as one nation and still be Muslims and Believers."[86] Moreover, the Azad Kashmir Legislative Assembly gave impetus to the anti-Ahmadi campaign when it passed a resolution in April 1973 to declare Ahmadis non-Muslims.[87] It is evident from this fact that the Ahmadis "were publically humiliated and harassed by fanatics . . . The fanatics also threatened Bhutto [with] dire consequences in case he failed to resolve the controversy through legal and constitutional measures."[88]

---

81. Syed Rashid Ali, "Pakistani Constitutional Amendments of 1974: Declaring Qadianis as a non-Muslim Minority," online.

82. Telegram, "Political Situation in Punjab (June 17, 1974)," Public Library of US Diplomacy (Plus D), online.

83. Ibid.

84. Lutful Islam, "Qadiani Issue: 1974 – IV – The Background," *Ahmadiyya Times*, 31 October 2012.

85. Kaushik, *Ahmadiya Community*, 42.

86. Maududi, *Qadiani Problem*, 103.

87. Telegram, "Reimposition of Section 144 in Lahore (May 11, 1973)," Public Library of US Diplomacy (Plus D), online.

88. Kaushik, *Ahmadiya Community*, 43.

On 22 May 1974, in response to the anti-Ahmadi movement, Ahmadis attacked a train carrying a group of students from Nishtar Medical College, Multan at Rabwah railway station. The *Daily Jasarat* reported that "fifty students were badly injured with 13 in critical condition."[89] However, an Ahmadi site has a different view about this event.[90] This incident further aggravated the situation, and following the incident the whole of Pakistan was engulfed in anti-Ahmadi riots. The media was used to encourage Muslims to boycott the Ahmadis socially. As a result, "dozens of Ahmadis [were] killed across the country and many thousands made homeless due to arson and looting . . . mobs killed the victims and mutilated their bodies and burned them with their homes and possessions."[91] Anti-Ahmadiya processions, condemning the Ahmadiyas as foreign agents, were held in various towns across the country.[92]

Pressure mounted to change the legal status of Ahmadis. *Majlis Tahafuz-ē-Khatm-ē-Nubūvat* (Committee for protecting the last prophethood), a grand alliance of eighteen religio-political parties, condemned Bhutto for his failure to resolve the Ahmadi issue, and demanded his resignation if this issue was not resolved. This demand exerted tremendous pressure on Bhutto, who brought the issue forward to the Parliament of Pakistan. Subsequently, a constitutional amendment was passed unanimously by the Parliament on 7 September 1974, in which Ahmadis were declared non-Muslims.[93] (Since then, Ahmadis have been prohibited to use loudspeakers for the *azān* [call for prayer] and the *khuṭaba* [Friday Sermon] in Pakistan.)[94] It was unprecedented that "for the first time the Parliament passed judgment on the beliefs of a

---

89. *Daily Jasarat*, Karachi, May 31, 1974, cited on http://alhafeez.org/rashid/constipak.html, (accessed 6 July 2013).

90. http://cultgirlahmadiyya.blogpost.com.au/2012/07/refutation-allegation-ahmadi-muslim_26.html, (accessed 6 July 2013).

91. Islam, "Qadiani Issue."

92. Kaushik, *Ahmadiya Community*, 45.

93. *Act 49 of 1974: Constitution (Second Amendment) Act*, 425. Article 260 of the Constitution was amended with the following new clause: "a person who does not believe in the ***absolute and unqualified*** finality of the Prophet-hood of Muhammad . . . or claims to be a Prophet in ***any sense of the word*** or of ***any description whatsoever*** after Muhammad or recognizes such a claimant as a Prophet or a religious reformer, is not a Muslim for the purposes of the Constitution or Law." (emphasis added)

94. Antonio R. Gualtieri, *The Ahmadis: Community, Gender, and Politics in a Muslim Society* (Montreal: McGill-Queen's University Press, 2004), 36.

community and declared it non-Muslims."[95] Some considered that the state had gone far beyond its mandate because the matter of someone's belief is a personal issue between him and God and should not be the business of the state:[96] as Jinnah had clearly said, "you belong to any religion or caste or creed that has nothing to do with the business of the State."[97]

The Fourth Wave of the Anti-Ahmadi Campaign (1980–1984)
It is a common view in Pakistan that Ahmadis are following the agenda of Israel and that they have links with the Jews. This perception can be traced back to 1976, when Maulana Zafar Ahmad Ansari quoted a reference from Naamani's book *Israel: A Profile*, that there are six hundred Ahmadis living in Israel who had joined the Israeli army.[98] This news spread like wildfire throughout the country because "Pakistani Muslims had always been sensitive towards the Zionist state and such news generated more hostilities between them and Qadianis."[99]

At around this time, General Zia's dictatorial rule began and under his rule (May 1977 until August 1988) persecution of Ahmadis intensified. Zia's era brought a massive campaign against Ahmadis, due to the re-emergence of conservative Islam, which was promoted by Zia himself because of a combination of his Islamic convictions and his political motives. In 1980, Zia imposed mandatory Islamic taxes, *zakāt* (wealth tax) and *ushr* (agricultural tax), on Muslims.[100]

In response, *Jamait-ē-Ahmadiyya* declared on 28 July 1980 that "Ahmadiyya are Muslims and they will continue to pay *zakāt* and *ushr* as they have been doing previously."[101] However, this statement refueled anti-

---

95. Shaikh Aziz, "A Leaf from History: The Ahmadi Issue," *Dawn*, 24 February 2013, online.

96. Yasser L. Hamdani, "The 1974 National Assembly Proceedings on the Ahmadi Issue," *Daily Times*, 22 October 2012, online.

97. Jinnah, *Quaid-i-Azam*, 9.

98. Israel T. Naamani, *Israel: A Profile*, Pall Mall Country Profiles (London: Pall Mall Press, 1972), 75.

99. Syed Rashid Ali, "Post Anti-Qadiani Ordinance of 1984," online.

100. *Ordinance 28 of 1980: Zakat and Ushr Ordinance* (20 June 1980) 32 PLD Central Statutes (1980), 97. This ordinance authorized the government to deduct 2.5% from bank deposits and to levy one tenth (1/10) on gross proceeds of land possessed by the Muslims.

101. Kaushik, *Ahmadiya Community*, 60.

Ahmadi sentiments in orthodox circles. Now anti-Ahmadi forces reorganized themselves under the umbrella of *Tehrik-ē-Khatam-ē-Nubūvat* (movement for last prophethood) and demanded that Zia-ul-Haq resolve the confusion which still existed regarding the status of Ahmadis in Pakistan, despite the fact that they had been declared constitutionally non-Muslims in 1974.[102] Zia met the demand of the anti-Ahmadis on 8 April 1981 by passing the Provisional Constitutional Order, which, in sections 1-A (a) and (b), defined Muslims and non-Muslims.[103] Furthermore, the Lahore High Court ruled in April 1981 that "there is no succession either way between Muslims and non-Muslims" therefore Ahmadis (as non-Muslims) cannot inherit the property from Muslims, finding that Article 260(3) of the constitution of Pakistan was a declaratory judgment (i.e. Ahmadis had always been non-Muslims).[104] Again, on 12 April 1982, Zia clarified the State's position through a presidential order which reaffirmed that Ahmadis are non-Muslims.[105]

Nevertheless, none of these measures satisfied the demands of the TKN. They kept insisting that Ahmadis were anti-Pakistani and that they spied for India and Israel. TKN further alleged that Ahmadis had links with the Al-Zulfikar militant organization, which had been founded by Bhutto's son, Mir Murtaza Bhutto, with the aim of getting his father, who had been arrested by Zia, released. TKN put pressure on Zia, renewing their demands for "immediate implementation of the Islamic punishment for apostasy which is not less than [the] death sentence; [a] complete ban on the publication and distribution of Ahmadiya literature; and [that] immediate steps be taken to check the anti-national activities of the Ahmadiyas."[106] Zia acceded to their demands, but in a slightly different way, by issuing Ordinance 20 in 1984,

---

102. Ibid.

103. "'Muslim' means a person who believes . . . in the absolute and unqualified finality of the Prophethood of Muhammad (PBUH), the last of the prophets, and does not believe in or recognize as a religious reformer, any person who claimed or claims to be a prophet . . . after Hazrat Muhmmad (PBUH); and 'non-Muslim' means a person who is not a Muslim and includes a person belonging to the Christian, Hindu, Sikh, Budhist or Parsi community, a person of Quadiani group or the Lahori group (who call themselves Ahmadis or by any other name), or a Bahai and a person belonging to any of the scheduled castes." *CMLA Order 2 of 1981: Provisional Constitution (Amendment) Order*, 310–311.

104. *Muhammad Ashraf v. Niamat Bibi*, 33 PLD 520, 532–533 (1981).

105. *President's Order 8 of 1982: Amendment of the Constitution (Declaration) Order* (12 April 1982) 34 PLD Central Statutes (1982), 164–165.

106. Kaushik, *Ahmadiya Community*, 63.

which added two new sections, 298-B and C to the PPC.[107] This Ordinance prohibited Ahmadis from calling their *Azan* (Prayer-call), preaching and propagating their faith, calling their faith "Islam," or presenting themselves as Muslim.[108]

Ordinance 20 caused great concern to Ahmadis and they immediately approached the Federal Shariʿat Court, asking it to exercise its mandate under Article 203-D[109] of the constitution of Pakistan to examine whether or not Ordinance 20 was in conflict with the injunctions of the Qur'an and Sunnah.[110] However, the FSC upheld the validity of Ordinance 20 and dismissed the petition with the following ruling:

> The prohibition against calling their places of worship as Masjid or calling Azan for prayer is thus consequential to the declaration of the Ahmadis or Qadianis as non-Muslims or prohibition against posing them as Muslims. The Qadianis can call their places of worship by any other name and call the adherents of their religion to prayer by use of any other method. This does not amount to interference with the right to profess or practice their religion.[111]

After losing their battle in the FSC, a large number of Ahmadis were prosecuted and convicted in the different courts of the country. In response, Ahmadis decided to challenge Ordinance 20 on constitutional grounds. Two petitions were filed by the Ahmadis in the Lahore High Court; both were dismissed.[112] The Ahmadis were left with no choice but to knock on the door of the SCP. To this end, eight appeals were registered in the SCP claiming that Ordinance 20 violates the fundamental rights guaranteed

---

107. For the full text of clauses 298-B & C, see 37–38

108. *Ordinance 20 of 1984*, 102–103.

109. *President's Order 1 of 1980*. Article 203-D states: "If any law or provision of law is held by the Court to be repugnant to the Injunctions of Islam" and "Such law or provision shall, to the extent to which it is held to be so repugnant, cease to have effect on the day on which the decision of the Court takes effect." See also *President's Order 5 of 1982*, 155–156.

110. *Majibur Rehman and 3 Others v. Federal Government of Pakistan*, 17.

111. Ibid.

112. *Muhammad Aslam v. Federation of Pakistan*; *Majeeb-ur-Rehman Dard v. Federation of Pakistan*.

under Article 20 of the constitution of Pakistan.[113] One of the legal counsels of the Ahmadiyya community, Majib-ur-Rehman, argued that Article 20 "cannot be suspended even under emergency declared under Article 232 of the Constitution."[114] Despite their best efforts, on 3 July 1993, the SCP dismissed all eight appeals on two grounds: first, the religious practice of Ahmadis offends the majority of Muslims in Pakistan; and second, the Islamic use of epithets by Ahmadis violates the company and trademark laws.[115] With this judgment by the top judiciary of the country, all the legal doors for the Ahmadis have been completely shut in Pakistan. Since then, the situation of the Ahmadiyya community has rapidly deteriorated in Pakistan: as Hoodbhoy noted, "Ahmadis are the lightning rod that attracts more hatred than any other sect."[116] Likewise, Rashid also noted that "Ahmadi Muslims have been called the most persecuted Muslim religious group today."[117]

The post-1984 era was marked by an increasingly difficult period for the Ahmadiyya community in Pakistan. Since 1984, hate-filled posters, stickers, fliers and calendars have been openly distributed, inciting people to kill Ahmadis in Pakistan.[118] For example, pamphlets were distributed in Faisalabad in 2011 "audaciously displaying names and addresses of 50 prominent Ahmadis who were to be eliminated. The incendiary pamphlets were signed by the student wing of *Khatam-ē-Nubūvat*."[119] Furthermore, Hamdani notes that "one of the prominent activists of [the *Khatam-ē-Nubūvat*] forum said, by grace of God Mirzais [Ahmadis] had been reduced to the level of *Chuhras* (Christian sweepers) and soon they will be cleaned

---

113. Article 20 (a) "Every citizen shall have the right to profess, practice and propagate his religion; and (b) "Every religious denomination and every sect thereof shall have the right to establish, maintain and manage its religious institutions."

114. Mujeeb-ur-Rehman, *Error at the Apex* (Ontario, Canada: Oriental Publishers, 2002), online.

115. *Zaheeruddin v. State*, 1753–1754.

116. Hoodbhoy cited in Zofeen T. Ebrahim, "Ahmadis: The Lightning Rod That Attracts the Most Hatred," *Dawn*, 28 October 2011, online.

117. Qasim Rashid, "Pakistan's Failed Committment," *RJGLB* 11, no. 1 (2011): 24.

118. Staff Reporter, "Hate Campaign against Ahmadis Reaches New Height " *Daily Times*, 5 May 2012, 16.

119. Editor, "A Community No One Cares About," *The Express Tribune*, 18 June 2012, 16.

up together."[120] Likewise, Amir Liaquat Hussain, Pakistan's former federal minister for religious affairs, declared on his popular television show "Aalim Online" on 8 September 2008 that Ahmadis are infidels and it was both necessary and Islamic to kill them.[121] Even the government offices in Lahore display a poster containing hate speech against Ahmadis. "One of the posters at the Lahore's Custom House reads: *Qādiani ka jo yār hai ghaddār hai ghaddār hai* (whoever is a friend of an Ahmadi is a traitor)."[122] Another poster in front of the banking court in Lahore reads: "When a Muslim befriends a [Qādiani] he causes anguish to the Holy Prophet."[123] It is apparent that the government in Pakistan, far from failing to discourage the anti-Ahmadi campaign, actually encourages it. From this, it can be deduced that the government was frightened by the religious forces. As the adviser to the Chief Minister of Punjab, Zaeem Qadri admitted that the government did not remove the threatening banners, and "this was to prevent an adverse reaction against the government."[124]

As a result of the hate posters, many Ahmadis were killed in several parts of Pakistan. The campaign against Ahmadis reached its zenith on 28 May 2010, when two Ahmadi worship places in Lahore were attacked by religiously motivated attackers with modern weapons, who killed ninety-five Ahmadi worshippers and severely injured over one hundred twenty.[125] The Taliban's spokesman, Muhammad Omar, said to the media that "Ahmadis [had long been] a target for the militants"[126] due to their religious beliefs. He congratulated "the whole nation on what brave *Mujāhidin* (holy warriors) did yesterday in Lahore."[127] He further said that "on the whole we do like

---

120. Yasser L. Hamdani, "Do Ahmadis Deserve to Live in Pakistan?" *Friday Times*, 31 August–6 September 2012, online.

121. The program "Aalim Online" telecasted on Geo TV on 8 September 2008.

122. Hamdani, "Do Ahmadis Deserve?"

123. Ibid.

124. Zaeem Qadri, Advisor to the Chief Minister of Punjab. Interview telecasted on Dunya TV on 30 May 2010.

125. Salman Aslam, "Ahmadis Worship Places Hit – 80 Killed," *Dawn*, 29 May 2010, 1; Faisal Ali, "95 Killed in Lahore Claim Ahmadis," *Dawn*, 30 May 2010, 1.

126. Rahimullah Yusufzai, "Ahmadis Were Target for the Militants since Long," *The News*, 30 May 2010, 2.

127. Staff Reporter, "Taliban Claim Responsibility for Lahore Attacks," *Daily Times*, 30 May 2010, 4.

to encourage the nation for increasing such activities like targeted killings of Qādianis."[128] This was all based on the ideology that paradise can be secured by killing Ahmadis who are *Kāfir* (infidels). The Ahmadiyya community expressed their feelings in a letter to the President and Prime Minister of Pakistan, saying that "we have been left by the state at the mercy of the militants and miscreants who are thirsty for Ahmadi blood."[129]

The hatred towards Ahmadis persists even after their death, which is evident from the fact that Ahmadis are not safe in their graves in Pakistan. On 3 December 2012, a dozen armed men demolished one hundred twenty graves of Ahmadis in Lahore.[130] Their reasoning seems to be that Ahmadis had offended against 298-C, which prohibits Ahmadis from posing as Muslims even at their burial sites. This is evident from the desecration of the grave of Dr Abdus Salam (1926–1996), a renowned scientist and Nobel award holder, who is buried in Rabwah. Under court orders, the word "Muslim" has been deleted from his epitaph, which read, "First ——— Nobel Laureate."[131]

The *Khatam-ē-Nubūvat* conference, held in September 2012 at Lahore, demanded that the "religious activities of Ahmadis should be banned in Pakistan and their social activities should be monitored."[132] With regard to a social boycott of Ahmadis, the Lahore Bar Association had already taken a practical step with a unanimous vote at its meeting in February 2012 to ban the sale of Shezan Juice (a soft drink produced by a company owned by the Ahmadiyya community) within the premises of the Lahore High Court.[133] The president of the Bar Association, Hamid Khan, said that "stern action would be taken against the retailers who are caught selling the product."[134] Moreover, posters were displayed with calls for a boycott of the Ahmadiyya product: "O the drinker (sic) of Shezan! Do not invite God's wrath upon

---

128. Ibid.

129. Saba Imtiaz, "As Death Toll Mounts Ahmadis Fight Back with Letters," *The Express Tribune*, 2 November 2012, 2.

130. Staff Reporter, "120 Graves of Ahmadis Desecrated," *Dawn*, 4 December 2012, 17.

131. Murtaza Razvi, "Salaam Abdus Salam," *Dawn*, 21 November 2011, online.

132. Staff Reporter, "Khatm-e-Nubuwat Moot Calls for Restrictions on Ahmadis," *Pakistan Today*, 11 September 2012, 3.

133. Harris B. Munawar, "Ahmadis, Leprosy and Plague," *Pakistan Today*, 14 February 2012, 1, online.

134. Ibid.

you by drinking Shezan. Do not take this obnoxious drink of the apostates lest you suffer from any disease and you lose the pleasure of life."[135]

Our above discussion shows that Ahmadis have been facing religious, legal, social and political discrimination which made them one of the most vulnerable minority groups in Pakistan. The Ahmadiyya community migrated to Pakistan in 1947 with high hopes for a better life in a Muslim country but it proved completely the opposite. Now many of them seek asylum in Europe, the USA or Australia.

Christianity in Pakistan

Historical Overview of Christianity in Pakistan

The Christian mission towards the West from Antioch in the first centuries after Christ is well documented and is much better known than the progress of the Christian gospel towards Eastern lands. Yet, the same Christian message was carried down the valley of the Euphrates to Babylon, and then reached Arabs and even further afield took root among Persians, and from there it continued onward by both land and sea until it reached the peoples of India and China.[136] There has been a tendency among church historians to follow the pattern of Dr Luke in Acts to present the expansion of the church from Jerusalem to Rome.[137] Nevertheless, some fragmentary information is available about the spread of Christianity in the northern part of India, now Pakistan. When we turn the pages of Christian history, we do not find any evidence of the church's presence in that part by the eleventh century. Neill argued that the Islamic invasion by the Arabs took complete possession of the Indian seas and would have undermined the church.[138] Moreover, the *sūfī*-generated movements attracted not only low-caste Hindus but also the

---

135. Ibid.

136. Robert Eric Frykenberg, "Christians in India: An Historical Overview of Their Complex Origins," in *Christians and Missionaries in India*, ed. Robert Eric Frykenberg (London: RoutledgeCurzon, 2003), 33.

137. Philip Jenkins, *The Lost History of Christianity* (Oxford: Lion, 2008), 46–47; Michael Nazir-Ali, *From Everywhere to Everywhere: A World View of Christian Witness* (London: Collins, 1990), 23.

138. Stephen Neill, *The Story of the Christian Church in India and Pakistan* (Madras: CLS, 1972), 21–22.

fragile Christian community, which were in isolated pockets by the end of the first millennium. "Such Christian groups and individuals as survived must have succumbed to these mass movements."[139] It appears that they were completely eliminated by the eleventh or thirteenth century. Thus, there is no claim of continuity in the history of Christianity in Pakistan.

Christianity in present-day Pakistan spread through the modern missionary movement, "which began from the west in the sixteenth century, gained momentum in the eighteenth and reached its zenith in the nineteenth century."[140] Missionaries came into India with the intention of converting the high-caste people, but they could not attract many to Christianity.[141] One of the pioneer missionaries in the Punjab, Andrew Gordon, who began work in 1855, says, "I began with the educated classes and people of good social position, but ended among the poor and lowly."[142] Some missionaries were really troubled about mission work among the low castes. This we see from the letter of J. C. R Ewing to the Board of Foreign Missions dated 19 March 1894, in which he described this trend of poor, low-caste people becoming Christians as "raking in rubbish into the church."[143] Gordon also reports that a missionary remarked publicly at a missionary conference that "it was 'bad policy' to receive such low persons at the beginning of our work."[144] Some other missionaries in their reports hesitated to mention these converts' social background, and they were described more ambiguously as "common villagers" or "illiterate menials."[145] Nevertheless, in the nineteenth century, both Catholic and Protestant missionaries tended to focus on the

---

139. John Rooney, *Shadows in the Dark: A History of Christianity in Pakistan up to the 10th Century*, Pakistan Christian History (Rawalpindi: CSC, 1984), 98.

140. Michael Nazir-Ali, *Islam: A Christian Perspective* (Carlisle: Paternoster, 1983), 143.

141. J. H. Beaglehole, "The Indian Christians – A Study of a Minority," *MAS* 1, no. 1 (1967): 59–60.

142. Andrew Gordon, *Our India Mission* (Philadelphia: Inquirer Printing Co., 1886), 446.

143. John C. B. Webster, *The Christian Community and Change in Ninteenth Century India* (Delhi: Macmillan, 1976), 60.

144. Gordon, *Our India Mission*, 178.

145. Mark Juergensmeyer, *Religion as Social Vision: The Movement against Untouchability in 20th Century Punjab* (Berkeley, CA: University of California Press, 1982), 186.

low castes as these people were more attracted to Christianity as a group than the higher castes.[146]

Christianity attracted several groups from the low castes, like the *Megs* and the *Chamars*, yet the largest group that converted to Christianity in Punjab was the *Chuhras*, who were considered the lowest of all the scheduled castes. They were despised by the high castes because their work involved menial jobs such as removing and skinning dead animals.[147] Moreover, they ate the flesh of animals which had died a natural death and collected leftover food from their landlords. This was counted as highly disgraceful in Hindu society.[148]

There are several traditions regarding the origins of the *Chuhras*, which are outside of our subject matter here, but it is clear that there was no place in Hindu society for them, as they were considered "untouchables." They had no social connections with the upper castes, because they were considered polluted and were not allowed to use certain roads used by the upper class.[149] Even their shadows were carefully avoided by the high-caste people lest they be defiled.[150] The humiliation and degradation of the low castes was extreme in the Hindu dominated society. The *Chuhras* were despised "like the leper of old [who] must stop and give warning whenever there is any danger of contact."[151] So, they were not even allowed to hear the gospel alongside other castes in public, but "if they wish to hear, must stand apart by themselves."[152]

A mass conversion movement began among *Chuhras* in 1873 with the conversion of a lame and illiterate man called "Ditt."[153] Despite all oppo-

---

146. Kenneth and Helen Ballhatchet, "Asia," in *Oxford Illustrated History of Christianity*, ed. J. McManners (Oxford: Oxford University Press, 1990), 495.

147. Gordon, *Our India Mission*, 173.

148. Godfrey E. Phillips, *The Outcaste's Hope: Work among the Depressed Classes in India* (London: YPMM, 1912), 8; J. W. Youngson, *The Chuhras* (Bombay: Education Society's Press, 1907); Frederick and Margaret Stock, *People Movements in the Punjab* (Pasadena, CA: William Carey Library, 1975), 57.

149. John C. B. Webster, "Dalits and Christianity in Colonial Punjab: Cultural Interactions," in *Christians, Cultural Interactions, and India's Religious Traditions*, eds. Judith M. Brown and Robert Eric Frykenberg (London: Routledge Curzon, 2002), 95.

150. Stock, *People Movements*, 59.

151. Gordon, *Our India Mission*, 174.

152. Ibid.

153. Ibid., 421–427.

sition from his clan, he remained faithful to his new faith, saying, "Your opposition will never induce me to deny Christ."[154] More than that, he was determined to share the gospel message with his fellow *Chuhras*. Ditt's work among the *Chuhras* produced amazing results for which Pickett gives him credit, arguing that "the real founder of the Church in Sialkot was not Gordon but Ditt."[155] What Ditt began was to become the largest, but not the only, mass conversion movement in the Punjab. Other group movements were initiated in other low-caste groups in the late nineteenth century.[156] This approach of focusing attention on low-caste people was used by both Catholic and Protestant missionaries to convert groups of low-caste people, and it gave birth to a "mass movement."[157] In Northern India, of which the largest section is Punjab, more than 90 percent of the Christians come from low-caste backgrounds.[158] "By 1915, the United Presbyterians [in Punjab] had become an overwhelmingly *Chuhra* Church."[159]

Although there are many more low-caste Christians than high-caste Christians in Pakistan, it is not a religion only of low-caste people: there is substantial evidence that a considerable number of Muslims, Hindus and Sikhs in Pakistan have also embraced Christianity. Nonetheless, it is an undeniable fact that the church in Pakistan today is mainly the result of a mass movement in which untouchable groups such as *Chuhras* embraced Christianity, both Catholic and Protestant. This brief historical overview of the origins of Christianity in Pakistan provides a context for the following discussion of the Christians' experience in the minority context of Pakistan.

---

154. Ibid., 424.

155. J. Waskom Pickett, *Christian Mass Movements in India* (Lucknow: LPH, 1933), 55.

156. Stock, *People Movements*, 33–63.

157. During the mass movement, people had mixed motives for embracing Christianity, including to throw off their yoke of oppression, and "the desire for emancipation, dignity and socio-economic improvement." John O'Brien, *The Construction of Pakistani Christian Identity* (Lahore: Research Society of Pakistan, 2006), 562–563. Pickett observed that "the motives that lead Indian people to Christ in mass movements are the motives that lead people anywhere to him." Pickett, *Christian Mass Movements,* 160.

158. James Massey, "Christianity among the Dalits in the Northern India with Special Reference to Punjab," in *Christianity in India: Search for Liberation and Identity*, ed. F. Hrangkhuuma (Dehli: ISPCK, 1998), 3.

159. John C. B. Webster, "The Legacy of John Charles Heinrich," *IBMR* 37, no. 1 (2013): 34.

Pakistan Experience

There is substantial evidence that Christian politicians, S. P. Singha, C. Gibbons, Joshua Fazal Din and Chundu Lall, played a significant role in the making of Pakistan. They were instrumental in advocating the case for a separate nation of Pakistan. S. P. Singha, the Speaker of the Punjab Legislative Assembly, gave his casting vote, in line with the Muslim League in 1945, that the Punjab should be included in Pakistan.[160] However, this Christian heritage has since been lost, largely because, during the 1980s, there was a great move from Zia-ul-Haq to revise the curricula of state schools in order to promote Islam over other religions, portraying Hindus, Jews and Christians as enemies of Islam.[161] Since then, there have been strong feelings among Christians that due recognition has not be given to the Christians' support of the "Pakistan Movement" in the history books of school curricula in Pakistan.[162] As a result some Christians unsuccessfully appealed to the Lahore High Court to direct the government to "include in syllabus of all level of achievements and sacrifices of Christians in the creation of Pakistan."[163]

Chapter 1 showed that initially minorities were hesitant to support the demand for a separate Muslim country, but minorities, including Christians, came to support the idea because of Jinnah's assurance that no one in Pakistan would be discriminated against on the basis of religious allegiance.[164] However, this assurance died with Jinnah and the process of constitutional discrimination against minorities began and has continued throughout the history of Pakistan. We will now look at Christian experience in the minority context of Pakistan.

---

160. Samson S. Sharaf, "Pakistan's Unsung Hero," *The Nation*, 23 February 2013, 6; Salamat Akhter, *Tahrek-e-Pakistan ke Gumnam Kirdar* [The Anonymous Characters of Pakistan Movement] (Rawalpindi: CSC, 1997), 62–63.

161. For good analysis of this subject, see K. K. Aziz, *The Murder of History: A Critique of History Text Books Used in Pakistan* (Lahore: Sang-e-Meel Publications, 2010); Pervez A. Hoodbhoy and Abdul M. Nayyer, "Rewriting the History of Pakistan," in *Islam, Politics and the State: The Pakistan Experience*, ed. Mohammad Asghar Khan (London: Zed Books, 1985), 164–177.

162. Jennifer Jivan and Peter Jacob, "Life on the Margins" (Lahore: NCJP, 2012), 20.

163. Staff Reporter, "Plea for Highlighting Christians' Role," *Dawn*, 23 August 2011, 17.

164. Jinnah, *Quaid-i-Azam*, 9.

Untouchables

Some scholars argue that the term "untouchables" was used for various categories, but Crooke argues convincingly that the untouchables were specifically the forerunners of the *Chuhras*.[165] As we noted above, a large proportion of Pakistani Christians are of Punjabi origin[166] from the low castes, especially *Chuhras*. The Christians' social background was one of the major reasons why they were despised by the Hindus before Partition in 1947 and are despised now by Muslims in Pakistan. Ideally, there is a strong element of equality in Islam but, in the case of Pakistan, this element failed to break the social pattern of the society set by Hinduism.[167] In this regard O'Brien notes, "Despite the fact that Pakistan was now a Muslim country, already on its way to becoming an Islamic state, and that they, as Christians, were, according to Islamic ideology, *ahl-ē-kitāb* (People of the Book), the determining factor in all social intercourse was – as it still is – caste!"[168] The majority of Pakistani Christians still do menial jobs. The phenomenon of social degradation is deeply rooted in Pakistani society and thus Christians, who are mostly the descendants of low-caste people, have not escaped the stigma of untouchability by becoming Christians, as they are still tainted, both by their origins and by their menial work.[169]

Although the social origins of Christians account for much of the discrimination against them, the element of religious allegiance cannot be ignored when it comes to discrimination and prejudice in Pakistani society. In this regard Green notes, "Since the 1970s, fuelled by the rise of Islamism,

---

165. William Crooke, *The Tribes and Castes of the North-Western Provinces and Oudh*, 4 vols., vol. 2 (Calcutta: Office of the Superintendent of Government, 1896), 260–262.

166. Moghal and Jivan claim that "98% Pakistani Christians are ethnically Punjabis, though many do not live in the Punjab." Dominic Moghal and Jennifer Jivan, *The Christian Church in Pakistan* (Rawalpindi: CSC, 1997), 10.

167. Chuhras who adopted Islam were called *chhote musallis* (polluted) and not accepted as full Muslims. They were obliged to appoint their own Mullahs (Islamic clerics) as they were not allowed to worship with other Muslims and not intermarry with them.

168. O'Brien, *Construction of Pakistani Christian Identity*, 588.

169. Freda Carey, "Dalit, Dhimmi or Disciple," MTh Thesis (Edinburgh: University of Edinburgh, 1999), 32.

alongside and even eclipsing the old epithet of 'sweeper' [untouchable], is the more recent one of *kāfir* ('infidel')."[170]

Most Muslims despise all Christians in Pakistan by calling them *Chuhras* or *Isai* (followers of Isa, Arabic word for Jesus), labels which are often employed as terms of abuse.[171] To try to avoid this social and religious degradation, some Christian leaders in Pakistan protested and filed a petition in the Lahore High Court that they should be called *masihi* ("Masih" from Messiah) instead of *isai*.[172] Pakistani Christians face social stigma and discrimination irrespective of their actual caste background or occupation. (Even Christians from the West are labeled with this title by Muslims in Pakistan). To avoid this, Christians sometimes hide their identity in the market place. If they reveal their identity as Christians, Muslim shopkeepers might refuse to sell them food items. Some Muslims regard it as unacceptable for Christians to drink water from the same place where they drink. A reluctance to share water was the motivation behind the case of Asia Bibi, who is still in prison in Pakistan facing charges of blasphemy.[173]

The social stigma of untouchability affects even Christians who belong to non-sweeper classes: they tend to look down on sweeper-class Christians and treat them in the same manner as Muslims do. They remain distant from them socially and refuse to eat and drink with them. Some argue that well-off Christians try to show that "they originally don't belong to the Chuhra community"[174] and so they need not mix with sweeper-class Christians and even avoid eating and drinking with them which shows that "this behavior is not adopted for hygienic purposes."[175]

---

170. Timothy Green, "Identity Issues for Ex-Muslim Christians," *SFM* 8, no. 4 (2012): 454.

171. Ali Waqar, "Hate Mongering Worries Minorities," *Daily Times*, 25 April 2006, online.

172. Khaled Ahmed, "Word For Word: Masihi Instead of Isai," *Daily Times*, 17 April 2005, online.

173. Asia Bibi with Anne-Isabelle Tollet, *Blasphemy: The True, Heart – Breaking Story of a Woman Sentenced to Death over a Cup of Water* (London: Virago Press, 2012), 19–23.

174. Yunis Khushi, "Being a Christian in Pakistan," *Focus* 10, no. 4 (1990): 255.

175. Dominic Moghal, *Human Person in Punjabi Society: A Tension between Religion and Culture* (Rawalpindi: CSC, 1997), 47.

Ghettoization

At the beginning of the nineteenth century, Protestant and Catholic missionaries acquired cultivated land in irrigated areas in which they established villages for scattered and economically depressed Christians. Missionaries took this initiative to give native Christians a standing in the society by changing their status from *kammi* (slave worker) to *zamindār* (landowner). O'Brian notes, "There was a strong humanitarian and even liberationist element in developing these agricultural colonies."[176] However, the establishment of these villages may have had a negative effect on the church in Pakistan. Some have made the charge that these separate Christian villages caused the further isolation of Christians. In this regard Moghal argued, "They [missionaries] brought the scattered converts together, keeping them away from the rest of the community. As a result religious identity became associated with separateness, which increased the marginalization of the community."[177] Moghal mainly held the missionaries responsible for the ghettoization of Christians by establishing Christian villages and *bastis* (slums).

While Moghal may be partly correct in his analysis with regard to the urban *bastis* for Christians, his argument does not stand up in the case of Christian villages. These villages were successful in completely changing the outcast status of these marginalized people from *kammi to zamindār*. This move gave a new identity and status to the Christians, who could then stand on the same platform as other landowners, which is a great sign of *izzat* (honour) in the Punjab. "In fact, their new enhanced status gave them opportunity to meet with outsiders on something approaching equality, for the first time in their long history of struggle for dignity."[178] Moreover, these villages gave them such an environment of freedom and economic prosperity that this even affected the physical appearance of their new generations.[179]

Moghal also overlooked the other side of the picture, which was that these people had been ghettoized for centuries anyway. They came to Christianity

---

176. O'Brien, *Construction of Pakistani Christian Identity*, 451.

177. Dominic Moghal, "Alienation of the Local People: The Future of Religious Minorities in Pakistan," *Al-Mushir* 37, no. 2 (1995): 40.

178. O'Brien, *Construction of Pakistani Christian Identity*, 460.

179. Walbridge observed that "many canal colony Christians do not look physically like the Chuhras, who are generally small built and dark." Linda S. Walbridge, *The Christians of Pakistan: The Passion of Bishop John Joseph* (Richmond: RoutledgeCurzon, 2003), 19.

along with their inherent ghettoization. They were ghettoized in the villages by the Hindus before the creation of Pakistan, and later by the Muslims. Christians who live in Muslim villages in present-day Pakistan are segregated in their own section of the village, usually on the outskirts. This writer has observed that Christians generally live on the low side of the villages, near the village drain, which is a place of humiliation. The other factor is that when floods hit, those on the lower parts of the village are vulnerable to greater destruction. These untouchables (later Christians) had been used as a protection wall by the superior castes, previously Hindus and later Muslims in Pakistan.

The majority of Christians live together in ghetto-like *bastis* in the urban areas because their poverty and social background have pushed them to live in the slums, which have such poor facilities that no well-off people would want to live there. When the Roman Catholic Church saw the economic plight of the Christians, they established Christian residential colonies in the urban areas to accommodate the many Christians who had migrated to cities after partition, looking for employment.

The other main reason that Christians live together in a ghettoized situation is the security factor. Due to the rise of extremism in Pakistan, Christians feel insecure living among Muslims, so they tend to move to the Christian colonies and prefer to live among their co-religionists for the sake of their security.[180] Christians working among Muslims face prejudice from colleagues and superiors, therefore Christians often prefer to work among other Christians within the church. There is a vicious circle, in which discrimination and marginalization have made Christians more isolated which, in turn, has reinforced ghettoization.

Despite all the factors mentioned above, Pakistani Christians are also responsible for their ghettoization. It can be argued that they tend to segregate themselves from the majority of the community for fear of losing their Christian identity. They live with such a sense of insecurity about their

---

180. Tariq C. Qaiser, a Christian politician and former member of the parliament, shifted his residence from a more affluent Muslim area to a Christian colony in Sargohda, Pakistan, because his house was attacked by the Muslim fanatics and he felt insecure being a single Christian family living among the Muslims. This author has firsthand knowledge of this, being his fellow villager.

identity that they build high walls of so-called "church culture" around them. Their sense of vulnerability keeps them locked into a ghetto mentality.

Exploitation

The partition of India and Pakistan took place in 1947, accompanied by the violent deaths of half a million people and the mass migration of people on both sides. Due to the migration of a large number of Hindus and Sikh landlords to India, a vast number of Christian tenants and agricultural workers lost their agricultural jobs.[181] Large numbers of Muslim migrants, known as *muhājirs* (refugees), were initially treated sympathetically and preferred over Christian agricultural labourers and tenants by the native Muslims.[182] As a result, a massive number of Punjabi Christian agricultural labourers and tenants who had formerly tilled the land became unemployed. This situation forced them to move towards cities in search of employment. Unfortunately, there was no option for these unskilled and illiterate agricultural labourers other than to take up the work of sweepers.[183]

Of those Christians who stayed behind in the villages, some were employed by their new Muslim landowners as *athri* (who worked exclusively on the agriculture land) and *seyp* (who worked for a number of masters to do the lowest form of work, including cleaning the cattle yards/pens and the removal of night soil).[184] These village labourers were exploited by their employers because their wages were not paid in cash but in kind at harvest times. Thus, if the landowner had a low crop due to natural causes, he would pay less to his *seyps*. This economic exploitation is common in rural Pakistan and most of the victims were Christians because they could not raise their voice about this exploitation and injustice. The economic exploitation of Christians continues and they live under a constant feeling of socio-economic strangulation. This has been expressed by one of the bishops of the Church of Pakistan, Manuwar Rumalshah:

---

181. M. K. Kariakosi, *Conditions of Christians in East Punjab following Partition: Source Materials* (Delhi, 1982), 385-88.

182. John Rooney, *Into Deserts: A History of the Catholic Diocese of Lahore (1886–1986)*, Pakistan Christian History (Rawalpindi: CSC, 1986), 99.

183. Streefland notes that there was a migration of Christianized Punjabis to the towns before 1947 but that the numbers were negligible compared with what came after. Pieter H. Streefland, *The Christian Punjabi Sweepers* (Rawalpindi: CSC, 1974), 40.

184. O'Brien, *Construction of Pakistani Christian Identity*, 446.

> There are no opportunities for advancement. We are in a situation like the old European Jews and old South Asians, where the majority communities would not give them jobs. The few jobs that open up are offered first to relatives, then clan, then tribe, then to someone recommended to you, regardless of qualifications. Christians are last in line.[185]

According to a conservative estimate, 60 percent of Christians are dependent on church-provided employment in Pakistan. If this source of employment is not available, then it would be hard, if not impossible, for Christians to survive there.

On the other hand, it has a negative impact on the psychology of the Christians to be dependent on church-based jobs. There was a big blow to the Christian community in October 1972 when all private educational colleges and schools were nationalized under the policy of socialism by Zulfikar Ali Bhutto. This severely undermined the educational and economic development of the Christian community.

When Forman Christian College was denationalized in 2003, Dr Peter Armacost, a missionary of the Presbyterian Church of the USA, took over as principal. He had a series of meetings with various Christian leaders about the value of the college and how it could best serve the Christian community. The universal response had nothing to do with education but was only that it was a place where Christians could get jobs.[186]

Spies and Enemies of the State

Since the creation of Pakistan, Christians have made a significant contribution in the sectors of Education and Health and have also served in the armed forces of Pakistan and sacrificed their lives during wars. In the 1965 war against India, Flight Lieutenant Marvin Lesly fought bravely at the Karachi front and won fame as "a defender of Karachi." The services of Squadron Leaders Peter Christy and Cecil Chuhdhary have also been acknowledged.[187] Despite this, during the wars with India in 1965 and 1971, Christians

---

185. Charles Strohmer, "Taliban Neighbors: Christian Witness in Pakistan," *Christian Century* 126, no. 1 (2009): 11.

186. James A. Tebbe, email message to author, 8 July2013.

187. Azam Mairaj, "The Story of Christian Martyrs," *The Nation*, 6 September 2012, 24.

were falsely accused of spying for the Indian Army. Many Christian pastors were interrogated by the Pakistan army in the 1965 war and brutally tortured. Now Christians are labeled as "American *Jāsūs*," who are spying for Americans. In this regard Maulana Tahir Ashrafi, Chairman of the Pakistan Ulamā Council, admitted in a recent interview that the main perception among the masses in Pakistan is that "Christian citizens of Pakistan are not loyal to the country, they are loyal to either US or Europe."[188]

Christians in Pakistan today are often perceived in the same way as Christians under Persian rule were perceived – as enemies of the state who have no loyalty to the land to which they belonged. In AD 337, war broke out between two old rivals, Rome and Persia. The Christians living in Persia associated themselves with Rome on the grounds of common faith and declared Rome to be on God's side.[189] When the Persian emperor, Shapur II, heard this about the Christians, he got furious and issued a decree to the princes of his empire, saying, "They [Christians] live in our territory, but their sympathies are with Caesar, our enemy."[190]

Christians living in the Persian Empire in the fourth century showed their loyalty to the western Roman Christian Empire on the basis of a common faith and, as a result, Christians were justly perceived to be enemies of the state. Likewise, the Armenians in Turkey in 1915 were accused by the Ottoman Turks of being disloyal to the state on the grounds that many of them had dual nationality or worked in the embassies with foreign governments.

Although the situation for Christians in Pakistan today is not exactly the same as in earlier history, there are similarities. In some way, local Christians are responsible for this view, as sometimes Christians take the side of Americans and other Western countries in discussion with their Muslim colleagues, friends and neighbours about the actions and policies of America and the West regarding the Muslim world. It has also been observed that Christian youth sometimes favour Western teams in sports against Pakistan.

---

188. Mohammad Shehzad, "Interview: Allama Tahir Ashrafi on Blasphemy Laws," *Newsline*, April 2013, 47.

189. William G. Young, *Patriarch, Shah and Caliph* (Rawalpindi: CSC, 1974), 23.

190. Ibid., 24.

There may be two motivations behind this behaviour: one is a response to the discrimination that Christians face in every sector of life in Pakistan, including in national level sports; and the other factor is that their faith overrides their nationalism. (Pakistani Christians often naively presume that Western nations and sporting teams ARE Christians – but in practice they are generally not!)

The perception of Pakistani Christians as pro-Western is widespread. Global socio-political and cultural tensions, caused by such events as the Western-backed invasions of Afghanistan and Iraq and other international issues that may arise, do sometimes cause a negative backlash towards Christian communities, who tend to be seen as "anti-state," "belonging to the enemy," and "supporters of foreign interests." This gives Christians an increased sense of uncertainty and insecurity, and local Christian communities have to bear the brunt when tensions arise.

Allies of the US and West

It is a commonly held view among Muslims in Pakistan that Christianity is a Western religion and therefore Christians are associated with the West on religious grounds. When the US attacked Afghanistan and later Iraq, in retaliation for the 9/11 attacks on New York, it was perceived by Muslims in Pakistan that the Christian West had invaded their Muslim countries. Both wars were regarded as being between Christians and Muslims. Lieven writes, "The deep hostility to US even among the senior officers of the Pakistan army comes from anger at perceived US domination and subjugation of the Muslim world."[191]

The framing of the conflict along religious lines was reinforced by Osama bin Laden, who issued a *fatwā* (religious verdict) against America, known as the "World Islamic Front Statement," and signed by several militant Islamic leaders. It stated that "it was the duty of all Muslims to comply with God's order by killing Americans and their allies [because they are infidels]."[192] Many in Pakistan took this ruling seriously and retaliation against the US invasion resulted in terrorist attacks on Christians in Pakistan. On 17 March 2002, there was a terrorist attack on the Protestant International Church

---

191. Lieven, *Pakistan*, 187.
192. Hussain, *Frontline Pakistan*, 72.

in Islamabad, in which six people were killed and forty-two badly injured, including the Sri Lankan ambassador. Five months later, on 5 August 2002, Murree Christian School was targeted by the terrorists. Four days later, on 9 August 2002, a Christian hospital in Taxila was hit by the terrorists. As people were coming out of a church service in the Taxila Hospital, attackers threw hand grenades at the worshippers, killing five people and injuring twenty, most of them women.

The government of Pakistan did not condone these attacks. After sustained effort by the investigation agencies, some of the culprits were arrested. They include the mastermind behind these attacks, Saif-ur-Rehaman Saifi. The former president of Pakistan, Pervez Musharraf, states in his book: "Under interrogations he [Saifi] claimed that the motive behind the attacks was retaliation against the United States for its invasion of Afghanistan, and the treatment meted out to Muslims in Afghanistan."[193] It was also revealed by the terrorists that they were given instructions by their leadership to attack Christians in Pakistan.[194]

Pakistani Christians have felt strongly that the US invasion of Afghanistan and Iraq has put Pakistan's Christian community in a difficult situation. Catholic Archbishop Lawrence Suldana says that "the wars in Afghanistan and Iraq have increased discrimination against Christians significantly in this context."[195] Islamic Zealots seeking revenge for American bombings in Afghanistan massacred eighteen Christian worshippers in a Bhawalpur Church on 28 October 2001. Zahid Husain, a Pakistani scholar, writes that, "this barbaric action was apparently inspired by the rhetoric of war between 'Islam and Christianity.'"[196]

One village pastor shared his experience that when the Iraq war started. The chief men of the Muslim community came to him and insisted that he phone his "Christian brother President George Bush" to ask him to stop bombing their Muslim brothers and sisters in Iraq. The poor village pastor was confused and surprised to hear from the Muslim village chiefs, and

---

193. Pervez Musharraf, *In the Line of Fire: A Memoir* (New York: Free Press, 2006), 230.
194. Ibid., 231.
195. Theodore Gabriel, *Christian Citizens in an Islamic State: The Pakistan Experience* (Hampshire: Ashgate, 2007), 66.
196. Hussain, *Frontline Pakistan*, 47.

replied humbly that there was no way he could get access to the President of the Super Power; instead, they should ask the President and Prime Minister of Pakistan to contact him.[197]

To correct the misperception that Christians in Pakistan are inevitably allied with the West, Christian leaders in Pakistan have been continuously denying their association with the West. Nonetheless, in the wake of 9/11 and the ensuing "War on Terror," Christian minorities in Muslim countries have increasingly been viewed as "Allies of the West." In this regard Shah notes, "Terrorists have repeatedly [been] blaming these minorities [Christians] [for] supporting the United States and its European allies."[198] Likewise, Gabriel also notes that "the blasphemy law has become a convenient tool for expressing hostility against Christians, who are erroneously perceived to be the allies of the USA and West."[199]

Other factors, apart from the wars against Afghanistan and Iraq, have fuelled the misperception that the Christian West is in conflict with the Muslim world. The freedom of speech promoted in the West has resulted in several incidents that have been highly offensive to many Muslims. For example, the Danish Cartoons, Salman Rushdie's book, *The Satanic Verses*, Florida Pastor Terry Jones' call to burn the Qur'an, and a film about the prophet of Islam produced in the US and perceived to be blasphemous, have all been seen as acts committed by the Christian West against Muslims. This is due to the misconception that everything which comes out of the US and other Western countries is Christian. Unfortunately, Muslims in Pakistan associate these acts with local Christians on the grounds of common faith, with results that can be violent. For example, on 9 March 2013 in Lahore, two hundred houses of Christians were burned in the name of blasphemy. The Law Minister of Punjab, Rana Sanaullah, commenting on this incident, said "that incident of violence against the minorities are reactions to the blasphemous acts committed on US and European soil."[200]

---

197. BM/C 21 December 2012.

198. Sabir Shah, "Minorities Including Christians at Receiving End in Pakistan," *The News*, 15 March 2013, online.

199. Gabriel, *Pakistan Experience*, 66.

200. Mohammad Shehzad, "Murder by Law," *Newsline*, April 2013, 40.

Concluding Summary

Ahmadis have a bitter experience as a minority group in Pakistan, and the persecution of the Ahmadis is solely religiously based. They have been facing severe hostility from orthodox Sunni Muslims who consider them not only theologically different but also *kāfir* who are deserving of death. The Ahmadiyya community migrated to Pakistan in anticipation of a better life in a new Muslim country, because they identify themselves as Muslims. However, orthodox Muslims did not accept them as Muslims and consequently succeeded in excommunicating the Ahmadis from Islam in Pakistan in 1974. Anti-Ahmadi forces continue to work towards completely eradicating Ahmadis from Pakistan. It is evident that the more religious or Islamic Pakistan has become, the more sectarian it has become.

Like Ahmadis, Christians are also a minority group facing persecution. However, the discrimination against Christians is based on a number of factors, not just on their religious beliefs. These include the Christians' social backgrounds, as well as their perceived association with the West. Ahmadis and Christians anticipated a better future in a Muslim state than in a Hindu state, and so gave preference to Pakistan over India. However, their hopes were disappointed and the reality proved completely the opposite.

CHAPTER 5

The Experience of Christians and Ahmadis under Pakistan's Blasphemy Laws

Introduction

In the previous chapter, we looked at the overall situation of Christians and Ahmadis living as minorities in the context of Pakistan. We now move from a general to a specific analysis, therefore this chapter will focus on the experience of both communities under Pakistan's blasphemy laws.

When it comes to the application of the blasphemy laws in Pakistan, human rights activists repeatedly point out that these laws are discriminatory and violate human rights guaranteed by the constitution of Pakistan as well as international treaties (as seen in chapter 3). However, the supporters of the blasphemy laws vehemently disagree with this view. They argue that Pakistan's blasphemy laws:

1. are not discriminatory and apply equally to all citizens of Pakistan. In support of this, they offer the evidence that the majority of those accused of blasphemy belong to the Muslim community.
2. actually protect those accused of blasphemy by preventing people taking the law into their own hands. They argue that, without the blasphemy laws, anarchy would prevail.
3. are not being misused. As evidence for this, they point out that no one has been executed yet under these laws.

4. secure the minorities. They are argue that, if blasphemy laws are amended, minorities will be unsafe.
5. operate in the context of Pakistan's judicial system, a free media, and a civil society, all of which are strong enough to prevent the misuse of these laws.

The main objective of this chapter is to examine these arguments in the light of the experience of minorities living under the blasphemy laws. Undoubtedly, the blasphemy laws have affected, to a greater or lesser extent, all the minority groups in Pakistan. However, this thesis will focus on Christians and Ahmadis because these two minorities are most affected by the blasphemy laws in Pakistan.

Argument # 1

Pakistan's blasphemy laws are not discriminatory and apply equally to all citizens of Pakistan. The supporters of Pakistan's blasphemy laws argue that more Muslims than non-Muslims have been tried under these laws. In this regard, the adviser to the Prime Minister on Human Rights, at Pakistan's Universal Periodic Review hearing in UN in 2012, stated that "there was a misunderstanding that this law was used to target only minorities. The majority of cases registered under this section had been against Muslims."[1]

While this is true, it ignores two significant facts: first, that there are proportionally far more Muslims (96.28%) in Pakistan than minorities (3.72%), so it would be reasonable to expect more Muslims to be charged; and, second, that the blasphemy laws discriminate against every religion other than Islam. So far as the design of Pakistan's blasphemy laws is concerned, the legal analysis of the blasphemy laws in chapter 3 demonstrated that the underlying intention and purpose of the Zia-framed clauses of the blasphemy laws, enacted in the 1980s, was to protect only one religion – Islam. This intention is evident from the fact that the clauses (295-B, C; 298-A, B, C) pertain only to offences against Islam. Those of other religions have no recourse if their religion is insulted. Moreover, Clauses 298-B and C deal

---

1. Report of Working Group on the Universal Periodic Review, Human Rights Council, 22nd Session, UN Doc. A/HRC/22/12 (26 December 2012), 10; Najam U Din, "State of Human Rights in 2012" (Lahore: HRCP, 2012), 116.

specifically with the Ahmadis: in Clause 298-B, they were restricted from using descriptions and titles which are reserved for certain holy personages and places of Islam; and Clause 298-C forbids anyone from the Ahmadi sect calling himself a Muslim or preaching or propagating his faith as Islam. This bias in the design of the Zia-framed clauses of the PPC undermines the argument that "they are equally applied to all citizens of Pakistan therefore are not discriminatory."

On further examination, this assertion does not support the argument that the law applies equally to all in Pakistan. According to the *Dawn* newspaper report, 1,274 people were charged under the blasphemy laws between 1986 and 2010.[2] Most newspapers and human rights reports cite the data collected by the National Commission for Justice and Peace (NCJP) in Pakistan. According to its annual report for 2012–2013[3], the number of blasphemy cases against different religious communities in Pakistan was as follows:

Chart 5.1. Blasphemy Cases in Pakistan 1986–2012

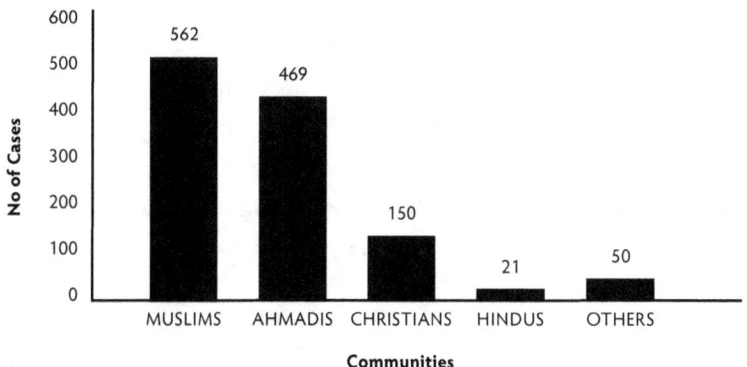

The data in chart 5.1 shows that the majority of those accused under the blasphemy laws belong to the Muslim community. It is important to note here that the data about Muslims accused of blasphemy does not distinguish between Shia and Sunni. The Human Rights Commission of Pakistan (HRCP) has observed that the Shia community is the most persecuted in

---

2. Staff Reporter, "Timeline."
3. Jacob, "Human Rights Monitor 2012–13," 203–204.

Pakistan:[4] nevertheless, it does not distinguish between Sunni and Shia in its report about the blasphemy cases.[5] When we make the distinction between Sunni and Shia communities in the blasphemy cases it becomes evident that nearly all those accused of blasphemy are minorities (whether Ahmadis, Christians or Shia Muslims).

Although the Shia community is not the focus of this thesis, nevertheless it is important to mention them for the purposes of examining this claim that more Muslims than minorities have been charged under the blasphemy laws. The tension between Shia and Sunni is not new in Pakistan. The latest poll by the US-based Pew Research Centre reports that 50 percent of Sunni Muslims in Pakistan believe that Shias are non-Muslims.[6] (Thus comes from what the Shia leaders had foreseen at the time of the formation of Pakistan: that Shia Muslims would face discrimination in a majority Sunni Muslim state.) Some Sunni militant groups like *Sipāh-ē-Sihāba* Pakistan (SSP) and *Lashkar-ē-Jhangvi* (LeJ) have demanded that the government declare the Shia community non-Muslim, just like the Ahmadis.[7] In this regard SSP developed and promoted this slogan: *"Agar Pakistan men musalmān bun kar rahnā hai, tau Shi'a ko kāfir kahnā hai"* (if you want to live in Pakistan as Muslim, then Shia must be declared infidels).[8]

The supporters of this view have vigorously pursued their agenda by violent means to eliminate the Shias from Pakistan, as they consider them heretics as well as infidels and worthy to be killed. This is evident from the fact that "the anti-Shia campaign is now nationwide and affecting every city and province . . ."[9] As a result, over 400 people of the Shia community have

---

4. HRCP states that 758 members of the Shia community have been killed in Pakistan from 2008 till 2012. Din, "State of Human Rights in 2012," 63.

5. See ibid., 50–53.

6. Pew Research Center, "The World's Muslims: Unity and Diversity – Boundaries of Religious Identity," 9 August 2012, online. This is also confirmed by Salahuddin, a Pakistani journalist, that "a large number of Sunni Muslims do not accept Shias as Muslims." Ghazi Salahuddin, "Kingdom of Fear," *Newsline*, November 2012, 37.

7. P. R. Kumaraswamy and Ian Copland, *South Asia, the Spectre of Terrorism* (New Delhi: Routledge, 2009), 134.

8. Seyyed V. R. Nasr, "The Rise of Sunni Militancy in Pakistan," *MAS* 34, no. 1 (2000): 163.

9. Ahmed Rashid, "Pakistan Is in the Grip of Chaos," *BBC News*, 25 January 2014, online.

been killed in 2013 alone.[10] The hatred against Shia is also evident from this report that cardboard shooting targets with the inscription "*Shi'a kāfir*" were recovered from one of the training camps of anti-Shia militant groups in Khuzdar, Baluchistan.[11]

Thus Shia Muslims should properly be considered a minority group in Pakistan; and, as part of the anti-Shia campaign in Pakistan, the blasphemy laws have become an easy way for the Sunni majority to entangle the Shia minority in blasphemy cases. Most blasphemy cases are brought against Shias during the month of *Muḥarram,* because that is the time when Shias, mostly, show their antagonism to the first three caliphs of Islam, as well as to the Prophet Muhammad's youngest wife, Aisha, all of whom are very revered personalities according to Sunni beliefs.[12] There have been multiple examples of this. According to newspaper reports on 17 January 2012, five men from the Shia community were arrested for allegedly using offensive language against the *sahaba* (the companions of the Prophet of Islam). They were accused of writing derogatory remarks against the *sahaba* on the walls of a train.[13] Another man, named Iftkhar Ali, a Shia Muslim, was accused of blasphemy for allegedly using foul language against the first three caliphs of Islam.[14] A FIR (First Information Report) was lodged against 150 unidentified and 72 nominated members of the Shia community on 25 November 2012 for committing blasphemy during the Shia ritualistic procession of mourners.[15]

The NCJP, in its annual report for 2012–2013, highlighted the discrimination against Shia by distinguishing between those accused of blasphemy from Sunni and Shia communities.[16]

---

10. Staff Reporter, "World Report 2014: Pakistan" (Human Rights Watch, 2014), online.

11. Saher Baloch, "Silence of the Grave," *Dawn,* 16 February 2014, 16.

12. SSP introduced the *Nāmūs-ē-Sihābah* (Honor of the Companions of the Prophet) bill in the National Assembly, which sought to add the name of the four Rightly-Guided caliphs to the list of those covered by the Blasphemy Law. Nasr, " Rise of Sunni Militancy," 161.

13. The Express Tribune, 18 January 2012.

14. *Ahmadiyya Times,* 5 April 2012.

15. Owais Jafri, "Secterian Violence: Procession Mourners Accused of Blasphemy," *The Express Tribune,* 27 November 2012, online.

16. Jacob, "Human Rights Monitor 2012–13," 146.

Chart 5.2. Blasphemy Cases in Pakistan in 2012, with Shia/Sunni Distinction

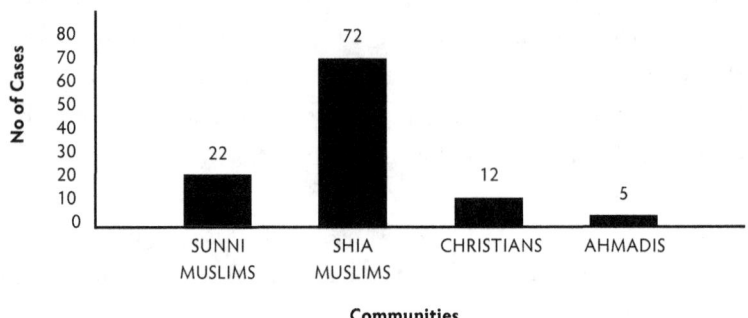

Chart 5.2 shows that there were many more Shia accused than Sunnis. During my personal research in November–December 2013 in Pakistan, I was able to talk to the director of the NCJP, who confirmed the fact that about 70 percent of Muslims accused of blasphemy belong to the Shia community.[17]

If we analyze blasphemy cases according to the proportion of each community's population in Pakistan, then we get a surprisingly contrary picture. According to government statistics, the percentage of Muslims is 96.28 percent of the total population of Pakistan, Hindus are 1.60 percent, Christians are 1.59 percent and Ahmadis are 0.25 percent. The total population is over 182 million. Pew Research estimates that, of the Muslims in Pakistan, 87 percent are Sunni and 13 percent are Shia.[18] Some other sources confirm this figure.[19] It can therefore be argued that the number of Sunni Muslims accused in blasphemy cases (22 in 2012) is insignificant, given that they account for about 84 percent of the population (87% of 96.28%). In contrast, Ahmadis, who account for 0.25 percent of the total population, and

---

17. SS/C 28 November 2013.
18. Pew Research Center, "The Future of the Global Muslim Population: Sunni and Shia Muslims," 27 Jan 2011, online.
19. Martin Walker, "The Revenge of the Shia," *The Wilson Quarterly* 30, no. 4 (2006): 17; Paul Liben and Jessica Sarra, "USCIRF: Annual Report for 2013" (Washington: USCIRF, 2013), 119.

Christians, who account for 1.59 percent, were the accused in half of all blasphemy cases between 1986 and 2012 (see chart 5.1).[20]

The following chart compares a percentage of blasphemy cases with the proportion of population of each community in Pakistan.

Chart 5.3. Percentage of Blasphemy Cases in Pakistan 1986–2012, with Proportion of Population

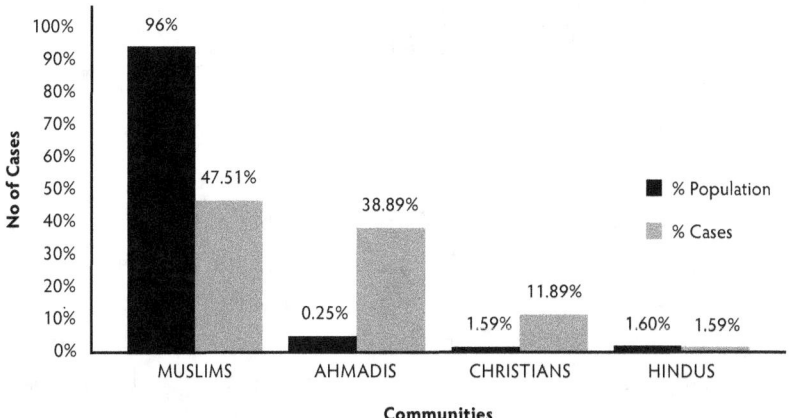

The above chart shows that, in comparison to population, Ahmadis are by far the most targeted group, followed by Christians, while Muslims are at the bottom of the ladder. This demonstrates that Muslims, especially Sunni, are least likely to be accused of blasphemy when compared to the minorities in Pakistan. This analyis leads us to conclude that it is not true, as argued by supporters of the blasphemy laws, that these laws are applied equally to all citizens of Pakistan.

Furthermore, it is worth noting the distribution of blasphemy cases across the four provinces of Pakistan (see chart 5.4 below).

---

20. Nina Shea and Paul Marshall, "Blasphemy in Pakistan," *The Weekly Standard*, 24–31 January 2011, online.

Chart 5.4. Blasphemy Cases in Pakistan 1986–2012, by Province

Province	% of Cases
PUNJAB	74.07%
SINDH	22.79%
K.P.K.	2.74%
BALUCHISTAN	0.40%

Source: NCJP

According to chart 5.4 above, 74 percent of blasphemy cases occurred in the province of Punjab in Pakistan. Further classification of these cases reveal that 80 percent of cases in Punjab were from eight districts in central Punjab: Lahore, Faisalabad, Toba Tek Singh, Gujranwala, Sheikhupura, Sialkot, Gujrat and Kasur.[21] The majority of Christians and Ahmadis in Pakistan live in these eight districts of central Punjab.[22]

Several other reasons for the high ratio of blasphemy cases in the central Punjab are offered by analysts.[23] However, one of the main reasons for the high ratio of blasphemy cases in these districts is the larger presence of Ahmadi and Christian communities, who are disproportionally accused of blasphemy. In contrast, there are far fewer blasphemy cases in K.P.K and Baluchistan provinces, which are far more religiously conservative. It can be argued that one of the reasons for less blasphemy cases in these provinces is the smaller presence of Christians and Ahmadis.

In summary, our analysis has shown that the blasphemy laws are largely used against minorities, especially Ahmadis and Christians, and that most

---

21. Marco Tosatti, "Blasphemy: A Law of Blood," *Vatican Insider*, 16 June 2011, online.

22. Mansoor Raza, "Blasphemy Laws: A Fact Sheet," *Dawn*, 15 April 2010, online.

23. Asif Aqeel, a Pakistani Christian researcher, held this view that Punjab has been more influenced by the process of "merging of Brahmanic Hinduism's ritual impurity with Islamic ceremonial uncleanness" with regard to untouchables who mostly converted to Christianity in Punjab. As evidence, he points out that several blasphemy cases against Christians have been rooted in such caste-based discrimination. Asif Aqeel, "Pakistan's Christian Sanitation Workers Swept into Societal Gutter," *WorldWatch Monitor*, 7 July 2011, online.

of the Muslims accused of blasphemy are Shias, who can also be considered a minority group in Pakistan. We conclude by arguing that the blasphemy laws are not equally applied to all citizens in Pakistan and that they are, in fact, discriminatory and applied in violation of human rights.

Argument # 2

We now turn to examine and respond to a second argument for Pakistan's blasphemy laws; that is, the argument that these laws actually protect those accused of blasphemy by preventing people taking the law into their own hands. It is argued that, without the blasphemy laws, anarchy would prevail.

In support of this view, Rafiq Tarar, the former president of Pakistan, stated, "If this law is not there the doors to courts will be closed on the culprits and the petitioners provoked by them, and then everyone will take the law in his own hands and exact revenge from the criminals. As a result anarchy will prevail in the country."[24] Likewise, Imran Khan, the leader of Pakistan Tehreek-e-Insaf (PTI), argued that in the absence of this law "people would be lynched and there would be anarchy. The stern law, therefore,

Chart 5.5. Blasphemy Cases in the Eras before and after the Establishment of Pakistan's Blasphemy Laws

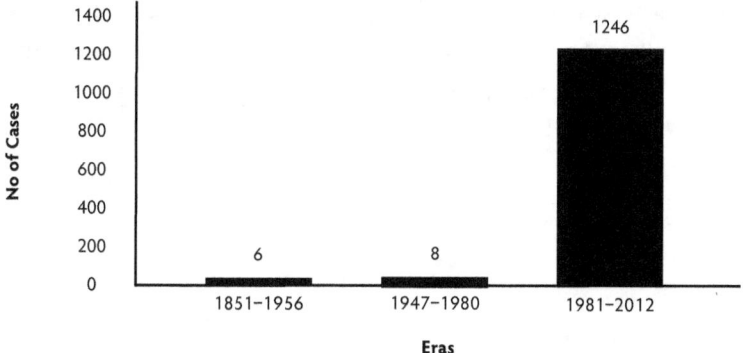

---

24. Qureshi, *Nāmūs-ē-Rasūl*, 17.

also helps those accused of blasphemy."[25] Another prominent advocate of this view, Mian Nazir Akhtar, former Chief Justice of Lahore High Court, claimed that "if blasphemy laws were abolished, Muslims would take revenge themselves by following in Ghazi Ilam Din Shaheed's footsteps."[26]

In order to assess this argument, we will examine the data concerning blasphemy cases in the eras before and after the Zia-framed clauses of blasphemy laws.

As can be seen from chart 5.5, there were very few cases of blasphemy during the period of British rule (1851–1946): in fact, only six cases in nearly one hundred years. In our analysis here, we will focus on the period starting from the creation of Pakistan in 1947. The chart shows that there were only eight blasphemy cases in Pakistan in the thirty-three years between 1947 and 1980; that is, before the harsher clauses of the blasphemy law were enacted. In contrast, 1,246 blasphemy cases have been registered in the thirty-one years since these harsher clauses were introduced (1981–2012).

This comparison explicitly reveals that blasphemy was not an issue in Pakistan before these laws were enacted. However, after the promulgation of the new laws, blasphemy has become a very significant phenomenon in Pakistan. Blasphemy cases have increased significantly. There has been an average of thirty-nine cases per year since the harsher clauses of the blasphemy law have been framed (especially Clause 295-C in 1986).

Supporters of the blasphemy laws argue that these harsher clauses were added in order to discourage blasphemy.[27] However, as the chart below shows, the number of blasphemy cases has increased significantly since the introduction of these harsher laws.

---

25. Aakar Patel, "Pakistan's Blasphemy Law," *The Express Tribune*, 26 August 2012, online.

26. "Holy Prophet (pbuh) Awarded Death Sentence for Blasphemy," *Pakistan Today*, 13 December 2010, online.

27. Qureshi, *Messenger of God*, 69–70.

Chart 5.6. Blasphemy Cases 1981–2012, by Decade (last column covers only two years)

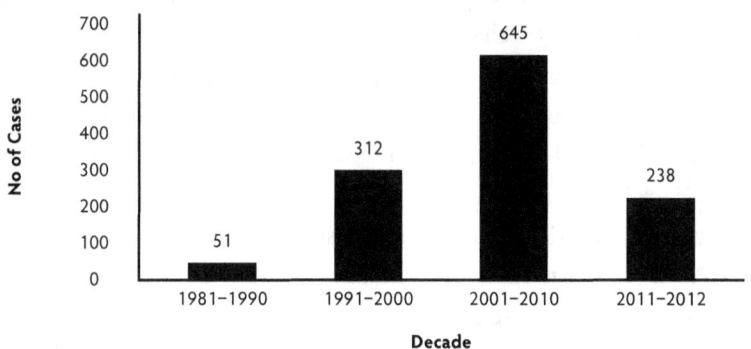

Source: NCJP

Chart 5.6 shows that blasphemy cases have increased significantly in the decades since 1981, from 51 cases in the 1980s to 312 in the 1990s and 645 in the years from 2001–2010.

It is important to note here that 1991 was the year when the death sentence for blasphemy was made mandatory in Clause 295-C by the Federal Shariat Court (FSC) and furthermore that the penalty for "outraging the religious feelings of any class" was extended from two years to ten years in Clause 295-A, which was passed by the Parliament.

Chart 5.7. Extrajudicial Killings after Blasphemy Allegations Cases 1991–2012

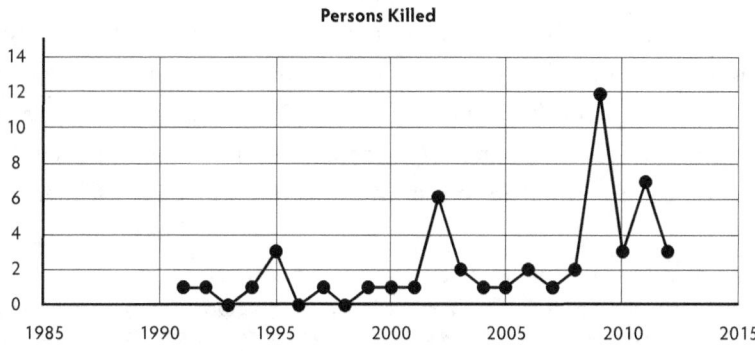

In marked contrast to the claims of the supporters of the blasphemy laws, it seems that (as seen in chart 5.6) one of the fundamental causes of the increased number of blasphemy cases and the extrajudicial killings after blasphemy allegations (as chart 5.7 shows) in the decades from 1991 to 2012 has been the harsher penalties for blasphemy added in 1991. This increasing number of blasphemy cases indicates clearly that the laws have become an easy tool in the hands of people, who use them prolifically.

The special report of Freedom House, an independent human rights monitoring organization, stated that "Pakistan's blasphemy laws are routinely used to exact revenge, apply pressure in business or land disputes, and for other matters entirely unrelated to blasphemy."[28] The victims of the misuse of blasphemy laws are inevitably Pakistan's minorities, especially Ahmadis and Christians, who are more vulnerable to charges leveled against them largely for ulterior motives.

The above is evident from the fact that there were only eight blasphemy cases between 1947 and 1980 in Pakistan.[29] All these cases were ones in which Muslims were accused of blasphemy, either by other Muslims or by non-Muslims. Not a single case of blasphemy – committing an act of profanity against the Prophet of Islam or defiling the Qur'an – was reported against non-Muslims.[30] This is evidence that there was no trend among non-Muslims to commit blasphemy against the religion of the majority population in Pakistan. However, in contrast, it is apparent from chart 5.1 above that 451 Ahmadis and 193 Christians have been charged with blasphemy since the promulgation of the harsher clauses of the blasphemy law.

The quoted data raises a serious question: why have so many non-Muslims started committing blasphemy after the introduction of the laws with stringent penalties, when there were no records of incidents of blasphemy by non-Muslims in Pakistan before these laws? There is a compelling argument that the apparent change in the behaviour of non-Muslims is indeed not a behavioural problem of non-Muslims but rather a consequence of

---

28. Prud'homme, "Policing Belief," 74.

29. *Khawaja Nazir Ahmad v. State; The Punjab Religious Book Society v. State; Okil Ali and Others v. Behari Lal Paul; Muhammad Khalil v. State; Abdul Karim v. State; Fazal-I-Raziq v. Riaz Ahmad; Shafiqur Rehman v. State; Qaiser Raza v. State.*

30. Mohammad Nafees, "Blasphemy Laws in Pakistan: A Historical Overview" (Islamabad: CRSS, 2013), 23.

the new laws. It has been pointed out by human rights groups, academics, civil society and journalists that the blasphemy laws are often misused, as the "case studies reveal that ulterior motives [exist] behind the framing of blasphemy cases against innocent individuals."[31]

The misuse of the laws is evident from the fact that, in the handful of appeals against the lower courts' decisions which have been heard by the superior courts in Pakistan, all the decisions of the lower courts against Christians were overturned on the grounds that the accusations had been fabricated. For example, one of the most highly publicized blasphemy cases in Pakistan was that of *Salamat Masih vs. State*. The charge against Salamat and two co-accused, Rehmat and Manzoor Masih, was that they wrote offensive words on the wall of a mosque. During the trial at session court, Manzoor was assassinated by the militants. Salamat and his uncle Rehmat Masih were sentenced to death on 9 February 1995 by the Sessions Court in Lahore, but were acquitted by the Lahore High Court (LHC) on appeal on 23 February 1995. In this case, eight amicus curiae were requested by the court to render their assistance to the court. Seven of them argued that the case was unsupported by evidence and had resulted in baseless convictions.[32] The LHC acquitted the appellants, declaring that the prosecution's witnesses "utterly failed to prove the case of the prosecution."[33] The LHC also criticized the trial court along with the investigating agency and the public prosecutor who "failed to perform their duties in a case based on serious charges."[34]

In another case, Rimsha Masih, a mentally challenged teenage girl, was accused of burning pages of the Qur'an in August 2012. Justice Rehman of Islamabad High Court remarked that "on one hand the complainant in the FIR said that the accused carried a polythene bag containing verses of the Holy Qur'an but failed to explain how he had suspected it when the verses were not visible from the bag."[35] It was later disclosed by two of the assistants that their senior cleric, Khalid Jadoon Chishti, the imam of a local

---

31. Farieha Aziz, "In the Name of Religion," *Newsline*, February 2011, 35.
32. *Salamat Masih v. State*, 818–823.
33. Ibid., 826.
34. Ibid.
35. Web Desk, "Threatened in Pakistan, Rimsha Masih Escapes to Canada," *The Express Tribune*, 30 June 2013, online.

mosque, had added pages from the Holy Qur'an to concoct evidence against Rimsha, a resident of a slum in Islamabad. The purpose of this conspiracy was to force the Christians to flee from the neighbourhood as cleric Chishti "allegedly issued a decree on his mosque's loudspeaker to burn Christians of the *Mehrabadi* village alive."[36]

Numerous other examples can be cited to show that people misuse this law for ulterior motives. These examples show that, instead of protecting people, as supporters of the blasphemy laws claim, the laws provide an easy way for malicious people to settle personal scores. Iqbal Haider, the federal law minister, who conducted a survey in 1994 of all the blasphemy cases in Pakistan, concluded that "95% of the cases were based on personal enmity, sectarian prejudice, religious dislike, and sometimes even because of marriage and property disputes."[37]

Supporters of the harsh blasphemy laws argue further that the absence of blasphemy laws would result in people taking the law into their hands. However, it is notable that no one accused of blasphemy was killed between 1947 and 1980. In contrast, as the following chart 5.8 shows, fifty-one people accused of blasphemy have been killed extrajudicially during the period 1990–2012.

Chart 5.8. Extrajudicial Killings of Those Alleged to Have Committed Blasphemy 1990–2012

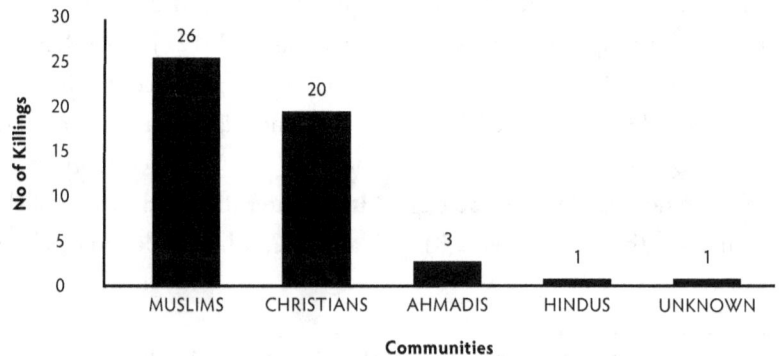

Sources: NCJP

---

36. Ibid.
37. Aziz, "Interview: Iqbal Haider," 37.

The extrajudicial killings started in 1991: that is, the year when the Federal Shariʿat Court made the death penalty mandatory for the offence of blasphemy under Clause 295-C.[38] Subsequently, the first person to be murdered extrajudicially for the alleged crime of blasphemy, Ahmer Naimat, a Christian school teacher, was killed in 1991. Since then fifty-one persons accused of blasphemy have been killed extrajudicially. Twenty of those have been Christians. Some may argue that the number of Muslims killed has been much higher, but if this number is seen in the light of the proportion of the population of the communities, then Christians, who are 1.59 percent of the total population, can be seen to have suffered disproportionally from extrajudicial killings. Some of them were killed soon after their acquittal from the court, an act that was criminal as well as contemptuous to the court.

This leads us to argue that the mandatory death penalty for the offence of blasphemy in Clause 295-C seems to have provided instigators with a legal as well as a religious ground for taking the law into their hands. Some members of the judiciary have even expressed support for extrajudicial killings. For example, Mian Nazir Akhtar, former justice of Lahore High Court, remarked that "no one had authority to pardon blasphemy and anyone accused of blasphemy should be killed on the spot as a religious obligation."[39] Maulana Yousef Qureshi, the senior clergyman of a major mosque in the northwestern city of Peshawar, publically announced that "anyone who kills Asia [a Christian woman] will be given 500,000 rupees in reward from Masjid Mohabat Khan."[40] Likewise, Rehman Malik, former Interior Minister, said that "he would shoot any blasphemer himself."[41]

It is statements like this that provoke those who undertake extrajudicial killings. In July 2010, two Christian brothers accused of blasphemy were shot and killed as they were leaving a hearing at a Faisalabad court house. They had been accused of writing a pamphlet that criticized the prophet of Islam. In the first quarter of 2011, two high-profile people accused of

---

38. *Muhammad Ismail Qureshi v. Pakistan*, 35.

39. Cited in Nafees, "Blasphemy Laws in Pakistan," 40.

40. Rob Crilly, "Pakistani Cleric Puts Bounty on Christian Woman's Head," *The Telegraph*, 3 December 2010, online.

41. Carlotta Gall, "Assassination Deepens Divide in Pakistan," *The New York Times*, 6 January 2011, A4.

blasphemy were murdered in the capital city of Pakistan in daylight. First, the Muslim governor of Punjab, Salman Taseer, was gunned down by one of his security guards, Mumtaz Qadri, on 2 January. Soon after, on 3 March, a Christian federal minister, Shahbaz Bhatti, was killed for opposing Pakistan's blasphemy laws.

These events demonstrate that Pakistan's blasphemy laws, instead of protecting the accused, are provoking people to take the law into their own hands. This assertion is strengthened by Mehreen Malik, a Pakistani researcher, who stated that the "very existence of laws regarding blasphemy promotes antagonism towards minorities and gives Muslim fanatics a warrant to take the law into their hands."[42] Likewise, Akbar says that blasphemy laws "provide the murderers a license to kill people and easily get away with such heinous crimes in the name of religion."[43] This is evident from these episodes that Mumtaz Qadri, assassin of Governor Taseer, was showered with rose petals and lauded by calling him a "soldier of Islam" by the lawyer community in the court of the capital city of Pakistan.[44] Farooq Ahmad, the 20-year-old convicted murderer of Naimat Ahmer (a Christian school teacher), was garlanded at the police station in Faisalabad by his supporters and glorified with the claim that he had won "heavens" by killing a *kafir* (infidel) for blasphemy.[45]

Our analysis has shown that, instead of protecting people, blasphemy laws have actually become a tool in the hands of those who wish to misuse them for ulterior motives. In this regard, minorities, especially Ahmadis and Christians, are the most vulnerable. We conclude by arguing that the blasphemy laws fail to fulfill their underlying objective, which, according to their advocates, is to prevent people from taking the law into their hands. Instead, they have had the opposite effect, resulting in tragic extrajudicial killings of those accused of blasphemy.

---

42. Mehreen Z. Malik, "The Gojra Murders and the Blasphemy Law," *Pakistaniaat: JPS* 1, no. 2 (2009): 121.

43. Akbar, "Who Benefits."

44. Zahid Hussain, "The Ideological Divide," *Newsline*, February 2011, 18.

45. Naeem Shakir, "Fundamentalism, Enforcement of Shariah and the Law on Blasphemy in Pakistan," *Al-Mushir* 34, no. 4 (1992): 116.

Argument # 3

The third argument put forward by the advocates of blasphemy laws in support of their assertion that blasphemy laws are not being misused. As evidence for this, they point out that no one has yet been executed under these laws.

In this regard, Babar Awan, the former minister for law in Pakistan, rejected the view that the blasphemy law has been used to target many, stating:

> Pakistan being a very responsible state was capable of creating such lego-constitutional mechanism of trials, appeals and constitutional and other procedural remedies that even since 1986 till date, reportedly, no execution has taken place under this law so far.[46]

The cursory reading of this assertion – that "no execution has taken place under this law" – gives the impression that nobody has yet been sentenced to death under the blasphemy laws. That is not true, as in fact, many people have been convicted of blasphemy and sentenced to death by the lower courts. However, the punishment given by the lower courts has never been implemented yet in Pakistan, because none of their convictions have been ratified by the Supreme Court of Pakistan (SCP). On the basis of this fact, the advocates of the blasphemy laws argue that the blasphemy laws are not being misused.

It is true that no one has as yet been executed by the state under Clause 295-C (there has been a defacto moratorium on civil hangings in Pakistan since 2008).[47] Nevertheless, chart 5.8 above explicitly shows that there have been fifty-one extra-judicial killings of people accused of blasphemy, half of whom belong to minority groups (20 Christians, 3 Ahmadis, 1 Hindu). This shows that the accuser often becomes prosecutor, judge and executioner. At times the blasphemy laws, especially Clause 295-C, have had the effect of providing a legal as well as a religious ground for accusers to play the role

---

46. Ansar Abbasi, "Awan Advises against Amending Blasphemy Law " *The News*, 8 February 2011, online.

47. The Government of Pakistan lifted a moratorium on capital punishment in December 2014 after a deadly attack on a school in Peshawar in which more than 150 school pupils and teachers were killed by the Taliban.

of judge as well as executioner. It would be fair to say, however, that this is not the stated intent of the law, and that extrajudicial killings are just as illegal in Pakistan as they are in other countries! Such events are therefore clear evidence of the misuse of blasphemy laws, creating a pressing need for these laws to be repealed or drastically changed.

In contrast, Mairaj-ul-Huda Siddiqui, *Amir Jamait-ē-Islami* Karachi, argued, "People contend that false cases are registered under the Blasphemy Law, but does the same not happen under other laws? Are cases of theft not falsely registered and who knows what else? Does that mean that all the laws in Pakistan should be abolished?"[48] Although Siddiqui is correct in pointing out the flaws in Pakistan's judicial system where almost all laws can be abused to a greater or lesser extent, he fails to identify the severity of the consequences of the misuse of blasphemy laws, compared to other laws in Pakistan. For example, if someone is falsely accused of theft or murder, the accused person will be directly affected and his family indirectly impacted. By contrast, when a person is accused of blasphemy, it is not only the accused and his family who suffer, but the whole community of which he or she is a part – even before the court decides whether the accusations are false or true.

This is evident from incidents in which one individual was accused of blasphemy, but the whole community was punished. For example, in February 1997, the twin Christian villages of Shantinagar in Multan Division were looted and burned by 20,000 Muslim citizens with the support of 500 policemen. The *Friday Times* noted, "The police first evacuated the Christian population of 15,000, then helped the raiders use battle-field explosives to blow up their houses and property."[49] On 12 November 2005, the Christian community of Sangla Hill in Faisalabad District in Punjab experienced a day of violence and vandalism. The editorial in the *Daily Dawn* of 15 November 2005 stated:

> The burning down of three churches, a missionary-run school, two hostels and several houses belonging to the Christian community by an enraged mob of some 3,000 people . . . Following

---

48. Farieha Aziz, "Interview: Mairaj-ul-Huda Siddiqui of the JI," *Newsline*, December 2010, 28.

49. Khaled Ahmed, "A Decaying State Kills Its Minorities," *The Friday Times*, 24 August–6 September 2012, online.

allegations of blasphemy leveled against one Yousaf Masih by his Muslim gambling partners who accused him of also torching the Holy Qur'an, calls were given from mosque loudspeakers to punish the local Christians.[50]

In another significant incident occurring subsequent to an accusation of blasphemy, on 1 August 2009, eight Christians were burned alive and about 100 homes were looted and burned with chemical explosive in Gojra in the district of Faisalabad (we will see the details of the Gojra incident in the next section). Again, on 9 March 2013, more than two hundred houses belonging to Christians were burned down at Joseph colony in Lahore, the capital city of Punjab, after Sawan Masih, a Christian sanitary worker, was accused of blasphemy against the Holy Prophet. Note, however, that the Supreme Court of Pakistan denied any link between the accusation of blasphemy and the subsequent arson. Chief Justice of SCP, Iftikhar Chaudhry, remarked during the hearing that "the arson attack did not seem to have stemmed from a blasphemy case. A land occupation issue might have been the trigger."[51] We have just mentioned a few significant incidents here, but several other incidents of this nature have taken place in Pakistan.

There were very few incidents of such a nature that have happened in the history of Pakistan before the establishment of the new blasphemy laws. By contrast, since the new laws have been introduced, they have been misused on a large scale, as the above-mentioned incidents clearly demonstrate. Although it is true that no one has been executed yet, the laws have had other significant negative effects, which cannot be discounted.

The lack of judicial executions does not support the argument that the laws are not being abused. Evidence that the laws are being abused can be seen in the fact that, in blasphemy cases, "the lower courts issue convictions based on minimal evidence, often in the context of intimidation and threats by religious extremists."[52] I. A. Rehman, Director of the Human Rights Commission of Pakistan, confirms that "the extremists do resort to violence and intimidation to coerce the police, politicians, courts and even

---

50. Editor, "Dawn – Editorial," *Dawn*, 15 November 2005, online.
51. Mudassir Raja, "Joseph Colony Case," *The Express Tribune*, 12 March 2013, online.
52. Prud'homme, "Policing Belief," 82.

the victims."⁵³ According to Human Rights Watch and the US Commission on International Religious Freedeom (USCIRF), at least sixteen people are currently on death row for blasphemy, while another twenty are serving a life sentence in Pakistan.⁵⁴ (All were convicted by the lower courts).

Furthermore, the process of appeals is complex and lengthy, especially in blasphemy cases. In Pakistan, it takes years for appeals to be heard by the superior courts. In this regard, the *Pakistan Today* editorial on Friday 20 September 2013 noted: "Once a person is arrested it takes years, sometimes eight to ten years, to prove his or her innocence in courts."⁵⁵ Consequently, this has led to those accused of blasphemy remaining in jail, in miserable conditions, for many years, bearing the unjustified punishment for a crime which they have not committed. We have noted above the former law minister's finding that 95 percent of blasphemy cases are based on fabrications for ulterior motives. This is contrary to the fundamental principle in criminal law attributed to William Blackstone: "It is better that ten guilty persons escape than that one innocent person suffers."⁵⁶ This principle is also found in Islamic law because of the saying of the Prophet of Islam that the "mistake of *qazi* (judge) in releasing a criminal is better than his mistake in punishing an innocent."⁵⁷

Thus it is contrary to the norms of English as well as Islamic law that a large majority of innocent people, as demonstrated above, suffer under blasphemy laws. Evidence of their innocence is found in the fact that, to date, all convictions in blasphemy cases have been overturned by the superior courts. This truth of baseless convictions has been acknowledged even by Ismail Qureshi, the main architect behind the move of the blasphemy laws in Pakistan. He acknowledged that "nobody has ever been sentenced to death by Federal Shari'at Court or Supreme Court on the indictment of blasphemy, as the prosecution or complainant could not prove the case

---

53. Talib Qizilbash, "Interview: I. A. Rehman, Director HRCP," *Newsline*, July 2010, 24.

54. Liben, "USCIRF: Annual Report for 2013," 118.

55. Editor, "Editorial," *Pakistan Today*, 20 September 2013.

56. Wilfrid Prest, *William Blackstone: Law and Letters in the Eighteenth Century* (Oxford: Oxford University Press, 2008).

57. Al-Tirmidhi Hadith–1011, http://www.alim.org/library/hadith/TIR/1011 (accessed 29 Aug 2017).

beyond reasonable doubt or where there was no conclusive proofs for conviction . . ."[58] However, the length of time it takes for someone accused of blasphemy to be cleared is a further injustice: someone accused of blasphemy has to wait for years to prove his/her innocence before the superior court. As bail is not granted in blasphemy cases, this means that the accused has to remain in jail during the whole period of their trial, which takes years.

This is evident from the case of Asia Bibi, a Christian woman, arrested on blasphemy charges on 19 June 2009 and given the death sentence on 29 November 2010 by the Sessions Court. Despite considerable international pressure from human rights groups, the appeal against her conviction was eventually heard by the Lahore High Court (LHC) after four years, on 16 October 2014. The LHC, after a four-hour hearing, upheld her death sentence. Now Asia's appeal is pending before the SCP. According to legal analysts, it will probably be at least three years before her appeal will be heard by the Supreme Court.[59] Asia has been in jail since June 2009.

Another highly publicized blasphemy case which, again, demonstrates the injustice of the blasphemy laws, is that of Ayub Masih, who was detained for six years before he was acquitted. He was arrested on 14 October 1996 after one of his neighbours, with whom he reportedly had had a dispute, claimed to have heard Masih utter praise for author Salman Rushdie's *Satanic Verses*. Masih was given the death sentence for the offence of insulting the Prophet of Islam, under Clause 295-C, by the session court in Sahiwal on 20 April 1998. (Bishop John Joseph, the first Roman Catholic Pakistani bishop, shot himself dead in front of the same court on 6 May 1998 as a protest against Ayub's conviction.) Ayub's sentence was confirmed by the Lahore High Court Multan Bench on 24 July 2001.[60] (This was the first blasphemy case in which the High Court had confirmed the sentence of capital punishment for blasphemy.) However, Masih was eventually acquitted by the Surpreme Court of Pakistan and released on 15 August 2002, after it was discovered that Masih had been falsely accused by his neighbour,

---

58. Qureshi, *Messenger of God*, 67.

59. Waqar Gillani and Salman Masood, "Pakistani Christian Woman's Appeal of Death Sentence Is Rejected," *The New York Times*, 17 October 2014, A11.

60. *Ayub Masih v. State*, 54 PLD 1048 (2002).

who had forced Masih's family off disputed land and taken it as his own.[61] Overall, it took about six years for Ayub to get an aquittal. The travesty of justice is that he was imprisoned for six years for an offence for which he was eventually declared innocent.

Those accused of blasphemy who belong to a minority, especially to the Christian or Ahmadi communities, are discriminated against by the jail authorities. For example, the team of Centre for Legal Aid, Assistance and Settlement (CLAAS) paid a visit to Younis Masih, a Christian man accused of blasphemy. He had been given the death sentence by the session court in May 2007, in Mianwali jail. He had been sent there to await his appeal to the Lahore High Court against his conviction. Masih told the CLAAS fact-finding team: "When I was shifted here in Mianwali, the jail authority tortured me severel times . . . the food quality is so poor and is not sufficient for eat. No appropriate medical facilities are available in the jail."[62] Similarly, Asia Bibi spent almost five years in jail in miserable conditions, where she faced bullying from fellow inmates and was badly beaten by a member of staff while at Sheikhupura jail.[63] The fact-finding report of CLAAS describes the plight of prisoners accused of blasphemy in Camp Jail, Lahore: "They were punished and kept in solitary confinement, without toilet, electricity and water . . . [and further they] are suffering with different medical problems such as skin allergy, stomach diseases, cardiac pain, and lung infections . . ."[64]

In conclusion, despite the fact that no one has yet been executed for blasphemy, serious and systemic abuses of the blasphemy law occur. Those accused of blasphemy spend years in jails, bearing both physical and psychological punishment. Many people suffer from false accusations of blasphemy. In fact, rather than being an argument in support of the blasphemy laws, the fact that no one has yet been executed is evidence of the misuse of the blasphemy laws, as, despite many accusations, to date no one has ultimately been found guilty of blasphemy.

---

61. Ibid., 1059.

62. Joseph Francis, "CLAAS Pakistan: Annual Report 2012" (Lahore: CLAAS, 2012), 121.

63. Tollet, *Blasphemy*, 48–49.

64. Francis, "CLASS Pakistan: Annual Report 2011," 168.

Argument # 4

We now turn to examine and respond to the fourth argument offered by the advocates of the blasphemy laws: that is, that if these laws are amended, minorities in Pakistan will be unsafe. Maulānā Muhammad Khan Shirani, the chairman of the Council of Islamic Ideology (CII), stated that "the minorities would become unsafe if amendments were made in the blasphemy law."[65] A few months later, after this statement, Maulana Tahir Asharfi, one of the leading members of the CII, stated on 19 September 2013 that blasphemy laws were being misused and that their misuse was virtually un-Islamic and equally blasphemous. Ashrafi also made it public through the media that CII decided "to fix the same penalty for the person who falsely accuses of blasphemy as the accused."[66] However, on 23 September 2013, CII retreated from this position and Shirani stated that there was no need to amend the law because laws dealing with false accusations already existed in the PPC (sections 194 and 211).[67]

It is appropriate to respond first to this assertion of Shirani, no one has been executed for blasphemy, because no one has been found guilty under Clause 295-C of the blasphemy laws, and all convictions by the lower courts have been overturned by the high courts or Supreme Court on the basis that the accusations made have been false. Despite this, no false accuser has been punished under Sections 194 and 211 in blasphemy cases in Pakistan.

Some may point out the Rimsha case as an example, in which a local cleric, Jadoon Chisti, was arrested on charges of falsifying evidence against Rimsha.[68] However, he was eventually cleared of the charges, as his two junior clerics retreated from their former assertion that they had been eyewitnesses of Chisti's act of adding pages from the Qur'an to a polythene bag carried by Rimsha. Even if Chisti was innocent (as declared by the court in

---

65. Staff Reporter, "Minorities to Be Unsafe If Blasphemy Law Amended: CII," *The News*, 30 May 2013, online.

66. Staff Reporter, "CII Suggests Amends to Blasphemy Laws " *The Nation*, 19 September 2013, 20, online.

67. Muhammad Anis, "Blasphemy Law Can't Be Amended: CII Chief," *The News*, 24 September 2013, online.

68. Matt Hoffman, "Modern Blasphemy Laws in Pakistan and the Rimsha Masih Case: What Effect – If Any – the Case Will Have on Their Future Reform," *WUGSLR* 13, no. 2 (2014): 386–392.

Islamabad), his two junior clerics therefore should have been punished by the court for being false witnesses. (Many believe that both witnesses had been threatened by extremists to withdraw their testimony, and that they subsequently said that they had been pressurized by the police to give false witness against Chisti.)

The fact that no one has yet been punished for producing false accusations in blasphemy cases may be one of the reasons for the significant growth in the number of blasphemy cases. If false accusers have been punished, this could have reduced the growing number of fabricated blasphemy cases. However, the majority of the members of the CII opposed the suggestion to amend the law to allow those convicted of falsely accusing others of blasphemy to face the same penalty as those convicted of blasphemy. Their justification was that "they did not want to discourage people from coming forward and [lodging] complaints against blasphemers."[69]

It is apparent that the CII does not seem interested in stopping the misuse of the blasphemy law. This leads us to argue that Islamic religious custodians like the CII in Pakistan are actually violating one of the fundamental principles of Islamic law laid down by its giver, Prophet Muhammad, that it is better to release a criminal than to punish the innocent.

We now turn to examine the main argument: that is, that minorities would be unsafe in the absence of this law. As we have noted above, blasphemy has become a very sensitive issue in Pakistan. Once a person has been accused of blasphemy, there is no way for him or her to live a normal life in Pakistani society, even if he/she is cleared of blasphemy charges by the court. This fact is evident from the following examples: although Salamat and Rehmat Masih were both declared innocent and acquitted by the Lahore High Court, Jamaat-e-Ahl Sunnat, a religious organization, offered a prize of 1 million rupees for the killing of the accused, according to Siddiqui and Hayat. Another religious organization, named the Mutahidda Ulama Council, announced a reward of 300,000 rupees for the same purpose.[70] Consequently, this left no hope for Salamat and Rehmat to live in the country, so they sought asylum in Germany in order to save their lives.

---

69. Ali, "CII Debate."
70. Siddique, "Unholy Speech," 334.

Both men, along with their families, secretly left for Germany in February 1995.[71] Similarly, after his acquittal, Ayub Masih managed to survive only by seeking asylum in Italy in 2002. After Rimsha Masih's acquittal, she and her family sought asylum in Canada in 2012. Tahir Naveed, Rimsha's counsel, commented during her trial, "Rimsha has lost her life, she cannot be part of normal society, even if she gets acquitted. She will have to hide and take shelter somewhere else. She cannot survive with this name and identity."[72]

The cases mentioned above are high-profile cases in which Western governments granted asylum to the victims. Many others, however, who have been unable to secure asylum, remain on the run for their safety. Some of them could not save their lives in this game of hide and seek. This is evident from the case of Mr Atiq Bajwa, an Ahmadi advocate from Vehari, who was charged on 10 November 1992 under 298-C for using the routine greetings of *assalām-u-alaikum* and for reciting *bismillāh*. The complainant said that these utterances had hurt his religious feelings. Mr Bajwa faced these charges for five years, without resolution, until, in 1997, he was murdered by an Islamic zealot.[73]

There are even more examples of people whose lives have been endangered by the blasphemy law, even while they have been in prison. Asia Bibi was given the death sentence by the lower court in November 2010. Governor Taseer sympathized with her by saying that he would seek a presidential pardon for her. In response, Maulana Yousaf Qureshi, the cleric of Mohabat Khan Mosque in Peshawar, stated that no president, parliament or government had the right to pardon a blasphemer; and he offered a reward of half a million rupees for anyone who would kill Asia Bibi.[74] He further said, "We expect her to be hanged and if she is not hanged then we will ask the Taliban to kill her."[75]

It is apparent from the above examples that there is no way for those accused of blasphemy to live a normal life in Pakistan, even after their

---

71. Ibid.

72. Nazar Ul Islam, "Burn the Girl Alive," *Newsweek*, 12–19 October 2012.

73. Press and Publication Desk, "Plight of Ahmadi Muslims in Pakistan" (Tilford: IIP, 2000), online.

74. Correspondent, "Blasphemy Case: Cleric Offers Rs.500,000 for Aasia's Execution," *The Express Tribune*, 4 December 2010, online.

75. Ibid.

innocence has been proven in court. This undermines the argument of the CII that the blasphemy law protects minorities, and that if it is amended, minorities will become unprotected. Our above discussion clearly demonstrates that minorities have become extremely vulnerable due to these laws. The mandatory death penalty for blasphemy, prescribed in Clause 295-C, in effect provides a religious as well as a legal justification for the accuser to become an executioner. This can be seen further from the following case study:

Case Study of Gojra Incident

On 25 July 2009, Talib Masih's son's wedding celebrations were under way. Masih's relatives and friends were throwing money in the form of notes on the groom.[76] During the celebrations, some children started throwing papers in the air, imitating the adults throwing notes on the groom. The next day, on 26 July, Muhammad Ashraf – a Muslim resident of the nearby village – alleged that he found pieces of papers inscribed with Qur'anic verses outside Talib Masih's house.[77] On 30 July, Ashraf, a local landlord, and over a dozen activists of religious parties, some of whom had come from outside the village, ordered Talib Masih to appear before the *panc' āyat* (the local committee of elders) and defend himself against the allegations made by Ashraf. Talib appeared before the *Panc' āyat* and denied defiling the Holy Qur'an. A quarrel broke out during the meeting and the Muslim members of the committee beat up Talib, before his wife and other women from the family came to rescue him.[78] Soon after, announcements were made through the loudspeakers of mosques in villages across the area, inciting local Muslims to punish the blasphemers.[79] According to the fact-finding report of the Human Rights Commission Pakistan (HRCP): "Without [verifying] the charge, scores of Muslim men from nearby villages attacked Christians' houses in *Koriān* within an hour of announcements from mosques . . . They set fire to 57 Christian houses after [looting] or destroying valuables."[80]

---

76. This is a common traditional practice in Punjab, in which currency notes are showered upon the groom by the relatives, friends and family members.
77. Talib Qizilbash, "No Room for the Other," *Newsline*, July 2010, 21.
78. Ibid.
79. Ibid.
80. HRCP Team, "Report of HRCP Fact-Finding Mission" (HRCP, 2009).

The matter did not end there, as the news that Christians had desecrated the Qur'an spread to surrounding areas. On 31 July, after the Friday prayers, an announcement was made in different mosques in Gojra city that a strike would be observed throughout the city and a protest rally organized against the alleged blasphemous act of the Christians.[81] On the following day, 1 August, the protest rally turned violent, marched towards the Christian colony in Gojra and started attacking Christians with stones. The Christians, along with the inadequate police force, managed to keep the mob at bay for some time before the violent mob wanting to eradicate the *kāfirs* (infidels), overpowered them.[82] The fact-finding report of the HRCP states:

> The attackers started looting valuable articles and smashing furniture and electrical appliances such as televisions, refrigerators, computers, crockery, kitchen utensils, etc. Destroyed furniture and electronics were later thrown out into the street. Around this time, witnesses reported seeing around 10 masked armed men, who were carrying unidentified inflammable substances, starting to set houses on fire.[83]

Eight Christians, including four women and a child, were burned alive, several were injured, and two churches and more than one hundred twenty Christian homes were destroyed.[84] This violence was the result of announcements made from the mosques urging Muslims to "make mincemeat of Christian[s]."[85] Despite the original incident in *Korāin*, and despite hearing the announcements from the mosques, the local administration and the police in Gojra did not take appropriate action and no adequate security measures were put in place to protect the Christian community in Gojra. A judicial inquiry of the incident, headed by Lahore High Court Judge Iqbal Hameedur Rehman, was completed in September 2009. The report says:

---

81. Mustafa Qadri, "Intolerance Is Sweeping across Pakistan," *The Guardian*, 24 August 2009, online.
82. Ibid.
83. Team, "Report of HRCP."
84. Aftab A. Mughal, "The Injustice Continues," *Newsline*, August 2010, 53.
85. Team, "Report of HRCP."

The tribunal reached the conclusion that the riots were a result of the inability of law-enforcement agencies to assess the gravity of the situation, inadequate precautionary and preventative measures taken by law-enforcement agencies, a lukewarm stance by the Toba Tek Singh DPO, the failure of intelligence agencies in providing prompt and correct information, a defective security plan, the irresponsible behaviour of the administration, [and] the complete failure of police while discharging their duties.[86]

The incident had terrible political and psychological effects on the horrified victims. One of the victims, on Pakistan day, celebrated in the same month as the attack (August), said, "We're still waiting for our freedom, if this was our country this would not have happened."[87] Another female victim, Margaret, shared her experience: "I was terrified, so frightened I couldn't think. I thought I was going to lose everything. My father had had heart surgery a few days earlier and when he went back and saw his house burned down, he got heart attack and died."[88] Another Christian Shamaun Masih, says that his children, who saw the rampage, are still traumatized. He said that "they start weeping whenever they see something unusual."[89]

Our analysis above and this case study in particular has shown that, instead of protecting minorities, the blasphemy laws have made them more vulnerable. This leads us to conclude that the argument of the Council of Islamic Ideology, that minorities will be unsafe in the absence of the blasphemy laws, seems very hard to justify.

Argument # 5

The final section of this chapter will examine the fifth argument in support of the blasphemy laws. This was presented at Pakistan's Universal Periodic Review hearing in UN in 2012, when the adviser to the Prime Minister

---

86. Inquiry Report of Gojra Incident 2009, available at http://www.punjab.gov.pk/?q=gojra_incident_2009.

87. Qadri, "Intolerance Is Sweeping."

88. Correspondent, "Blasphemy Case Evokes Fear in Pakistan Christian Town," *Dawn*, 1 September 2012, online.

89. Ibid.

on Human Rights argued that "an independent judiciary, free media and vibrant civil society also provided an effective safeguard against any misuse of the blasphemy law."[90] This argument was made in the light of the lawyers' movement for the independence of the judiciary in 2007, which became successful due to the support of the media and the civil society in Pakistan. We will examine this argument by consecutively reviewing all three elements: judiciary, civil society and media.

Judiciary

As demonstrated by the number of examples discussed previously, the lower judiciary in Pakistan has been notorious for making hasty and controversial decisions under pressure, especially in blasphemy cases. On 27 March 2014, Swan Masih, a sanitary worker from Joseph colony, was given the death sentence along with a fine of 200,000 rupees under 295-C by the session court in Lahore.[91] Throughout the trial, Masih had maintained his innocence and had argued that the real reason for the blasphemy allegation was a property dispute between him and his friend.[92] Previously, the SCP had denied any link between the accusation of blasphemy and the subsequent burning of two hundred houses belonging to Christians in Joseph colony.[93] On 4 April 2014, less than two weeks after Swan Masih's sentence, a session court in Toba Tek Singh sentenced a Christian couple, Shafqat Emmanuel and Shagufta Kausar, to death and fined them 100,000 rupees under 295-C. They had allegedly sent a text message, deemed insulting to the Prophet of Islam, to the cleric of a local mosque in July 2013.[94] However, the defence lawyer, Hassan, argued before the court that the text had originated from a cell phone which the couple had lost some time before the incident, and they could therefore not have sent the message.[95]

---

90. Din, "State of Human Rights in 2012," 116.
91. AFP, "Pakistan Court Sentences Christian Man to Death for Blasphemy," *The Guardian*, 28 March 2014, online.
92. Ibid.
93. Raja, "Joseph Colony Case."
94. AFP, "Couple Gets Death Sentence over Blasphemous Text Message," *The Express Tribune*, 5 April 2014, online.
95. Ibid.

Due to death threats from extremist forces against the accused, defence lawyers and judges, blasphemy cases are now tried in jails instead of in open courts. Even with this secrecy, the judiciary is not free from pressure from extremist forces. Despite the fact that the allegations were lacking concrete evidence in the two cases mentioned above, the session court passed the death sentence. In an interview with Majeeb-ur-Rehman, a renowned advocate from the Ahmadi community, claimed that if the lower courts set the accused free then they would be attacked, therefore the lower courts sentence left the matter for superior courts to review it. In that way, the lower courts avoided a sword hanging over their heads.[96] The view that the judiciary in Pakistan is not independent or fair has been advocated by *Manzil*, an independent think-tank based in Karachi, which conducted a study on the judicial system of Pakistan. It concluded that,

> the independence of judiciary in Pakistan has been jeopardized by pressure and threats brought by Islamic fundamentalists. Many lower court judges genuinely fear reprisals should they render acquittals against accused blasphemers . . . Lower Court judges are forced to convict accused blasphemers on weak evidence rather than face the prospect of verbal and physical attacks for releasing them.[97]

Likewise, Gabriela Knaul, the United Nations special rapporteur on the independence of judges and lawyers, expressed her concerns. Knaul noted during her visit to Pakistan from 19–29 May 2012:

> I am especially concerned about cases brought under the "so-called blasphemy law" as it was reported to me that judges have been coerced into deciding against the accused even without supporting evidence; as for the lawyers, in addition to their reluctance to take up such cases, they are targeted and forced not to represent their clients properly.[98]

---

96. MR/A 5 December 2013.

97. Hamza Hameed and Kamil Jamshed, "A Study of the Criminal Law and Prosecution System in Pakistan " (Karachi: Manzil, 2013), 13.

98. Hasnaat Malik, "Coercion Rules in Blasphemy Cases: UN Expert," *Daily Times*, 30 May 2012, online.

Consequently Sherry Rehman, a former parliamentarian in Pakistan, proposed in her private bill that the blasphemy law should be amended so that blasphemy cases would be taken up directly by the high court instead of heard in the lower courts. The lower judiciary is clearly more vulnerable to intimidation and pressure, which stop them providing justice to those accused of blasphemy.

Although the higher judiciary is much more resistant to external pressure, even it is not free from threats by extremists. This can be tragically seen in the fact that Justice Arif Iqbal Bhatti, the senior member of the Lahore High Court bench, was assasinated on 10 October 1997 because he had aquitted Salamat Masih and Rehmat Masih in 1995. In another recent example, Syed Pervez Ali Shah, a judge of the anti-terrorist court, who sentenced to death Mumtaz Qadri, the assassin of Governor Taseer, subsequently started recieving death threats from extremists. He was forced to take refuge with his family in Saudi Arabia.[99] The extremist forces are able, through such incidents, to exert pressure even on the superior judiciary. When Ayub Masih was convicted of blasphemy in a session court, and sentenced to death, he subsequently appealed to the Multan Bench of the Lahore High Court in Pakistan on 25 July 2001. It is generally believed that his appeal was turned down as a result of "immense pressure brought by fundamentalists who, on the day of the appeal, surrounded the High Court to intimidate the proceedings."[100] So the assertion that blasphemy laws cannot be abused because they operate in Pakistan's free judicial system, put forward by the adviser of the prime minister, does not stand up in the light of the evidence.

Another factor which disproves the argument that blasphemy laws are dealt with under a free judiciary is that blasphemy cases are mostly decided on the basis of religious emotionalism. It has been observed that even some judges in the high courts have been swayed by religious bias in blasphemy cases. In two cases filed under the same section of the blasphemy laws, a court applied a different yardstick for a Muslim and a Christian. In 2008, Khawaja Sharif, then Chief Justice of Lahore High Court, did not quash a case against a Christian woman named Martha Bibi. Her counsel cited an earlier decision

---

99. Zulqernain Tahir, "Qadri Case Judge Sent Abroad," *Dawn*, 24 October 2011, online.
100. Hameed and Jamshed, "Study of the Criminal Law," 13.

in which the same judge had quashed a case against one Qari Muhammad Yunus on the grounds, among others, that the complaint was not registered with the permission of the government, even though 295-C does not carry this requirement.[101] In Asia Bibi's case, the Lahore High Court prevented President Asif Zardari from granting a presidential pardon to Asia.[102] Ali Dayan Hussain, spokesperson of Human Rights Watch, commented:

> The Pakistani Constitution is absolutely categorical on the president's right to pardon . . . In preventing the pardon, in preempting it in fact, the court did something quite surreal. It actually stopped an executive action from taking place. And, by doing so, compounded the suffering of a woman who was unjustly convicted under a discriminatory law.[103]

For the Ahmadi community, religious prejudice is evident even at the level of the superior judiciary in Pakistan. For example, in 1993, in the case of *Zaheeruddin versus State*, the Supreme Court's majority verdict was: "When an Ahmadi or Ahmadis display in public, on a placard, a badge, or a poster, or write on walls, or ceremonial gates or buntings, the Kalima (Islamic creed) or chant other Shari'a Islam, it would amount to publicly defiling the name of the Holy Prophet."[104] According to prominent human rights lawyer and Supreme Court advocate Hina Jilani, Pakistan now has "a judiciary that has been influenced by Islamization."[105] It could be argued that this is one of the reasons that appeals against convictions of blasphemy go on for years is, as pointed out by Senior Supreme Court lawyer Abid Hassan Minto, "judges and prosecution lawyers use delaying tactics to keep the accused in jail as long as they possibly can without his or her trial reaching a conclusion."[106]

---

101. Jamal, "Herald Exclusive."
102. Crilly, "Pakistani Cleric."
103. Farieha Aziz, "Interview: Ali Dayan Hassan," *Newsline*, April 2011, 33.
104. *Zaheeruddin v. State*, 1778.
105. Hameed and Jamshed, "Study of the Criminal Law," 11.
106. Jamal, "Law of Diminishing Utility."

Civil Society

Now we move to the issue of civil society. Following the successful lawyers' movement for the independence of the judiciary in 2007, in which civil society and a free media had played an integral role, there was much anticipation that a civil society would play a significant role in making changes to the blasphemy laws. In anticipation of this, Sherry Rehman, then Information Minister, tabled a private bill to the National Assembly with proposed amendments to the blasphemy laws. For this task, Rehman sought "full and active support from civil society and media."[107] However, very little support was offered by the civil society and media for her move to bring some procedural changes to Pakistan's blasphemy laws. Instead, the religious rightwing forces launched a massive campaign against her proposed bill. They showed their street power by organizing huge rallies all over Pakistan, especially in the big cities of Karachi and Lahore. Thousands of their supporters demonstrated in Karachi, Lahore and Islamabad, demanding that Pakistan's blasphemy laws remain intact. The *New York Times* reported: "A crippling strike by Islamist parties brought Pakistan to a standstill on Friday as thousands of people took to the streets, and forced businesses to close, to head off any change in the country's blasphemy law . . ."[108] It was observed by the international press that the popular power which religious forces hold in Pakistan contrasts sharply with the relatively ineffectual and weak influence of civil society.[109] Dr Mehdi Hasan, the chairman of the Human Rights Commission in Pakistan, said that "the liberal and democratic forces in the country have retreated so much . . ."[110] Likewise, Ahmad Rashid, a Pakistani researcher, asserted that the "civil society has largely gone into hiding."[<?>] Similarly, Javed Ghamdi, a renowned Islamic scholar in Pakistan, echoed this, saying that "they [extremists] have become stronger, because they have street power behind them, and the liberal forces are weak and divided."[111]

---

107. Reporter, "Civil Society, Media Asked to Help Repeal Blasphemy Law," *Dawn*, 10 December 2009, online.

108. Salman Masood, "Pakistanis Rally in Support of Blasphemy Law," *The New York Times*, 1 January 2011, A4.

109. Ibid.

110. Ibid.

111. Declan Walsh, "Islamic Scholar Attacks Pakistan's Blasphemy Laws," *The Guardian*, 21 January 2011, online.

After the assassinations of Salman Taseer and Shabaz Bhatti at the beginning of 2011, liberal voices have been intimidated to a greater extent and many fear to speak out. This is largely due to the *Tālibāns'* warning pamphlet found at the place where Shahbaz Bhatti was assassinated: "This is the fate of that cursed man. And now, with the grace of Allah, the warriors of Islam will pick you out one by one and send you to hell, God willing."[112] The retreat of the liberal voices is illustrated by Javed Ghamdi, an outspoken Islamic scholar whose voice had stood out because he had critiqued blasphemy laws on religious grounds. He fled to Malaysia with his family after police discovered a plot to bomb his house in Lahore. Fears that moderates would be oppressed and silenced became true, when a few months following the *Tālibāns'* warning, *Tālibān* gunmen assassinated Dr Farooq Khan, an outspoken ally of Ghamdi, at his clinic in the northwestern city of Mardan.[113]

When it comes to the Ahmadi community, the positive influence of civil society is even more questionable. "While a minority sponsored and promoted persecution of innocent Ahmadis, the majority facilitated the evil by remaining silent."[114] Saleem-ud-Din, a spokesperson of Jama'it Ahmadiyya Pakistan, pointed out that ninety-five Ahmadi worshippers had been killed and over one hundred twenty severely injured in Lahore on 28 May 2010. No Chief Minister or any Cabinet Minister then visited the attacked worship places or even made a single statement of condemnation of the incident in order to console the bereaved Ahmadi community.[115]

Media

Third, we now take a brief look at the role of the media, especially with regard to the blasphemy issue in Pakistan. A recent study conducted by Sana McMillion on the role of the media in Pakistan, indicates that the English-language newspapers generally project a moderate view by addressing the problem of the rise of extremism and how to bring about reform in the blasphemy laws. A poll of the readers of *The Nation*, a Pakistani English-language newspaper, on 19 March 2014, showed that 68 percent of them believed the

---

112. Shehrbano Taseer, "Pakistan Has Abdicated Its Responsibilities," *The Guardian*, 3 March 2011, online.

113. Walsh, "Islamic Scholar."

114. https://www.persecutionofahmadis.org/the-society/ (accessed 13 April 2014)

115. SD/A 5 December 2013.

blasphemy law should be repealed.¹¹⁶ In contrast, Urdu newspapers, which are read by an overwhelming majority of Pakistanis, tend to promote a religious ideology that glorifies Islam.¹¹⁷ For example, the Ahmadiyya central office in *Rabwāh* Pakistan released its 2012 annual press report, which states: "In 2011 the Pakistani Urdu press continued the publication of baseless news stories. During the year more than 1173 news stories were published against Ahmadis."¹¹⁸ In another example, Hamid Mir, a prominent journalist in Pakistan, in his article in the *Jang* daily Urdu newspaper, noted that Jinnah, the founder of Pakistan, had been the defence council in the High Court case of Ilam Din, the assassin of the Hindu publisher of a blasphemous book against the Prophet of Islam.¹¹⁹ Allama Iqbal, a philosopher and creator of the idea of Pakistan, actively participated in his funeral along with six million Muslims, and Iqbal praised his martyrdom. Mir argued that people like Jinnah and Iqbal, enlightened Muslims of their time, had supported the act of Ilam Din on the basis of their religious convictions.¹²⁰ Reading between the lines, Mir is trying to legitimize the act of a Muslim zealot by asserting that he was praised by the founding fathers, enlightened Muslim figures, of the nation. In the same manner, Mumtaz Qadri, the assassin of Governor Taseer, was described in most circles of Pakistan's media as a latter-day Ilam Din and showered with rose petals by hundreds of lawyers in front of the court room. Hoodbhoy says, "Glib-tongued television anchors sought to convince viewers that Taseer had brought ill unto himself."¹²¹ In an interview with the BBC Urdu, Abbas Athar, a Pakistani journalist, alleged that Taseer's killer had been the Pakistani media.¹²²

---

116. "Do You Think That the Blasphemy Law Should Be Repealed?" *The Nation*, 19 March 2014, 7.

117. Sana M. McMillion, "Crucial Reform of Pakistan's Blasphemy Laws Remains a Distant Dream" (Norway: NPRC, 2012), 6.

118. https://www.persecutionofahmadis.org/the-media-2012/ (accessed 13 April 2014).

119. Jinnah argued that Raj Pal hurts the feelings of Muslims which caused Ilam Din to stab Pal so Din should be tried under IPC 308, not under IPC 302. *Ilam Din v. Emperor*.

120. Hamid Mir, "Iqbal, Quaid-i-Azam and Ghazi Ilam Din," *Jang*, 11 January 2012, online.

121. Pervez Hoodbhoy, "Remembering Salman Taseer," *The Express Tribune*, 1 January 2012, online.

122. http://www.bbc.co.uk/urdu/multimedia/2011/01/110110_abbas_athar_media_taseer_uk.shtml (accessed 27 April 2014).

Although the media in Pakistan is free, however, they have not demonstrated impartiality in reporting, and do not uphold recognized codes of media ethics. The electronic media in Pakistan is fairly new and tends to focus mostly on ratings, and, as a result, on sensationalism at the expense of journalistic ethic. "Sensational journalism, weak ethics and lack of trained reporters has added a competition between TV channels over the breaking news syndrome."[123] This prevents most TV channels from playing an effective role in the objective analysis of issues, and from speaking up for tolerance and the peaceful resolution of perceived conflicts. It is the general view of the media analysts in Pakistan that many television channels have been active in spreading rumours, inflaming sentiments and giving space to speakers who are intolerant and who promote violence.

At times, the fairly new and thriving media industry has played a positive role, but on the other hand it has also been responsible for sensationalizing events and pursuing ratings rather than upholding journalistic standards. For instance, in 2008, Dr Amir Liaquat Hussain, a prominent television anchor, proclaimed on Alim Online, a religious affairs program on popular Geo TV, that Ahmadis are *wājibu'l-qatl* (deserving to be killed). In the 48 hours after the broadcast, this led to the killing of two prominent members of the Ahmadiyya community in Karachi and two more Ahmadis were lynched later in the year.[124] (These later deaths were also attributed to Hussain's comments.)

The media's bias can be further seen from the fact that on 6 July 2012, the Pakistan Telecommunications Authority (PTA) banned a website, alislam.org, which belonged to the Ahmadi community. *The Nation* daily newspaper reported that "the site was accused of blasphemy against the Holy Prophet (PBUH) and the Muttahida Ulema Board had demanded that the PTA close down the site."[125] Moreover, the PTA routinely bans thepersecution.org, a site that documents crimes committed against Ahmadis.[126] Saleem-ud-Din, an Ahmadi leader in Rabwah, mentioned that they even "give

---

123. Ibid.
124. "Pakistan: No Action Taken against Geo TV Presenter," *Asian Human Rights Commission*, 18 September 2008, online.
125. Staff Reporter, "PTA Bans Ahmadi Website," *The Nation*, 6 July 2012, 14.
126. Huma Yusuf, "No Room to Breathe," *Dawn*, 9 July 2012, online.

money to the press to publish their news but they do not entertain them. Once a newspaper agreed to publish our news but at the last moment, its management refused by saying that they could not print Ahmadi news."[127] Likewise, Majeeb-ur-Rehman pointed out that one of the TV channels wanted to interview him with regard to the incident of the massacre of ninety-five Ahmadis in Lahore on 28 May 2010, but later he was informed that it was not possible to air an Ahmadi voice.[128] These incidents demonstrate that the opportunity for members of religious minorities to air their voices is shrinking.

It is clear that an independent judiciary, free media and vibrant civil society are not an effective safeguard against any misuse of the blasphemy laws. Our analysis of the judiciary, civil society and the media demonstrates that none of the three stakeholders have been able to stop the misuse of the blasphemy laws. A recent report from a US government advisory panel pointed out that Pakistan used blasphemy laws more than any other country in the world. Our study reveals that, instead of being a safeguard against the misuse of the blasphemy laws, these stakeholders became, in many cases, an instrument for the misuse of blasphemy laws.

Concluding Summary

We have examined and responded to five arguments put forward by the supporters of blasphemy laws. Our analysis shows that these arguments are not justified by the facts.

First, advocates of the blasphemy laws claim that they were equally applied to all citizens of Pakistan without any discrimination, since more Muslims than non-Muslims had been charged with blasphemy. However, our analysis demonstrates that the blasphemy laws are disproportionally used against minorities, especially Christians and Ahmadis, and that most of the Muslims accused of blasphemy were Shias, who could also be considered a minority group in Pakistan.

Second, they argued that Pakistan's blasphemy laws actually protected those accused of blasphemy by preventing people taking the law into their

---

127. SD/A 05Dec2013.
128. MR/A 05Dec2013.

own hands. By contrast, our analysis revealed that, instead of protecting people, the blasphemy laws had become a tool in the hands of those who wish to misuse them for ulterior motives. The punitive laws have had the effect of indirectly giving legitimacy to people who take the law into their own hands, resulting in tragic extrajudicial killings of those of accused of blasphemy.

Third, it was asserted that the blasphemy laws were not being misused because no one had yet been executed in Pakistan under these laws. However, our analysis demonstrated, although no one has been executed yet, the laws have had other significant negative effects, which cannot be discounted. These include serious and systematic abuses of the blasphemy law in which innocent people suffer terribly.

Fourth, it has been argued that if the blasphemy laws were amended, minorities in Pakistan would be unsafe. In contrast, our analysis demonstrated that minority groups, especially Christians and Ahmadis, have become extremely vulnerable under these laws. Multiple examples demonstrate that there is no way for those accused of blasphemy to escape penalties even after their innocence has been proven in court, especially if they belonged to a minority group.

Fifth, it was argued that blasphemy laws operated in the context of an independent judiciary, a free media and a vibrant civil society, all of which provided an effective safeguard against any misuse of the laws. However, our analysis demonstrated that none of the three stakeholders have been able to stop their misuse. In some cases, these agencies have become instruments for the misapplication of blasphemy laws. This chapter concludes by arguing that Pakistan's blasphemy laws are discriminatory and are being misused against minorities, especially Christians and Ahmadis, for ulterior motives. Accordingly, there is a pressing need to repeal or drastically change these laws in order to stop their misuse.

PART III

RESPONSE

CHAPTER 6

An Exploration and Comparative Analysis of Christian and Ahmadi Responses to Pakistan's Blasphemy Laws

Introduction

In chapter 4 we looked at the overall experience of Ahmadis and Christians living as minorities in the context of Pakistan. The following chapter specifically focused on the experience of Ahmadis and Christians under Pakistan's blasphemy laws. This chapter aims to explore and analyze the response of both communities to the situation arising from Pakistan's blasphemy laws. In November and December 2013 in Pakistan, forty-two interviews were conducted with academics, intellectuals, religious leaders, politicians, lawyers, activists and people affected by blasphemy laws from Ahmadi and Christian Pakistanis, 25 percent of whom were women. For the purpose of fair analysis, both communities have been given an equal weight in data collection, as 50 percent of the interviews were held with members of each community.

The findings with regard to the response of Ahmadi and Christian communities to Pakistan's blasphemy laws will be analyzed according to first similarities and then dissimilarities respectively. Under the section on dissimilarities will first look at how Ahmadis and Christians are reacting in different ways; and, second and more specifically, the reasons why they are responding differently despite living under the same circumstances.

Similarities

A Sense of Fear and Insecurity

During my personal research in late 2013 in Pakistan, the obvious similarity which I observed between Ahmadis and Christians regarding their response to Pakistan's blasphemy laws was a keen sense of fear and insecurity. When I approached the interviewees, seeking their consent to be interviewed about the subject of blasphemy laws, the initial response from most of them was a reluctance to speak on this subject, because they consider it a highly sensitive issue in Pakistan. One of the bishops to whom I spoke repeatedly insisted during the interview that his name be not disclosed in any comment related to this subject.[1] A Pakistani Christian researcher told me that he had conducted a survey which found that 65 percent of working Christians avoid any religious discussion because of the fear of blasphemy laws.[2] Moreover, when I approached a university professor from the Ahmadi community, he straightforwardly refused, saying that he did not want to speak on this highly sensitive subject.

This obvious attitude of intimidation is due to the fact that it is tragically easy to entangle anyone in a blasphemy case in Pakistan. USCIRF, in its annual report for 2013, notes that the blasphemy laws are easily misused because they "do not provide clear guidance on what constitutes a violation, empowering accusers to apply their personal religious interpretations."[3] It is evident from the following incident how easy it is to entangle someone in a blasphemy case. On 13 May 2014, in the city of Jhang, sixty-eight lawyers from the Muslim community were charged with blasphemy following a protest in which they had shouted slogans against a senior police officer, Umar Daraz. A member of *Ahle Sunnat Wal Jammat Pakistan* (ASWJP)[4]

---

1. IJ/C 17Dec2013. As we mentioned in the research methodology, the identity of the interviewees has been concealed. However, for sake of clarity, Christians are identified by the letter "C" and Ahmadis by the letter "A" in the footnotes. The date marks out when the interview was conducted by the author.

2. AA/C 24Nov2013.

3. Paul Liben and Jessica Sarra, "USCIRF: Annual Report for 2014" (Washington: USCIRF, 2014), 78.

4. In 2002, Musharraf banned Sipah-e-Sahaba Pakistan (SSP), but it continued their activities under the new name, ASWJP.

complained that his religious feelings had been offended because lawyers used foul language against Umar Daraz, who shares his first name with Umar bin Khattab, a revered personality from early Islam.[5]

It is clear that if Muslims can so easily be accused of blasphemy, then non-Muslims are extremely vulnerable to the charge. A Muslim tenant of an Ahmadi house owner, in the city of Kunri in the south of Pakistan, did not pay rent for several months. When he was asked to pay the rent by his Ahmadi landlord, the tenant instead framed a blasphemy case against him.[6] An experienced Ahmadi lawyer commented that the blasphemy laws are so vague that "if someone says that he does not like eating pumpkin and that person can be accused of insulting the Prophet because the Holy Prophet liked eating pumpkins."[7] He goes on to say that, for the Ahmadis, citing the name of the Holy Prophet puts them at great risk of being accused of blasphemy.[8]

Likewise, the Christians in Pakistan live in fear because of the blasphemy laws. One of the former bishops in Pakistan said that "this law has destroyed Christian community in Pakistan, as it has become a weapon which can be used against any one of us, anytime, anywhere. The fear of the blasphemy laws has so much hold on us that we cannot talk about the Prophet of Islam and are always reluctant to say his name."[9]

The fear and insecurity of minorities is heightened by the way the power and impartiality of the judiciary has been compromised by the misuse of blasphemy laws. Once the blasphemy issue comes up in Pakistan, extremist elements urge people to take the matter into their own hands, rather than to wait for the judiciary to do justice. This is evident from several recent examples.

On 16 May 2014, Khalil Ahmad, a 65-year-old man from an Ahmadi community, who was in police custody, having been charged with blasphemy, was shot dead. His murderer was a teenager who, disguised in a police

---

5. Syed R. Hassan, "Pakistani Police Charge 68 Lawyers with Blasphemy over Protest," *Reuters*, 13 May 2014.
6. MA/A 05Dec2013.
7. MR/A 05Dec2013.
8. MR/A 05Dec2013.
9. MS/C 06Dec2013.

uniform, had walked into the police station and shot Khalil dead while he was in police custody.[10] According to Salim-ud-din, a spokesperson of the Ahmadi community in Pakistan, Khalil and three others had been arrested for blasphemy because he had asked a Muslim shopkeeper in his village to remove from his shop inflammatory stickers denouncing the Ahmadi community.[11]

Second, Junaid Hafeez, a Fulbright scholar and lecturer of English at a university in Multan, was accused of posting blasphemous comments on his Facebook page. For months Hafeez's father tried to find a lawyer,[12] but no lawyer was prepared to take up the case because of fear of reprisals from extremist religious groups. Finally, Rashid Rehman, a human rights advocate, dared to defend Hafeez. Rehman told a press reporter that defending a blasphemy case in Pakistan is like a "walking into the jaws of death."[13] During court hearings on 9 April 2014, Rehman was openly threatened by the prosecution lawyers in the presence of the judge that by the next hearing "he would not exist anymore."[14] This proved true, as on 7 May 2014, Rehman was gunned down in his office along with two of his colleagues who were critically injured. The spokesperson for the UN High Commissioner for Human Rights, Rupert Colville, stated in a press briefing in Geneva that the assassination of Rehman has "brought into stark focus the climate of intimidation . . . in the country."[15]

The extrajudicial killing of Rehman was justified by many rightwing groups, who argue that anyone who does not consider a blasphemer as a blasphemer commits a blasphemy too. In support of this view, a slogan is being promoted in Pakistan that "one who sympathizes with the blasphemer is also blasphemer."[16] This belief became the grounds for the killings of

---

10. Katharine Houreld, "Teenager Kills Man Accused of Blasphemy in Pakistan Police Station," *Reuters*, 16 May 2014, online.

11. Ibid.

12. Ali Sethi, "Pakistan's Tyranny of Blasphemy," *The New York Times*, 21 May 2014, SR10.

13. Ibid.

14. Ibid.

15. http://www.ohchr.org/EN/NewsEvents/Pages/DisplayNews.aspx?NewsID=14583&LangID=E (accessed 20 May 2014)

16. Damaris, "Pakistan's Blasphemy' Laws Pose Growing Threat," *WorldWatch Monitor*, 13 May 2011, online.

Governor Taseer and Minister Bhatti in 2011. It is even dangerous to call Mumtaz Qadri, the assassin of Governor Taseer, a murderer, because he is considered by many to be a pious man. A newly built mosque in the capital of Pakistan, "the Jāmiā Masjid Mumtaz Qadri," has been named after Qadri, as a tribute to a man regarded as a religious hero who killed a man who sympathized with a blasphemer. Ashfaque Sabri, a cleric of Qadri Mosque, implicitly praised Qadri's action, saying that "my faith is not that strong otherwise I and every other Muslim would also do what Mumtaz Qadri did."[17]

The fact that the role of the judiciary is being lessened in blasphemy issues is further evident from another recent incident on 14 May 2014, when a prominent Geo TV station in Pakistan was charged under Sections 295-A and C and 298-A for airing a program which was considered blasphemous. (The channel broadcast images of dance with Sufi lyrics and music which, according to Muslim tradition, refers to the Prophet Muhammad and his family.) The session court in Islamabad ordered the police to register a blasphemy case against the owner of Geo TV, the program hostess and two guests. This matter has been inflamed by other media groups and has turned into a big issue. The Pakistan Electronic Media Regulatory Authority (PEMRA) claimed that it has received over 5,000 complaints against the program.[18] Before the PEMRA or the judiciary probed into the matter, a *fatvā* (verdict) had been issued by *Sunni Ittehād Council* (SIC), along with nearly nineteen militant Islamic organizations, declaring that it is *harām* (sinful) to watch Geo TV.[19]

Since then, several violent attacks on this media group have been reported. Imran Aslam, a president of the Geo channel, said that "it's a very dangerous situation because it puts all our staff at risk."[20] Even the country's most popular TV station Geo, belonging to one of the biggest and most powerful media groups, the *Jang* group, "is not immune" from blasphemy charges.[21] What would the situation be of the people from the minorities

---

17. Mehreen Z. Malik, "Footprints: Mumtaz Qadri Mosque, Memorial to Our Misdeeds," *Dawn*, 11 May 2014, online.

18. Correspondent, "Geo TV Faces Blasphemy Case " *The Hindu*, 18 May 2014, online.

19. Jon Boone, "Pakistan's Geo News Becomes Latest Target in Blasphemy Accusation Trend," *The Guardian*, 22 May 2014, online.

20. Ibid.

21. Ibid.

who are incomparably weaker and downtrodden? Undoubtedly, they face an even higher degree of vulnerability with regard to blasphemy accusations. This phenomenon of fear and insecurity is causing psychological stress to Ahmadis and Christians in Pakistan. One Ahmadi man said, "I gave ten thousand rupees more to a property dealer in fear that if I argue with him on the price of the property he may accuse me of blasphemy."[22] A well-off Christian businessman in Karachi checks the rubbish bin in his office very carefully every day, because he said, "you never know, a stray scrap of paper can ruin you, your family and your business."[23]

We have pointed out in chapter 4 some historical reasons for the ghettoization of the Christians in Pakistan. However, the fear of blasphemy has now become an integral factor to the further ghettoization of the Christian community. A Christian leader observed this when he was conducting interviews for a position in his institution:

> I was surprised to know that most of young Christians were having professional qualifications. I asked them why you want to work in Christian institution where you would not get handsome salary package as compared to what is offered in the open market. The common answer was that it is safe here to work in the Christian environment. There are so many risks to face working among the Muslim community, and indeed the greater one is the blasphemy.[24]

A former bishop of one of the dioceses of the Church of Pakistan confirmed that Christians preferred to work in church institutions, even if this was on a low salary, because of concerns for their safety.[25] Likewise, another Christian leader commented, "We are so afraid of blasphemy laws that we avoid to intermingle with the majority Muslim community."[26] This is causing a huge pressure on church-related jobs. The Moderator Bishop of the Church of Pakistan reported that 60 percent of Christians rely on jobs

---

22. Journalist/A 05Dec2013.
23. Mohammed Hanif, "How to Commit Blasphemy in Pakistan," *The Guardian*, 6 September 2012.
24. MA/C 20Nov2013.
25. MS/C 06Dec2013.
26. AS/C 17Nov2013.

provided by the church.²⁷ Christian students in colleges and universities keep to themselves and never try to relate to the majority Muslim students.²⁸

This phenomenon of ghettoization is also being faced by the Ahmadi community. As their students cannot live with other Muslim students in the same hostel, they have developed their own residential hostels for Ahmadi students in the big cities. Furthermore, the Ahmadi community has developed its own system of secondary education and has been affiliated with the Agha Khan Board of Shia Ismaili community²⁹ instead of with the government boards of secondary education in Pakistan. The pursuit of a safe environment is pushing both communities into further isolation.

Our discussion above demonstrates that minorities are so intimidated that they cannot freely express their concerns about the misuse of blasphemy laws due to their sense of fear and insecurity. In fact, the fear of being accused of blasphemy is pushing minorities to the position where they have to consider themselves as *dhimmi* (paying tax and submitting to a number of restrictions), unable to claim their status as equal citizens of Pakistan – a status which was promised by the nation's founder as well as guaranteed by its constitution.

A Trend of Exodus

Ahmadis and Christians alike are fleeing Pakistan in response to the blasphemy laws. The majority of Pakistani Christians were of Punjabi origins and came from socially depressed classes, and there was also a sizeable number of westernized Christians including Anglo-Indians and Goans.³⁰ These communities were mainly located in urban hubs, like Karachi and Lahore, and were Roman Catholic. Both these communities have dwindled to a considerable extent in Pakistan since the 1960s, which marked the beginning of the exodus of Anglo Christians. This exodus gained momentum in the 1970s and reached its zenith in the 1980s when Zia-ul-Haq extended

---

27. SA/C 21Nov2013.
28. SS/C 17Nov2013, AS/C 17Nov2013.
29. AM/A 04Dec2013.
30. Joseph C. Cordeiro, "The Christian Minority in an Islamic State: The Case of Pakistan," in *The Vatican, Islam, and the Middle East*, ed. Kail C. Ellis (New York: Syracuse University Press, 1987), 280.

his rule in the name of *niẓām-ē-muṣṭafā* (system of the Prophet of Islam). Andrew D'Mello, a Goan immigrant to Australia, states:

> As a Pakistani Goan I can relate to the Zia-ul-Haq era when he introduced strict laws to curb singing and dancing and closed the Catholic club in Lahore, which was used by the English-speaking Christian community, Goans and Anglos, for fun and entertainment . . . After Zia instilled those policies in Pakistan, it became very difficult for minorities to enjoy and celebrate their holidays (Christmas, Easter, New Year) . . . Islam was being forced down the throats of people who were not Muslim. This occurred in the late 70's and by the 80's Anglos and Goan communities started leaving in droves . . .[31]

On the other hand, others vehemently disagree with this view:

> As they [Anglo-Indians] had the European parentage, so they were given preference over local Indians, both in education and services by our colonial masters . . . So after the Independence it was quite natural that local population was encouraged to get education and enter in services by breaking the monopoly enjoyed the Anglo Indians thenceforth. They had to share/surrender their services with local population which were sacrosanct before partition. Anglo Indian might have thought that the new entrants are not as civilized as they were or culturally different. So they might have felt alienated themselves in what were their exclusive preserves, hence they decided to move to their fatherlands.[32]

Our space does not allow us to do a thorough analysis of this debate. However, it is an undeniable fact that the majority of Anglo Christians left Pakistan due to the process of Islamization which reached its height in Zia's era.

---

31. Comment posted on 6 October 2011 by Andrew D'Mello from Australia at: http://www.thefridaytimes.com/beta2/tft/article.php?issue=20110930&page=24#sthash.bZTNIhK1.dpuf (accessed May 21, 2014).

32. Comment Posted on October 02, 2011 by Balachandran from Chennai India at: http://www.thefridaytimes.com/beta2/tft/article.php?issue=20110930&page=24#sthash.bZTNIhK1.dpuf (accessed May 21, 2014).

Compared to Anglo Christians, there had been no trend among the Punjabi Christians to flee Pakistan, although some emigrated for economic reasons. This is, perhaps, due to the fact that most Punjabi Christians were socially depressed and uneducated and therefore had less opportunity to leave the country. Perhaps, also, their very long history of social discrimination (because of their social status), compared to the Anglo Christians, had resigned them to living in difficult circumstances.

When traditional Islam re-emerged in Pakistan, social discrimination blended with religious discrimination against Christians, many of whom came from the lower classes. Asif Aqeel, a Christian Pakistani researcher, notes that in Pakistan, "ultimately there was a merging of Brahmanic Hinduism's ritual impurity with Islamic ceremonial uncleanness with regard to sweepers, almost all of whom were Hindu "untouchables" who converted to Christianity . . ."[33] The process of blending social and religious discrimination affected the Punjab region most greatly, compared to other parts of Pakistan. For example, Rubina Bibi, a Christian woman from Alipur Chattha in the Punjab, bought *desi ghee* (cooking oil) from a local seller but found that it was not pure. When she complained to the seller that it was substandard and she therefore wanted to return it and have her money refunded, the shopkeeper argued that the oil had been polluted by having been poured into the bowl of a Christian, so it could never be returned. The ensuing argument led to blasphemy charges against Rubina Bibi.[34] Our study of the previous chapter revealed that 74 percent of blasphemy cases in Pakistan occurred in the province of Punjab. Further classification showed that a majority of blasphemy cases occurred in the eight districts of the Punjab province where the majority of Christians are located.

The majority of those acccused of blasphemy come from the socially poor class of people. A female lawyer from the Ahmadi community said, "The upper class or educated class of Pakistan, even from Ahmadis, have not been affected by the blasphemy laws because the people from the upper class, mostly educated, have no concern with the religion."[35] Similarly,

---

33. Asif Aqeel, "Christian Sanitation Workers Swept into Societal Gutter," *Daily Times*, 12 July 2011, online.

34. Ibid.

35. NA/A 13Dec2013.

a Christian researcher says that "our discrimination is based on the lower side [the socially downtrodden] of the pyramid. As we move towards top [socially upper class], this discrimination gets lesser."[36] More than 90 percent of Pakistani Christians are of Punjabi origin and the majority of them remain in the lower strata of society. These are the people most affected by the blasphemy laws.

In the past, Punjabi Christians, due to their social background, might have been relatively inured to discrimination and difficult circumstances. However, there is now an increasing trend for Punjabi Christians to seek refugee status, especially through Thailand and Sri Lanka, which are easy escape routes from Pakistan. One of the bishops in Pakistan related that, nowadays, he frequently receives phone calls from unfamiliar cell numbers and 80 percent of them are requesting a church letter to support an application to the UN for refugee status.[37] They want to go abroad, even if this is to Sri Lanka or Thailand, where the plight of asylum seekers is so bad that some even live in containers.[38] This writer has first-hand knowledge that many Punjabi Christians have abandoned their jobs and sold their properties in order to seek refugee status. There are reports that people have paid bribes of 30,000 to 40,000 rupees to immigration staff at the exit airports, Lahore and Karachi, to board a plane to Thailand or Sri Lanka in order to seek refuge there. It seems that the immigration officers asked for such substantial bribes because they sought to exploit people who were desperate enough to seek asylum. This writer has personally visited some Christian refugee families in Sri Lanka who have been living in a desperate situation (their survival was heavily dependent on the generosity of Sri Lankan Christians). When I asked one of the refugee families whether it would not have been better to die in Pakistan than to live this refugee life, the head of the family commented that, despite all difficulties here, "we are, at least, free from the fear of being accused of blasphemy in Pakistan."[39]

Although blasphemy laws are not the sole reason for Punjabi Christians to leave the country, the fear and insecurity which they engender have certainly

---

36. AA/C 24Nov2013.
37. MS/C 06Dec2013.
38. MS/C 06Dec2013.
39. SM/C 13Feb2010.

encouraged many to flee from Pakistan. Moreover, Christians perceive, in the light of several defeated efforts, that these laws are not going to change and that they will continue to be misused in Pakistan. In the words of one bishop, "Pakistan's blasphemy laws are not going to change till the day of judgment."[40] This leads us to argue that fear and insecurity, coupled with pessimism about the possibility of change, have led Punjabi Christians to flee from Pakistan in order to secure a future for their children, just like Anglo Christians did decades ago. Flight is the response of a frightened as well as defeated community, who have no hope for their survival in Pakistan.

The Ahmadi community in Pakistan, who face similar persecution, have responded similarly. It has been observed that "Ahmadis have been at the receiving end of what is called an unparalleled persecution in the modern era."[41] Circumstances have not been favourable for Ahmadis in Pakistan, as is evident from the 1953 disturbances against Ahmadis and their excommunication from the fold of Islam by the Parliament of Pakistan in 1974. Consequently Ahmadis have fled Pakistan. On 26 April 1984, Sections 298-B and C which make it a criminal offence for Ahmadis to pose themselves as Muslims, were passed by General Zia. Following this, Mirza Tahir Ahmad (the fourth caliph of the Ahmadiyya community) was compelled to leave Pakistan, along with his family and several associates, for London, where he established the headquarters of his community. His departure was followed by a widespread exodus of Ahmadis from Pakistan.

Since then, thousands of Ahmadis have secured asylum in Europe, Canada, the USA and Australia. Many initially go to Thailand and Sri Lanka to seek UN refugee status there. More recently, there has been a new development, as Ahmadis are now seeking asylum in China as well. The *Daily Times* reported that 35 out of 500 UN registered asylum seekers and refugees in China are Pakistani Ahmadis.[42] Although China signed up to the UN's refugee protocol in 1982, it does not have proper mechanisms to handle refugees. Francis Teoh, a senior UNHCR protection officer, has commented on the situation, saying, "I wonder how these individuals survive . . . the

---

40. MS/C 06Dec2013.

41. Hamdani, "Do Ahmadis Deserve," online.

42. Amir J. Bobra, "Ahmadis Seeking Refuge in China," *Daily Times*, 20 June 2014, online.

assistance we provide is barely enough."[43] Despite all this, one asylum seeker said, "I am happy here compared with Pakistan."[44] Another asylum seeker said, "there is killing and persecution of minorities every day [in Pakistan]."[45]

Those Ahmadis who wish to flee the country but cannot do so immediately take refuge within Pakistan in Rabwah, where there is a temporary shelter for persecuted and displaced Ahmadis. During my visit to Rabwah in late 2013, I was able to see the facility, where seven hundred people at a time can stay and eat, and I met several displaced people, including some accused of blasphemy, who had been provided with shelter for the short term.

When I commented to the Ahmadi community in Rabwah that, if this trend of fleeing the country continued, their community would get weak, Ahmadi leaders acknowledged that the exodus was affecting their community in a significant way, but that there was no other way to secure the life of their people.[46]

An Exclusive Approach

The history of the last four decades of Pakistan reveals that extremism has gradually increased and its levels are continuously rising. As a result, tragically, tolerance towards minorities has shrunk to a considerable extent in Pakistani society. As a consequence, all minority groups, to a greater or lesser extent, face discrimination and intolerance in Pakistan. This led I. A. Rehman, General Secretary of HRCP, to say that "the future seems quite dark, if not for women, but surely for the minorities in Pakistan."[47] In any case life in Pakistan is difficult for all people, regardless of whether they are a majority or a minority. As a result, every minority group in Pakistan presents and broadcasts its own face of suffering in order to attract the international community to its own predicament rather than that of others.

In other words, each minority group tends to advocate only for its own people.[48] When Shias are killed in Pakistan, it is only members of the Shia

---

43. AFP, "Ahmadis Find Refuge in China," *The Express Tribune*, 19 June 2014, online.
44. Ibid.
45. Bobra, "Ahmadis Seeking Refuge."
46. MR/A 05Dec2013.
47. Cited in Din, "State of Human Rights in 2012."
48. There are, however, human rights organizations, like HRCP, which advocate on behalf of all oppressed and persecuted people, without partiality

community who protest and raise their voices: no other minority group visibly stands with them. In the same way, Hindus highlight their own ill-treatment. In a recent incident, in which there was a protest in front of the federal Parliament in Islamabad against the desecration of Sikhs' religious books in Mirpur Sindh, it was clear from the media coverage that all the protesters belonged to the Sikh community, as they were easily distinguished by their turbans: no representatives of other minority groups were seen with them.[49]

Ahmadis and Christians in Pakistan, who both suffer from the misuse of the blasphemy laws, nevertheless also tend to highlight their own predicament and ignore that of others. Both communities think and communicate that their group of people is more persecuted than any other minority group in Pakistan. For example, I was recently invited to a church gathering in Melbourne, Australia, and asked to comment on Pakistan's blasphemy laws. When I presented the statistics on blasphemy cases, which showed that the Ahmadi community, number wise, has been most affected of all the minority groups in Pakistan, one Pakistani Christian leader objected, saying, "You are misrepresenting the data."[50] He insisted, despite the evidence, that Christians are the most affected by blasphemy laws in Pakistan. In the same way, I observed the same attitude being shown, consciously or unconsciously, by Ahmadi leaders, during my interviews with them in Rabwah, Pakistan, in late 2013.[51] Members of each community tend to think that they are the most persecuted minority group in Pakistan. Perhaps this attitude undermines their willingness to raise their voices about the plight of others. Linda Walbridge's research in Pakistan strengthens this view: "it was obvious that the two communities [Ahmadis and Christians] had never empathized with each other's plights."[52]

Ahmadi leaders justify this attitude by arguing that if Ahmadis and Christians worked together then they would be more likely to provoke a

---

49. Iftikhar Firdous, "Sikh Community Storms Parliment to Protest against Alleged Desecration of Their Holy Books," *The Express Tribune*, 23 May 2014, online.
50. BP/C 07July2013.
51. HR/A 04Dec2013; YM/A 04Dec2013; AZ/A 05Dec2013
52. Walbridge, *Christians of Pakistan*, 55.

counter reaction from the majority Muslim community.⁵³ Salim-ud-Din noted that "at one or two places we supported Christians and we were blamed by the Islamic clerics that we are involved in conspiracy against the Muslims."⁵⁴ Likewise, Christians have the same fear of incurring more hatred from the majority community if they speak up for Ahmadis or stand with them.⁵⁵ They fear that standing together might create more difficult circumstances for the Christian community.

The narrow focus by each community on their own plight can be further seen from the example of the Shia community which has also been affected heavily by Pakistan's blasphemy laws (as seen in ch. 5). Despite the fact that they suffer from the same abuses as other minority groups, there is no evidence of any explicit voice or demand from the Shia community for amending these laws. In fact, the general perception in Pakistan is that the demand to repeal or amend blasphemy laws comes from non-Muslims. It is, perhaps, due to this perception that Shias don't want to object to the blasphemy laws, lest they be reckoned as non-Muslims.⁵⁶ (Note that 50 percent of the Sunni Muslims in Pakistan already consider Shias non-Muslims.) It can be argued that the Shia community is reluctant to support any demands to repeal or amend the blasphemy laws out of fear that this support would put them in a more vulnerable position. It could inflame calls to excommunicate Shias from the mainfold of Islam as happened to Ahmadis in Pakistan in 1974.

Our above discussion demonstrates that each minority group in Pakistan remains in a confined circle of its own and refrains from interacting with and supporting one another due to fear that their support may increase the antagonism of the majority community. They refuse to speak up for other communities for fear that the majority community might perceive that the minorities are trying to form a grand alliance against Islam. As a result,

---

53. MR/A 05Dec2013.

54. SD/A 05Dec2013.

55. MA/C 20Nov2013; JF/C 22Nov2013

56. When General Zia imposed Zakat as compulsory tax on Muslim in 1980's, the Shia community agitated aggressively on the basis of their tradition that it is a voluntary tax. As result, Shias were exempted from the compulsory Zakat Tax like other minorities in Pakistan. Some argue that, by doing so, the Shia community enlisted itself among minorities. Since then, there are strong feelings among the Sunni Muslims that Shias have declared themselves to be out from the mainstream of Islam by rejecting one of the five pillars of Islam.

minority groups become self-centred, each focused exclusively on their own suffering, and never speaking up for the plight of others. Each minority group, especially Christians and Ahmadis, is more concerned about its own survival in Pakistan than the welfare of others. As long as they are safe, they do not seem to care what happens to other minority groups.

A Sense of Disillusionment

Another similarity between Christians and Ahmadis is that both communities feel hopeless about the possibility of any substantial amendment to the blasphemy laws in the near future. Ahmadi leaders offer the following reasons for their despair: they say "we went against the sections of 295-C and 298-C in the courts but the decision was always against us."[57] Ahmadis believe that it is useless to go to any court in Pakistan to have the laws revised.[58] This disillusionment is based on the fact that they lost their religious battle in the Federal Shariʿat Court (FSC), in 1985, to have Sections 295-B and C changed. This was followed by their legal defeat in the SCP in 1993 (as seen in ch. 4).

Moreover, widespread discrimination against Ahmadis has meant that any move by the Pakistani government to improve the status of Ahmadis has met with opposition. For example, on 27 February 2002, the then military ruler General Pervez Musharraf issued an order, Chief Executive's Order No.7, to abolish Pakistan's separate electorate system, so that Muslims and non-Muslims would be enlisted on the same electoral roll.[59] However, shortly afterwards, on 17 June 2002, he issued another order, Chief Executive's Order No.15, which reversed the previous order and stipulated that the names of Ahmadis were to be deleted from the joint electoral rolls and placed on a supplementary voter list.[60] This is despite the fact that all other religious minorities are listed on the joint electoral lists: it is only Ahmadis for whom there is a separate electoral system.

---

57. AM/A 04Dec2013.

58. CS/A 04Dec2013; AM/A 04Dec2013; MR/A 05Dec2013.

59. *Chief Executive's Order 7 of 2002: Conduct of General Elections Order*, (27 February 2002) 54 PLD Central Statutes (2002), 197.

60. *Chief Executive's Order 15 of 2002: Conduct of General Elections (Second Amendment) Order*, (17 June 2002) 54 PLD Central Statutes (2002), 247–248.

This discrimination against Ahmadis can be further seen from an abortive attempt by General Musharraf in late 2004 to remove the religious identification column in Pakistani passports, which would have enabled Ahmadis to participate in the *hajj* (pilgrimage) to Mecca in Saudi Arabia. Ahmadis are forbidden to offer this religious rite, the *hajj*, because the Saudi government also considers them non-Muslims. Musharraf seemed under pressure to reverse his initiative, in 2005, when he himself restored the religious identification column. (Moreover, in order to obtain a Pakistani passport, the Muslim applicant is required to sign a religious affirmation denouncing the founder of the Ahmadi faith, Mirza Ghulam Ahmad, as an imposter.)[61] Reports have surfaced that pressure is being mounted on the Pakistani government by rightwing groups to change national identification cards so that, like passports, they include an entry labeled "Qadiani," which is a pejorative term for Ahmadis.[62] If this new scheme is passed, it would make Ahmadis more vulnerable to discrimination at all levels. With this context in view, one Ahmadi female lawyer said, "God may bring change through supernatural ways but if we see the ground realities, the change in blasphemy laws does not seem to come."[63]

The Christian community feels similar despair. It can be traced back to the suicide, in 1998, of Bishop John Joseph, a human rights activist and a great advocate for the rights of minorities in Pakistan. The bishop took his life on 6 May 1998 in front of the very court in Sahiwal where a Christian man, Ayub Masih, was given the death sentence in a blasphemy case. According to the Roman Catholic Church (whose explanation is popularly supported), Bishop Joseph took his life as a protest against the blasphemy laws.[64] Despite other, less popular, explanations for his death which have circulated in the media, the Christian community in Pakistan is quite convinced that he gave his life in protest against the misuse of the

---

61. See the Application Form for Pakistani Passport. Available at http://www.pakistan.org.au/upload/new-form-a.pdf

62. Paul Liben and Jessica Sarra, "USCIRF: Annual Report for 2012" (Washington: USCIRF, 2012), 111.

63. AN/A 13Dec2013.

64. Owen Bennett-Jones, *Pakistan: Eye of the Storm*, 2nd ed. (London: Yale University Press, 2003), 19.

blasphemy laws, and he is therefore remembered as a martyr with respect to blasphemy laws.

Another reason for the despair of the Christian community is that three major attempts to amend the blasphemy laws have been drastically defeated (as seen in ch. 1). During the rule of General Musharraf, in 2004, one small procedural change was introduced: a blasphemy case could only be registered by a senior police officer of a rank of the Superintendent of Police (SP). However, the police department did not take any heed of this amendment and it has never been implemented. This shows that even the powerful autocratic government of the military general, Pervez Musharraf, was not able to implement such a minor procedural change in the blasphemy laws. Any democratic government will struggle to take action on an issue as sensitive as blasphemy. Moreover, the killings of Governor Taseer and Minister Bhatti in 2011 shattered the hopes of the Christian community for any change in Pakistan's blasphemy laws. Following the assassination of these two high-profile figures, Asma Jhangir, the chairperson of HRCP, said, "I am not optimistic that [the blasphemy] laws will be repealed."[65] In such circumstances, it is natural that the Christian community in Pakistan feels hopeless and despairing. As one of the bishops commented that these laws cannot be changed until the day of judgment.[66]

The above discussion demonstrates that both the Ahmadi and the Christian communities are disillusioned about the possibility of any change to Pakistan's blasphemy laws in the near future. Accordingly, both communities have had to look outside Pakistan, towards the international community, to appeal to them to plead the case of these minorities with the government of Pakistan. We will discuss this in the next section.

A Dependent Approach

The Christian community in Pakistan has become a community that is dependent on foreign help, and their dependency on the West is not only financial but in terms of advocacy as well. It is a commonly held view in Pakistan that the West, including the USA, is Christian, and the policies of their governments are therefore perceived as Christian policies. (The majority

---

65. Cited in Din, "State of Human Rights in 2012."
66. MS/C 06Dec2013.

of people in Pakistan do not make a distinction between secularism and Christianity, perhaps because of the strong notion of the politico-religious government or state religion in Islam). Due to this perception, if anything happens in the West against Islam, this is perceived as the anti-Islamic acts of Christians. Furthermore, Christians in Pakistan are held responsible for the perceived anti-Islamic acts of the "Christian" West, because they are associated with the West on religious grounds.[67] It is therefore Pakistani Christians who face the wrath of extremists who express their grievances over the actions of individuals or governments in the West (including the US) against Muslims. For example, on 21 September 2012, the Federal Government of Pakistan declared a "Day of Love for the Prophet" and called upon people to demonstrate peacefully against an amateurish anti-Islamic film, *The Innocence of Muslims*, which had been produced by Nakoula Basseley in the USA and uploaded onto YouTube. The film stirred the religious sentiments of Muslims worldwide and provoked a strong reaction, particularly in Muslim countries. A mob protesting against the film in the city of Mardan in Pakistan torched St Paul's Lutheran Church, a Christian high school, a library, a computer laboratory and the houses of clergymen. Another church was attacked in Hyderabad and Christians were beaten.[68] (Moreover, a Pakistani government minister, Ghulam Ahmad Bilour, offered a bounty for the killing of Nakoula Basseley, and YouTube has since been blocked in Pakistan). In the same way, when western governments or human rights organizations raise their voice to protest against the mistreatment of Christians in Pakistan, this is generally seen merely as other Christians sympathizing with and supporting their co-religionists.

The Christian community is also dependent on the West financially. Because of the socio-economic position of Christians in Pakistan, Christian NGOs as well as the church establishment are heavily dependent on foreign mission agencies for financial support.[69] This reinforces the impression that Pakistani Christians have strong links with the West. This foreign dependency

---

67. There is strong sense of the concept of *ummah* (universal community) among Pakistani Muslims, meaning that anything that happens anywhere to Muslims affects the worldwide Muslim community. Perhaps they see in the same manner that whatever is done by the West is related to the worldwide Christian community.

68. Din, "State of Human Rights in 2012," 154.

69. Sookhdeo, *People Betrayed*, 342.

may also be partly because of their social backgrounds. As pointed out by Godfrey, the ancestors of Christians in Pakistan "think of themselves as naturally dependent upon others . . . This tendency has been engrafted in them for 1,000 years, and is now part of their very nature."[70] Whenever anything wrong happens to the Christian community in Pakistan, they look towards the West, particularly the US, to intervene and rescue them. (A poor Christian lady asked why America did not send airplanes and take all Pakistani Christians to USA). For example, in the case of Asia Bibi, Michael Nazir Ali, a Pakistani origin bishop in England, appealed to "the international community, the UN, the Commonwealth and the EU [to] do everything they can to make sure this vulnerable woman [Asia Bibi] does not suffer the extreme penalty . . ."[71] Furthermore Pope Benedict XVI, on 17 November 2010 at St Peter's Square, called the world's attention to the plight of Asia:

> Over these days the international community is, with great concern, following the situation of Christians in Pakistan, who are often victims of violence or discrimination. In particular, I today express my spiritual closeness to Asia Bibi and her family while asking that, as soon as possible, she may be restored to complete freedom.[72]

When her husband told Asia in jail that the pope had talked about her, she responded: "I leap out of my chair and jump for joy, shouting, I don't believe it!"[73] Similarly, the pope's advocacy on their behalf was well received by Christians in Pakistan. However, media reports reveal that it was not well received by the majority of the Muslim community in Pakistan. Some Christian ideologues in Pakistan are even of the opinion that Asia's case has lingered on because of the involvement of the international community.[74]

---

70. Phillips, *Outcaste's Hope*, 16.

71. Michael Nazir-Ali, "Repeal Pakistan's Blasphemy Law," *The Guardian*, 13 November 2010, online.

72. Pope, "Respect the Rights of Christians," https://www.youtube.com/watch?v=f7k2EQZWbQw.

73. Tollet, *Blasphemy*, 90.

74. AA/C 24Nov2013.

The Ahmadi community does not depend upon the West for financial support because they are quite strong financially and giving is highly encouraged as a religious duty. On the other hand, the Ahmadi community does depend a lot on the advocacy of the international community because they think that "if the international community intervenes it is much better."[75] During my interviews with Ahmadis, I wanted to know how they lobbied for their case. One Ahmadi female activist replied that they lobbied with governments abroad because their top leadership, Khalifa, was based in London. As a result, the Canadian prime minister spoke out for the plights of Ahmadis in Pakistan. Furthermore, when international high officials come for diplomatic visits, they raise Ahmadi issues with the government of Pakistan.[76] An Ahmadi lawyer responded that they provided reports to embassies and kept them informed about the ill-treatment of Ahmadis in Pakistan.[77] Western support to the Ahmadi community reinforces the commonly held view among Muslims in Pakistan that Ahmadis are Western agents. This notion has existed since the inception of the Ahmadiyya movement when its founder, Ghulam Ahmad, taught that Jihad against the British is not lawful. This was seen as a sign of sympathy with the West.

Our above discussion demonstrates that both Christian and Ahmadi communities depend heavily on the international community in the West to speak out for their plight and advocate on their behalf. Consequently, others in Pakistan perceive that both communities have strong links with the West and they are therefore labeled as anti-Pakistan as well as anti-Islamic. It can be argued that this perception has contributed to the failure of both communities to win the sympathies of the majority Muslim community for their plight. This dependent behaviour furthermore becomes a hindrance in acquiring substantial support from the moderate Muslim community to stand up for their rights in Pakistan.

---

75. MR/A 05Dec2013.
76. UK/A 13Dec2013.
77. AM/A 05Dec2013.

Dissimilarities

This section on dissimilarities will firstly look at how Ahmadis and Christians are reacting in different ways to the blasphemy laws; and, second and more specifically, the reasons why they are responding differently, despite living under the same circumstances.

When it comes to retaliation, agitation, protest or public demonstrations against the misuse of the blasphemy laws or against any mistreatment of minorities in Pakistan, the Ahmadi community is notably unified in their response of saying no to all aforementioned forms of agitation. For example, in May 2010, eighty-six Ahmadis were killed and one hundred twenty injured in an attack on their two worship places in Lahore. Despite this huge atrocity, no public demonstration was held by the Ahmadi community in any part of the country. General Shuja Pasha, the former Director General of Inter-Services Intelligence (ISI), told the judicial commission probing into the Abbottabad raid by the US Military that killed Osama bin Laden in May 2011, that the Lahore police protected the attackers of Ahmadis in 2010 and even directed them to the hospital where the wounded Ahmadis were being treated so that they could attack them again there.[78] Even then, no public protest against the Punjab police or the government was held by the Ahmadis.

In another significant instance, on 27 July 2014 in the city of Gujranwala, a violent mob set ablaze the houses and belongings of the Ahmadi community after an Ahmadi boy was accused of posting a blasphemous picture of the Kaaba on his Facebook page. As a result, four people, including a woman with an unborn child and two minors, were burned alive. Salim-ud-din, the spokesperson of Ahmadiyya Jamait, told the media that "he had personally been in touch with federal minister, local police officials and the inspector general of police but no one had listened or bothered [to respond to prevent the violence]."[79] The Station Head Officer (SHO) of the local police stated, "*sāḍay vas di gal naïn* (it is not something that we can control)."[80] The media

---

78. Correspondent, "Pasha's Abbottabad Briefing," *Pakistan Today*, 11 July 2013, online.
79. Rana Tanveer, "Gujranwala Blasphemy Case: Ahmadis Point Fingers at Silent Spectators," *The Express Tribune*, 28 July 2014, online.
80. Rabia Mehmood, "Ahmadis, Seared to the Wall," *Dawn*, 30 July 2014, online.

reported that the mob first looted the Ahmadis' homes and shops and then burned them, but the police stood there as silent spectators.[81] Despite this injustice, the Ahmadi community buried all their deceased without any public demonstration or agitation.[82] Mirza Masroor Ahmad, the current *khalifa* of the Ahmadi community based in London, issued a press release in response to the above-mentioned incident in which he reaffirmed the standpoint of the Ahmadi community: "Let it be clear that we Ahmadi Muslims will never undertake any worldly protest and nor will ever take to streets. Our response to all of the sustained persecution that we face is, and will always remain, to bow down before Allah the Almighty and to seek His help and mercy."[83] This response reflects the motto of the Ahmadiyya community, "Love for All, Hatred for None." The above examples show that this response is collectively followed by the whole community. It is not the case that the leadership says one thing and the people do the opposite: a consensus exists among the Ahmadi community on the policy of non-retaliation in response to any mistreatment of them in Pakistan.

In contrast, the response of Pakistani Christians is characterized by a lack of unity. Sookhdeo's observation is worth noting: "A series of initiatives – usually completely separate from one another – have come from individuals in the Church hierarchies and from Christian politicians."[84] Christians in Pakistan have been responding in a variety of ways to the misuse of blasphemy laws and any other kind of mistreatment. For example:

1. Some Pakistani Christian leaders are of the view that Christians should not show weakness but they should rather be prepared to retaliate. One of the advocates of this view justifies his position with these examples: In village No 136, a clash occurred between Christians and Muslims and, in retaliation, two Muslims were shot dead by the Christians. In an incident in Gojra in 2009, when the Christian colony was attacked, a young Christian man with a gun kept the crowd away from the community for four

---

81. Tanveer, "Gujranwala Blasphemy Case."
82. Ibid.
83. "UK: Statement of His Holiness Mirza Masroor Ahmad Following Attacks on Ahmadis in Gujranwala, Pakistan," *Ahamdiyya Times*, 28 July 2014, online.
84. Sookhdeo, *People Betrayed*, 303.

hours. This response prevented the Christians there from bearing a huge loss.[85] The advocates of this view argue that Christians have the right of defence and therefore Christians are allowed to arm themselves for this purpose.[86] Some Christian leaders in Pakistan have warned the government that if the violence and discrimination against Christians continue, then the possibility of forming *Sipāh-ē-Masihā* (soldiers of Christ) – like *Sipāh-ē-Sihāba* and *Sipāh-ē-Muhammad* – cannot be ruled out.[87] This view is justified by some Christian preachers in Pakistan on theological grounds: they point to Jesus' words where he said to his disciples: "And the one who has no sword must sell his cloak and buy one" (Luke 22:36).[88]

2. Other Christians are of the view that they should protest, but peacefully, raising their voices through rallies and protests. However, most of the protests that have been held have turned violent. For example, in response to the burning of 150 houses of Christians in the Joseph Colony in Lahore on 9 March 2013 by a violent mob of Muslims, Christians protested violently, breaking into a Metro Bus office at Ferozpur Road and damaging state property in Lahore. A large contingent of police had to resort to shelling tear gas at the protesters to stop further damage.[89]

3. Other Christians hold the view that, because they are a tiny minority and cannot face the brunt of the majority community, retaliation should be avoided as it will result only in more bloodshed. Instead, Christians should advocate through the international community to put pressure on the government of Pakistan to stop persecution of minorities.

4. Still others say that they should demand a separate province for Christians on the basis of the number of Christians in Pakistan.

---

85. JF/C 22Nov2013.
86. JF/C 22Nov2013; JN/C 12Nov2014.
87. Alexander Malik, cited in Sookhdeo, *People Betrayed*, 340.
88. JN/C //Nov2014.
89. Web Desk, "Joseph Colony Backlash: Enraged Protesters Smash Metro Bus Office," *The Express Tribune*, 10 March 2013, online.

However, it is unlikely that Christians could justify this demand as, according to government statistics, Christians make up just 1.59 percent of the total population, which is a very small proportion. (Note, however, that the majority of Pakistani Christian leaders believe that the government is understating their numbers, though they have no statistical evidence with which to refute government data.)

The unified response of the Ahmadi community can also be seen from the way they react to elections in Pakistan. General Zia introduced separate electorates on religious grounds in 1985. Since then, the Ahmadi community has boycotted the election as a protest against this discrimination.[90] Similarly, in 2002, when President Musharraf reintroduced the joint electorate, but maintained a supplementary voter list for Ahmadis only, the Ahmadi community decided to stay away from elections until this discrimination was ended.[91] The Ahmadi boycott is evident from the fact that the local council in Rabwah does not have a single representative from the Ahmadi community despite over 90 percent of its residents belonging to the Ahmadiyya community.[92] (It is important to note that the Ahmadi community has been boycotting the elections in a unified and peaceful manner.)

When separate electorates were introduced in 1985 on religious grounds, Christians, unlike Ahmadis, responded in inconsistent ways. Some Christian leaders were of the opinion that the separate electorate was a move to isolate Christians from mainstream society, and they therefore opposed it. Others saw the separate electorate as an opportunity to get a voice in the political system, so they supported it. Some others argued that minorities should have a dual right of vote – meaning that they could vote for both Muslim as well as Christian representatives.[93] No unified practical step was taken by Christians to challenge the discriminatory system in the way that the Ahmadis did.

---

90. SD/A 05Dec2013.

91. AFP, "Pakistan's Ahmadis to Boycott Elections," *Newsweek*, 23 April 2013, online.

92. MR/A 05Dec2013.

93. James A. Tebbe, "Interviews with Christian Members of National Assembly," *Al-Mushir* 27, no. 2 (1985): 99–100.

The separate electorate was replaced by a joint electorate in 2002; three general elections (2002, 2008 and 2013) have been conducted under this system. The Human Rights Commission of Pakistan pointed out in its special report, *Religious Minorities in Elections*, that there were several pockets in Punjab province where the minority vote could sway the election results.[94] Despite this fact, not even a single Christian candidate was nominated for a general seat by any mainstream political party in Punjab. It is disappointing, that the Christian community has not worked together to raise a unified voice against this discrimination and put together nominations for general seats to the mainstream political parties. (Note, however, that many Pakistani Christians believe that the representatives nominated by the political parties for reserved seats are not true representatives of their community.)[95]

This shows that the Christian community, unlike the Ahmadis, has not challenged the discrimination in the political system of Pakistan in a unified manner. Whatever political system is adopted by the government, no matter how discriminatory it is, the Christian community tends to become part of that system. Although the HRCP vividly highlights the discriminatory nature of the political system of Pakistan, no unified voice has been heard from the Christian community challenging it. This shows that Christians are a fragmented community compared to the Ahmadis. One Christian social activist rightly elaborates the state of Pakistani Christians by using a Punjabi idiom: "*Chovi (24) churay tey panji (25) huqay*" (twenty-four Chuhras and twenty-five smoke pipes).[96] The lack of unity of the Christian community means that they can be ignored. Consequently, political parties and government never give any weight to the needs of Christians.

Now a serious question arises: Why are Ahmadis unified and Christians fragmented in their responses to discrimination, despite the fact that they are living in the same circumstances and facing more or less the same kind

---

94. Staff Reporter, "Religious Minorities in Elections: Equal in Law, Not in Practice" (Lahore: HRCP, 2013), 8–9.

95. Staff Reporter, "Seperate Electorate Urged for Minorities," *Dawn*, 12 August 2014, online.

96. AA/C 24Nov2013. This Punjabi idiom is commonly used to describe disunity among the Christian community in Pakistan. One smoke pipe is sufficient for a group of people sitting around which they share. But in case of Pakistani Christians, instead of sharing, each has his own smoke pipe which describes figuratively the picture of disunity among them.

of challenges? This question can be answered by looking at sociological, religious and political reasons for the integrated and disintegrated responses of both communities.

Sociological Reasons

Social Stigma

The overwhelming majority of Punjabi Christians belonged to one of the socially depressed groups known as Chuhras, who were considered the very lowest class and were despised and exploited in India. Pickett points out in his classic study, *Christian Mass Movements in India*, that 70 percent of those who converted to Christianity from the depressed classes did not have a spiritual motive.[97] Instead, as the majority of sociological and historical accounts of depressed classes in India agree, one of the dominant motives for the depressed classes, especially Chuhras, to convert to other religions was to acquire a social standing on equal footing with others in a society where they had been under oppression for centuries. In Stock's words: "Their consuming desire was for freedom from oppression and a rise in social status."[98] For this purpose, the majority of them converted to Sikhism, Islam or Christianity.

However, they soon found that their dream of improving their social standing did not come true. In the Sikh religion, they were relegated to an inferior group called the *Mazhabi* Sikhs. Hutton states that a Chuhra's origin "prevents him ever being admitted to full social equality with the Sikh from *rājpūt* or *jat* origin, despite the Sikh repudiation of caste."[99] Cunningham also points out that "they found that [the] equality their religion promised them existed in theory rather than in fact."[100] Likewise, Chuhras were not accepted fully in Islam by their Muslim co-religionists: they were distinguished as *musalis* (little Muslims) despite the fact that Islam proclaims equality (Q.49:13). This shows that Chuhras were not able to acquire equal social standing with their co-religionists by adopting the religions of Sikhism and

---

97. Pickett, *Christian Mass Movements*, 164.

98. Stock, *People Movements*, 179.

99. J. H. Hutton, *Caste in India, Its Nature, Function and Origins*, 4th ed. (Bombay: Oxford University Press, 1963), 39.

100. J. D. Cunningham and H. L. O. Garrett, *A History of the Sikhs* (London: Oxford University Press, 1918), 72.

Islam. Nevertheless, there was some benefit: at least, they were able to get rid of their old identity as "Chuhras," which had been a huge social stigma for them in the class-conscious society in India.

In contrast, Chuhras in the northern part of India (now Pakistan) who converted to Christianity found that they were not able to escape this social stigma. Instead of their status being improved by the adoption of a new religion, the status of Christianity became stigmatized by association with Chuhras. The American United Presbyterian Mission was the pioneer in reaching Chuhras for Christianity in the middle of the nineteenth century, followed later by other missions. A newly established indigenous Presbyterian church was called "Chuhra Church."[101] Moreover, the missionaries and their local workers in the villages were mocked as *chuhra ka guru* (teachers of Chuhras).[102]

It is tragic that, even after more than 150 years of the Pakistani church, Christians in Pakistan are still called Chuhras; still tainted, both by their origins as well as by their menial work. I was told by a Christian politician that the Punjab government had appointed a Christian as a health minister, but that the Muslim community were very reluctant to accept him as their health minister. On several occasions, people commented about him in a derogatory fashion: "See, Chuhra is coming."[103] Similarly, when a Christian, Joseph Zacharias, was appointed as Station Head Officer (SHO) at the police station in Raiwind, the local *mullahs* (Muslim clerics), along with leading men of the local Muslim community, approached the Chief Minister of Punjab to protest: "If one has to use an abusive language to us,[104] then at least it should not happen through a Chuhra." Consequently he was transferred from there.[105]

Even more unfortunately, the word Chuhra is commonly used within Christian circles to show contempt for others. In O'Brien's words, "[there is] a sizeable minority [within the Pakistani church] whose social mobility

---

101. Webster, "Legacy of John Charles Heinrich," 34.
102. Webster, "Dalits and Christianity," 102.
103. MG/C 23Nov2013.
104. Pakistani Police often use abusive language with the common people, though it is not permissible by law.
105. MG/C 23Nov2013.

had brought them to the point where they not only wished to repress and deny their history, but wanted no social intercourse – even in the church – with those involved in sweeping."[106] This social stigma of a shameful social background has continued to trouble the Christians in Pakistan, resulting in what O'Brien calls, a "chronic inferiority complex."[107] On the one hand, Pakistani Christians have been suffering this social stigma for such a long time that there seems no way to escape it. In consequence, the stigma seems to have been internalized by Christians. On the other hand, discriminatory laws, like *Ḥudūd Laws*, *Qānūn-ē-Shahādat* (Law of Evidence) and blasphemy laws (as seen in ch. 1), have created a deep sense among the Christians that they are being treated as second-class citizens of the country.

The social stigma, coupled with the cumulative effects of the discriminatory laws, have increased the intensity of the inferiority complex of Christians, which is already chronic in its nature. Consequently, the confidence of Christians as a community within Pakistani society has been undermined. A recent study indicates that religious minority adolescents (Christians and Hindus) in Pakistan are susceptible to lower self-esteem as compared to the youth belonging to mainstream religious groups.[108] One young Christian commented that the inferiority complex of Christians has led them to become a defeated community.[109] Likewise, a female Christian politician said that the inferiority complex was affecting their youth psychologically and shattering their confidence as Christians on a massive level.[110] As a result, Christian youth suffer from internalized oppression as well as external discrimination.

Paulo Freire, a Brazilian organizer and educator who worked with people who were exploited and oppressed, wrote in his book *Pedagogy of the Oppressed* that "the oppressed can change their circumstances through *praxis* – reflection and action – and that in order to do that, they have to

---

106. O'Brien, *Construction of Pakistani Christian Identity*, 507.

107. Ibid., 504.

108. Shahid Iqbal, Riaz Ahmad and Nadia Ayub, "Self-Esteem: A Comparative Study of Adolescents from Mainstream and Minority Religious Groups in Pakistan," *JIMH* 15, no. 1 (2013): 54.

109. SC/C 27Nov 2013.

110. MG/C 23Nov2013.

learn to analyze their lives and to throw aside internalized oppression."¹¹¹ In the case of Pakistani Christians, they have to deal with both internalized oppression as well as external discrimination. In other words, they are burdened by both internal feelings of oppression and worthlessness, but also by the socio-political reality of oppressive and discriminatory laws. In many countries, groups that were discriminated against have overcome their situations through education, organization, economic advancement, or some other avenue.¹¹²

The present situation of the Christian community in Pakistan reveals that they are far behind in all these areas. For example, a recent sociological survey indicates that 72 percent of Christians in Lahore were illiterate.¹¹³ If this is the case of Christians in Lahore, where there are many more Christian educational institutions than in other parts of the country, how much worse the situation must be elsewhere in Pakistan. Moreover, a conservative estimate is that 80 percent of Christians live below the poverty line and are engaged with cleaning work, which is regarded as menial and is one of the reasons that Christians are called Chuhras. Unless the Christian community in Pakistan finds ways to deal with its internalized oppression, it will be difficult, if not impossible, for the community to stand together with confidence to resist any kind of external discrimination.

Insofar as the Ahmadi community is concerned, they do not suffer from the problem of internalized social stigma. Instead their discrimination is completely objective. During my interviews with the Ahmadi community, I noticed that nearly 95 percent of those whom I interviewed clearly stated at the beginning of our talk that although the State of Pakistan considered them non-Muslims, they never consider themselves non-Muslims; instead, they ardently teach their children that they are Ahmadi Muslims.¹¹⁴ One Ahmadi leader said, "Although I cannot call myself Muslim in Pakistan

---

111. http://ctb.ku.edu/en/table-of-contents/culture/cultural-competence/healing-from-interalized-oppression/main (accessed 30 August 2014).
112. http://ctb.ku.edu/en/table-of-contents/culture/cultural-competence/healing-from-interalized-oppression/main (accessed 30 August 2014).
113. Noel Alter, "Socio-Economic Conditions of Christians in Lahore, Pakistan" (Lahore: Forman Christian College University, 2011), 4.
114. NA/A 13Dec2013; CS/A 04Dec2013; HR/A 04Dec2013; AM/A 04Dec2014.

because of law but I can consider myself Muslim which I do."[115] This is a good example of the way the Ahmadi community prevents any kind of religious inferiority complex becoming internalized. The Christian community in Pakistan could learn from the Ahmadis' example how to counter their internalized inferiority complex in order to assert that their social status is not that of Chuhras (this point will be discussed at length in the next chapter).

Sense of Community

When a minority group lives in difficult circumstances, a sense of community is one of the protective factors for the survival of the group. There is a great sense of community among the Ahmadis, which can be seen from multiple examples. On 28 May 2010 in Lahore, two worship places of Ahmadis were attacked during Friday prayers and ninety-four people were killed – most of them the breadwinners for their families. In response to this catastrophe, the Ahmadi community built residential flats in Rabwah for those families who had lost their breadwinners. I was told during my visit to Rabwah in 2013 that the Ahmadiyya Jamait had not demanded any help from the government for these families, who are being completely supported by the Ahmadi community.[116] This process of support will continue until their children complete their education and get employment. One Ahmadi official mentioned that when you help your people in difficult circumstances, it gives a powerful message of comfort and encouragement that they have not been left alone. Furthermore, it gives them a strong bond to their community and, when somebody else faces difficult circumstances, these people show more sympathy than anyone else.[117]

The sense of community among the Ahmadis is further illustrated by their giving to community-based charity programs. One Ahmadi leader mentioned that income tax officers had asked in surprise how they could collect such huge amounts. The leaders replied that every Ahmadi was supposed to give a monthly offering, whether he/she earned one rupee or one million rupees. It is all done on a voluntarily basis.[118] I also witnessed in Rabwah that

---

115. HR/A 04Dec2014.
116. AM/A 05Dec2013.
117. AM/A 05Dec2013.
118. MS/A 25Nov2013.

community members are served regardless of their social background and religious identity. This is evident from the common kitchen where food is served without partiality to all those who are staying for temporary shelter.[119] This policy of the Jamait helps significantly in creating stronger bonds of love and sympathy, especially among the marginalized in the community.

In contrast, this sense of community is largely missing among Christians in Pakistan. Most Christians prioritize their personal benefit over that of the community. Previous sociological studies about the Christian community in Pakistan have indicated that the Christian community is divided along the lines of the *birādari* (network of kinship) system. Robert Tebbe, who served as an educationist in Pakistan, observed that the Christian community is "often torn by strife [and] divided into *birādaris* which contend with each other."[120] McClintock, a sociologist, noted that, among Punjabi Christians, especially those in church leadership, "they are expected to use their position within the church to provide economic and political support to the immediate family and to other members of their *birādari* as well. If they ignore the requests of their relatives for jobs or other material aid, their relationship with other members of the *birādari* become very strained."[121] Some other studies about Punjabi Christians have supported this observation.[122] Now the focus of concern of Christians has narrowed still further. Over the past few decades, the concept of *birādari* has faded to a great extent, and has been replaced with concern for "me and my family." Sometimes Christians fail to show concern even for their extended family. For example, one researcher told me about two Christian sisters who were in Thailand, applying for refugee status, along with their families. One of them got her case approved but the other sister, instead of rejoicing with her, challenged the ruling, telling the UN officials that her sister's case was false and hers was true. As a result, both applications had been put on hold for further investigation.[123] Similarly, when a Christian leader finds an op-

---

119. KI/A 04Dec2013.

120. Robert F. Tebbe, "Education in Pakistan: A Minority Perspective," *Al-Mushir* 25, no. 3&4 (1983): 184.

121. Wayne McClintock, "A Sociological Profile of the Christian Minority in Pakistan," *Missiology* 20, no. 3 (1992): 349–350.

122. Moghal, *Human Person,* 65–66; Sookhdeo, *People Betrayed,* 308–310.

123. AA/C 24Nov2013.

portunity to meet with government officials, he usually puts forward his own case instead of advocating on behalf of the community.[124]

The question arises why this selfish approach exists among Christians in Pakistan. Much can be attributed to the fact that the majority of Christians come from a socially weak background characterized by extreme poverty, insecurity and dependence upon others for their livelihood.[125] Although a small number of Christians are able to escape the social stigma of poverty through education and hard work, most Christians remain affected by the "attitude of scarcity" which still exists and which they try to satisfy through illicit means. In other words, a desperation to provide for their families leads them to focus on the interests of their immediate family, rather than considering the interests of the broader Christian community. For instance, Christian leaders are often involved in selling church property for personal gain. This attitude of scarcity leads Christian leaders to behave selfishly, without regard for the broader community. This selfishness has been one of the great obstacles to the formation of a genuine Christian community in Pakistan. Unless a sense of community is generated, it would be challenging for the Christians in Pakistan to stand together for their rights and come up with an integrated response to the blasphemy laws.

Religious Reasons

Factionalism

As mentioned previously, a split occurred in the Ahmadi community in 1914, in the early years of the movement. Consequently, two groups came into existence known as the Lahore and Qadian groups. The majority remained loyal to the Qadian group which is the main Ahmadi group worldwide. According to Ahmadi sources, "it spans over 200 countries with membership exceeding tens of millions."[126] However, it is a surprising factor that in the century (1914–2014) since this major split took place, there has been no further denominational split in the Ahmadiyya Jamait. This is reckoned

---

124. MA/C 20Nov2013.

125. Webster, "Dalits and Christianity," 95.

126. Ahmadiyya Muslim Community: An Overview, at http://www.alislam.org/introduction/ (accessed 21 August 2014).

to be one of the main reasons why the Ahmadis have remained intact as a united community.

In contrast, denominational divisions have been a huge phenomenon for the Christian church in Pakistan, just as they have been for the Christian church globally. According to the Centre for the Study of Global Christianity at Gordon-Conwell Theological Seminary, there were an estimated 34,000 denominations in 2000, rising to an estimated 43,000 in 2012. These numbers have exploded from 1,600 in the year 1900.[127] It is beyond the scope of our subject here to investigate the causes of factionalism in the Christian church worldwide. However, this phenomenon of rapid increase in Christian denominations has affected the Christian community in Pakistan to a great extent. Western Christianity is playing a significant role in bringing to Pakistan new denominations, cults and many other new groups with their distinctive teaching and labels. As Christians in Pakistan are struggling economically, they are vulnerable to such groups, who start new denominations with Western money. Nowadays, South Korean Christianity is also playing a major role in forming new denominations in Pakistan. Although there is no actual data available on new denominations in Pakistan, *Operation World* estimates that there were sixty-four denominations in Pakistan in 2010.[128] This data focused on major denominations but there are also many new small churches with distinct identities which are operating in Pakistan; and this trend is increasing.

The important point to note here is that, due to the restrictions on conversion from Islam, the conversion rate from Islam is negligible. Likewise, instances of conversion from other religions are very rare. Consequently, the formation of new churches actually means the further division of existing churches. The enthusiasm of the new denominations often leads them to steal sheep from other Christian pastures instead of preaching

---

127. http://www.gordonconwell.edu/resources/documents/StatusOfGlobalMission.pdf (accessed 21 August 2014).

128. Protestant 25, Independent 37, Catholic 1 and Marginal 1. Jason Mandryk, ed. *Operation World* (Colorado Springs: Biblica, 2010), 658. See also Peter Brierley, ed. *World Churches Handbook* (London: Christian Research, 1997), 648–651; "Pakistan," in *World Christian Encyclopedia*, ed. David B. Barrett (Nairobi: Oxford University Press, 1982), 542–545.

to non-Christians. Unfortunately, this trend is on the rise, especially in Protestant circles in Pakistan.

The Pakistani Christian community is also beset by many internal conflicts, especially in Protestant circles. For example, in 1968 the United Presbyterian Church was split over a power struggle. Since then, factionalism has been the characteristic of this church until the present. The Church of Pakistan (COP) formed in November 1970 from a union of Anglican, Methodist, Lutheran and Church of Scotland. This was a good example of unity but tragically the internal conflicts have affected the COP significantly. For instance, in 1997, the Rev Ijaz Inayat was elected Bishop of Karachi. Shortly before his consecration, a rival faction within the diocese charged the election was unlawful and received an injunction from a civil court blocking the consecration. In 2002, the Rev Sadiq Daniel was elected in an election boycotted by supporters of Bishop Inayat. This dispute is still going on in the court over the legitimacy of the Bishop of Karachi. A Muslim judge criticized both parties and rebuked them to settle their disputes among themselves, as commanded in the New Testament.[129] This phenomenon of internal conflicts has not been restricted to the major churches, but it has affected the churches within Pentecostal and Brethren circles as well. The Brethren church had a strong ministry of revival among the nominal Christians in Pakistan, but unfortunately it could not prolong its reputation as division occurred over leadership and property issues.

Denominational divisions, coupled with internal conflicts, have affected the unity of the Christian community to a great extent in Pakistan. These are also correlated with the *birādaris* and *zāts* (castes) factors that have contributed to factionalism in the church.[130] This phenomenon has much less of an impact in secular or majority Christian countries. However, it has huge implications for Christians living in the minority context of Pakistan. William Young, who explored the challenges faced by the Eastern Church in the first millennium, advised the church living in the minority context: "For [the] spiritual health of the Church, and to ensure its security and respect in

---

129. Gerald Mall cited in Sookhdeo, *People Betrayed*, 310–311.

130. See for good discussion on Biradheri and Zat factors, McClintock, "Sociological Profile," 349–350; O'Brien, *Construction of Pakistani Christian Identity*, 628–632.

a non-Christian State, it is absolutely essential that Christians lay to heart the importance of avoiding in-fighting or inter-denominational conflicts."[131]

Our above discussion demonstrates that denominational divisions along with internal conflicts have resulted in a further disintegration of the Christian community in Pakistan. These factors have hindered Christians from being united on one platform. A few years ago, the government of Punjab added a provision in the prison manual to give six months' remission in sentence to those prisoners who completed a basic Islamic studies course. On the basis of this, some Christian organizations put a demand before the government that this same provision should be available for Christian prisoners who completed a Christian education course. The government of Punjab agreed and asked for the curriculum which was to be taught to the Christian prisoners. This writer was part of the committee formed to plan a curriculum which would be submitted to the government. After several meetings of the committee, no consensus was found among members of the different denominations represented on the committee. Each denomination advocated for its own agenda and a lot of time was wasted in discussing non-essential issues. Consequently, the opportunity was lost and the cause of the Christian community was damaged because of denominational differences.

Central and Credible Leadership

Ahmadiyya Khilafat (caliphate) was formally established in 1908. Since then, there have been five spiritual leaders and its fifth and current Khalifa (caliph) is Mirza Masroor Ahmad, who is based in London. (In 2008 the Ahmadiyya Muslim Community celebrated 100 years of their caliphate.) Although Ahmadis claim that the "Ahmadiyya Caliphate" is purely spiritual in nature, its other dimensions cannot be ignored. The Khalifa serves as the worldwide spiritual and administrative head of an international religious organization with tens of millions of members spread across 200 countries.

The important point to note here is that the Ahmadi community is very much connected to the Khalifa. I was told that Ahmadi parents even get the consent of the Khalifa for the marriages of their children.[132] An Ahmadi educationist, Bashir Ahmad, the head of Business School at Forman Christian

---

131. Young, *Patriarch, Shah and Caliph*, 182.
132. AM/A 04Dec2013.

College – A Chartered University, wrote to the Rector of the university to say that "everything he did in life was guided by whether or not he had the approval of his caliph."[133] The office of Khalifa is highly respected among the Ahmadi community. An eyewitness told me that, when the present Khalifa, Mirza Masroor Ahmad, was elected to this lifelong position on 22 April 2003, there were thousands of Ahmadis gathered in London to hear who their new leader was going to be, despite the fact that, at that time, the weather in London was very cold and there was heavy rain. The new Khalifa came out wearing an old coat and told all the people to sit; immediately, they all sat to witness his oath ceremony.[134] Ahmadis follow what the Khalifa says. Although he is living in London, he is easily accessible to Ahmadi Muslims worldwide who seek guidance through emails, letters and his weekly sermons broadcasted live into various languages on MTA International, an Ahmadi Satellite television station, established in 1994. He also meets with individual members of the community on a daily basis which shows his concern for the community. The office of the Khalifa plays a significant role in binding the Ahmadi community together. Nowadays the Ahmadiyya Muslim Community is the only Muslim sect in the world that is united under one leader. The Ahmadis believe that "the institution of [the] Khilafat is the source of the Community's unity, vibrancy, organization, progress and its focus on peace."[135] Although the Khalifa is based in London, there is a chain of leadership which reaches into Ahmadi communities around the world. For example, each country has one spokesperson who gives policy statements to the media on behalf of the Ahmadi community. In Pakistan, the current spokesperson is Saleem-ud-din.

In contrast, there is no single recognized leader of the Christian community in Pakistan. Although the leader of the Roman Catholic Church is the pope, who is recognized as the spiritual head of the church, his role is much more symbolic. No fair parallel can be drawn between the pope and the Ahmadiyya Khalifa. Furthermore, the Roman Catholic Church is only one of a multitude of denominations represented in Pakistan. The Christian community has become a disintegrated community. Every Christian leader,

---

133. James A. Tebbe, email message to author, 30 Sep 2014.
134. MS/A 27Nov2013.
135. MR/A 27Nov2013.

political or religious, likes to speak to the media. There is competition among Christian leaders to become celebrities: they are desperate to be seen on television. One negative effect of this is that various accounts of news related to the Christian community circulate in the media, and sometimes the media are confused about who is the true representative of the Christian community. A female Christian politician observed that Christians in Pakistan have never been together, as they have neither a clear leader nor a strong sense of community.[136] Another Christian leader said, "We all are leaders and do not want to listen to anyone. Everybody cares for his own self."[137]

Another related issue for the Christian community is the credibility of their leadership. During my interviews with the Ahmadis, nobody voiced any complaint that their leadership was involved in corruption, whether at a higher or a lower level of leadership. They have full confidence in their leadership, and people love to follow their leaders. In contrast, there is huge concern about the credibility of Christian leadership in Pakistan. It is very common for political leaders to be accused of involvement in corruption scandals but, sadly, Christian leaders are not immune to this allegation. During my interviews with Christians, I sensed a clear voice of deep concern, particularly from Christian youth, alleging that the Christian church leadership is almost uniformly corrupt.[138] The corruption allegations have discredited the Christian leadership and therefore people do not trust their leaders. Christian leaders in Pakistan have failed to provide direction to the community. One Christian youth said, "They didn't have a good role model in their leadership to follow."[139] The Christian community, if not quite like a flock without shepherds, is surely a flock without good shepherds. The lack of godly and effective leadership is one of the key reasons for the Christians behaving as a directionless community. Without credible leadership it is hard for such a community, which is already disintegrated, to stand together for its rights.

---

136. MG/C 23Nov2013.
137. SR/C 20Nov 2013.
138. AS/C 14Nov2013; SS/C 14Nov213; KR/C 09Dec2013.
139. KR/C 09Dec2013.

Political Reasons

Political Awareness

During my personal research in Pakistan, I observed that the overwhelming majority of Ahmadis whom I interviewed, were politically aware, with a good knowledge of the blasphemy laws and their implications. One obvious reason for this political awareness, of course, is the high literacy rate in the Ahmadiyya community. Ahmadis claim that the literacy rate for Ahmadis living in Rabwah is about one hundred percent.[140] One Ahmadi leader explained that they set a target for their children that there should be no one in their community with less than an intermediate level of education.[141] Moreover, the Ahmadiyya Jamait continue to educate their community on political matters by holding seminars. One female educationist said that she had learned about the discriminatory nature of the blasphemy laws and the political system in a seminar organized by the Jamait, where one of the leading lawyers, Majib-ur-Rehman, gave a comprehensive presentation about discriminations that Ahmadis face, both legally and politically.[142]

During my interviews, I asked Ahmadis why they did not become involved with the political process in Pakistan. It was surprising that over 90 percent of them responded adequately with political and legal reasons to justify why Ahmadis did not get involved in politics in Pakistan where a significant majority of people are politically ignorant. For example, one woman responded that because the joint electorate system in Pakistan includes all minorities except Ahmadis, in protest Ahmadis will not become part of this discriminatory political system.[143] Another reason for their lack of political involvement was highlighted by another Ahmadi woman: "If we accept the existing system of reserved seats for minorities then we have to be recognized as non-Muslims, which is unacceptable to us. That is why we do not become part of this system."[144]

---

140. HR/A 04Dec2013; AM/A 04Dec2013.
141. AM/A 04Dec2013.
142. UK/A 13Dec2013.
143. NA/A 13Dec2013.
144. UK/A 13Dec2013.

The above responses demonstrate that Ahmadi women are just as politically aware as men. This is remarkable in the context of a male-dominated society, where females have less status and opportunity in all areas of life. It can be argued that the political awareness of Ahmadis, both men and women, is one of the key reasons for the Ahmadis' united response, as the majority of community members, including women, are aware of the challenges they are facing as a minority group in Pakistan. They have understood how important unity is for their survival in Pakistan.

Moreover, the Ahmadi leadership is also concerned with their community and gives priority to community issues over personal ones. For example, when the late Benazir Bhutto came to Pakistan in 1988 to campaign for election, she met Mirza Tahir Ahmad, the fourth K̲h̲alifa of the Ahmadi community, to request his support in the election. Tahir Ahmad, instead of asking personal benefits, raised a community issue with her. His words were, "I am ready to support you: [but] please tell me what you would do with the second amendment."[145] Benazir replied that she was not able to do anything because the law had been passed by her father. Mirza Tahir then responded, "I have nothing to discuss with you."[146]

In contrast to the Ahmadis, members of the Christian community do not seem to have much political awareness. The majority of Christians in Pakistan do not consider that the blasphemy laws are really an issue that they can address. This is evident from the fact that the Christian community does not raise this as an issue during election campaigns, or present it as a demand before political parties and their election candidates. Most politicians from the main political parties assert that Christians are not concerned about the blasphemy laws because they never present a case against the laws during election campaigns.[147] Although it is true that this is a highly sensitive issue and that politicians are reluctant to touch this law, Christians' silence on blasphemy laws during elections provides justification to political parties to remain indifferent to this issue.

---

145. Ahmadis were declared non-Muslim minority by the parliament of Pakistan in 1974 during the premiership of the Zulfikar Ali Bhutto, father of Benazir Bhutto.

146. MS/A 25Nov2013.

147. AA/C 24Nov2013.

When Christians do become politically involved, their demands tend to concern issues such as sewerage, electricity, water and roads in their localities. One Christian politician told me that she had received applications from different Christian localities to repair the walls of Christian cemeteries. She was disappointed about the community's demand, and commented that "we [Christians in Pakistan] are concerned about dead ones but have no concern for our living ones."[148] This kind of demand shows the lack of awareness by the Christian community about their real issues.

Some Pakistani analysts held Christian foreign missionaries responsible for this lack of political awareness among the Christian community in Pakistan. For example, Dominic Moghal argued that, as it was not possible for missionaries as foreigners to take part in national politics, therefore they never encouraged local Christians to take part in politics.[149] In other words, it is argued that their attitude was, what we cannot do, we will not allow you to do. Likewise, Zafar Ismail asserted that "the missionaries would often actively discourage or prevent the Pakistani Christians in their compound from political involvement, because any antagonism the Christians might inadvertently produce could have resulted in the missionaries losing their visas."[150] Similarly, Salmat Akhtar said that local Christians "were indoctrinated to abstain from politics as if it was the forbidden tree."[151]

These ideologues may be partly right, but it is not justifiable to hold missionaries exclusively responsible for the failure of local Christians to get involved in politics. These ideologues have overlooked the social background of those in the Christian community, especially Punjabi Christians, who come from the lowest level of society, where they had been oppressed; socially, morally, economically, ethically and politically, for centuries. How was it possible for these people to gain confidence just by becoming Christians? As we pointed out earlier, a significant number of people from oppressed classes had embraced Christianity because of the protection it offered from oppressors as well as for material gains. This view is strengthened by what Campbell informs us: "There was such eagerness among Chuhras to leave their old life

---

148. MG/C 23Nov2013.
149. Moghal, "Alienation of the Local People," 39.
150. Zafar Ismail cited in Sookhdeo, *People Betrayed*, 312.
151. Akhter, *Tahrek-e-Pakistan*, 21.

and status that many thousand enrolled themselves as Christians without the knowledge of missionaries."[152] Such converts were termed *rice Christians*. Their self-seeking attitude has been transferred to following generations which is reflected in the fact that, during the May 2013 elections, some of these so-called Christians agreed to vote for a particular candidate in return for payment of Rs.500 or Rs.1000 (equal to US$5 or $10).[153] The election candidates knew that votes could be purchased from Christian localities. I was even told that there were some local Christian leaders who asked Muslim politicians for money to purchase Christians' votes.[154] It may be argued that this occurred because of poverty, but poverty alone does not account for this phenomenon: the vote-selling reflects the lack of political awareness of Christians who do not value their vote. This attitude is also the product of an oppressed and defeated community which has no confidence that it can make any contribution to change. One Christian politician commented, "We are a sick community: when there is [a] healing crusade, thousands of Christians get together. But for [a] national issue, no one would dare to come."[155] This writer witnessed this behaviour of the Christian community during his visit to Pakistan in November 2014, when a very few Christians came out in protest against an inhuman act of the burning alive of Shehzad and his five months pregnant wife, Shama Masih, in a brick kiln in Kot Radha Kishan in eastern Pakistan by a violent mob on the accusation of desecrating the Qur'an on 4 November 2014.

Our above discussion shows that the level of political awareness in the Christian community is desperately disappointing. Unless the Christian community is properly politically aware, it is unrealistic to expect that they will stand together for their rights.

---

152. Ernest Y. Campbell, "The Church in the Punjab: Some Aspects of Its Life and Growth," in *The Church as Christian Community*, ed. Victor E. W. Hayward (London: Lutterworth, 1966), 151.
153. SR/C 28Nov2013.
154. SR/C 28Nov2013.
155. MG/C 23Nov2013.

Concluding Summary

In order to explore and analyze the Ahmadi and Christian responses to Pakistan's blasphemy laws, the study of this chapter was divided into two major sections – similarities and dissimilarities. Our study on similarities has indicated that both communities are so intimidated by their sense of fear and insecurity that they cannot freely express their concerns about the misuse of blasphemy laws.

The fear of being accused of blasphemy is pushing minorities to the state where they have to consider themselves as *dhimmi*, unable to claim their status of equal citizens of Pakistan, despite this having been promised by the founder of Pakistan as well as guaranteed by the constitution of Pakistan.

Second, due to their fear of blasphemy laws, both Christians and Ahmadis are fleeing the country, and this trend is weakening both communities.

Third, we have argued that minority groups refuse to speak up for other minority communities for fear that the majority community might perceive that the minorities are trying to form a grand alliance against Islam. As a result, minority groups become self-centred, each focused exclusively on their own suffering, and never speaking up for the plight of others. Each minority group, especially Christians and Ahmadis, is more concerned about its own survival in Pakistan than the welfare of others.

Fourth, our study has demonstrated that both communities are disillusioned about the possibility of any change to Pakistan's blasphemy laws in the near future because, so far, all efforts to amend the blasphemy laws have been defeated.

Fifth, we have seen that both communities look towards outside help and depend significantly on the international community for advocacy. Both communities strongly believe that unless the West intervenes, nothing is going to be solved for them in Pakistan. We have argued that this dependent behaviour becomes a hindrance in acquiring substantial support from the moderate Muslim community to stand for their rights within the country. Furthermore, this dependent approach is leading both communities, Christians and Ahmadis, to lose their confidence and courage to stand against any discrimination. As a result, defeated communities have come into existence who have no trust in the efficacy of their own struggle as well as no hope for their future.

The section on dissimilarities looked at how Ahmadis and Christians are reacting in different ways to the blasphemy laws and other kinds of mistreatment. Our comparative analysis demonstrates that the Ahmadi community in Pakistan is notably unified in their response. By contrast, the Christian community is characterized by a lack of unity in their response. Further, our analysis focused more specifically on the reasons why these communities are responding differently, despite living under the same circumstances and facing more or less the same kinds of challenges. This study demonstrates that there are great sociological, religious and political obstacles that prevent Christians from becoming a genuinely unified Christian community which could stand together for their rights in Pakistan.

Our sociological analysis indicates that social stigma, coupled with the cumulative effects of discriminatory laws, have increased the intensity of the inferiority complex of Christians, which is already chronic in its nature. Consequently, the confidence of Christians as a community within Pakistani society has been undermined. This inferiority complex has led the Christians to become a defeatist community. Unless the Christian community in Pakistan finds ways to deal with its internalized oppression, it will be difficult, if not impossible, for the community to stand together with confidence to resist any kind of external discrimination. By contrast, the Ahmadi community does not suffer from the problem of internalized social stigma. Instead, their discrimination is completely objective.

When a minority group lives in difficult circumstances, a sense of community is one of the protective factors for the survival of the group. We have seen that there is a great sense of community among the Ahmadis. However, this sense of community is largely missing among Christians in Pakistan. This study demonstrates that Christian leaders often behave selfishly, without regard for the broader community. This selfishness has been one of the great obstacles to the formation of a genuine Christian community. We have argued that unless a sense of community is generated, the dream of Christians standing together for their rights is not going to come true.

Apart from the first division in 1914 there has been no denominational split in the Ahmadiyya Jamait. This is reckoned to be one of the main reasons why the Ahmadis have remained intact as a united community. In contrast, factionalism has been a huge phenomenon for the Christian church in Pakistan. The Pakistani Christian community is beset by many internal conflicts among churches. We have argued that factionalism, coupled with internal conflicts, has resulted in further disintegration of the Christian community in Pakistan.

Further, this section's study also highlights that Ahmadis have a credible leadership which is evident from the fact that nobody from the Ahmadi community voiced any complaint that their leadership was involved in corruption. They have full confidence in their leadership and people love to follow their leaders. In contrast, there is huge concern about the credibility of Christian leadership in Pakistan. Allegations of corruption have discredited Christian leadership and therefore people do not trust their leaders. The lack of godly and effective leadership is one of the key reasons for the Christians behaving as a directionless community. Without credible leadership, it is hard for such a community, which is already disintegrated, to stand together for their rights.

Finally, our analysis of political reasons demonstrates that the Ahmadi community is far ahead of the Christian community in political awareness. We have argued that unless the Christian community become properly aware of their political rights and duties, they are highly unlikely to stand up for their rights.

CHAPTER 7

Theological and Contextual Reflections on the Christian Response to Pakistan's Blasphemy Laws

Introduction

Chapter 6 looked at the ways in which Christians and Ahmadis respond to the blasphemy laws, recognizing that in some ways, their responses are similar, while in other ways, each community reacts in different ways. We examined some reasons why their responses are so different, despite the fact that they are living under the same circumstances. We now move to reflect upon these responses using theological and contextual lenses, focusing on the Christian community. Thus our theological and contextual reflection in this chapter will focus on the Christian community's response to Pakistan's blasphemy laws.

This will assist us to offer a way for the Christian church in Pakistan to deal with their circumstances arising from Pakistan's blasphemy laws.

Reflection: Sense of Fear and Insecurity

Chapter 6 demonstrated that there is a great sense of fear and insecurity among the Christians in Pakistan because of the blasphemy laws. This level of fear has been intensified due to a horrific incident on 4 November 2014 in which a Christian couple, Shahzad Masih and his five months pregnant wife, Shama Masih, were tortured and afterwards incinerated in a brick kiln located near the town of Kot Radha Kishan in eastern Pakistan, by a violent mob, who had accused them of desecrating the Qur'an. The media reported that authorities at the local mosques had used the mosques' loudspeakers to command the mob to punish the couple on the grounds that they had insulted the Qur'an. The media also reported that, before the arrival of the mob, both husband and wife were locked up in a room adjacent to the brick kiln by their employer, Yusuf Gujar, who had a dispute over money with the couple, both of whom worked as bonded labourers at the brick kiln. The victims had four children.[1] A daily newspaper, *Pakistan Today*, published the story of the incident based on the account of eyewitnesses:

> According to Yasmeen [eyewitness], the mob then opened the door from inside and brought the couple into open, where highly-charged protesters were baying for their blood. They beat them with wood clubs on their head, and hatchets, before they were both tied to a tractor and pulled out onto an under-construction road covered with crushed stones. Mukhtar [another eyewitness] said, Shama had succumbed to the torture while Shahzad was unconscious, but still breathing, but the mob was still not willing to leave them alone. The mob then took some petrol from the tractor and doused their bodies and threw them in the kiln."[2]

This horrific incident has, understandably, terrified the Christian community across the country. It has also raised several theological questions with which Christians in Pakistan are wrestling. During my visit to Pakistan in November 2014, I found that members of the Christian community were asking several questions, especially after the above-mentioned incident. For example:

1. Where is God when it hurts? Why is God absent from their suffering? Why doesn't God interfere in their circumstances as he did in Daniel 3?

---

1. Waqar Gillani, "Pakistani Christian Couple Are Tortured and Burned to Death by Angry Mob," *The New York Times*, 5 Novmber 2014, A10.

2. Asher John, "Christian Couple Tortured, Bodies Burned over 'Blasphemy,'" *Pakistan Today*, 6 November 2014, 3.

2. Do God's promises (such as those in Isa 43:2 and Ps 66:12) stand true today? Does God's word have any significance for them today?
3. What is the point of living in the context of suffering when their sufferings do not make any sense to them?

When Christians do not get satisfactory answers to such questions, their response tends to be to seek ways of avoiding suffering which seems to them purposeless and incomprehensible. The two main ways that Pakistani Christians seek to do this are by:

1. Abandoning the faith.
2. Fleeing the country.

Two pertinent questions arise in response to these reactions:

1. The question of Christian ethics.
2. The question of the church's survival.

We will reflect upon each of these in turn.

Abandoning the Faith

There are Islamic institutions in Pakistan – the Badshahi Mosque, Jamia Ashrafia and Jamia Naeemea, all in Lahore – which maintain records of converts to Islam. Aoun Sahi, a Pakistani journalist, reports:

> Officials at the Madrassa [Jamia Naeemea] say the number of people converting from other religions, especially Christianity, to Islam is on the rise here. At least 50 to 60 Christians embrace Islam each month by signing [declaration] . . . that they accept Islam without any greed or pressure and promise to "remain in the religion of Islam for the rest of the life."[3]

He further notes:

> Badshahi Mosque is another institution that issues [a] certificate to those who convert to Islam. Muhammad Yousuf, assistant protocol officer at the mosque, says rarely a day goes without some cases of conversion. "Sometimes dozens of people convert

---

3. Aoun Sahi, "Pakistani Christians Convert to Islam because of Threats and Intimidations," *AsiaNews.it*, 16 March 2011, online.

to Islam during a day. Overwhelming, [the] majority of them come from [the] Christian minority, . . .⁴

Sometimes media reports of conversions are exaggerated. Therefore, in order to confirm this reported data, this writer requested his colleagues at the Open Theological Seminary (OTS) to do an independent inquiry into the conversion of Christians as reported by these two institutions in Lahore. They found that, at Jamia Naeema, eight to ten Christians come for conversion each month,⁵ and that at the Badshahi Mosque in Lahore, there were approximately twelve to fourteen cases of conversion each month.⁶ The officials at both institutions elaborated that more cases of conversion come in the month of Ramadan (a month of fasting in the Islamic calendar) and that the majority of them are from a Christian background.⁷

It is pertinent to ask about the motivations behind these conversions. This question has also been investigated during the visits to these institutions. Raghib Naeemi, the principal of Jamia Naeemia, stated the following reasons behind the conversion of Christians to Islam:

1. Some fell in love with a Muslim and converted in order to marry him or her.
2. Servants working in Islamic institutions (e.g. sweepers) wanted to improve their social status.
3. Some of them wanted to end their marriage, which is not easy in Christianity.
4. Some of them were truly impacted by the teachings of Islam.⁸

According to Orangzaib Ali, the Assistant to the Director of the Ulama Committee at Badshahi Mosque:

1. Most of coverts genuinely turned to Islam because of its message.
2. Some of them convert because they wanted to improve their social status.

---

4. Ibid.
5. MI/M 26Jan2015; RN/M 26Jan 2015.
6. OA/M 26Jan2015.
7. MI/M 26Jan2015; OA/M 26Jan2015.
8. RN/M 26Jan2015.

3. Sometimes labourers and domestic workers were obligated by their employers to change their religion in order to keep their job.[9]

In contrast, Pakistani Christians suggest different reasons for the conversion of their co-religionists to Islam. For example, Peter Jacob, a Christian human rights activist, thinks that security fears have become a major reason why members of the marginalized and discriminated Christian community convert to Islam. He further said, "Blasphemy laws are also being misused to pressurize Christians to convert to Islam."[10] Joseph Francis, another Christian human rights activist, explained that some conversions take place when Christian girls are abducted and married off to a Muslim, as once they have come into the circle of Islam, there is no way for them to return to Christianity.[11] Others have suggested that nominal Christians are more likely to be attracted to Islam because they do not have a deep understanding of their faith in Christ. As an example of this, they mention Yousuf Youhana, a Christian cricket star who converted to Islam in 2005, having been easily influenced by his fellow Muslim cricketers. He later played international cricket as Muhammad Yousuf.[12]

The rates of conversion cited above are from Lahore, where Christians are relatively privileged compared to those in other parts of the country. If Christians are converting to Islam at such rates in Lahore, then Christians living in the other parts of the country, especially rural areas, are even more vulnerable to giving up their faith. Although various reasons have been suggested above for why Pakistani Christians convert to Islam, an underlying factor seems to be the fragile state of Christianity in Pakistan, which is quite often shallow and cannot stand firm in times of trial and suffering.

Our above discussion reflects the context in which Pakistani Christians are living presenting great challenges to them. Pakistani Christians face completely different circumstances and challenges from those faced by Western Christians. In this regard, it is unhelpful that Pakistani Christians tend to look to Western Christianity as the ongoing standard for themselves.

---

9. OA/M 26Jan2015.
10. Sahi, "Pakistani Christians Convert."
11. Francis, "Annual Report 2012," 150–154, 276–279.
12. AM/C 19Nov2014; GA/C 19Nov2014.

(This is perhaps due to the historical reason that Christianity in present-day Pakistan was spread through the Western missionary movement.) Accordingly, Western Christian thoughts or movements often easily influence Christianity in Pakistan.

For example, prosperity theology (sometimes referred to as the "prosperity gospel," the "health and wealth gospel," or the "gospel of success"), which emerged in modern Western society, has had a big influence in Pakistan. According to prosperity theology, life revolves around the notion of individual freedom and happiness, and therefore teaching on suffering is not commonly associated with prosperity gospel teaching. This theology promotes the notion that believers in Christ should not expect to face hardships.[13] In the light of this theology, it is easy for those who are suffering to conclude that either they do not have enough faith (which leads to them feeling guilty) or that God does not love them. This theological teaching has spread rapidly, especially in poor contexts around the world, because of its attractive message that "it is God's will for all believers to be rich, healthy, and successful."[14] Believers are taught that a suffering-free life is guaranteed through faith in Christ.

This form of Western Christianity has influenced Pakistani Christians to a considerable extent, mostly through Pentecostal circles and independent groups, because it offers tremendous promises to economically and socially deprived people. Anwar Fazel, a well-known Pakistani healer, currently holds a healing meeting every week in Lahore. It is attended by 6,000 to 7,000 people, who come with all sorts of health, economic and social needs. (Due to the multitude of people, traffic police face huge difficulties in managing the traffic in that area.) Following his pattern, there are other groups who have started this kind of meeting in different areas of Lahore where the prosperity gospel is propagated. Three cities, Lahore, Karachi and Faisalabad, are very popular locations for healing crusades, because a significant number of Christians reside in these cities. Despite the government of Pakistan warning that such big gatherings are an easy target for terrorists in Pakistan,

---

13. Naomi Haynes, "Affordances and Audiences: Finding the Difference Christianity Makes," *Current Anthropology* 55, no. S10 (2014): 359; Philip Yancey, *Where Is God When It Hurts* (Grand Rapids, MI: Zondervan, 1997), 92–95.

14. Haynes, "Affordances and Audiences," 359.

people are so desperate to have their needs fulfilled that they never pay any attention to these threats. The doctrine of health and wealth theology is very attractive to people living in poverty and suffering.

Unfortunately, however, this doctrine has detrimental results when the promises preached to downtrodden people do not come true in their lives. When their theology does not match their experience, they begin to question their faith in God, asking, "Where is he? Why he is absent? Why does he not intervene in their circumstances?" Sometimes they feel guilty, presuming that their faith is not strong enough and that they are not good Christians. As their Christian faith (based on prosperity theology) was already shallow, they are unable to deal with the realities of suffering. Whether there is a direct correlation between those who hear prosperity teaching and convert to Islam when disappointed, or not, the theology based on this philosophy underlies the predominant thinking in the Pakistani Church today. Undoubtedly, this Christian theology is not biblical and is insufficient to sustain a community in times of persecution, so it is not surprising that many Christians in Pakistan are abandoning their faith.

In contrast to the mindset of many present-day Christians, for whom the existence of suffering makes their faith vulnerable to criticism and doubt, early Christians saw the pain and adversity of life as one of the main reasons for embracing faith. "Early Christian speakers and writers not only argued vigorously that Christianity's teaching made more sense of suffering than other religions, they insisted that the actual lives of Christians proved it."[15] Other early Christian writings, like Ignatius of Antioch's *To the Romans* and Polycarp's *Letter to the Philippians,* pointed "to the poise with which Christians faced torture and death for their faith. Christians used suffering to argue for the superiority of their faith because they suffer better than the pagans."[16]

The Greeks taught that the very purpose of philosophy was to help people face suffering and death. On this basis, Christian writers such as Cyprian, Ambrose, and later Augustine made the case that Christians suffered and died better than others and that this was empirical, visible evidence that

---

15. Timothy Keller, *Walking with God through Pain and Suffering* (London: Hodder & Stoughton, 2013), 41.
16. Ibid., 41–42.

Christianity was the "supreme philosophy."[17] Classics scholar Judith Perkins cites Ignatius of Antioch, who was the first writer to use the word "Παθος" (suffering) to describe Christ's death: "Christ's suffering is his essential message, and Christians' acceptance of suffering is the sign of their commitment to his message."[18] After unpacking the early Christians' experience, Perkins argues that "the Greek philosophical tradition's account of suffering was neither practical nor satisfying for the average person. The Christian approach to pain and evil, with both greater room for sorrow and greater basis for hope, was a major factor in its appeal."[19]

Instead of the false theology of prosperity, Christians in Pakistan need to learn the theology of suffering – in Luther's words, the "theology of the cross" – which enabled the primitive church to endure through pain and suffering. The Pakistani church needs to look to the early church as a standard and role model, rather than to the Western church. Furthermore, the Pakistani church needs to focus more on the poverty and faith of the early church instead of the luxury and resources of the Western church. Following the pattern of the early Christians, Pakistani Christians need to adopt walking through suffering as a lifestyle, as this is actually the lifestyle of Jesus. His call is, "Whoever wants to be my disciple must deny themselves and take up their cross daily and follow me" (Luke 9:23). What the cross looks like will vary from context to context, but the imagery of suffering conveyed in the vivid word "cross" is very relevant to Pakistani Christians.

Moreover, the Pakistani church needs to learn from its own history as well because this church, in its early history, handled persecution and difficulties quite well. The beginnings of the revival in this land went back to a person, named Ditt, who suffered significantly for his faith until others joined him.[20] Likewise Sadhu Sundar Singh suffered enormously for the sake

---

17. Ibid., 42.

18. Judith Perkins, "The 'Self' as Sufferer," *The Harvard Theological Review* 85, no. 3 (1992): 263.

19. Judith Perkins, *The Suffering Self: Pain and Narrative Representation in the Early Christian Era* (London: Routledge, 1995).

20. Gordon, *Our India Mission*, 423–424.

of his Christian faith.[21] Another example is that of Labu Mall, first local theological teacher in the Gujranwala Theological Seminary in Pakistan, who refused to work unless he would be supported by his own people. Instead of taking a regular house, he insisted on living in servants' quarters.[22]

The Christian church in Pakistan needs to take courage from the fact that their God is not aloof from their pain and suffering, as he suffered in Christ and experienced their pain, abandonment and suffering, and even death on the cross. Alister McGrath puts it this way:

> God is not like some alleged hero with feet of clay, who demands that others suffer, while remaining aloof from the world of pain himself. He has passed through the shadow of suffering himself. The God in whom Christians believe and trust – is a God who himself suffered, and by doing so, transfigures the sufferings of his people.[23]

Dembski reinforces this point by making a helpful distinction between knowledge by description and knowledge by acquaintance. "Knowledge by description is available from books. But knowledge by acquaintance means getting your hands dirty in the nitty-gritty of human experience. On the cross, Christ has done exactly that."[24] Moreover, he still suffers through the sufferings of his church and "senses our sufferings as his own."[25] This is evident from Jesus' words, "Saul, Saul, why do you persecute me?" (Acts 9:4).

In the light of our above discussion we can conclude that there is a great need to confront biblically the issue of suffering, which is actually at the heart of the Christian story. This needs to be the basis of the preaching of Christian theology in Pakistan, instead of "prosperity theology." The Pakistani church needs to inject the theology of the cross more vigorously

---

21. Arthur Parker, *Sadhu Sundar Singh: Called of God* (Calcutta: CLS, 1920), 29–40; C. F. Andrews, *Sadhu Sundar Singh: A Personal Memoir* (London: Hodder & Stoughton, 1934), 76–85.

22. James A. Tebbe, email message to author, 22 Jan 2015.

23. Alister E. McGrath, *Suffering,* http://www.bethinking.org/suffering/suffering-problem (accessed 29 December 2014); Alister E. McGrath, *Suffering of God* (Grand Rapids, MI: Zondervan, 1995), 26.

24. William A. Dembski, *The End of Christianity: Finding a Good God in an Evil World* (Carlisle: Paternoster, 2009), 19.

25. Keller, *Walking with God,* 53.

into its teaching and preaching in contrast to the view presented by prosperity theology. When this is done, the theology that is taught will match the experience of people's lives, instead of contradicting it. Such faithful teaching with true biblical theology will both produce deeper faith, which will sustain Pakistani Christians in their suffering; and give meaning to their suffering, which will ultimately provide a sense of purpose for persevering in the context of suffering.

Fleeing the Country

The overwhelming majority of Christians in Pakistan are from the socially deprived classes and their social origin accounts for much of the discrimination and prejudice they face in a class-conscious society such as Pakistan. Given this social context, it is fair to ask whether Pakistani Christians are suffering because of their faith or simply because of their low social background. This question is being debated among Christians in Pakistan.

There is a strong evangelical voice in the church in Pakistan, especially within Protestant circles, that the existing sufferings of Christians in Pakistan cannot be reckoned as suffering for their faith, unless their suffering is directly linked to their proclamation of the gospel.[26] In support of their view, they argue that more blasphemy cases have been framed against the socially deprived, therefore they consider that the present sufferings of Christians in Pakistan are due to their social identity rather than religious reasons.[27]

This view can be countered with the example of Christians in Iraq and Syria, who are not being persecuted for proclaiming the gospel but just because of their allegiance to the Christian faith; in other words, because of their identity as Christians. Likewise, on 22 September 2013, two suicide bombers carried out an attack at the end of a Sunday service at All Saints Church, Peshawar, killing eighty-five people and injuring more than one hundred.[28] This suffering happened because they were Christians, not because they were personally proclaiming the gospel. In the same way, the multiple examples mentioned above demonstrate that Christians do face the brunt of persecution by the majority community because they are Christians

---

26. SS/C 17Nov2013; AS/C 17Nov2013.
27. AA/C 21Nov2013; SS/C 17Nov2013.
28. Jon Boone, "Pakistan Church Bomb," *The Guardian*, 25 September 2013, online.

(whether they are genuine believers or nominal Christians). This debate about the cause of suffering has not been explored rationally in Pakistan and therefore the variety of views is causing confusion for the Christian community in Pakistan.

During my interviews in 2013 and 2014 in Pakistan, I sensed clearly that the majority of Christians do not understand why they are suffering in this context. They get confused and discouraged when their sufferings do not make any sense to them. They think that their suffering is useless. Despite the importance for Christians in Pakistan of understanding the reasons for and purpose of their suffering, no sincere academic effort has been made by the Christian church in Pakistan to reflect theologically upon this issue within their context, in order to help the Christian community make sense of their suffering. This is evident from the fact that this writer has not come across a single book in Urdu, written by a Pakistani Christian, which deals in depth with this subject. Christians get confused and frustrated when their sufferings do not make any sense to them and this is exactly what is happening with the overwhelming majority of Christians in Pakistan.

When suffering does not make any sense to Pakistani Christians, then it is easy for them to think that there is no point in enduring and therefore that it is better to flee from this situation. According to Nazir Bhatti, a Christian human rights activist, "90% [of] Pakistani Christians favour refugee status from UN after rising violence."[29] This ambition is reflected in the views of a young Pakistani Christian who pleaded, "*Ap sab mil key Christian countries ko request karein key wo ham sab ko Pakistan se nikal le jaein*" (You all [Christian NGOs and religious leaders] request Western Christian countries to give all of us refuge in their countries).[30] It has been reported that, in the last two years, the number of Christian asylum seekers especially from Pakistan has increased due to the persecution of minorities. "In some instances, framing of charges against them for acting against some religious laws including blasphemy and in some cases because of their forced conversion . . . There

---

29. Nazir S. Bhatti, "90% Pakistani Christian Favour Refugee Status from UN after Rising Violence," *Pakistan Christian Post*, 14 May 2014, online.
30. Ibid.

are a number of Christians in Sri Lanka, Indonesia, Papua New Guinea, Fiji, Christmas Island, Greece, Kenya and the island nation of Malta."[31]

Another report estimated that about 26,300 Pakistanis, the highest number ever recorded, have applied for asylum in 2014 and a very large number of them are non-Muslims, especially Christians.[32] There are certainly a variety of reasons and motives behind the exodus, but it can be argued that it happens most when people do not find any sense of purpose behind their sufferings.

Sociologists like Max Weber, Frederick Nietzsche and others have argued that "when no explanation at all is given – when suffering is perceived as simply senseless, a complete waste, and inescapable – victims can develop undying anger and poisonous hate that was called *ressentiment* . . ."[33] In order to avoid this *ressentiment*, sociologists say that every society must provide a "discourse" through which its people can make sense of suffering. One of the world's leading sociologists, Peter Berger, writes that every culture has provided an "explanation of human events that bestows meaning upon the experiences of suffering and evil."[34] Further, sociologists insist that a society equip its people for the battles of living in this world.[35] We argue that in the context of suffering, it is one of the church's fundamental responsibilities not only to provide an explanation for suffering but to help people to be faithful to the central message of the Christian faith – the message of the cross. This is a message of suffering that is at the heart of the Christian story and through which the church can equip its people to be prepared to bear their cross. What this looks like will, of course, vary from context to context.

In this regard, the Pakistani church could benefit from the example of the Ahmadi community in Pakistan. They have a much more robust understanding that their suffering in Pakistan is not in vain. For example, I was told during my interviews with them that they compare themselves to

---

31. Emanuel Sarfraz, "Another Exodus of Refugees from Pakistan," *The Nation*, 19 March 2014, online.

32. Nasir Jamal, "Destination: Aslyum Abroad," *Dawn*, 16 May 2015, 3.

33. Cited in Keller, *Walking with God*, 14. See Max Weber, *The Sociology of Religion* (Boston: Beacon, 1993), 110–115.

34. Peter Berger and Hansfried Kellner, *The Homeless Mind: Modernization and Conciousness* (New York: Vintage, 1974), 185.

35. Keller, *Walking with God*, 14.

the early Christians who went through a great persecution in the first three centuries of Christianity. Likewise the Ahmadis accept that they have to go through tribulations in Pakistan. They also believe that, as circumstances changed in the Christians' favour after three centuries, when Constantine became a Christian, the time will come when the situation will improve for Ahmadis. They believe that this goal cannot be achieved without suffering now, therefore they perceive their sufferings are a journey towards that goal. This is, perhaps, why the Ahmadi community, much more than the Christian community, bears calmly the mishaps that happen to them, because they are more prepared for this task and moreover their sufferings make sense to them.

The Pakistani church therefore needs to realize its responsibility to faithfully communicate what the Bible teaches about the place of suffering in Christian discipleship. One way to do this would be to provide a theological course at different levels through which people could get an explanation for their suffering in their minority context.

Another way could be to highlight the role models of the Pakistani church, from its own early history. Examples are, as noted above, Ditt, Sadhu Sundar Singh and Labu Mall who, despite all their sufferings, remained faithful to their call to follow Jesus.

Question of Christian Ethics

As noted above, many Christians in Pakistan respond to their suffering by attempting to flee the country and seek asylum elsewhere. This obviously weakens the church in Pakistan. However, it also raises another serious issue, which is that of Christian ethics. Those seeking asylum must present a strong case to show that there are serious threats to their lives if they remain in Pakistan. This presents a very real temptation to make up false stories in order to gain asylum. A Christian researcher told me that, in order to strengthen their claims to asylum, some Christians register a false blasphemy case against themselves by bribing the police Rs. 40,000 to 50,000 in order to get the copy of a false FIR to support their case for asylum.[36] However, the majority of Christian asylum seekers use letters from their church to support their claims of persecution. As we noted in chapter 6, one of the bishops

---

36. AA/C 24Nov2013.

told me during an interview that he received numerous phone calls and that 80 percent of them related to requesting a church letter in support of applications for asylum.[37] I interviewed six of Pakistani Christians who sought asylum in Australia among whom five have false letters from the church.[38]

This shows, regrettably, that an overwhelming majority of Christian asylum seekers from Pakistan make false claims. Despite knowing the truth, the majority of pastors, especially in Protestant circles, are willing to provide letters in support of their false claims that their lives are under threat. During my interviews with Christian leaders, I raised this question. One pastor argued that while the church had no solution for the problems facing the Christian community there, they had to help, in any way, anyone striving for a better future for his children.[39]

The advocates of the above view claim that there is biblical justification for lying in order to save a life. They cite the examples of the Hebrew midwives in Exodus 1 and Rahab in Joshua 2, whom they see as saintly liars. John Frame, one of the leading proponents of this view, claims, along with a number of other theologians, that it is acceptable to make exceptions to normal ethics in extreme cases such as war and in order to save the life of another.[40] The proponents of this view frequently refer to one of the most famous ethical dilemmas, when some Christians sheltered Jews in their homes during World War II. In this context, Frames argues, there is "no obligation to tell the truth to people who, for example, seek innocent life."[41] In a theological support of this view, they cite those biblical references in which someone misleads an enemy, without incurring condemnation, and sometimes even being commended.[42] Luther defended the case for lying for

---

37. MS/C 6Dec2013.

38. JM/C 26Jan2015; SM/C 26Jan2015; PM/C 26Jan2015.

39. MA/C 20Nov2013.

40. John M. Frame, *The Doctrine of the Christian Life* (Phillipsburg, NJ: P&R, 2008), 834–840.

41. Ibid., 839.

42. Hebrew midwives in Egypt (Exod 1:15); Rahab's concealment (Josh 2:6; 6:17; Heb 11:31; Jas 2:25); the Ambush at Ai (Josh 8:3–8); Jael and Sisera (Judg 4:18–21; 5:24–27); Samuel misleads Saul (1 Sam 16:1–5); Michal deceives her father (1 Sam 19:12–17); David lies to Achish (1 Sam 27:10); God sends lying spirit against Ahab (1 Kgs 22:19–23); Elisha misleads the Syrian troops (2 Kgs 6:14–20); Jeremiah lies to the Princes (Jer 38:24–28) and sends a powerful delusion (2 Thess 2:11).

the sake of good and the church, arguing that a lie in case of necessity is a useful lie. Such lies, he said, "not be against God."[43]

On the other side, the predominant view among Reformed Christians is that of Augustine, Calvin and John Murray who argued that we should never tell lies under any circumstance.[44] In this regard, Murray says, "Truth and untruth are antithetical because God is truth. And this is the reason why truthfulness and untruth do not cohere."[45] Likewise, Wayne Grudem argues in favour of never lying "in every situation and every circumstance of life, and this will be true for all eternity."[46] The proponents of this camp note that Jesus referred to Satan as "a liar and the father of lies" (John 8:44). By contrast, Jesus declared himself to be the Truth (John 14:6). They argue that lying is more Satan-like than Christ-like.

This brief analysis shows that both sides have strong arguments with substantial biblical support for their positions. Vern Poythress rightly makes a notable point in analyzing this debate that "neither side has succeeded in presenting an argument that would convince everyone on the other side."[47]

However, when it comes to the Pakistani Christian pastors who are issuing false letters as well as Christian asylum seekers who are making up false stories for the purpose of asylum, their act cannot be justified theologically because of the following reasons:

1. Pastors are helping those whose lives may not actually be in danger. Instead they are supporting mostly wealthier Christians who ask for letters to support their asylum applications. (This is against the biblical principle to rob others rights. Phil 2:4; Luke 6:31; Rom 15:2.)

---

43. Cited in Uri Gneezy, "Deception: The Role of Consequences," *AER* 95, no. 1 (2005): 384.

44. Augustine (AD 354–430), the most famous defender of the view that lying is always wrong. See the extensive discussion in Paul J. Griffiths, *Lying: An Augustinian Theology of Duplicity* (Grand Rapids: Brazos, 2004). John Murray, *Principles of Conduct* (London: Tyndale, 1957), 123–148.

45. Murray, *Principles of Conduct*, 148.

46. Wayne Grudem, "Why It Is Never Right to Lie: An Example of John Frame's Influence on My Approach to Ethics," in *Speaking the Truth in Love: The Theology of John Frame*, ed. John J. Hughes (Phillipsburg, NJ: P&R, 2009), 801.

47. Vern S. Poythress, "Why Lying Is Always Wrong: The Uniqueness of Verbal Deceit," *WTJ* 75, no. 1 (2013): 83.

2. The issuing of false letters damages the reputation of the Christian community in Pakistan in particular, as well as the country in general, reinforcing the belief that Pakistanis are not reliable and are prone to cheating.
3. A few decades ago, Christians in Pakistan were considered trustworthy and honest people. This helped them to win the confidence of Muslim merchants who hired Christians in preference to Muslims. But this image of the Christian community has been distorted to a considerable extent. Now there are many cases of Christians involved in embezzlement, corruption, deception and many other immoral activities. Christian pastors, by issuing false letters, and Christians, by making false statements contribute to the moral decay of the Christian community, instead of building up the Christian character of the community – something which is very much needed.
4. Strengthening the integrity of the Christian community would help it to regain a good reputation within the country and, as Christians are also Pakistani citizens, so it may contribute to improving the image of Pakistan in the world.
5. Christians are called to be salt and light in society (Matt 5:13–16), but the actions of these pastors undermine the Christian character and such deeds, especially by church leaders, are a great hindrance in the way of spreading the gospel message in Pakistan. In this regard Mahatma Gandhi rightly pointed out few decades ago, ". . .all of you Christians . . . must begin to live more like Jesus Christ. Practice your religion without adulterating it or toning it down,"[48] and "people will come to see the source of your power."[49] For this reason, Jones wrote that "God has used Gandhi to help Christianize unchristian Christianity."[50]

---

48. E. Stanley Jones, *Mahatma Gandhi: An Interpretation*, 1st ed. (London: Hodder & Stoughton, 1948), 70.
49. Ibid., 83.
50. Ibid., 102.

Question of Church's Survival

Whenever the suffering of the church is discussed, Tertullian's theology of martyrdom is mentioned. Tertullian, a second-century church father, theologian and apologist, developed his theology of martyrdom in the context of the courage of the Christians in Carthage who were being thrown to lions and burned in public, and the blood of the martyrs that was regarded as the foundation of the church.[51] He admired the courage of the Christians[52] and wrote to the Roman authorities to tell them that persecution of the Christians was producing results opposite to what was intended: "The more we are mown down by you, the more numerous we grow; blood of the Christians is seed" (which is often misquoted as "the blood of the martyrs is the seed of the church").[53] Tertullian's statement has been used repeatedly over the centuries to support the notion that persecution always causes church growth as well as purifying the church. Thus, persecution is seen as a great benefit to the church. Undoubtedly, the persecution of the primitive church pushed it out of Jerusalem and eventually caused the gospel to be spread swiftly in different directions across three continents (Europe, Africa and Asia) over the first three centuries. In modern times, the underground church in China has also grown in the midst of persecution. Yung states emphatically that "suffering has refined and strengthened the church in China."[54] Likewise, one pastor of the house church in China, states, "Persecution is good for the church. More persecution, more growth."

However, this notion of "suffering has strengthened the church" has not come true in many parts of the world, especially in the Muslim world, including the northern part of India, which is now Pakistan. (Other parts of the Muslim world are beyond the scope of our studies here so we will confine ourselves to the geographical area of what is now Pakistan.)

There exists substantial evidence that, until the end of the first millennium, Nestorian Christianity had a strong presence in the northern part

---

51. Gerald Bray, "Tertullian," in *The Dictionary of Historical Theology*, ed. Trevor A. Hart (Carlisle: Paternoster, 2000), 538.

52. It is presumed that perseverance of the Christians under severe persecution in Carthage led Tertullian to Christianity. Jonathan Hill, *The History of Christian Thought* (Oxford: Lion, 2003), 30.

53. Ibid.

54. Hwa Yung, "The Church in China Today," *Transformation* 21, no. 2 (2004): 127.

of India, now Pakistan.⁵⁵ This has also been confirmed by archaeological discoveries which have shown that the Nestorians were a vital community in Asia.⁵⁶ Some Church historians, like John Rooney, are of the view that the ancient Christianity in the northern part of India had vanished by the eleventh century.⁵⁷ Others like Barkat Ullah suggest that it survived longer – to some point in the fourteenth century.⁵⁸ Christian communities lived in the various parts of Punjab, Sindh and Baluchistan, covering the areas in Pakistan and Afghanistan in the first millennium. Their disappearance has been a genuine puzzle to church historians. Why could that church not survive? It is true that we do not have definite answers, but we will attempt to trace the major reasons for the collapse of the ancient church in the northern part of India.

First, Christians suffered as a result of Jihad by Muslims. One of the characteristics of the Muslim conquest of India was the establishment not only of the Muslim empire but of the Muslim faith. This meant a huge setback to Christianity in the North of India.⁵⁹ Second, the heavy burden of tax as *dhimmi* made Christians rethink their loyalty to their faith.⁶⁰ Stewart notes that "numbers of nominal Christians adopted the faith of their new masters, while others fled into more distant places."⁶¹ Third, the Sufi-generated movements attracted not only low-caste Hindus but also members of the fragile Christian community.⁶² This demonstrates that the Christians could not sustain their faith in the face of the harsh conditions inflicted by Islamic invaders on the subdued minorities.

It would be easy to blame the demise of Christianity in Pakistan on external factors, but it would be unfair to overlook the internal factors which equally contributed to the elimination of Christianity. For example,

---

55. John Stewart, *Nestorian Missionary Enterprise: The Story of a Church on Fire* (Edinburgh: T&T Clark, 1928), 14.

56. Kahar Barat, "Aluoben, a Nestorian Missionary in 7th Century China," *JAH* 36, no. 2 (2002): 185.

57. Rooney, *Shadows in the Dark*, 98.

58. Barkat Ullah, *Saleeb Key Harawal* [Guardians of the Cross], 4 vols., vol. 2 (Lahore: NCCP, 2010), 110–114; Stewart, *Nestorian Missionary Enterprise*, 230.

59. Titus, *Islam in India*, 15; Stewart, *Nestorian Missionary Enterprise*, 232–234.

60. Rooney, *Shadows in the Dark*, 96.

61. Stewart, *Nestorian Missionary Enterprise*, 216.

62. Rooney, *Shadows in the Dark*, 98.

Nestorian Christianity was very accommodative: they indiscriminately incorporated the customs of the local religions into their own brand of Christianity.[63] The corruption of the Nestorian church, coupled with its eventual failure to fulfill its great commission despite early successful missionary outreach, was another reason for the church's demise. Some viewed the decline of the church as evidence of God's swift judgment upon it.[64] Overall, historians attribute "the decline of Christianity in this region [to] . . . a general weakness in the Church in Persia, which brought about that Church's steady disintegration."[65]

The circumstances of the ancient church, which led to its decline, are disturbingly similar to those of the present church in Pakistan. While the external circumstances are not as difficult as they were for the ancient church, the internal situation is very similar – perhaps even worse. Our above discussion demonstrated that Christians in Pakistan are abandoning their faith and fleeing the country because of their difficult circumstances, including the implications of the blasphemy laws. This raises a serious concern: if Christians in Pakistan are so frightened that they are abandoning their faith and/or fleeing the country, how would they respond if the circumstances became even more difficult, as in IS-controlled areas in Iraq and Syria, where the three options for non-Muslims are, convert to Islam, pay *jizya*, or prepare to be slaughtered?

If Pakistani Christians encountered this situation, would the existing church in Pakistan be able to stand firm? The present attitude of Christians, many of whom are leaving the country or converting to Islam in circumstances of less intense persecution, reveals that the answer is "perhaps not." The past eclipse of Christianity in Pakistan is a warning to the Christian church to hold on to her faith. A robust biblical faith is a powerful phenomenon which provides people with the strength to endure in the most difficult circumstances. There is a desperate need for the church in Pakistan to strengthen the believers in their Christian faith.

---

63. G. W. Houston, "An Overview of Nestorians in Inner Asia," *CAJ* 24, no. 1/2 (1980): 65.

64. E. W. McDowell, "The Ancient Nestorian Church and Its Present Influence in Kurdistan," *JRD* 2, no. 1 (1911): 70.

65. Rooney, *Shadows in the Dark*, 107.

Reflection: Social Stigma

The overwhelming majority of Christians in Pakistan come from one of the depressed groups known as the Chuhras, who were considered the lowest class and were despised and exploited in India. Many have viewed their conversion to the Christian faith as a part of their struggle for a new identity and dignity and as a means of overcoming oppression and dehumanization.[66] However, as our study in chapter 6 demonstrated, the Chuhras' conversion to Christianity did not enable them to escape the social stigma affixed to their old identity. This stigma persisted, even within their own Christian circles where the word Chuhra is commonly used to show contempt. As a consequence, this negative social stigma seems to have been internalized by a majority of Pakistani Christians, even those who are not Chuhras. Moreover, we have shown that the prejudicial implementation of discriminatory laws, such as the blasphemy laws, has deeply undermined the Pakistani identity for Christians, creating a deep sense of worthlessness that they are not equal citizens of Pakistan.

As a result of these two factors, Pakistani Christians are burdened by both internal feelings of oppression as well as external discrimination. In the light of this reality, we have argued that unless the Christian community in Pakistan finds ways to overcome its internalized oppression it will be difficult, if not impossible, for the community to stand together with confidence to resist any kind of external discrimination. This reality of the social stigma faced by Pakistani Christians needs to be dealt with at least three levels: theological, social and political.

Theological Perspective

As we have seen, Christians in Pakistan are stigmatized due to their low social background. It is unfortunate that in India neither Christianity nor other religious movements were able to break the social pattern of the Hindu class system. Instead, these other religions have been influenced by the caste system, and have more or less followed the same divisions. This is evident from the fact (noted above) that Christians use the term Chuhra to ridicule their poor fellow Christians, especially those who are still involved in menial

---

66. John O'Brien, *The Unconquered People: The Liberation Journey of an Oppressed Caste* (Karachi: Oxford University Press, 2012), 309–310.

work. Those Christians who have been able to advance socially through education and hard work take care to disassociate themselves from those in the sweeper class. Christians from the canal colonies,[67] who became landowners through the generosity of missionaries, now deny their low social background altogether, claiming instead to be *Jats* (agricultural clan in North India) or *Rajputs* (literally meaning, "Sons of a king"),[68] and they despise Christians from the urban sweeper class.[69]

This behaviour illustrates the fact that "Congress leadership, during the freedom movement, demanded the ending of segregation in South Africa but did nothing concrete to end segregation within India."[70] Similarly, Christian leaders, both past and present, have protested against the discrimination against Christians in Pakistan,[71] but have failed to end discrimination within the church circles. The majority of Pakistani Christians face discrimination in society because of their low social background, but it is unfortunate that they face the same experience, perhaps with even more intensity, within Christian circles. Consequently, the majority of poor Christians are dually marginalized and victimized.[72] Tragically, the latter experience of marginalization is all the more painful because it is from their own people and occurs within

---

67. During the British rule in India, canal construction led to the establishment of canal colonies in the Punjab. Some of the colonies were established by Christian missionaries by acquiring agricultural land for socially deprived Christians. See section on ghettoization in chapter 4.

68. J. C. Heinrich worked (from 1932–40) as missionary in one of the Christian canal colonies known as Martin Pur where he minutely observed the psyche of Chuhra background Christians. He found the most common reaction among them was to show one's superiority over the other and were seen in "establishing a pseudo-superiority by lowering and disparaging rivals or apparent superiors" J. C. Heinrich, *The Psychology of a Supressed People* (London: Allen & Unwin, 1937), 60. See for good review of Heinrich's work, Webster, "Legacy of John Charles Heinrich," 34–37.

69. Despite the fact, with a few exceptions, they all were from the same class. See Pickett, *Christian Mass Movements*, 111.

70. M. J. Audi, "Ambedkar's Struggle for Untouchables: Reflections," *IJPS* 50, no. 3 (1989): 313.

71. There has been persistent demand from the Pakistani Christians that they should not be referred as *Isai* (employed as term of abuse). For example, on the social media, many Pakistani Christians posted their protest against the CDA (Capital Development Authority) for using the word *Isai* in the religious column for Christians in the Birth Registration Certificate.

72. O'Brien and Walbridge also pointed out that "the sweeper class is thus doubly marginalized." O'Brien, *Construction of Pakistani Christian Identity*, 459; Walbridge, *Christians of Pakistan*, 19.

church circles. Their marginalization within the church is more damaging than that outside the church because it not only hurts their social identity but also creates doubts about their spiritual identity – whether "all are one [and equal] in Christ Jesus" (Gal 3:28).

Churches in Pakistan preach that Christian believers have a new identity in Christ. This involves the rejection of status (1 Cor 1:26–31; Phlm 16) and the dissolution of all barriers which separate human beings from one another (Gal 3:27–28). Paul discussed the issue of new identity in Christ in a context where Jews claimed spiritual superiority and Greeks claimed cultural superiority. "Despite their different identities, they have become a reconciled community with diverse cultural-religious backgrounds, who live together as the church, representing the new creation."[73] Others, such as Campbell, argue that "the identity of all believers is transformed in Christ but not so as to obliterate their previous social identity,"[74] and therefore Jews and Gentiles in Christ need to accept and create space for each other. Campbell resists the historic claim that Paul saw the church as a new Israel that replaced Israel.[75] Nevertheless, there is consensus among the NT scholarship that for Paul the equality in Christ requires the abrogation of difference. It meant that all their social, racial, ethnic, and religious superiority or inferiority has vanished. On a more serious note, Paul addressed this issue in the Corinthian church where "[t]he high-status Corinthians may look down their noses at their uncouth lower-class brothers and sisters in the faith, regarding them as something of an embarrassment, but Paul insists that they must be 'clothed' with dignity and honour."[76] This is the theology taught to Pakistani Christians, but our discussion above demonstrates that there is a contradiction between theology and practice within the Christian church in Pakistan.

As noted above, one of the major reasons for Christians to change their religion is to acquire a new identity in order to improve their social standing in society. In the context of Pakistan, identifying as Muslim improves

---

73. Christoffer H. Grundmann, "Reconciliation and the New Identity in Christ," *IRM* 97, no. 386–387 (2008): 262.

74. William S. Campbell, *Paul and the Creation of Christian Identity* (London: T&T Clark, 2008), 129.

75. Ibid.

76. Roy E. Ciampa and Brian S. Rosner, *The First Letter to the Corinthians*, ed. D. A. Carson, PNTC (Nottingham: Apollos, 2010), 607.

one's social standing. Marginalized Christians in Pakistan are desperate to do this, which is evident from the fact that the majority of converts to Islam are from a low social background, as noted by Jamaia Naeemia and the Badshai Mosque.[77] Surprisingly, it is rare that anyone from the Ahmadi community comes to convert to Islam,[78] despite the fact that they too are highly vulnerable to all sorts of violence and discrimination due to their faith. This suggests that, compared to Christians in Pakistan, they are relatively secure in their spiritual identity. We noted previously that the government of Pakistan has endorsed a particular definition of a Muslim to which Ahmadis do not conform. Consequently they were officially declared non-Muslims in 1974. Undoubtedly, this was a strategic move to undermine their spiritual identity by trying to invalidate their beliefs. To counter this move, Ahmadis put a huge emphasis on their spiritual identity. They not only regard themselves as Muslim, but as true Muslims. They regard themselves as spiritually privileged because they are part of the reformist renewal movement, which started towards the end of nineteenth century, and which they consider was actually the rebirth of true Islam.[79]

The Christian community could learn from the Ahmadis' example on how to counter their inferiority complex by asserting their spiritual identity in Christ over their social status as Chuhras. Tragically, however, Pakistani Christians still recognize their fellow Christians by their social identity instead of their spiritual identity, thus creating Christians who are victims of double marginalization. Ahmadis are better able to withstand marginalization because they face this externally but not internally. If Christians could more accurately reflect their equality based on their new identity in Christ and practice it within Christian circles, this would significantly help the majority of Pakistani Christians to overcome their internal inferiority complex which, in turn, would enable them to have self-confidence in order to deal with external pressures.

---

77. R/M 26Jan2015; MI/M 26Jan2015; OA/M26Jan2015.

78. R/M 26Jan2015; MI/M 26Jan2015; OA/M26Jan2015.

79. Antonio R. Gualtieri, *Conscience and Coercion: Ahmadi Muslims and Orthodoxy in Pakistan* (Montreal: Guernica, 1989), 109.

Social Perspective

The overwhelming majority of researchers agree that the depressed classes were the original inhabitants of this land. When the invaders came, they plundered them and deprived them of all the resources of their land. They were pushed out of society and forced to become a class dispossessed of their rights. Historians inform us that from about 2000 BC, semi-nomadic tribes from Poland to Central Asia, collectively called Aryans, conquered the aboriginal inhabitants of North India and made them slaves.[80] The Aryans ultimately adopted the Hindu Religion based on the *Rig Vedas* (sacred text of Hindu Religion) which divided society into four classes: *Brahmin* (the priestly class or ruling class), *Kshatriya* (the warrior class), *Vaisiya* (the trading class) and *Shudra* (the serving class). The invaders classified the aboriginal people as even lower than the lowest caste, Shudra: they were called outcastes, a people without caste in a caste-ruled society.[81]

These outcastes were originally the aboriginal rulers of Punjab but later became crushed tribes known as untouchables.[82] Crooke argues convincingly that they were the forerunners of the Chuhras.[83] Likewise, O'Brien notes, "The aboriginal . . . tribes [were] reduced to servitude by the Aryan conquests, who are called Chandala in classical Brahminic literature [but] designated as Chuhra in the census of India (1868–1931) and in contemporary Pakistan are known as the Punjabi Christians."[84] These aboriginal people have been denied their religious and social privileges for centuries and were instead restricted to the most degrading occupations and condemned to a lifelong experience of devastating poverty, without opportunities for social advancement.

Several attempts have been made to socially emancipate these depressed classes in India. For example, *Ad-Dharm* was an early twentieth-century emancipation movement among the oppressed of the Punjab which claimed that they were the original inhabitants of the land, and constructed

---

80. O'Brien, *Construction of Pakistani Christian Identity*, 11.
81. Pickett, *Christian Mass Movements*, 24.
82. O'Brien, *Unconquered People*, 23.
83. Crooke, *Tribes and Castes*, 26–32.
84. O'Brien, *Unconquered People*, xiii.

Ad-Dharm as their "original religion" – the literal meaning of this expression.⁸⁵ This movement demanded that depressed classes be called *Adi Hindus* which means "aboriginal residents of India."⁸⁶ Another significant attempt was made by B. R. Ambedkar, who himself came from the untouchables. He was a brilliant lawyer who later secured the position of India's first Minister of Law, became an architect of India's constitution, and was a great advocate for the political rights of untouchables. Ambedkar argued that "just as it was intolerable for one country to rule another, it is equally true that no class is good enough to rule over another."⁸⁷ His passion for the liberation of depressed classes led him to assert that "the liberation of Dalits no longer lay within Hinduism but rather from Hinduism."⁸⁸ This assertion was a great blow to the Hindu majority in India. To counter this move, in order to keep the untouchables in the fold of Hinduism, Gandhi coined a term *harijans*⁸⁹ (literally meaning "children of God") as a way to give social standing and dignity of life to the depressed classes in India.

Sometimes, Christians in Pakistan hide their identity as Christians because they are associated with a low social background. Moreover, discriminatory laws, especially the blasphemy laws, threaten to deny Christians even their Pakistani identity as equal citizens. Consequently, the majority of Christians in Pakistan sometimes feel that Pakistan is not their country. However, if they could be shown like Dalits in India that their association with this land goes back centuries and that they are the *adi-peoples* (original habitants of this land), this could have a very positive psychological impact on Christians in Pakistan. It could also be beneficial to educate Pakistani Christians that the term "Churha" was originally an ethnographic term

---

85. Ibid., 11.

86. Pickett, *Christian Mass Movements*, 25.

87. O'Brien, *Unconquered People*, 197.

88. Arvind Sharma, "Dr. B. R. Ambedkar on the Aryan Invasion and the Emergence of the Caste System in India," *JAAR* 73, no. 3 (2005): 865.

89. Wolpert claims that the term *Harijans* was actually first coined by Narasinh Mehta, the father of Gujarati Poetry, but later it was made popular by Gandhi as a way to give dignity to millions of outcastes in India. Stanley Wolpert, *Gandhi's Passion: The Life and Legacy of Mahatma Gandhi* (New York: Oxford University Press, 2001), 168.

which only later came to be used in a pejorative way to describe association with menial work (cleaning work).⁹⁰

Political Perspective

Pakistani Christians must deal with this notion that Pakistan was created only by Muslims and only for Muslims, for it creates an inferiority complex for minorities implying that Pakistan is not their country. They need to know that the term *dhimmi* comes from the Arabic word *dhimma,* meaning protection. It is used to describe non-Muslims who were conquered or had surrendered to Muslim forces. In order to live under the protection of their Muslim conquerors (rather than being killed), *dhimmis* pay *jizya* (poll tax) to the Islamic state. (When the Taliban were ruling over some of the northern part of Pakistan, they began to charge this tax from non-Muslims).

There is another example from Islamic history of how to deal with non-Muslims: as those with whom Muslims made a treaty. In this case, non-Muslims were designated as *Mu'ahids* (non-Muslims with whom a treaty has been made). For example, the Christians of Najran were called *Mu'ahids* who agreed to pay *jizya* for religious freedom, peace and protection.⁹¹ But the important fact to note is that "the [Christians] in Pakistan are neither a conquered people (*dhimmi-s*), not a people with whom some treaty has been made (*mu'ahid-s*)."⁹² On the contrary, Christians lived in the territory before the creation of the nation of Pakistan. And more importantly, Christians living in the Punjab preferred Pakistan over India.⁹³ It was choice, not conquest, that placed them there.

---

90. O'Brien, *Unconquered People*, 23.

91. Mahan H. Mirza, "A Delegation of Christians from Najrān Visits the Prophet Muḥammad: Contemporary English Sīrah Literature for a Western Audience," *Islamic Studies* 50, no. 2 (2011): 165. For primary source for Najran treaty, see Ishaq, *Life of Muhammad*, 270–277.

92. Charles Amjad-Ali, "The Role of Christian Youth in a Non-Christian Society," *Al-Mushir* 28, no. 1 (1986): 16.

93. First, on 23 June 1947, S. P. Singha, a Christian representative and speaker of the Punjab Assembly used his casting vote for the inclusion of the Punjab in Pakistan. Second, on 25 July 1947, Christian leaders, S. P. Singha, C. E. Gibbon and Fazal Elahi, pleaded to the Boundary Commission, responsible for the demarcation of boundaries of India and Pakistan, while deciding about the Punjab, the Christian population be included with the Muslim population. See for good discussion on Christians' contribution in the formation of Pakistan. Emmanuel Zafar, *A Concise History of Pakistani Christians* (Lahore: Humsookhan, 2007), 62–68, 117–127.

Unfortunately this contribution of Christians to the history of Pakistan has been eliminated from the school text books. There is a demand from the Christians in Pakistan that their contribution should be included in the curriculum of Pakistan history so that new generations of Muslims, as well as minorities, will be acquainted with this historical fact. It is pertinent to note here that due to the rise of prejudice, intolerance and sectarianism in Pakistan, there is now a great realization at the level of civil society, as well as at government level, to rewrite text books to encourage more tolerance and an appreciation of diversity.[94] This would help diminish the notion among Muslims that Pakistan was created only by Muslims and only for Muslims. It would also boost the confidence of Christians, as they recognize that they have made a significant political contribution to the creation of Pakistan and that they have an equal right to live in it. In other words, this suggestion may help Pakistani Christians in reclaiming identity by regaining history.

Reflection: A Sense of Disillusionment

Our discussion in chapter 6 indicated the reasons for both the Ahmadi and the Christian communities' disillusionment about the possibility of any change to Pakistan's blasphemy laws in the near future. This is the case despite a lot of pressure from the international community and human rights groups on the past and present government of Pakistan to amend the blasphemy laws because of their misuse. No government in Pakistan, autocratic or democratic, has been able to make any substantial amendment to these laws, due to the overwhelming support of the general public, along with that of extremist elements, for these laws. The extremist groups are powerful enough to threaten the government with violence if they consider any change to the blasphemy laws. The assassinations in 2011 of two high-profile government figures, the governor of Punjab, Salman Taseer, and the Religious Minorities Minister, Shahbaz Bhatti, resulted in speaking out against the misuse of the laws. As a consequence, civil society, human rights activists and minorities are disillusioned about any possible change to these laws in the near future. One of the bishops in Pakistan, cited above,

---

94. Asad Zia, "Revised Curriculum: JI Pushes through Its Agenda on Textbooks in KP," *The Express Tribune*, 27 October 2014, online.

expressed his desperation by saying that he did not think he would see any change in these laws until the day of judgment.[95]

Here now a pertinent question arises: if these laws are not going to be changed, then is there anything else that can be done? The fact of the matter is that there is no escape from this painful reality in Pakistan. Our focus in this chapter is how Christians can learn to live in such circumstances. A key aspect of their circumstances is to understand the sensitive nature of the context in which they are living.

Contextual Sensitivity

One of the few high-profile blasphemy cases which attracted the attention of the world media was that of Rimsha Masih, a Christian teenager with Downs syndrome. She was accused on 16 August 2012 of burning pages from the Qur'an in a locality called Mehrabad in the surroundings of the capital city of Islamabad. Later she was exonerated of the charges when it was revealed by Muhammad Zubair, one of the assistants to a Muslim cleric at the local mosque, Muhammad Khalid Jadoon Chishti, that he (Chishti) had placed pages of the Qur'an into a plastic bag of ashes in order to strengthen the case against the Christian girl. Zubair testified, "I asked him what he was doing and he said this is the evidence against them and this is how we can get them out from this area."[96] This exposed the plot against the Christians living in that locality, most of whom earn money as sweepers or sanitation workers. It was revealed through media reports that Chishti has long campaigned against the Christians, seeking to oust them from the locality of *Mehrabad*. The main reason for this campaign, according to Chishti, was "the noise made by [Christian] services held at its tiny churches." Chishti "had welcomed the departure of most of the area's Christians as a result of Masih's arrest."[97]

The whole incident was designed to dislocate the Christian people because the local imam and his Muslim congregants were not comfortable with the Christians' noisy worship, especially during the Muslims' prayer times.

---

95. MS/C 6Dec2013.

96. Jon Boone, "Pakistani Mullah Accused of Trying to Frame Girl in Blasphemy Case," *The Guardian*, 3 September 2012, online.

97. Jon Boone, "Pakistan Drops Blasphemy Case against Christian Girl," *The Guardian*, 20 November 2012, online.

The imam said that the Christians had been repeatedly told not to engage in loud activities during Muslim prayer times because it caused a disturbance. However, the Christians did not heed his warning, which caused enmity between Christians and Muslims in that area.

This case study shows that the churches and the local Christians at *Mehrabad* did not care for the sensitivity of their context with regard to their worship style. As a consequence, the whole Christian community in that area bore the price. All Christian families in the area fled for their safety, along with Rimsha, who was beaten up by the mob and faced the blasphemy charges. Loud music in church meetings is very popular in Christian colonies in Pakistan due to the influence of the new Pentecostal movement and televangelists. Sometimes churches in the same locality compete with each other in their lively worship style with dance and loud music. This worship style does not make any sense to the Muslim-majority community and it seems irreverent to them. Historically, Christian worship in Pakistan has been strongly influenced by Hindu worship in which music and dance play a significant part.[98] However, the loud music and dance about which the imam in Mehrabad complained is a new phenomenon. It is influenced by the unrestrained worship style of western churches, which Pakistani Christians believe expresses their freedom in Christ.

The Apostle Paul devoted substantial attention in his letter to the Corinthians to dealing with public worship in the Corinthian church (1 Cor 14:1–24). This demonstrates Paul's concern for communal worship. Garland's commentary on verse 23 regarding its impact on unbelievers is noteworthy: "They [unbelievers] will not be impressed by this spiritual outburst but will conclude that these Christians are stark raving mad."[99] This is exactly what the Muslims in Pakistan think about the noisy Christian worship style. As seen above, this has caused trouble for the Christians in Mehrabad who had ignored the sensitivities of their context.

---

98. *Bhajans* are largely religious songs and they have more to do with Hindu worship. The Bhajan type of song is the most commonly used in the Pakistani church, especially Punjabi *Zaburs* (Psalms) which are often referred to as Punjabi *Bhajans*. Frank Y. Pressly, "The Punjabi Zabur: Its Composition, Use and Influence," in *Reader in Contextualization for Pakistan*, ed. Freda Carey (Lahore: OTS), 94–95.

99. David E. Garland, *1 Corinthians*, ed. Robert W. Yarbrough, BECNT (Grand Rapids, MI: Baker, 2003), 651.

Another issue of contextual sensitivity concerns the lifestyle of Christians in Pakistan. The incident in the Joseph colony in Lahore in March 2013, where two hundred houses of Christians were burned, can be used as a case study. The popular version of the story is that the Christians were being terrorized by the "land mafia" to make the Christians sell their property to Muslim industrialists. This could have contributed to the burning of the colony. But the specific events which triggered this incident, identified by the police during their investigations, tells us more. According to the police investigation, "Imran Shahid, a Muslim, had been drinking with Sawan Masih, a Christian sanitary worker, when a drunken row erupted over religion. Shahid accused his friend of making derogatory remarks about the Prophet Muhammad as their argument turned ugly."[100] Sawan's brother, in an interview on Geo TV, confirmed that Sawan used to provide alcohol to Shahid and that they used to drink together. This shows that Imran was a customer of Sawan's. I was told during my interviews with Christians in Pakistan that, due to the liquor business and other things considered immoral, the Joseph colony was called *Dozekh colony* (place of hell) by local Muslims.[101] This name was given to the locality because, in the eyes of Muslims, Christians were spreading evil in society. They provided an opportunity in the blasphemy laws to punish them for polluting the society.

The government of Pakistan has given provision to Christians to buy alcohol from certain places on religious grounds (Christians are permitted to buy but not sell alcohol). However, some have taken advantage of this provision to run an underground liquor trade. On a few occasions, Christian wine merchants have taken out public demonstrations to demand a higher quota on the basis that alcohol is an essential part of their religion.[102] Christians themselves often drink too much. On Christmas Eve, it is normal to find drunk young Christians in every street of the big Christian localities in Pakistan. Many Pakistani Christians brazenly defy the constraints of their cultural context by their lifestyle (specifically their misuse of alcohol).

---

100. Rob Crilly, "Mob Burns Christian Homes in Pakistani City," *The Telegraph*, 10 March 2013, online.

101. SS/C 28Nov2013.

102. Qaiser Julius, "The Place of Mosaic Law in the Christian life and its Implications for the Church in the Sharia Context," (University of Bristol, 2007), 51.

Pakistani Christians copy western cultural norms, which may be fine in a western cultural context, but are not acceptable in the Islamic legalistic context.[103]

Another important issue of contextual sensitivity concerns religious discussion in Pakistan. When we study cases in which Christians have been accused of blasphemy, a number of cases, including Anwar Masih's case in 1993, Ayub Masih's case in 1996, Younis Masih's case in 2007 and Asia Bibi's case in 2009 show interpersonal conflict resulting in Christians making unfavourable comparisons between Christ and the Prophet of Islam. Christians did not pay due regard to the cultural context. For example, Younis Masih from Lahore was accused in 2007 of telling the *qawāl* (singer): "Don't sing *qawāli* (praise song) for your Prophet because he is dead; instead, sing songs of Jesus who is alive."[104] Anwar Masih from Sumdari in 1993 was also accused of comparing Muhammad and Jesus, saying, "Your Prophet is dead and our Prophet is alive in the heavens."[105] Likewise, Ayub was accused of arguing that "his religion was real and true, whereas theirs [was] absolutely false and incorrect . . . and [their Prophet] hopelessly wrong."[106] Some cases, like those of Asia Bibi, show the inflammatory comments that Christians had made were in response to Muslims' derogatory words about Christ and Christians. However, although the Muslims in those cases had insulted Christians and their religion, they did not suffer the same consequences as the Christians did for insulting Islam and the Prophet.

When we probe the reasons why Christians in Pakistan sometimes make this sort of comparison between religions, it may have been due to the influence of some Protestant missionaries, like C. G. Pfander, who used such methods for evangelism in India. One of the popular methods is polemics (contentious argument), through which the superiority of the Christian faith was shown by asserting that Christianity's founder is alive and Islam's founder is dead. This method was inherited by national Christian apologists like

---

103. Qaiser Julius, "The Importance of Contextual Sensitivity for the Church in the Islamic Context," in *Reader in Contextualization for Pakistan*, ed. Freda Carey (Lahore: OTS, 2013), 35.

104. *State v. Younis Masih*, Session Court Lahore, 2–3 (2007).

105. *State v. Anwar Masih*, Session Court Samundri, 1 (1998).

106. *Ayub Masih v. State*, 1053.

Imad ud-din, Abdul Haq, Sultan Muhammad Paul and many others, who adopted a confrontational approach in their debates with Muslims.[107] No doubt, these apologists had a great influence on the Christians in northern India and still are lauded as heroes of Christian faith in Pakistan.

Before the re-emergence of radical Islam in Pakistan, such comparisons had been tolerated, but since the introduction of blasphemy laws, the religious context in Pakistan has completely changed. There is now almost zero tolerance to any such comparisons. Thus Christians should therefore avoid making these comparisons, as they mostly cause problems for themselves rather than yielding any benefit for Christianity in Pakistan. It is not being proposed here that Pakistani Christians should stop witnessing to Muslims – not at all – but instead that they have to find appropriate ways to share their faith effectively, taking the context into account instead of using a confrontational approach.

All three case studies above show that Christians brought problems on themselves due to their lack of sensitivity to the cultural context. In the first case, it was their worship style; in the second, their attitudes towards alcohol reflecting their social lifestyle; and in the third case, the unnecessary mention of religious differences in the context of personal disputes. This demonstrates that Christians in Pakistan sometimes fail to accommodate themselves to their cultural context in many ways, causing them to be regarded as aliens, and Christianity to be seen as an imported western religion. For the sake of their own safety, and for the sake of an effective Christian witness, it is important for Pakistani Christians to be more sensitive to cultural constraints.

For our theological reflection, let's see how Paul deals with the issue of contextual sensitivity. Paul was the main advocate of the Gentile church and no doubt a heroic figure who played a key role in the Gentile mission. He argued passionately that there was no theological justification for Gentiles being forced to adhere to the ritual dimension of the law. However, Paul showed consideration of his context when he circumcised Timothy (Acts 16:1–3). Some see Paul's teaching and action as irreconcilable, arguing that "he was acting in an unprincipled manner, since he regarded a circumcision

---

107. Avril A. Powell, "Pillar of a New Faith: Christianity in Late-Nineteenth-Century Punjab from the Perspective of a Convert from Islam," in *Christians and Missionaries in India*, ed. Robert E. Frykenberg (London: RoutledgeCurzon, 2003).

as a matter of indifference (Gal 5:6)."[108] Baur wrote, "the Paul of the Acts is manifestly quite a different person from the Paul of the Epistles."[109] Several battles have been fought between scholars on what Paul is actually saying. Wright perceptively notes, "Luther thought Paul was against the law, Calvin thought he was in favour of it, Schweitzer thought the question was wrongly put, and the twentieth century has been writing footnotes to all three."[110]

The narrative of Acts informs us that Paul circumcised Timothy "because of the Jews who lived in that area" (Acts 16:4). Marshall, Bruce and Peterson are all of the view that Paul did this to assist Timothy in his future ministry among the Jews.[111] He considered Timothy's context and put into practice this principle: "To those under the law I became like one under the law. To those not having the law I became like one not having the law" (1 Cor 9:20–21).

Some years later Paul joined in certain Jewish purification rites in Jerusalem, having taken a Jewish Nazirite vow (Acts 21:17–26). Some interpreters think that Paul took this Jewish vow to try to bring harmony between Jewish and Gentile churches. Some Jewish Christians were offended by rumours that Paul taught all Christians (including the Jews) to abandon the law of Moses. So it seems that Paul considered the context of the Jerusalem church and accepted James's proposal to undergo the purification rituals of the law. These two examples reveal how much Paul valued contextual sensitivity, and how he put into practice the principle of 1 Corinthians 9:20–21. Perhaps some people would take it that legalism is being suggested with this analysis, but the principle being put into practice by Paul is not legalism but contextual sensitivity. Paul makes this concept clear in his letter to the

---

108. E. Haenchen cited in I. Howard Marshall, *Acts*, ed. Leon Morris, TNTC (Nottingham: IVP, 1980), 276.

109. F. C. Baur cited in John Stott, *Acts*, ed. John Stott, BST (Leicester: IVP, 1991), 257.

110. N. T. Wright, *The Climax of the Covenant* (London: T&T Clark, 1991), 137.

111. Marshall, *Acts*, 276; F. F. Bruce, *The Book of the Acts*, ed. Gordon D. Fee, NICNT (Grand Rapids, MI: Eerdmans, 1988), 304; David G. Peterson, *The Acts of the Apostles*, ed. D. A. Carson, PNTC (Nottingham: Apollos, 2009), 450–451.

Romans,[112] and it needs to be taken into account seriously by Pakistani Christians living in an Islamic context.[113]

The three case studies above suggest some contextual insensitivity on the part of Christians. It can be argued that if Christians showed more sensitivity to the Islamic context of Pakistan in which they were living these incidents may have been avoided. It is therefore important for Pakistani Christians to be sensitive to the context in which they are living and to mould their religious and social lifestyles accordingly.[114] By doing so, accusations of blasphemy in Pakistan may in future be avoided to some extent.

Concluding Summary

Our theological and contextual reflection has focused on the Christian community's response to their situation arising from Pakistan's blasphemy laws. This study reveals that several theological questions are being raised by Pakistani Christians in response to their circumstances. When they do not find satisfactory answers to their questions, they respond in two main ways: abandoning their faith, or fleeing the country. Both of these undermine Christianity in Pakistan.

In order to deal with this situation, we have argued that the Pakistani church needs to inject the theology of the cross more vigorously into its teaching and preaching, in contrast to the prevailing prosperity theology. This will, instead of contradicting, match the experience of people's lives. Teaching from a perspective of a biblical theology could produce deeper faith, which will sustain Pakistani Christians in their suffering, and give meaning to their suffering. That will ultimately provide a sense of purpose for persevering in the context of suffering. In the context of suffering, it is one of

---

112. "As one who is in the Lord Jesus, I am fully convinced that no food is unclean itself. But if any one regards something as unclean, then for him it is unclean. If your brother is distressed because of what you eat, you are no longer acting in love . . . Do not destroy the work of God for the sake of food. All food is clean, but it is wrong for a man to eat anything that causes someone else to stumble. It is better not to eat or drink wine or to do anything else that will cause your brother to fall." (Rom 14:14–15, 20–21).

113. Julius, "Place of Mosaic Law," 52.

114. With this argument, it is not being proposed here that Christians should abandon any distinctive about their faith and religion and become Muslims in order to fit into the Islamic context.

the church's fundamental responsibilities not only to provide an explanation for suffering but also to help people to be faithful to their Christian faith and to equip them to bear their cross. To survive in Pakistan, the Pakistani church needs to adopt "walking through suffering" as a lifestyle.

The church also needs to address the sense of inferiority experienced by most Pakistani Christians, which is due to both internal and external factors. We have seen that Christians are despised and exploited because of their low social background. This stigma has persisted, even within Christian circles, where the word Chuhra is commonly used to show contempt. As a consequence, this negative social stigma seems to have been internalized by the majority of Pakistani Christians. Moreover, this study demonstrates that the prejudicial implementation of discriminatory laws, such as the blasphemy laws, has deeply undermined Christians' identity as Pakistani citizens. It has created a deep sense of worthlessness and the perception that they are not equal citizens of Pakistan.

Pakistani Christians are burdened by both internal feelings of oppression as well as by external discrimination. In order to deal with their social stigma, we have argued that the Christian community in Pakistan needs to find ways to overcome its internalized oppression so that the community can stand together with confidence to resist external discrimination. If Christians in Pakistan could more accurately reflect their equality based on their new identity in Christ and live this out within Christian circles, it would significantly help them to overcome their internal inferiority complex. This, in turn, would give them the self-confidence to deal with external pressures.

Finally, we have argued that Pakistani Christians need to be sensitive to the Islamic context in which they are living and mould their religious and social lifestyles in such way as to the cultural environment to avoid giving offence unnecessarily. By doing so, it may be possible, to some extent, to avoid some incidents in which Christians are accused of blasphemy.

CHAPTER 8

Conclusion: A Way Forward for the Christian Church in Pakistan

This study has been structured into three major parts.

Part I comprised three chapters. The first chapter explored the historical development of Pakistan's blasphemy laws as a background to this research issue. This enquiry has demonstrated that Pakistan has drifted away from its founder's vision of a secular democracy, and started to move towards Islamization. Although the process of Islamization continued over the years, it intensified throughout the rule of General Zia-ul-Haq (1977–1988), and Islam re-emerged in Pakistan in a more traditional way than any era before or since. Our examination of Zia's era demonstrated that his Islamic orientation, coupled with his political motives, led him to introduce five additional clauses to the blasphemy laws in the PPC which Pakistan had inherited from the British. The changes that Zia made to the Islamic judicial system and, in particular, the creation of the Federal Shariat Court (FSC), made the blasphemy laws significantly harsher. Although major efforts have been made by three post- Zia governments to bring procedural changes to the blasphemy laws in order to reduce their misuse, all these efforts have been conclusively defeated, leaving doubt over any possibility of change in Pakistan's blasphemy laws in the near future.

Chapter 2 assessed the extent to which Pakistan's blasphemy laws were consistent with Islamic Sharia. First, we specifically analyzed the question of whether the Qur'an mandates capital punishment for blasphemy. Our study demonstrated that modernists and traditionalists employ different hermeneutical approaches towards interpreting the text of the Qur'an, through which they come up with opposite conclusions. Our analysis has argued that there is no explicit evidence or clear Qur'anic mandate for capital punishment for blasphemy.

Second, the case for capital punishment for blasphemy was analyzed in the light of the *sunna*, which is the second fundamental source of Islamic Sharia. Confusingly, both traditionalists and modernists use the same sources to argue for their own different positions. The traditionalists argue that there is clear evidence in the *sira* and *ḥadith* literature that the Prophet of Islam authorized the execution of his vilifiers. By contrast, modernists claim that in those incidents, the sentence was carried out by Muhammad as the ruler (rather than as Prophet), therefore those actions and rulings were related to the original context of the Prophet and cannot be applied to succeeding generations. We have argued that if the modernists' argument is true, then there is no theological justification for blasphemy laws in the Penal Code of Pakistan.

Third, we examined whether the *fiqh* of four Sunni schools support Pakistan's blasphemy laws. Our analysis has demonstrated that the majority of the *hanafi* and *shafii* jurists, though not those of the *maliki* and *hanabali* schools, are of the opinion that a blasphemer should be given the opportunity to repent and that, if he repents, he should be forgiven. The *hanafis* have an even more lenient position with regard to women and non-Muslim offenders. In our analysis, we raised three points of concern:

- First, the framers of the blasphemy laws in Pakistan and later the FSC did not acknowledge the principle of Islamic law which demands that more weight should be given to the earlier opinion (in this case, that of the *Hanafi* school).
- Second, the majority of Muslims in Pakistan and, indeed, worldwide, follow the *Hanafi* school. Despite this, the position of this school has been largely ignored by the framers of the blasphemy laws and later by the FSC, in favour of other schools whose followers are in the minority. This demonstrates that a minority view has been imposed on the majority.
- Third, the constitution of Pakistan declares that the country is the *Islami Jamhūria Pakistan* (Islamic Republic of Pakistan). The word *jamhūr* means "people," so the title affirms that Pakistan is democratic as well as Islamic. We have argued that Pakistan's

legislature and judiciary have violated the norms of Islamic law, in which early legal opinion has more weight than later opinions, as well as the norms of democracy, where the view of the majority should be implemented.

The final section of chapter 2 focused on Muslim scholarship in the modern period generally with regard to the applicability of Sharīa and blasphemy laws and specifically to opinions about whether these laws are man made or divine in origin. The traditionalists have held to the pre-modern position that Sharīa is divine and that the blasphemy laws, being a part of Sharīa, are also divine in origin and therefore must be implemented according to the letter and the spirit of the historical Sharīa. By contrast, modernists have argued that Sharīa is not divine, but evolved through the hermeneutical efforts of the medieval jurists living in the context of the Islamic state. The blasphemy laws were the creation of the Islamic political regimes that used these laws to subdue their political opponents. They argue that these laws were man made and therefore subject to change.

After this theological analysis of the blasphemy laws, in chapter 3 we presented a legal analysis of these laws. First, our analysis demonstrated that the Zia-framed clauses explicitly favoured the religion of the majority in Pakistan. By contrast, the British-framed clauses had provided protection to all religions and even to sects within religions. Second, the Zia-framed clauses were seriously flawed, as they lacked the requirement of intent, which was a salient feature of the British-framed clauses and a key factor in the prevention of their misuse. Third, the Zia-framed clauses are so vague and depend so much upon interpretation that their ambit is dangerously open to misuse. Fourth, because the Zia-framed clauses were cognizable, police could arrest the accused on the complaint of any individual without having to verify the accusations. Fifth, these laws were contrary even to Pakistan's own mental health laws, as people with mental disorders suffer under these laws because of their ambiguity. Finally, the laws are incompatible with the international human rights covenants signed by Pakistan over the years.

In summary, Part I has argued that Pakistan's blasphemy laws cannot be justified either on the theological grounds of Islamic Sharīa or on legal grounds. In other words, these laws are contrary to Islamic law as well as to the British law which formed the basis of Pakistan's legal system.

The second major part of our study (chs. 4 and 5) explored the experience of both Ahmadi and Christian communities of living as minority groups in the context of Pakistan and, specifically, how they have been affected by Pakistan's blasphemy laws. Chapter 4 explored the nature of oppression for Ahmadis and Christians in Pakistan. Originally, the Ahmadiyya community migrated from India to Pakistan in anticipation of a better life in a new Muslim country. However, orthodox Muslims did not accept them as Muslims and consequently succeeded in excommunicating them from Islam in Pakistan. We have seen that the persecution of the Ahmadis is solely religiously based. They have been facing severe hostility from orthodox *sunni* Muslims who consider them not only heretics but also *kāfirs* who deserve death. In the light of the experience of the Ahmadis, we have argued that the more religious or Islamic Pakistan has become, the more sectarian it has become.

Like Ahmadis, Christians are also a minority group facing persecution in Pakistan. However, discrimination against Christians is based on a number of factors, not just on their religious beliefs. These other factors include the Christians' social background, as well as their perceived association with the West. Both Ahmadis and Christians anticipated a better future in a Muslim state than in a Hindu state, and so gave preference to Pakistan over India, but the reality for both groups proved completely the opposite.

After this survey of the overall situation of Christians and Ahmadis in Pakistan, we moved to a specific analysis of the experience of both communities under Pakistan's blasphemy laws. In the light of their experience, chapter 5 examined and responded to five arguments put forward by the supporters of blasphemy laws.

First, advocates of the blasphemy laws argue that they are equally applied to all citizens of Pakistan without any discrimination, and that this can be seen by the fact that more Muslims than non-Muslims have been charged with blasphemy. However, our analysis demonstrated that the blasphemy laws have been disproportionally used against minorities, especially Christians and Ahmadis, and that most of the Muslims accused of blasphemy are *shi'as*, who could also be considered a minority group in Pakistan.

Second, they argued that Pakistan's blasphemy laws actually protected those accused of blasphemy by preventing people taking the law into their own hands. In contrast, our analysis revealed that, instead of protecting people, the blasphemy laws had become a tool in the hands of those who wished to misuse them for ulterior motives.

Third, it was asserted that the blasphemy laws were not being misused because no one has yet been executed in Pakistan under these laws. However, as our analysis demonstrated, although no one has yet been executed legally, the laws have had other significant negative effects, which cannot be discounted. These include serious and systematic abuses of the blasphemy law in which innocent people suffer terribly. The punitive laws have had the effect of indirectly giving legitimacy to people who take the law into their own hands, resulting in tragic extrajudicial killings of those of accused of blasphemy.

Fourth, it was argued that if the blasphemy laws were amended, minorities in Pakistan would be unsafe. In contrast, our analysis demonstrated that minority groups, especially Christians and Ahmadis, have become extremely vulnerable under these laws. Multiple examples were given to demonstrate that there is no way for those accused of blasphemy to escape penalties, even after their innocence has been proven in court, especially if they belong to a minority group.

Fifth, it was argued that the blasphemy laws operate in the context of an independent judiciary, a free media and a vibrant civil society, all of which provided an effective safeguard against any misuse of the laws. By contrast, our analysis of the judiciary, civil society and the media demonstrated that none of the three stakeholders were able to stop the misuse of these laws. In fact, our analysis demonstrated that, in some cases, these agencies have contributed to the misuse of blasphemy laws. This analysis of the experience of minorities under blasphemy laws has led us to argue that there is a pressing need to repeal or drastically change these laws in order to stop their misuse.

Having explored the experience of Ahmadis and Christians under these laws, Part III of our study examined how Ahmadis and Christians were reacting in different ways to the persecution they suffered and, more specifically, why they were responding differently despite living under the same circumstances in Pakistan.

In order to explore and analyze the Ahmadi and Christian responses to Pakistan's blasphemy laws, chapter 6 was divided into two major sections:

similarities and dissimilarities. Our study of the similarities between these groups indicated that both communities were so intimidated by their sense of fear and insecurity that they could not freely express their concerns about the misuse of blasphemy laws. We have argued that the fear of being accused of blasphemy is pushing minorities to the point where they have to consider themselves as *dhimmi*. They are unable to claim their status as equal citizens of Pakistan, despite this having been promised by the founder of Pakistan as well as guaranteed by the constitution of Pakistan. Second, due to their fear of the blasphemy laws, both Christians and Ahmadis are fleeing the country, and this trend is weakening both communities. Third, we have shown that minority groups refuse to speak up for each other for fear that the majority community might perceive that they are trying to form a grand alliance against Islam. As a result, minority groups became self-centred, each focused exclusively on their own suffering, and never speaking up for the plight of others. Each minority group, especially Christians and Ahmadis, is more concerned about its own survival in Pakistan than the welfare of others. Fourth, our study demonstrated that both communities were disillusioned about the possibility of any change to Pakistan's blasphemy laws in the near future because, so far, all efforts to amend them have been defeated. Fifth, both communities looked towards outside help and depended significantly on the international community for advocacy.

We have argued that this dependent behaviour becomes a hindrance to acquiring substantial support from the moderate Muslim community within Pakistan to stand up for the rights of these minorities within the country. Furthermore, this dependent approach is leading both communities, Christians and Ahmadis, to lose their confidence and courage to stand against any discrimination. As a result, these defeated communities have come into existence which have no trust in the efficacy of their own struggle as well as no hope for their future.

The section on dissimilarities demonstrated that the Ahmadi community in Pakistan was notably unified in their response while, in contrast, the Christian community was characterized by a lack of unity in their response. Our analysis focused more specifically on the reasons why these communities are responding differently, despite living under the same circumstances and facing more or less the same kinds of challenges. This study demonstrated that there were great sociological, religious and political obstacles that prevented Christians from becoming a genuinely unified community which could stand together for their rights in Pakistan.

Our sociological analysis indicated that social stigma, coupled with the cumulative effects of discriminatory laws, increased the intensity of the inferiority complex of Christians, which was already chronic in its nature. Consequently, the confidence of Christians as a community within Pakistani society has been undermined. We have argued that this inferiority complex has led the Christians to become a defeatist community. Unless the Christian community in Pakistan finds ways to deal with its internalized oppression, it will be difficult, if not impossible, for the community to stand together with confidence to resist any kind of external discrimination. By contrast, the Ahmadi community did not suffer from the problem of internalized social stigma. Instead, their discrimination was completely external.

When a minority group lives in difficult circumstances, a sense of community is one of the protective factors for the survival of the group. Our study demonstrated that there was a great sense of community among the Ahmadis. In contrast, it was largely missing among the Christians in Pakistan. We have argued that unless this sense of community is generated, the dream of Christians standing together for their rights is not going to come true.

Our analysis of religious factors indicated that there had been no denominational split in the Ahmadiyya *Jamait*. This is reckoned to be one of the main reasons why the Ahmadis have remained intact as a united community. By contrast, factionalism has been a huge phenomenon for the Christian church in Pakistan. The Pakistani Christian community is beset by many internal conflicts among churches. We have argued that factionalism, coupled with internal conflicts, has resulted in further disintegration of the Christian community in Pakistan.

Further, this section's study highlighted the fact that the Ahmadis appear to have credible leadership, as nobody from the Ahmadi community has voiced any complaint that their leadership was involved in corruption. They showed full confidence in their leadership and people loved to follow their leaders. By contrast, there was huge concern about the credibility of Christian leadership in Pakistan. Their leaders often behave selfishly, without regard for the broader community. This selfishness has been one of the great obstacles to the formation of a genuine Christian community. Allegations of corruption have discredited Christian leadership and therefore people do not trust their leaders. The lack of godly and effective leadership is one of the key reasons for Christians behaving as a directionless community. Without credible leadership, it is hard for such a community, which is already disintegrating, to stand together for their rights.

Finally, our analysis of political reasons has demonstrated that the Ahmadi community was far ahead of the Christian community in political awareness. We have argued that unless the Christian community becomes properly aware of their political rights and duties, they are highly unlikely to undertake a sustainable struggle for their rights.

Next, we undertook a theological and contextual reflection on the Christian community's response. This reflection revealed that several theological questions were being raised by Pakistani Christians in response to their circumstances. When they did not find satisfactory answers to their questions, they were responding in two main ways: by abandoning their faith, or by fleeing the country. Both of these responses undermine Christianity in Pakistan. In order to deal with this situation, we have argued that the Pakistani church needs to inject the theology of the cross more vigorously into its teaching and preaching, in contrast to the prevailing prosperity theology. When this is done, the theology that is taught will match, instead of contradict, the experience of people's lives. Faithful teaching of true biblical theology will both produce deeper faith, which will sustain Pakistani Christians in their suffering, and give meaning to their suffering. This will ultimately provide a sense of purpose for persevering in the context of suffering. When Christians are living in the context of suffering, it is one of the church's fundamental responsibilities not only to provide an explanation for suffering but to help people to be faithful to their Christian faith and to equip them to bear their cross. For this purpose, we have argued that the Pakistani church needs to adopt "walking through suffering" as a lifestyle.

In order for Christianity to survive and thrive in the hostile context of Pakistan, the church also needs to address the sense of inferiority experienced by most Pakistani Christians, which is due to both internal and external factors. We have seen that Christians are despised and exploited because of their low social background. This stigma has persisted, even within Christian circles, where the word *chuhra* is commonly used to show contempt. As a consequence, this negative social stigma seems to have been internalized by a majority of Pakistani Christians.

Moreover, our study demonstrated that the prejudicial implementation of discriminatory laws, such as the blasphemy laws, has deeply undermined Christians' identity as Pakistani citizens. This has created a deep sense of worthlessness and the perception that they were not equal citizens of Pakistan. As a result of these two factors, Pakistani Christians are burdened by both internal feelings of oppression as well as by external discrimination. In order to deal with their social stigma, we have argued that the Christian community needs to find ways to overcome its internalized oppression in order for the community to stand together with confidence to resist external discrimination. If Christians could more accurately reflect their equality based on their new identity in Christ and live this out within Christian circles, this would significantly help Pakistani Christians to overcome their internal inferiority complex which, in turn, would help them to have the self-confidence to deal with external pressures.

We have also argued that Pakistani Christians need to be sensitive to the Islamic context in which they are living and mould their religious and social lifestyles to the cultural environment in such a way as to avoid giving unnecessary offence. By doing so, it may be possible, to some extent, to avoid some incidents in which Christians are accused of blasphemy.

Overall, this study indicates that there are a number of challenges facing the Christian church in Pakistan. This opens up several fronts as a way forward. Our main concern regarding our suggestions here will be what the Pakistani church can do for itself.

Theological Front

No comprehensive academic effort has been made by the Christian church in Pakistan to reflect theologically upon the issue of suffering within their context in order to help the Christian community make sense of their suffering. This is evident from the fact that this writer has not come across a single book in Urdu, written by a Pakistani Christian, which deals in depth with this subject. Consequently, the majority of Christians in Pakistan get confused and frustrated when their sufferings do not make any sense to them.

The Pakistani church needs to realize its responsibility to faithfully communicate what the Bible teaches about the place of suffering in Christian discipleship. One way to do this would be to provide a theological course, suitable for those at different levels of education, through which people could get an explanation for their suffering in a minority context. There are a few different forums that could provide such a course.

1. First, the Open Theological Seminary (OTS), based in Lahore, provides a Christian education on a non-denominational basis, and thus is a significant institution which could play a vital role by offering a course on suffering, suited for different levels. OTS already has a network of nearly 5,000 students throughout the country.[1] It would valuable for OTS to make it a priority to prepare a course on this subject.

2. The Theological Educators Forum (TEF) is a loose network of theological educators in Pakistan but nevertheless an important forum. It can be used to encourage theological educators to include this subject in their curriculums for theological courses in their colleges and seminaries in Pakistan.

3. Another possible forum is Christian publishers in Pakistan. *Masihi Ishait Khana* (MIK) in Lahore, one of the significant Christian publishers in Pakistan, and other Christian publishers can be encouraged to motivate Pakistan Christian authors to write on this subject in Urdu and their work should be published and made available to Christian readers in Pakistan. Moreover, the stories of Christian heroes who endured suffering with great courage, particularly from Pakistan's own Christian history, should be made available in Urdu so that young generations could be prepared and motivated for suffering.

4. Pastors can be encouraged through the Langham Expository Preaching Forum in Pakistan (a network of over 700 pastors and preachers throughout the country) to preach on this subject,

---

1. Field Staff, "Graduates in 2014," *Cup of Tee,* 2014, 5.

demonstrating a sound understanding of the biblical text and of the context of their local congregations.

When this biblical theology of suffering permeates the Pakistani church through theological colleges, OTS courses, published material and preaching in churches, it will help Pakistani Christians understand the meaning of their suffering and ultimately give them a sense of purpose for living in the context of suffering. It would also help Christians to be encouraged and deepened in their Christian faith, which will provide them with the strength to adopt a Christian lifestyle that can endure difficult circumstances.

Sociological Front

Pakistani Christians can counter their inferiority complex by focusing on their spiritual identity in Christ over their social status as *chuhras*. Kingsbury correctly observed that "while the Church only too readily emphasizes its lowly place in Pakistani society, it fails to balance this by giving due recognition to its dignified place in God's sight."[2] Moreover, it is a tragedy that Pakistani Christians tend to identify their fellow Christians by their social rather than their spiritual identity, thus creating Christians who are victims of double marginalization. If the Christian community could more accurately reflect the equality of all believers, based on their new identity in Christ, this would significantly help them to overcome their internal inferiority complex which, in turn, would enable them to have the self-confidence to deal with external pressures. Furthermore, the strongly hierarchical structures within the church in Pakistan, especially within the mainline denominations, convey a huge gap between members of a congregation and church leadership. This reinforces the sense of social inferiority felt by many Christians. In response, it would be helpful if the Church minimized its hierarchical structure so that the church leadership identified more with the common people.

The persecution experienced by Pakistani Christians can be exacerbated by their ghetto mentality. This isolation and stigmatization could be reduced if Pakistani Christians came out of their ghettos and integrated more with the majority community (without compromising their faith). The church

---

2. John R. Kingsbury, "The Social Responsibility of the Christian Church as a Minority Community in Pakistan," (Australian College of Theology, 2001), 379.

could do this by promoting a dialogue approach instead of a confrontational approach. This approach may help the Christian community to gain the confidence of moderate Muslims, who might then be willing to stand up for their protection. Christian leaders need to build good relations with Muslim intellectuals, writers and moderate religious scholars so that they will speak out against discrimination against minorities. The voice of moderate Muslims could play a vital role in Pakistan.

For example, Rimsha Masih, a teenage girl accused of blasphemy in 2013, was released within a month, primarily because Muslim voices through the media put huge pressure on the government and judiciary to provide justice to the teenager. Consequently, she was released and cleared of blasphemy charges more quickly than has ever happened before in the history of Pakistan. So it is important for the church to build good relations with the Muslim academia who can raise their voice through different means against the misuse of the blasphemy laws. For example, several secular Muslim organizations, notably the HRCP, are already advocating for this. Some churches, especially the Catholic Church, are doing relatively well in this area, but this needs to be done more strategically, especially by Protestants.

When Pakistani Christians have healthy relations with their Muslim neighbours this can do much to reduce the tension between the two communities. I was told by the security guard of the Open Theological Seminary, which is located in a Muslim-majority area, that, on 21 September 2012, there was a strong protest in that area against an amateurish anti-Islamic film, *The Innocence of Muslims*, which had been posted on YouTube. The film stirred the religious sentiments of Muslims worldwide and provoked a strong reaction. As the mob was protesting against the film in Lahore, the OTS office was threatened by protesters. However, Muslim neighbours realized the situation and asked the guard to go inside, lest he, as a Christian, come under attack. Instead, Muslim neighbours stood in front of the main gate and protected OTS and its security guard from any mishap. The security guard testified that this happened because of the healthy relations between OTS and its Muslim neighbours.[3]

---

3. SG/OTS, 07Nov2014.

As our study has indicated, most of the persecution in Pakistan occurs under the blasphemy laws, which some Muslims take advantage to settle personal disputes. Asif Mall, a Pakistani Christian human rights activist, has suggested the concept of "Mordecai Intervention," based on Esther 2:19–23. The idea of the Mordecai Intervention is to prevent atrocities by notifying authorities that they are about to occur so that police can arrest the plotters before the atrocity takes place. This requires "Mordecais" in the communities (that is, those who are influential members of the community; who are willing to speak up in defence of others; and who put justice above personal self-interest). Mall noted that "the system has worked on several occasions and has considerable potential."[4] This idea could be suggested to the local congregations in Pakistan to consider and see if potential people in the local congregations could be identified as Mordecais. A network of Mordecais throughout the country may help to reduce atrocities.

Political Front

We have seen that Christians in Pakistan do not seem to have much political awareness. Christians do not raise the blasphemy laws as an issue with their political representatives during elections or demand that political parties and their election candidates advocate to change the laws. Consequently, the main political parties believe that Christians are not concerned about the blasphemy laws. Although Christians are aware that amending the blasphemy laws is a highly sensitive issue which politicians are reluctant to touch, Christians' silence on blasphemy laws during elections provides justification to political parties to remain indifferent to this issue.

It is evident from our discussion above that the Christian community has so little political awareness that they often cannot distinguish between issues that are related to the National Assembly and those which are related to the local level. On 8 April 2014, the SCP directed the provincial governments to conduct city government elections in 2014/15.[5] Since then, it has seemed that the Christian community has had no strategy as to what demands they

---

4. Asif Mall, email message to author, 18 Mar 2015.
5. Supreme Court of Pakistan released detailed judgment in civil appeal nos. 38 to 45 of 2014, http://www.supremecourt.gov.pk/web/page.asp?id=1808 (accessed 12 May 2015).

should raise on the city government level and what should they do on the provincial and national level. This shows that there is a great lack of political awareness on the part of the Christian community in Pakistan.

Here the Christian community can learn from the Ahmadi community. One reason for the Ahmadis' increased political awareness is the high literacy rate in the Ahmadi community. Christians should work hard to motivate their community to invest in education, as this can contribute significantly to change. Moreover, Christians could also follow the example of the Ahmadi community by holding seminars on different levels, designed to educate their community on political matters.

As we have seen, for any political move to be successful it is important for a community to be unified. Unfortunately, Pakistani Christians can be characterized by a lack of unity as well as lack of effective leadership. This is evident from a recent incident which happened on 17 March 2015 in Youhanabad, Lahore, where two churches were attacked. In reaction, a Christian mob killed two suspects by burning them alive. This reaction caused huge damage to the community's image in the country and also jeopardized any political move of the community in future. This act of violence shows that the protesters acted on their own and were not willing to wait for the community's unified response. It also shows the acute failure of leadership on the part of Christian community. Sajid Ishaq, Chairman of the Pakistan Interfaith League, commented, "What I observed was that the political leaders and the church leadership [of Christians] were not on the same page. Even between the two churches that were attacked there was little to no coordination . . . A mob is like an unguided missile . . . when they reacted there was no one to handle them."[6]

Our study pointed out that when a minority group lives in difficult circumstances, a sense of community is one of the key protective factors for the survival of the group. We have seen that there is a great sense of community among the Ahmadis. By contrast, this sense of community is largely missing among Christians in Pakistan. Our study demonstrated that, generally, the Pakistani church is severely weakened by disunity and particularly by selfish leadership. Most Christians prioritize their personal benefit over

---

6. Luavut Zahid, "Youhanabad Incident," *Pakistan Today*, 21 March 2015, online.

that of the community. This selfishness has been one of the great obstacles to the formation of genuine Christian community in Pakistan. Moreover, denominational divisions, along with internal conflicts, have resulted in the further disintegration of the Christian community in Pakistan. These factors have hindered Christians from being on one platform. The lack of unity in the Christian community means that they can be more easily ignored by political parties and government, who never give any weight to the needs of Christians. Unless a sense of community can be generated, standing together for their rights will be a dream which will never come true for the Christians in Pakistan.

The Ahmadis' unity and effective leadership is also seen by the way they deal with the media. They have a central media cell from where they give a unified response to the media. By contrast, in the Christian community, every Christian leader speaks to the media and gives his own stance on an issue, further undermining any sense of unity among Christians.

The Christian church could make much better use of the National Council of Churches in Pakistan, which is an existing forum. If it could be strengthened and used effectively, it could help to bring the church denominations under one umbrella and present a unified voice to the media. All member church bodies should play their part to revive this forum and also include new church denominations, so that its voice could represent the Christians in Pakistan on wider scale.

Educational Front

Our study has noted previously that minority groups which have been discriminated against have, in many countries, overcome their situations through education, organization, community solidarity, political activism, strong leadership and economic advancement. We have demonstrated that Christians in Pakistan are far behind in all these areas. In terms of education, there is a high rate of illiteracy among Pakistani Christians. Economically, a conservative estimate is that 80 percent of Christians live below the poverty line and are engaged in cleaning work, which is regarded as menial work and is one the reasons that Christians are despised socially.

Overall, Christians' social profile, which correlates with their economic profile, is very low and needs to be raised to give social standing to the community in the society. As our study has demonstrated, most blasphemy cases involve those who are socially deprived and from a low strata of life. Raising the social profile of the Christian community may help to minimize occurrences of blasphemy cases. The only possible way to raise the social and economic profile of the Christian community in Pakistan is through education.

Here, Pakistani Christians can learn from Ahmadis, who set a target that there should be no one in their community with a level of education lower than a high school intermediate level. Christians should work hard to motivate their community to invest in education, as this can significantly change the profile of the community. It can be argued that Christian witness in Pakistan would be more bold and effective if their social standing was improved.

Forman Christian College was denationalized and returned to the church in 2003. Since then, it has played a significant role in providing quality higher education in Pakistan. Currently, nearly 950 out of its 6,500 students are Christians. If other Christian colleges, such as Murray College in Sialkot and Gordon College in Rawalpindi, which were nationalized in the 1970s, were returned to the church, they could make a considerable contribution to providing a high level of quality education to the Christian community in Pakistan. So the church in Pakistan should make a sustained effort to resume management of these colleges.

When the community is equipped with a higher level of education, its young educated Christians must be encouraged to compete for jobs in every sector of life in the country, especially the public sector (e.g. education, health, armed forces, civil services and business) and not just rely on the church to provide jobs. Having Christians represented in the public sector would help to raise the social and economic profile of the community. This would enable it to recover from its social decay and give the community a better social standing in the society and to prepare it for community witness in Pakistan.

Contextual Front

Our study has demonstrated that sometimes Christians invite problems for themselves because of their lack of sensitivity to their cultural context.

Conclusion: A Way Forward for the Christian Church in Pakistan

At times, Christians in Pakistan fail to accommodate themselves to their cultural context in many ways. As a result, "Christians are regarded as a group of foreigners in Pakistan."[7] For the purpose of their protection as well as their effective Christian witness, it is important for Pakistani Christians to be more sensitive to cultural constraints. The Pakistani church needs to help the Christian community to be aware of the sensitivity of their context. "Evangelicals in Pakistan have instead focused on presenting the context of traditional systematic theology, largely via translation models, which lack a sufficient analysis of local culture."[8] Here Sadhu Sundar Singh's comment is worth noting: "Indians do need the Water of Life, but not in the European Cup."[9]

In this regard, the Christian Study Centre (CSC) in Rawalpindi and *Maktaba-e-Anaveem* Pakistan in Muridkey have done a good job in producing helpful resources on the importance of contextual theology. But these efforts should be doubled to better help the church in Pakistan understand the sensitive nature of the context in which it now exists and to respond to its circumstances appropriately, socially, politically and theologically, in order for it to survive and thrive in the repressive religio- and socio-political context of Pakistan.

The author trusts that this study is a humble contribution to the scholarship in this field of research. However, the author's perspective, like that of anyone else, is limited and partial. The reader may judge if the study has grasped the heart of the reality of the researched phenomenon into which it enquired. An invitation is extended to other researchers to investigate this phenomenon from other angles and perspectives.

---

7. Pervaiz Sultan, "History of the Development of the Church of Pakistan," in *The Christian Church in Pakistan: A Vision for the 21st Century*, ed. Dominic Mughal and Jennifer Jivan (Rawalpindi: CSC, 1997), 17.

8. Kingsbury, "Social Responsibility," 487.

9. B. H. Streeter and A. J. Appasamy, *The Sadhu: A Study in Mysticism & Practical Religion* (Delhi: Mittal Publications, 1987), 228.

Glossary

ahl al-kitāb — people of the book, the Qur'anic expression used to describe people to whom a Holy book has been revealed (including Jews and Christians)

al-shahadatayn — the two testimonies

amicus curiae — literally, friend of the court. A lawyer who educates the court on points of law that are in doubt

ansār — citizen of Medina who helped the Prophet of Islam when he migrated from Macca to Medina

assalām-u-alaikum — Arabic greeting used by Muslims. Its translation is "peace be upon you"

athri — a worker who works exclusively on the agricultural land in the rural Punjab

azān — Islamic call to prayer

birādari — kinship group; patrilineage

basti — a slum characterized by substandard housing and squalor

bismillah — a term meaning "In the name of God" used by Muslims in a variety of contexts

brahmin — highest racially based class in Hinduism

chandala — conquered tribes of Punjab

dalit — collective term used for oppressed classes in India

dhimma — the pact that allows right of residence to non-Muslims in the Islamic state in return for payment of tax

dhimmi — non-Muslim resident of Islamic state

darūd sharif	blessing, holy sayings,
dozakh	hell, hades or the place of punishment
fasād	spreading mischief in a Muslim land
fatwā	legal opinion concerning Islamic Law
fiqh	Islamic Jurisprudence; science of the Sharīa
gharib hadith	a kind of categorization of hadith based on its chain that is not narrated through an abundance of narrators at each level of the chain
grundnorm	basic norm that forms an underlying basis for a legal system
ḥadd	the limit ordained by Allah, which includes the punishment for certain crimes
ḥadith	reports on the sayings and the traditions of the Prophet of Islam
ḥajj	annual Islamic pilgrimage to Macca
ḥanafi	one of the four school of Sunni Jurisprudence, named after Arab scholar *Abū Hanifa*
ḥanbāli	one of the four school of Sunni Jurisprudence whose origins are attributed to *Ahmad ibn Hanbāl* in Baghdad in the ninth century
ḥarām	an act that is forbidden by Allah
ḥarijan	children of God (Gandhian term for oppressed classes in India)
ḥudūd	the limits ordained by Allah including the punishment for certain crimes
ḥāfiẓ-ē-qur'an	literally meaning, "guardian," it is term used for someone who has completely memorized the Qur'an
ijma	the consensus of either the *umma* or just the *ulamā* – one of four bases of Islamic Law
ijtihad	individual inquiry to establish the ruling of Islamic law upon an issue
imām	leader of Muslim community in prayer

imām mahdi	meaning, "guided one." According to Sunni tradition *mahdi* will appear with prophet *isa* (Christ) before the end time. Shia tradition is different.
'isa	Islamic term for Jesus – Isa ibn Maryam
'isai	Islamic term for a Christian
'izzat	honour, respect, face
jāsūs	spy
jat	Indo-Scythian agricultural tribe
jihād	it can refer to a war or struggle against unbelievers or to the spiritual struggle within oneself against sin
jizya	protection tax paid by dhimmis to the Islamic state
jumhūr	people
kāfir	unbeliever, disbeliever or infidel
kalama ṭaiyiba	Islamic statement of belief: "There is no God besides Allah and Muhammad is the messenger of Allah."
kammi	a slave worker in the rural Punjab
khalifa	a successor or the Prophet, leader of the Muslim community
kharāj	land tax paid by *dhimmis* to the Islamic state
khatam-ē-nubuvat	finality of prophecy.
khulfa-ē-rāshdin	Sunnis consider the first four caliphs as the "rightly guided" caliphs: Abu Bakr, 'Umar, 'Uthman and 'Ali.
khuṭba	public address by *imam* delivered in the mosque at weekly (usually on Friday) or annual rituals
kshatriya	second racially based class in Hinduism
kufir	disbelieve or deny the truth of Islam
la'nat	curse, execration, or imprecation.

maliki	one of the four school of Sunni Jurisprudence. It was founded by the Imam Malik.
marham-ē-īsa	ointment of Jesus – according to Ahmadi tradition, it has been used to heal Jesus' wounds
masih	Urdu word for Christ
masihi	Urdu word for a Christian
mazhabi sikh	low-caste, or sweeper converted to Sikhism
mens rea	intention to commit a prohibited act
mu'ahid	one who enters into covenant with another
mufti	Islamic scholar who is interpreter or expounder of Islamic law
muhājir	migrant, the term is associated with the early Islamic history of the migration of Muslims from Macca to Medina. After the independence of Pakistan, a significant number of Muslims immigrated to Pakistan.
muhraba	rebellion
mujaddid	the Islamic term for one who brings renewal
munāfiq	a hypocrite who outwardly practices Islam while inwardly concealing his disbelief
murtadd	one who gives up Islam wilfully for another faith
mursal	with omissions in the chain
musali	low-caste, or sweeper converted to Islam
nāt	a poem that specifically praises the Prophet of Islam
nizām-ē-mustafā	system of the Prophet of Islam
pancāyat	local decision making council in the rural Punjab
qawāl	a performer of *qawāli*
qawāli	a form of sufi devotional music popular in South Asia
qazi	a judge ruling in accordance with Islamic law
rājput	landed dynasty claiming putative Ksatriaya Varna

ridda	apostasy, *ridda* wars are known as the Wars of Apostasy launched by the first caliph of Islam
rasūl	messenger or apostle
sabb	blasphemy: insulting God (*sabb Allah*) or Muhammad (*sabb ar-rasūl*)
sahāba	the companions of the Prophet of Islam
seyp	a worker employed by a number of families to do the lowest forms of work including the cleaning of cattle byres and the removal of night soil in the rural Punjab
shafi'i	one of the four school of Sunni Jurisprudence. It was founded by the Arab scholar *Al-Shafi'i* in the 9th century.
shirk	idolatry; polytheism; the sin of believing in any divinity except God and of associating other gods with God
shudra	the fourth racially based class in Hinduism
sira	life or biography of the Prophet Muhammad
sharia	the path to a watering hole; the ethical code and moral code based on the Qur'an and Sunna; basis of *fiqh*; Islamic law
shi'a	a branch of Islam who believe in Imam Ali and his sons (Hassan and Hussayn) as custodians of Islam by the will of the Prophet Mohammed
sufi	one who propagates *sufism*
sufism	mystical dimension of Islam
sunna	the practice of the Prophet of Islam
sunni	the largest denomination of Islam who accept the *sunna* and the succession of the first three caliphs
suo motu	an action taken by court as a legal process on its own without being requested to do so by either party in a case
sūrah	chapter; the Qur'an is composed of 114 surahs

ṭāghūt	originally Aramaic, meaning "false god"; also tyranny
takfir	declaration of individual or group who were previously considered Muslim as kaffir
tāzir	discretionary punishment – a sentence or punishment whose measure is not fixed by the Sharia.
taqlīd	to follow the scholarly opinion of one of the four Imams of Islamic Jurisprudence.
vaisiya	third racially based class in Hinduism
'ulamā	the leaders of Islamic society, including teachers, *imams* and judges (singular alim)
umma	(literally, nation) the global community of all Muslim believers
ummati nabi	follower of the prophet
ushr	a tax on the potential produce or output of a piece of land
wājib'l-qatil	obligatory or mandatory to be killed
zakāt	tax, alms, tithe as a Muslim duty; Sunnis regard this as the fourth Pillar of Islam
Zamindār	on the Indian subcontinent, someone who held enormous land and held control over peasants
zandaqah	heresy
ẓill	image or reflection
zinā	sexual activity outside of marriage (covering the English words adultery and fornication)
zinā bi'l-jabr	rape

Bibliography

Main Sources

Abbas, Shemeem B. *Pakistan's Blasphemy Laws: From Islamic Empires to the Taliban*. 1st ed. Texas: University of Texas Press, 2013.

Abbasi, Ansar. "Awan Advises against Amending Blasphemy Law." *The News*, 8 February 2011. http://www.thenews.com.pk/TodaysPrintDetail.aspx?ID=3853&Cat=13.

Abbasi, Yasir. "Mental Health Ordinance 2001 – Is It Really Being Used?" *JPMA* 58, no. 10 (2008): 578–580.

Abdal-Haqq, Irshad. "Islamic Law: An Overview of Its Origin and Elements." In *Understanding Islamic Law: From Classical to Contemporary*, edited by Hisham M. Ramadan. 1–42. Oxford: AltaMira Press, 2006.

Abou El Fadl, Khaled. *Rebellion and Violence in Islamic Law*. Cambridge: Cambridge University Press, 2001.

Abu-Zayd, Nasr Hamid. "Renewing Qur'anic Studies in the Contemporary World." In *Silenced: How Apostasy and Blasphemy Codes Are Choking Freedon Worldwide*, edited by Paul Marshall and Nina Shea. 289–294. Oxford: Oxford University Press, 2011.

"Act No. 25 of 1927: Criminal Law (Amendment) Act, (22 September 1927)." In *The Current Indian Statutes*. 138–141. Lahore: Law Times, 1927.

Adamec, L. W. *Islam: A Historical Companion*. Gloucestershire: Tempus, 2007.

Adamjee, Maheen B. "Interview: Sherry Rehman." *Newsline*, December 2010, 33–35.

Agence France-Presse. "Ahmadis Find Refuge in China." *The Express Tribune*, 19 June 2014. http://tribune.com.pk/story/724068/ahmadis-find-refuge-in-china/.

———. "Couple Gets Death Sentence over Blasphemous Text Message." *The Express Tribune*, 5 April 2014. http://tribune.com.pk/story/691720/couple-gets-death-over-blasphemous-text-message/.

———. "More Than 40,000 Protest Blasphemy Law Change." *Dawn*, 9 January 2011. http://dawn.com.

———. "'No Option' but to Abide by PM's Decision on Blasphemy: Sherry." *Dawn*, 3 February 2011. http://dawn.com/2011/02/03/no-option-but-to-abide-by-pms-decision-on-blasphemy-sherry/.

———. "Pakistan Court Sentences Christian Man to Death for Blasphemy." *The Guardian*, 28 March 2014. http://www.theguardian.com/world/2014/mar/27/pakistan-court-sentences-christian-man-death-blasphemy.

———. "Pakistan's Ahmadis to Boycott Elections." *Newsweek*, 23 April 2013. http://newsweekpakistan.com/pakistans-ahmadis-to-boycott-elections/.

———. "Qadri Indicted in Salman Taseer Murder Case." *Dawn*, 14 February 2011. http://dawn.com/2011/02/14/qadri-indicted-in-salman-taseer-murder-case/.

Ahmad, Irfan. "Genealogy of the Islamic State: Reflections on Maududi's Political Thought and Islamism." *The Journal of the Royal Anthropological Institute* 15 (2009): S145–S62.

Ahmad, Jamil-ud-Din, ed. *Speeches and Writings of Mr. Jinnah*. 6th ed. 2 vols. Vol. 1. Lahore: SMA, 1960.

Ahmad, Khurshid. "Pakistan: Vision and Reality, Past and Future." *The Muslim World* 96, no. 2 (2006): 363–379.

Ahmad, Khwaja Nazir. *Jesus in Heaven on Earth*. Woking, UK: Literary Trust, 1952.

Ahmad, Mirza Bashir-ud-Din Mahmud. *Hadhrat Ahmad*. Tilford: IIP, 1998. http://www.alislam.org.

———. *Khilafat-E-Rashidah*. Tilford: IIP, 2009.

———. *Truth about the Split*. New ed. Tilford: IIP, 2007.

Ahmad, Mirza Ghulam. "An Answer to Dr. Dowies Prediction of General Destructions of All Muhmmadans." *The Review of Religions* 1, no. 9 (1902): 337–349.

———. "The Appearance of Promised Messiah." *The Review of Religions* 1, no. 5 (1902): 205–208.

———. *The British Government and Jihad*. Tilford: IIP, 2006.

———. "The Early Life and Mission of the Promised Messiah." *The Review of Religions* 2, no. 2 (February 1903): 61–67.

———. *Fateh Islam* [Victory of Islam]. Tilford: IIP, 2002.

———. "The Future of Islam." *The Review of Religions* 3, no. 11 (1904): 391–425.

———. *Izāla-Ē-Auham* [in Urdu] [The Removal of Misconceptions]. Amritsar: Riād-ē-Hind Publisher, 1891.

———. *Masih Hindustan Mein* [Jesus in India]. Translated by Qazi Abdul Hamid and Muhammad Ali. New ed. Tilford: IIP, 2007.

———. *A Misconception Removed*. Rev. ed. Tilford: IIP, 2007.

———. "The Plague." *The Review of Religions* 1, no. 6 (1902): 241–252.

———. "A Proposal for the Utter Extinction of Jehad." *The Review of Religions* 1, no. 1 (January 1902): 1–10.

———. "Religious Controversies and Our Position in Them." *The Review of Religions* 1, no. 2 (February 1902): 43–63.

Ahmad, Mirza Tahir. "Punishment for Apostasy: A Scrutiny of the Qur'anic Teachings on Apostasy and How This Conflicts with Maududi's Analysis." *The Review of Religions* 101, no. 6 (2006): 50–63.

Ahmad, Mubasher. "Khilafat and Caliphate." http://www.alislam.org.

Ahmad, Rafi. "The Islamic Khilafat – Its Rise, Fall, and Re-Emergence." Accessed 6 May 2013. http://www.alislam.org.

Ahmad, Sahibzada M. M. "Exalted Status of the Holy Prophet as the Khatamun Nabiyeen." Accessed 30 May 2013. http://www.alislam.org.

Ahmed, Akbar S. *Journey into Islam: The Crisis of Globalization*. Washington: Brookings Institution Press, 2007.

Ahmed, Ishtiaq. "The 1947 Partition of Punjab." In *Region and Partition: Bengal, Punjab and the Partition of the Subcontinent*, edited by Ian Talbot and Gurharpal Singh. viii, 407. Oxford: Oxford University Press, 1999.

———. "Pakistan, Democracy, Islam and Secularism: A Phantasmagoria of Conflicting Muslim Aspirations." *Oriente Moderno* 84, no. 1 (2004): 13–28.

Ahmed, Khaled. "A Decaying State Kills Its Minorities." *The Friday Times*, 24 August–6 September 2012. http://www.thefridaytimes.com/beta3/tft/article.php?issue=20120831&page=2.

———. "Word for Word: Masihi Instead of Isai." *Daily Times*, 17 April 2005. http://www.dailytimes.com.pk/default.asp?page=story_17-4-2005_pg3_4.

Ahmed, Munir D., and Khalid Duran. "Pakistan." In *Islam in the World Today: A Handbook of Politics, Religion, Culture and Society*, edited by Werner Ende and Udo Steinbach. 325–350. London: Cornell University Press, 2010.

Ahsan, Abdullah. "Pakistan since Independence: An Historical Analysis." *The Muslim World* 93, no. 3/4 (2003): 351–370.

Akbar, Malik Siraj. "Who Benefits from Pakistan's Blasphemy Law." In *Huffington Post*, 2012.

Akhtar, Masud. "The Finality of Prophethood." *The Islamic Review* 6, no. 5 (1986): 8–15.

Akhter, Salamat. *Tahrek-E-Pakistan Ke Gumnam Kirdar* [in Urdu] [The Anonymous Characters of Pakistan Movement]. Rawalpindi: CSC, 1997.

Akyol, Mustafa. "Islam's Problem with Blasphemy." *The New York Times*, 14 January 2015.

al-Awa, Muhammad S. *Punishment in Islamic Law: A Comparative Study.* Indianapolis: American Trust Publications, 1982.

Al-Bukhari, Muhammad Ibn Ismaiel. *Sahih Al-Bukhari.* Translated by Muhammad Muhsin Khan. 9 vols. Vol. 6. Riyadh: Darussalam, 1997.

al-Jaza'iri, Abu Bakr. *Min Kitab Al-Fiqh Ala Al-Madhahib Al-Arba'ah.* Beirut: Dar al-Fikr.

al-Misri, Ahmad ibn Naqīb. *Reliance of the Traveller: The Classic Manual of Islamic Sacred Law.* Translated by Nuh Ha Mim Keller. Rev. ed. Maryland: Amana Publications, 1994.

Al-Mubarakpuri, Safiur-Rahman. *The Sealed Nectar: Biography of the Noble Prophet.* Rev. ed. Riyadh: Darussalam, 2002.

Al-Qayrawani, Abdullah ibn Abi Zayd. *The Risala: A Treatise on Maliki Fiqh.* http://www.nmnonline.net/e-books/The-Risala-A-Treatise-on-Maliki-Fiqh.pdf.

al-Shaybānī, Muḥammad, and Majid Khadduri. *Shaybānī's Siyar: The Islamic Law of Nations.* Baltimore: Johns Hopkins Press, 1966.

Ali, Abdullah Yusuf. *The Meaning of the Glorious Qur'an: Text, Translation and Commentary.* 2 vols. Vol. 1, Cairo: Dar Al-Kitab Al-Masri, 1934.

Ali, Faisal. "95 Killed in Lahore Claim Ahmadis." *Dawn,* 30 May 2010.

Ali, Kalbe. "CII Debate on Blasphemy Law." *Dawn,* 20 September 2013. https://www.dawn.com/news/1044163.

Ali, Mohammad. *The Holy Qur'an: Containing the Arabic Text with English Translation and Commentary.* Lahore: Ahmadiyya Anjuman-I-Ishaat-I-Islam, 1920.

Ali, Muhammad. *The Ahmadiyya Doctrines.* Lahore: AAII, 1932. http://www.aaiil.org.

———. *The Ahmadiyya Movement.* Translated by S. Muhammad Tufail. Lahore: AAII, 1973.

———. *The Split in the Ahmadiyya Movement.* Lahore: AAII, 1994. http://www.aaiil.org.

———. "Two Sections of the Ahmadiyya Movement." *The Islamic Review* 7, no. 4 (1987): 6–10.

Ali, Syed Anwer. *Qur'an: The Fundamental Law of Human Life.* 16 vols. Vol. 5. Karachi: Hamdard Foundation, 1989.

Ali, Syed Rashid. "Pakistani Constitutional Amendments of 1974: Declaring Qadianis as a Non-Muslim Minority." http://alhafeez.org.

———. "Post Anti-Qadiani Ordinance of 1984." http://alhafeez.org/rashid/constipak.html.

Alter, Noel. "Socio-Economic Conditions of Christians in Lahore, Pakistan." Lahore: Forman Christian College University, 2011.

Amjad-Ali, Charles. "The Role of Christian Youth in a Non-Christian Society." *Al-Mushir* 28, no. 1 (1986): 15–18.

Amjad-Ali, Christine, and Charles Amjad-Ali. *The Legislative History of the Shariah Act.* Rawalpindi: CSC, 1992.

An-Na'im, Abdullahi A. "Constitutionalism and Islamization in the Sudan." *Africa Today* 36, no. 3/4 (1989): 11–28.

———. *Islam and the Secular State: Negotiating the Future of Sharia.* Cambridge: Harvard University Press, 2008.

———. "The Islamic Law of Apostasy and Its Modern Applicability: A Case from Sudan." *Religion* 16 (1986): 197–224.

———. "Religious Minorities under Islamic Law and the Limits of Cultural Relativism." *Human Rights Quarterly* 9, no. 1 (1987): 1–18.

Andrews, C. F. *Sadhu Sundar Singh: A Personal Memoir.* London: Hodder & Stoughton, 1934.

Anis, Muhammad. "Blasphemy Law Can't Be Amended: CII Chief." *The News*, 24 September 2013. http://www.thenews.com.pk/Todays-News-13-25646-Blasphemy-law-cant-be-amended-CII-chief.

APP. "Govt Not Amending Blasphemy Law, Says PM." *Dawn*, 18 January 2011.

———. "UN Periodic Review: Islamabad Reaffirms Pledge to Human Rights." *The Express Tribune*, 31 October 2012. http://tribune.com.pk/story/458731/un-periodic-review-islamabad-reaffirms-pledge-to-human-rights/.

Aqeel, Asif. "Christian Sanitation Workers Swept into Societal Gutter." *Daily Times*, 12 July 2011. http://archives.dailytimes.com.pk/national/12-Jul-2011/christian-sanitation-workers-swept-into-societal-gutter.

———. "Pakistan's Christian Sanitation Workers Swept into Societal Gutter." *WorldWatch Monitor*, 7 July 2011. http://www.worldwatchmonitor.org/2011/07-July/article_114675.html/.

———. "A Renewed Debate over Blasphemy Laws." *WorldWatch Monitor*, 2 October 2013. http://www.worldwatchmonitor.org/2013/10/article_2733432.html.

Arzt, Donna E. "The Application of International Human Rights Law in Islamic States." *Human Rights Quarterly* 12, no. 2 (1990): 202–230.

Asad, Muhammad. *The Message of the Qur'an.* Lahore: Kazi Publications, 1980.

Asghar, Raja. "Javed Hashmi Assails Blasphemy Law in NA." *Dawn*, 25 September 2013. http://www.dawn.com/news/1045294/javed-hashmi-assails-blasphemy-law-in-na.

Ashrafi, Tahir. "He Died in Defence of Humanity." *Daily Times*, 4 January 2013. http://www.dailytimes.com.pk/default.asp.

Aslam, Salman. "Ahmadis Worship Places Hit – 80 Killed." *Dawn*, 29 May 2010.

Audi, M. J. "Ambedkar's Struggle for Untouchables: Reflections." *IJPS* 50, no. 3 (1989): 307–320.

Ayaz, Qazi. *Al-Shifa,* vol 2. Lahore: Maktaba Nabwaya, 1997. In Urdu.
Azad, Abu Al-Kalam. *Masla-E-Khilafat* [in Urdu] [The Issue of Caliphate]. Lahore: Maktabah Jamal, 2006.
Aziz, Farieha. "In the Name of Religion." *Newsline,* February 2011, 35–39.
———. "Interview: Ali Dayan Hassan." *Newsline,* April 2011, 32–34.
———. "Interview: Dr Khalid Zaheer, Religious Scholar." *Newsline,* December 2010, 28–29.
———. "Interview: Iqbal Haider." *Newsline,* December 2010, 37–38.
———. "Interview: Mairaj-Ul-Huda Siddiqui of the Ji." *Newsline,* December 2010, 27–28.
Aziz, K. K. *History of Partition of India: Origin and Development of the Idea of Pakistan.* 3 vols. Vol. 3, New Delhi: Atlantic, 1988.
———. *The Murder of History: A Critique of History Text Books Used in Pakistan.* Lahore: Sang-e-Meel Publications, 2010.
Aziz, Shaikh. "A Leaf from History: The Ahmadi Issue." *Dawn,* 24 February 2013. http://www.dawn.com/news/788358/a-leaf-from-history-the-ahmadi-issue.
Bader, Mohammad Jahangir. *The Constitutional History of Pakistan.* 2nd rev. ed. Lahore: Mansoor Book House, undated.
Bakhtiar, Laleh. *Encyclopedia of Islamic Law: A Compendium of the Views of the Major Schools.* Chicago: ABC International Group, 1996.
Bakshi, S. R. *The Making of India and Pakistan, Select Documents.* New Delhi: Deep Publications, 1997.
Ballhatchet, Kenneth and Helen. "Asia." In *Oxford Illustrated History of Christianity,* edited by J. McManners. Oxford: Oxford University Press, 1990.
Baloch, Saher. "Silence of the Grave." *Dawn,* 16 February 2014.
Bambale, Yahaya Y. *Crimes and Punishments under Islamic Law.* 2nd ed. Nigeria: Malthouse, 2003.
Barat, Kahar. "Aluoben, a Nestorian Missionary in 7th Century China." *JAH* 36, no. 2 (2002): 184–198.
Beaglehole, J. H. "The Indian Christians – a Study of a Minority." *MAS* 1, no. 1 (1967): 59–80.
Bennett-Jones, Owen. *Pakistan: Eye of the Storm.* 2nd ed. London: Yale University Press, 2003.
Berger, Peter, and Hansfried Kellner. *The Homeless Mind: Modernization and Conciousness.* New York: Vintage, 1974.
Bhatti, Nazir S. "90% Pakistani Christian Favour Refugee Status from UN after Rising Violence." *Pakistan Christian Post,* 14 May 2014. http://www.pakistanchristianpost.com/vieweditorial.php?editorialid=112.

Bhutto, Benazir. *Reconciliation: Islam, Democracy and the West*. 1st ed. New York: Simon & Schuster, 2008.

Bibi, Asia, with Anne-Isabelle Tollet. *Blasphemy: The True, Heart – Breaking Story of a Woman Sentenced to Death over a Cup of Water*. London: Virago Press, 2012.

Binder, Leonard. *Religion and Politics in Pakistan*. Los Angeles: University of California, 1961.

"Blasphemy Laws in Pakistan: Historical Overview." Islamabad: CRSS, 2012.

Bobra, Amir J. "Ahmadis Seeking Refuge in China." *Daily Times*, 20 June 2014. http://www.dailytimes.com.pk/region/20-Jun-2014/ahmadis-seeking-refuge-in-china.

Boone, Jon. "Pakistan's Geo News Becomes Latest Target in Blasphemy Accusation Trend." *The Guardian*, 22 May 2014. http://www.theguardian.com.

———. "Pakistan Church Bomb." *The Guardian*, 25 September 2013. http://www.theguardian.com/world/2013/sep/23/pakistan-church-bombings-christian-minority.

———. "Pakistan Drops Blasphemy Case against Christian Girl." *The Guardian*, 20 November 2012. http://www.theguardian.com/world/2012/nov/20/pakistan-drops-blasphemy-case-christian.

———. "Pakistani Mullah Accused of Trying to Frame Girl in Blasphemy Case." *The Guardian*, 3 September 2012. http://www.theguardian.com/world/2012/sep/02/pakistani-mullah-accused-girl-blasphemy.

The Dictionary of Historical Theology. Carlisle: Paternoster, 2000.

Brierley, Peter, ed. *World Churches Handbook*. London: Christian Research, 1997.

Bruce, F. F. *The Book of the Acts*. NICNT. Edited by Gordon D. Fee. Grand Rapids, MI: Eerdmans, 1988.

Bukhari, Mubasher. "Mentally Ill Persons Have Been Charged and Imprisoned without Trial for Years." *Reuters*, 22 July 2010. http://in.reuters.com.

Butt, Qaiser. "Top Islamic Body Proposes Changes in Blasphemy Law." *The Express Tribune*, 19 December 2010. http://tribune.com.pk/story/91838/council-of-islamic-ideology-top-islamic-body-proposes-changes-in-blasphemy-law/.

Butt, Usama. "Pakistan's Salvation: Islam or Western Inspired Secular-Liberal Democracy." In *Pakistan's Quagmire: Security, Strategy, and the Future of the Islamic-Nuclear Nation*, edited by Usama Butt and N. Elahi. 9–38. New York: CIPG, 2010.

Callard, Keith B. *Pakistan, a Political Study*. New York: Macmillan, 1957.

Campbell, Ernest Y. "The Church in the Punjab: Some Aspects of Its Life and Growth." In *The Church as Christian Community*, edited by Victor E. W. Hayward. 139–222. London: Lutterworth, 1966.

Campbell, William S. *Paul and the Creation of Christian Identity*. London: T&T Clark, 2008.
Carey, Freda. "Dalit, Dhimmi or Disciple." MTh Thesis. Edinburgh: University of Edinburgh, 1999.
Chaudhri, Muhammad Naseem. *Constitution of Islamic Republic of Pakistan of 1973 with Commentary*. Lahore: LTP, 2005.
Choudhury, G. W. "The Constitution of Pakistan." *Pacific Affairs* 29, no. 3 (1956): 243–252.
Ciampa, Roy E., and Brian S. Rosner. *The First Letter to the Corinthians*. PNTC. Edited by D. A. Carson Nottingham: Apollos, 2010.
Cohen, Stephen P. *The Idea of Pakistan*. Washington: Brookings Institution, 2004.
The Constitution of the Republic of Pakistan. Karachi: Government of Pakistan Press, 1962.
Constituent Assembly of Pakistan Debates 1, no. 76 (1956): 3376–3377.
Cordeiro, Joseph C. "The Christian Minority in an Islamic State: The Case of Pakistan." In *The Vatican, Islam, and the Middle East*, edited by Kail C. Ellis. 279–294. New York: Syracuse University Press, 1987.
Correspondent. "Advice to Legislature: No Need to Amend Blasphemy Law, Says CII." *The Express Tribune*, 20 September 2013. http://tribune.com.pk.
———. "Blasphemy Case Evokes Fear in Pakistan Christian Town." *Dawn*. 1 September 2012. http://dawn.com/2012/09/01/blasphemy-case-evokes-fear-in-pakistan-christian-town/.
———. "Blasphemy Case: Cleric Offers Rs.500,000 for Aasia's Execution " *The Express Tribune*, 4 December 2010. http://tribune.com.pk/story/85412/blasphemy-case-masjid-imam-offers-reward-to-kill-aasia/.
———. "Geo TV Faces Blasphemy Case." *The Hindu*, 18 May 2014. http://www.thehindu.com/news/international/south-asia/geo-tv-faces-blasphemy-case/article6021183.ece.
———. "Pasha's Abbottabad Briefing." *Pakistan Today*, 11 July 2013. http://www.pakistantoday.com.pk/2013/07/11/national/pashas-abbottabad-briefing-the-isi-chief-found-faults-with-everyone/.
———. "President Signs Convention on Civil, Political Rights." *Daily Times*, 4 June 2010. http://www.dailytimes.com.pk/default.asp?page=2010%5C06%5C04%5Cstory_4-6-10_pg7_18.
Cox, Neville. "The Clash of Unprovable Universalisms – International Human Rights and Islamic Law." *OJLR* (2013): 1–23.
Crilly, Rob. "Mob Burns Christian Homes in Pakistani City." *The Telegraph*, 10 March 2013. http://www.telegraph.co.uk/news/worldnews/asia/pakistan/9920465/Mob-burns-Christian-homes-in-Pakistani-city.html.

———. "Pakistani Cleric Puts Bounty on Christian Woman's Head." *The Telegraph*, 3 December 2010. http://www.telegraph.co.uk/news/religion/8179655/Pakistani-cleric-puts-bounty-on-Christian-womans-head.html.

Crooke, William. *The Tribes and Castes of the North-Western Provinces and Oudh.* 4 vols. Vol. 2, Calcutta: Office of the Superintendent of Government, 1896.

Cunningham, J. D., and H. L. O. Garrett. *A History of the Sikhs*. London: Oxford University Press, 1918.

Damaris. "Pakistan's Blasphemy' Laws Pose Growing Threat." *WorldWatch Monitor*, 13 May 2011. https://www.worldwatchmonitor.org/2011/05-May/article_112455.html/.

Dard, A. R. *Life of Ahmad: Founder of the Ahmadiyya Movement*. Tilford: IIP, 2008.

Dawud, Abu. *Sunan Abudawud*. Translated by Ahmad Hasan. 8th ed. 3 vols. Vol. 3. New Delhi: Kitab Bhavan, 2008.

Dehlvi, Anqa. "Pakistan's Blasphemy Law: The Great Untouchables." *Ahmadiyya Times*, 22 February 2013. http://ahmadiyyatimes.blogspot.com.au.

Dembski, William A. *The End of Christianity: Finding a Good God in an Evil World*. Carlisle: Paternoster, 2009.

Din, Najam U. "State of Human Rights in 2010." Lahore: HRCP, 2010.

———. "State of Human Rights in 2012." Lahore: HRCP, 2012.

Din, Najam U, and Saira Ansari. "State of Human Rights in 2007." Lahore: HRCP, 2007.

"Do You Think That the Blasphemy Law Should Be Repealed?" *The Nation*, 19 March 2014.

Durie, Mark. *The Third Choice: Islam, Dhimmitude and Freedom*. China: Deror Books, 2010.

Durrani, F. K. Khan. *The Ahmadiyya Movement*. Lahore: AAII, 1927.

Ebrahim, Zofeen T. "Ahmadis: The Lightning Rod That Attracts the Most Hatred." *Dawn*, 28 October 2011. http://dawn.com/2011/10/28/ahmadis-the-lightning-rod-that-attracts-the-most-hatred/.

Editor. "A Community No One Cares About." *The Express Tribune*, 18 June 2012.

———. "Dawn – Editorial." *Dawn*, 15 November 2005. http://www.dawn.com/news/1068475/dawn-editorial-november-15-2005.

Editor, "Editorial," *Pakistan Today*, 20 September 2013.

Ernst, Carl W. "Blasphemy: Islamic Concept." In *The Encyclopedia of Religion*, edited by Mircea Eliade, 242–245. New York: Macmillan, 1987.

Esposito, John L. "Islamization: Religion and Politics in Pakistan." *The Muslim World* 72, no. 3–4 (1982): 197–223.

Farmer, Ben. "Blasphemy Laws Must Not Be Scrapped, Says Musharraf." *The Telegraph*, 11 January 2011. http://www.telegraph.co.uk/news/worldnews/asia/pakistan/8264293/Blasphemy-laws-.

Farooq, Asad. "Fatwa Demands Death for Sherry." *Daily Times*, 9 January 2011. http://www.dailytimes.com.pk/?page=2011%5C01%5C09%5Cstory_9-1-11_pg1_1.

Faruki, Kemal A. "Pakistan Government and Society." In *Islam in Asia: Religion, Politics, and Society*, edited by John L. Esposito. 53–78. Oxford: Oxford University Press, 1987.

Feldman, Herbert. *A Constitution for Pakistan*. Karachi: Oxford University Press, undated.

Field Staff. "Graduates in 2014." *Cup of Tee*, 2014.

Firdous, Iftikhar. "Sikh Community Storms Parliment to Protest against Alleged Desecration of Their Holy Books." *The Express Tribune*, 23 May 2014. http://tribune.com.pk/story/712049/sikh-community-protests-against-alleged-insult-of-baba-guru-nanak/.

Firestone, Reuven. *Jihād: The Origin of Holy War in Islam*. New York: Oxford University Press, 1999.

Frame, John M. *The Doctrine of the Christian Life*. Phillipsburg, NJ: P&R, 2008.

Francis, Joseph. "CLAAS Pakistan: Annual Report 2010." Lahore: CLAAS, 2010.

———. "CLAAS Pakistan: Annual Report 2011." Lahore: CLAAS, 2011.

———. "CLAAS Pakistan: Annual Report 2012." Lahore: CLAAS, 2012.

Friedmann, Yohanan. *Tolerance and Coercion in Islam: Interfaith Relations in the Muslim Tradition*. New York: Cambridge University Press, 2003.

Frykenberg, Robert Eric. "Christians in India: An Historical Overview of Their Complex Origins." In *Christians and Missionaries in India*, edited by Robert Eric Frykenberg. 33–61. London: RoutledgeCurzon, 2003.

Gabriel, Theodore. *Christian Citizens in an Islamic State*. Aldershot: Ashgate, 2007.

———. *Christian Citizens in an Islamic State: The Pakistan Experience*. Aldershot: Ashgate, 2007.

Gall, Carlotta. "Assassination Deepens Divide in Pakistan." *The New York Times*, 6 January 2011.

Garland, David E. *1 Corinthians*. BECNT. Edited by Robert W. Yarbrough. Grand Rapids, MI: Baker, 2003.

Geijbels, M. "Pakistan, Islamization and the Christian Community." *Al-Mushir* 21, no. 2 (1979): 31–51.

———. "Pakistan, Islamization and the Christian Community. Part 2: The Status and Calling of Christians." *Al-Mushir* 22, no. 3 (1980): 99–116.

Ghamidi, Javed Ahmad. "Islamic Punishments: Some Misconceptions " http://www.al-mawrid.org.

———. "Punishment for Blasphemy against the Prophet (Sws)." http://www.al-mawrid.org.

Ghazi, Mahmud A. "The Law of Tawhin-I-Risalat: A Social, Political and Historical Perspective." In *Pakistan between Secularism and Islam*, edited by Tarik Jan. 209–240. Islamabad: Institute of Policy Studies, 1998.

Gibb, H. A. R., and J. H. Kramers. "Hudud Laws." In *Concise Encyclopedia of Islam*. Leiden: Brill Academic, 2001.

Gill, I. K. *Oppression and Injustice in Pakistan: Violation of Human Rights*. London: Hamilton, 1999.

Gillani, Waqar. "Hudood Laws Not Based on Reason or Religion." *Daily Times*, 25 June 2004. http://www.dailytimes.com.pk/default.asp?page=story_25-6-2004_pg7_24.

———. "Pakistani Christian Couple Are Tortured and Burned to Death by Angry Mob." *The New York Times*, 5 Novmber 2014.

Gillani, Waqar, and Salman Masood. "Pakistani Christian Woman's Appeal of Death Sentence Is Rejected." *The New York Times*, 17 October 2014.

Gneezy, Uri. "Deception: The Role of Consequences." *AER* 95, no. 1 (2005): 384–394.

Gordon, Andrew. *Our India Mission*. Philadelphia: Inquirer Printing Co., 1886.

Gour, Hari Singh. *The Penal Law of India: Being a Commentary – Analytical, Critical and Expository on the Indian Penal Code*. 11th ed. 4 vols. Vol. 3. Allahabad: Law Publishers, 2000.

Green, Timothy. "Identity Issues for Ex-Muslim Christians." *SFM* 8, no. 4 (2012): 435–481.

Griffiths, Paul J. *Lying: An Augustinian Theology of Duplicity*. Grand Rapids: Brazos, 2004.

Grim, Brian J., and Roger Finke. *The Price of Freedom Denied: Religious Persecution and Conflict in the 21st Century*. New York: Cambridge University Press, 2011.

Grudem, Wayne. "Why It Is Never Right to Lie: An Example of John Frame's Influence on My Approach to Ethics." In *Speaking the Truth in Love: The Theology of John Frame*, edited by John J. Hughes. 778–801. Phillipsburg, NJ: P&R, 2009.

Grundmann, Christoffer H. "Reconciliation and the New Identity in Christ." *IRM* 97, no. 386–387 (2008): 255–272.

Gualtieri, Antonio R. *The Ahmadis: Community, Gender, and Politics in a Muslim Society*. Montreal: McGill-Queen's University Press, 2004.

———. *Conscience and Coercion: Ahmadi Muslims and Orthodoxy in Pakistan*. Montreal: Guernica, 1989.

Guerin, Orla. "Pakistan Blasphemy Law Reformers' Death Threats." *BBC News*, 11 January 2011. http://www.bbc.co.uk/news/world-south-asia-12191082.

Haleem, Muhammad. "The Domestic Application of International Human Rights Norms." In *Developing Human Rights Jurisprudence*. London: HRUCS, 1988.

Hamdani, Yasser L. "The 1974 National Assembly Proceedings on the Ahmadi Issue." *Daily Times*, 22 October 2012. http://dailytimes.com.pk.

———. "Do Ahmadis Deserve to Live in Pakistan?" *Friday Times*, 31 August–6 September 2012. http://www.thefridaytimes.com/beta3/tft/article.php?issue=20120831&page=8.

———. "One Man's Qadri Is Another Man's Kafir." *Daily Times*, 21 January 2013. http://www.dailytimes.com.pk/default.asp?page=2013%5C01%5C21%5Cstory_21-1-13_pg3_3.

Hameed, Hamza, and Kamil Jamshed. "A Study of the Criminal Law and Prosecution System in Pakistan." Karachi: Manzil, 2013.

Hanif, Mohammed. "How to Commit Blasphemy in Pakistan." *The Guardian*, 6 September 2012.

Haqqani, Husain. *Pakistan: Between Mosque and Military*. Washington: CEIP, 2005.

Haqqani, Irshad Ahmad. "Failure of Democracy in Pakistan." *The Muslim World* 96, no. 2 (2006): 219–232.

Hasan, Masudul. *Sayyid Abul A'ala Maududi and His Thought*. 1st ed. 2 vols. Vol. 1, Lahore: Islamic Publications, 1984.

Hassan, Syed R. "Pakistani Police Charge 68 Lawyers with Blasphemy over Protest." *Reuters*, 13 May 2014.

Hayee, Bilal. "Blasphemy Laws and Pakistan's Human Rights Obligations." *UNDALR* 14, no. 3 (2013): 25–53.

Haynes, Naomi. "Affordances and Audiences: Finding the Difference Christianity Makes." *Current Anthropology* 55, no. S10 (2014): S357–S65.

Heinrich, J. C. *The Psychology of a Supressed People*. London: Allen & Unwin, 1937.

Hill, Jonathan. *The History of Christian Thought*. Oxford: Lion, 2003.

Hodson, H. V. *The Great Divide: Britain – India – Pakistan*. London: Hutchinson, 1969.

Hoffman, Matt. "Modern Blasphemy Laws in Pakistan and the Rimsha Masih Case: What Effect – If Any – the Case Will Have on Their Future Reform." *WUGSLR* 13, no. 2 (2014): 371–392.

"Holy Prophet (Pbuh) Awarded Death Sentence for Blasphemy." *Pakistan Today*, 13 December 2010. http://www.pakistantoday.com.pk/2010/12/13/city/lahore/holy-prophet-pbuh-awarded-death-sentence-for-blasphemy/.

Hoodbhoy, Pervez. "Remembering Salman Taseer." *The Express Tribune*, 1 January 2012. http://tribune.com.pk/story/315079/remembering-salmaan-taseer/?print=true.

Hoodbhoy, Pervez A., and Abdul M Nayyer. "Rewriting the History of Pakistan." In *Islam, Politics and the State: The Pakistan Experience*, edited by Mohammad Asghar Khan. 164–177. London: Zed Books, 1985.

Houreld, Katharine. "Teenager Kills Man Accused of Blasphemy in Pakistan Police Station." *Reuters*, 16 May 2014. http://www.reuters.com/article/2014/05/16/us-pakistan-blasphemy-killing-idUSBREA4F0HI20140516.

Houston, G. W. "An Overview of Nestorians in Inner Asia." *CAJ* 24, no. 1/2 (1980): 60–68.

Hussain, Rizwan. "Pakistan." In *The Oxford Encyclopedia of the Islamic World*, edited by John L. Esposito, 308–323. New York: Oxford University Press, 2009.

Hussain, Zahid. *Frontline Pakistan: The Path to Catastrophe and the Killing of Benazir Bhutto*. London: I. B Tauris, 2008.

———. "The Ideological Divide." *Newsline*, February 2011, 16–20.

———. "World News: Asia: Islamists Rally in Pakistan for Blasphemy Laws." *The Wall Street Journal Asia*, 2011.

Hutton, J. H. *Caste in India, Its Nature, Function and Origins*. 4th ed. Bombay: Oxford University Press, 1963.

Ibn, Warraq, ed. *Leaving Islam: Apostates Speak Out*. New York: Prometheus Books, 2003.

"Implementation of the Declaration on the Elimination of All Forms of Intolerance and of Discrimination Based on Religion or Belief." Accessed 13 March, 2013. http://www.unhcr.org.

Imtiaz, Saba. "As Death Toll Mounts Ahmadis Fight Back with Letters." *The Express Tribune*, 2 November 2012.

"International Covenant of Civil and Political Rights (ICCPR)." Accessed 13 March 2013. http://untreaty.un.org.

"International Religious Freedom Report 2010." US Department of State 2010.

Iqbal, Afzal. *Islamization of Pakistan*. Lahore: Vanguard Books, 1986.

Iqbal, Shahid, Riaz Ahmad, and Nadia Ayub. "Self-Esteem: A Comparative Study of Adolescents from Mainstream and Minority Religious Groups in Pakistan." *JIMH* 15, no. 1 (2013): 49–56.

Ishaq, Ibn. *The Life of Muhammad: A Translation of Ibn Ishaq's Sirat Rasul Allah*. Translated by A. Guillaume. Karachi: Oxford University Press, 2007.

Islam, Lutful. "Qadiani Issue: 1974 – IV – the Background." *Ahmadiyya Times*, 31 October 2012. Accessed 6 July 2013. http://ahmadiyyatimes.wordpress.com.

Islam, Nazar Ul. "Burn the Girl Alive." *Newsweek*, 12–19 October 2012.

Jacob, Peter. "Human Rights Monitor 2012-13: A Report on the Religious Minorities in Pakistan," 206. Lahore: NCJP, 2013.

Jafri, Owais. "Sectarian Violence: Procession Mourners Accused of Blasphemy." *The Express Tribune*, 27 November 2012. http://tribune.com.pk/story/471282/sectarian-violence-procession-mourners-accused-of-blasphemy/.

Jalal, Ayesha. "Conjuring Pakistan: History as Official Imagining." *IJMES* 27, no. 1 (1995): 73–89.

———. "The Past as Present." In *Pakistan: Beyond the Crises State*, edited by Maleeha Lodhi. New York: Columbia University Press, 2011.

Jamal, Asad. "Herald Exclusive: What the Law Says." *Dawn*, 15 February 2011. http://dawn.com/2011/02/15/herald-exclusive-what-the-law-says/.

———. "The Law of Diminishing Utility." *Herald-Exclusive*, February 2011. http://dawn.com/2011/02/15/herald-exclsive-the-law-of-diminshing-utility/print.

———. "Some Called for Changes." *The News*, 12–19 December 2010. http://jang.com.pk/thenews/dec2010-weekly/nos-12-12-10/dia.htm.

Jamal, Nasir. "Destination: Aslyum Abroad." *Dawn*, 16 May 2015.

Jenkins, Philip. *The Lost History of Christianity*. Oxford: Lion, 2008.

Jinnah, Mahomed Ali. *Quaid-I-Azam Mahomed Ali Jinnah: Speeches as Governor-General of Pakistan 1947–48*. Karachi: Pakistan Publications, 1962.

Jivan, Jennifer, and Peter Jacob. "Life on the Margins." Lahore: NCJP, 2012.

John, Asher. "Christian Couple Tortured, Bodies Burned over 'Blasphemy.'" *Pakistan Today*, 6 November 2014.

Jones, E. Stanley. *Mahatma Gandhi: An Interpretation*. 1st ed. London: Hodder & Stoughton, 1948.

Jones, L. Bevan. *The People of the Mosque: An Introduction to the Study of Islam with Special Reference to India*. Calcutta: Association Press, 1932.

Juergensmeyer, Mark. *Religion as Social Vision: The Movement against Untouchability in 20th Century Punjab*. Berkeley: University of California Press, 1982.

Julius, Qaiser. "The Importance of Contextual Sensitivity for the Church in the Islamic Context." In *Reader in Contextualization for Pakistan*, edited by Freda Carey. 30–40. Lahore: OTS, 2013.

———. "The Place of Mosaic Law in the Christian Life and Its Implications for the Church in the Sharia Context." University of Bristol, 2007.

Kamali, Mohammad H. *Freedom of Expression in Islam*. Kualalumpur: Berita, 1994.

———. "Punishment in Islamic Law: A Critique of the Hudud Bill of Kelantan, Malaysia." *Arab Law Quarterly* 13, no. 3 (1998): 203–234.

Kariakosi, M. K. *Conditions of Christians in East Punjab Following Partition: Source Materials*. Delhi, 1982.

Kathir, Ibn. *Tafsir Ibn Kathir*. 2nd ed. 10 vols. Vol. 2. Riyadh: Darussalam, 2003.

———. *Tafsir Ibn Kathir*. 2nd ed. 10 vols. Vol. 3. Riyadh: Darussalam, 2003.
———. *Tafsir Ibn Kathir*. 2nd ed. 10 vols. Vol. 4. Riyadh: Darussalam, 2003.
Kaushik, S. Nath. *Ahmadiya Community in Pakistan: Discrimination, Travail, and Alienation*. New Delhi: South Asian Publishers, 1996.
Kayani, M. Munir and M. R. Kayani. *Report of the Court of Inquiry Constituted under Punjab Act II of 1954 to Enquire into the Punjab Disturbances of 1953*. Lahore: Government of Punjab, 1954.
Keller, Timothy. *Walking with God through Pain and Suffering*. London: Hodder & Stoughton, 2013.
Khan, Azam. "Blaphemy Petition against Sherry Rehman Accepted." *The Express Tribune*, 18 January 2013. http://tribune.com.pk/story/495669/blasphemy-petition-against-sherry-rehman-accepted/.
Khan, Hamid. *Constitutional and Political History of Pakistan*. Karachi: Oxford University Press, 2001.
Khan, Khalid S. "What Is the Punishment of Blasphemy in Islam?" *The Review of Religions* 106, no. 9 (2011): 44–63. http://www.reviewofreligions.org.
Khan, Khalid Saifullah. "What Is the Punishment for Blasphemy in Islam." http://www.reviewofreligions.org.
Khan, Muhmmad Ayub. *Friends Not Masters: A Political Autobiography*. London: Oxford University Press, 1967.
Khan, Naveeda. *Muslim Becoming: Aspiration and Skepticism in Pakistan*. Durham: Duke University Press, 2012.
Khushi, Yunis. "Being a Christian in Pakistan." *Focus* 10, no. 4 (1990).
Kingsbury, John R. "The Social Responsibility of the Christian Church as a Minority Community in Pakistan." Australian College of Theology, 2001.
Kraan, J. D. "Religious Education in Islam, with Special Reference to Pakistan." *Al-Mushir* 25, no. 3 & 4 (1983): 107–182.
Kumaraswamy, P. R., and Ian Copland. *South Asia, the Spectre of Terrorism*. New Delhi: Routledge, 2009.
Küng, Hans. *Islam: Past, Present and Future* [Translated from the German.]. Translated by John Bowden. Oxford: Oneworld, 2007.
Lal, Nand. *The Indian Penal Code, Act 45 of 1860 with an Exhaustive, Explanatory, and Critical Commentary*. 2 vols. Vol. 2. Lahore: Krishen Lal & Co., 1929.
Larson, Warren F. *Islamic Ideology and Fundamentalism in Pakistan: Climate for Conversion to Christianity*. New York: University Press of America, 1998.
Lavan, Spencer. *The Ahmadiyyat Movement: A History and Perspective*. Delhi: Manohar Book Service, 1974.
Lewis, Bernard. *The Arabs in History*. 6th ed. New York: Oxford University Press, 1993.
———. "Behind the Rushdie Affair." *American Scholar* 60 (1991): 185–196.

———. *Discovery of Europe*. New York: Norton & Co., 1982.
Lewis, P. "News from the Country: The Women's Lobby." *Al-Mushir* 26, no. 1 (1984): 43–44.
Liben, Paul, and Jessica Sarra. "USCIRF: Annual Report for 2012." Washington: USCIRF, 2012.
———. "USCIRF: Annual Report for 2013." Washington: USCIRF, 2013.
———. "USCIRF: Annual Report for 2014." Washington: USCIRF, 2014.
Lieven, Anatol. *Pakistan: A Hard Country*. 1st ed. New York: Public Affairs, 2011.
Little, William, H. W. Fowler, Jessie Senior Coulson, C. T. Onions, and G. W. S. Friedrichsen. *The Oxford English Dictionary on Historical Principles*. 3rd ed. 2 vols Oxford: Clarendon Press, 1973.
Madani, Mohammad A. *Verdict of Islamic Law on Blasphemy and Apostasy*. Lahore: Idra-e-Islamiat, 1994.
Mairaj, Azam. "The Story of Christian Martyrs." *The Nation*, 6 September 2012.
Malik, Hasnaat. "Coercion Rules in Blasphemy Cases: UN Expert." *Daily Times*, 30 May 2012. http://www.dailytimes.com.pk/default.asp?page=2012%5C05%5C30%5Cstory_30-5-12_pg7_19.
Malik, Iftikhar H. *The History of Pakistan*. London: Greenwood Press, 2008.
Malik, Mehreen Z. "Footprints: Mumtaz Qadri Mosque, Memorial to Our Misdeeds." *Dawn*, 11 May 2014. http://www.dawn.com/news/1105513/footprints-mumtaz-qadri-mosque-memorials-to-our-misdeeds.
———. "The Gojra Murders and the Blasphemy Law." *Pakistaniaat: JPS* 1, no. 2 (2009): 120–124.
Malik, Saleem Nasir. "Muhammad – the Holder of the Seal." *The Review of Religions* 80, no. 5 (1985): 27–30.
Maluka, Zulfikar K. *The Myth of Constitutionalism in Pakistan*. Karachi: Oxford University Press, 1995.
Mandryk, Jason, ed. *Operation World*. Colorado Springs: Biblica, 2010.
Mansingh, Surjit. "Historical Setting." In *Pakistan, a Country Study*, edited by Richard F. Nyrop. 1–64. Washington: US Government Printing, 1984.
Marghīnānī, 'Alī ibn Abī Bak. *The Hedaya: A Commentary on the Islamic Laws*. Translated by Charles Hamilton. 2 vols. Vol. 2. New Delhi: Kitab Bhavan, 1985.
Marshall, I. Howard. *Acts*. TNTC. Edited by Leon Morris. Nottingham: IVP, 1980.
Mason, Herbert. *Al-Hallaj*. Surrey: Curzon Press, 1995.
Masood, Salman. "Pakistanis Rally in Support of Blasphemy Law." *The New York Times*, 1 January 2011.

Massey, James. "Christianity among the Dalits in the Northern India with Special Reference to Punjab." In *Christianity in India: Search for Liberation and Identity*, edited by F. Hrangkhuuma. Dehli: ISPCK, 1998.

Massignon, Louis. *The Passion of Al-Hallaj: Mystic and Martyr of Islam*. Translated by Herbert Mason. Bollingen Series. Abridged ed. Princeton: Princeton University Press, 1994.

Maududi, Abul Ala. *The Punishment of the Apostate according to Islamic Law*. Translated by Silas Husain and Ernest Hahn. Lahore: Islamic Publication, 1994.

———. *The Qadiani Problem*. Lahore: Islamic Publications, 1953. http://www.teachislam.com.

———. *Selected Speeches and Writings of Maulana Maududi*. Translated by S. Zakir Aijaz. Karachi: IIP, 1981.

Mawdudi, Abul Ala. *Tafhim Al-Qur'an: Towards Understanding the Qur'an*. Translated by Zafar I. Ansari. 8 vols. Vol. 2. Leicester: Islamic Foundation, 2001.

———. *Tafhim Al-Qur'an: Towards Understanding the Qur'an*. Translated by Zafar I. Ansari. 8 vols. Vol. 3. Leicester: Islamic Foundation, 2001.

McClintock, Wayne. "A Sociological Profile of the Christian Minority in Pakistan." *Missiology* 20, no. 3 (1992): 343–353.

McDowell, E. W. "The Ancient Nestorian Church and Its Present Influence in Kurdistan." *JRD* 2, no. 1 (1911): 67–88.

McGrath, Alister E. *Suffering of God*. Grand Rapids, MI: Zondervan, 1995.

McMillion, Sana M. "Crucial Reform of Pakistan's Blasphemy Laws Remains a Distant Dream." Norway: NPRC, 2012.

Mehmood, Rabia. "Ahmadis, Seared to the Wall." *Dawn*, 30 July 2014. http://www.dawn.com/news/1122333/ahmadis-seared-to-the-wall.

———. "Pakistan Blasphemy Laws Retake Center Stage." Accessed 22 January 2013. http://www.pbs.org/wnet/need-to-know/security/pakistan-blasphemy-laws-retake-center-stage/7546/.

Mir, Hamid. "Iqbal, Quaid-I-Azam and Ghazi Ilam Din." *Jang*, 11 January 2012. http://e.jang.com.pk/pic.asp?npic=11-01-2012%2FPindi%2Fimages%2F06_07.gif&fb_source=message.

Mirza, Mahan H. "A Delegation of Christians from Najrān Visits the Prophet Muḥammad: Contemporary English Sīrah Literature for a Western Audience." *Islamic Studies* 50, no. 2 (2011): 159–170.

Moghal, Dominic. "Alienation of the Local People: The Future of Religious Minorities in Pakistan." *Al-Mushir* 37, no. 2 (1995): 25–41.

———. *Human Person in Punjabi Society: A Tension between Religion and Culture*. Rawalpindi: CSC, 1997.

Moghal, Dominic, and Jennifer Jivan. *The Christian Church in Pakistan*. Rawalpindi: CSC, 1997.

Mughal, Aftab A. "The Injustice Continues." *Newsline*, August 2010, 52–53.

Mujeeb-ur-Rehman. *Error at the Apex*. Ontario, Canada: Oriental Publishers, 2002. http://www.thepersecution.org.

Munawar, Harris B. "Ahmadis, Leprosy and Plague." *Pakistan Today*, 14 February 2012. http://www.pakistantoday.com.pk.

Munir, Muhammad. *From Jinnah to Zia*. 2nd ed. Lahore: Vanguard Books, 1980.

———. "Precedent in Islamic Law with Special Reference to the Federal Shariat Court and the Legal System in Pakistan." *Islamic Studies* 47, no. 4 (2008): 445–482.

Murray, John. *Principles of Conduct*. London: Tyndale, 1957.

Musharraf, Pervez. *In the Line of Fire: A Memoir*. New York: Free Press, 2006.

Naamani, Israel T. *Israel: A Profile*. Pall Mall Country Profiles. London: Pall Mall Press, 1972.

Nadeem, Amer. "Blasphemy Laws in Pakistan: Make Them Better If Not Change." Accessed 20 January 2013. http://nomanquadri.blogspot.com/2010/12/blasphemy-laws-in-pakistan-make-them.html.

Nadwi, AbulHasan Al, and Zafar Ishaq Ansari. *Qadianism: A Critical Study*. 6th ed. Lucknow: AIRP, 1980.

Nafees, Mohammad. "Blasphemy Laws in Pakistan: A Historical Overview." Islamabad: CRSS, 2013.

Naqvi, Feisal. "Discretion and Valour." *The Express Tribune*, 4 February 2013. http://tribune.com.pk/story/502615/discretion-and-valour/.

Nasir, M. A. Khan. "Comment on Blasphemy by Leading Traditional Scholar." Accessed 3 October 2013.

Nasr, Seyyed V. R. "Islamic Opposition to the Islamic State." *IJMES* 25, no. 2 (1993).

———. *Mawdudi and the Making of Islamic Revivalism*. New York: Oxford University Press, 1996.

———. "The Rise of Sunni Militancy in Pakistan." *MAS* 34, no. 1 (2000): 139–180.

Nazir-Ali, Michael. *From Everywhere to Everywhere: A World View of Christian Witness*. London: Collins, 1990.

———. *Islam: A Christian Perspective*. Carlisle: Paternoster, 1983.

———. "Repeal Pakistan's Blasphemy Law." *The Guardian*, 13 November 2010. http://www.theguardian.com/commentisfree/belief/2010/nov/13/pakistan-blasphemy-law-asia-bibi.

Neill, Stephen. *The Story of the Christian Church in India and Pakistan*. Madras: CLS, 1972.

Nizam, Mubashar. "Government Has No Intention to Amend Blasphemy Law: PM." *Pakistan Times*, 31 January 2011. http://www.pak-times.com/2011/01/31/government-has-no-intention-to-amend-blasphemy-lawpm/.

Noorani, A. G. "Forbidden Pages." *Dawn*, 12 July 2014. http://epaper.dawn.com/DetailNews.php?StoryText=12_07_2014_009_004.

O'Brien, John. *The Construction of Pakistani Christian Identity*. Lahore: Research Society of Pakistan, 2006.

———. *The Unconquered People: The Liberation Journey of an Oppressed Caste*. Karachi: Oxford University Press, 2012.

O'Sullivan, Declan. "The Interpretation of Qur'anic Text to Promote or Negate the Death Penalty for Apostates and Blasphemers." *JQS* 3, no. 2 (2001): 63–93.

"The Objectives Resolution." *Islamic Studies* 48, no. 1 (2009): 89–118.

"Pakistan." In *World Christian Encyclopedia*, edited by David B. Barrett. Nairobi: Oxford University Press, 1982.

Pakistan. "The Code of Criminal Procedure." http://www.oecd.org/site/adboecdanti-corruptioninitiative/39849781.pdf.

———. *The Pakistan Code with Chronological Table and Index*. 3rd ed. Vol. 1 from 1836–1871. Karachi: Government of Pakistan, 1982.

Pakistan Penal Code (Amendment) Ordinance of 1982. March 18 34 Gazette of Pakistan, Extraodinary, Part I, March 18(1982).

"Pakistan Rally Backs Blasphemy Law." Al Jazeera (Qatar), 2011.

"Pakistan: No Action Taken against Geo TV Presenter." *Asian Human Rights Commission*, 18 September 2008. http://www.humanrights.asia/news/ahrc-news/AHRC-STM-244-2008.

"Pakistani Christian Sentenced to Death." *BBC*, 18 July 2002. http://news.bbc.co.uk/1/hi/world/south_asia/2136291.stm.

Parker, Arthur. *Sadhu Sundar Singh: Called of God*. Calcutta: CLS, 1920.

Patel, Aakar. "Pakistan's Blasphemy Law." *The Express Tribune*, 26 August 2012. http://tribune.com.pk/story/426498/pakistans-blasphemy-law/.

Patrick, Jeremy. "The Curious Persistence of Blasphemy." *FJIL* 23, no. 2 (2011): 187–220.

Perkins, Judith. "The 'Self' as Sufferer." *The Harvard Theological Review* 85, no. 3 (1992): 245–272.

———. *The Suffering Self: Pain and Narrative Representation in the Early Christian Era*. London: Routledge, 1995.

"Persecution of Ahmadis in Pakistan." 2010. Accessed 27 February 2013. http://www.thepersecution.org/dl/2010/annual_report2010.pdf.

Peterson, David G. *The Acts of the Apostles*. PNTC. Edited by D. A. Carson. Nottingham: Apollos, 2009.

Pew Research Center. "The Future of the Global Muslim Population: Sunni and Shia Muslims." 27 January 2011. Accessed 11 February 2014. http://www.pewforum.org/2011/01/27/future-of-the-global-muslim-population-sunni-and-shia/.

———. "The World's Muslims: Unity and Diversity – Boundaries of Religious Identity," 9 August 2012. Accessed 22 April 2014. http://www.pewforum.org/2012/08/09/the-worlds-muslims-unity-and-diversity-5-religious-identity/.

Phillips, Godfrey E. *The Outcaste's Hope: Work among the Depressed Classes in India*. London: YPMM, 1912.

Pickett, J. Waskom. *Christian Mass Movements in India*. Lucknow: LPH, 1933.

Pinault, David. "Losers' Vengeance." *America* 194, no. 13 (2006): 8–10.

Pirzada, Syed S., ed. *Foundations of Pakistan: All-India Muslim League Documents, 1906–1947*. Vol. 2, vol. 3. Karachi: NPH, 1970.

A Dictionary of Urdu, Classical Hindi and English. Lahore: Sang-e-Meel Publications, 2003.

Powell, Avril A. "Pillar of a New Faith: Christianity in Late-Nineteenth-Century Punjab from the Perspective of a Convert from Islam." In *Christians and Missionaries in India*, edited by Robert E. Frykenberg. 223–255. London: RoutledgeCurzon, 2003.

Poythress, Vern S. "Why Lying Is Always Wrong: The Uniqueness of Verbal Deceit." *WTJ* 75, no. 1 (2013): 83–95.

Press and Publication Desk. "Plight of Ahmadi Muslims in Pakistan." Tilford: IIP, 2000. http://www.thepersecution.org/archive/pl_blaw.html.

Pressly, Frank Y. "The Punjabi Zabur: Its Composition, Use and Influence." In *Reader in Contextualization for Pakistan*, edited by Freda Carey. 90–100. Lahore: OTS.

Prest, Wilfrid. *William Blackstone: Law and Letters in the Eighteenth Century*. Oxford: Oxford University Press, 2008.

Prud'homme, Jo-Anne. "Policing Belief: The Impact of Blasphemy Laws on Human Rights." Freedom House, 2010.

"Q&A: Pakistan's Controversial Blasphemy Laws." *BBC News – South Asia*, 20 November 2012. http://www.bbc.co.uk/news/world-south-asia-12621225.

Qadir, Manzoor. "No Amendments in Blasphemy Law Despite Recommendations." *Daily Times*, 28 August 2012. http://www.dailytimes.com.pk/default.asp?page=2012%5C08%5C28%5Cstory_28-8-12_pg7_20.

Qadri, Mustafa. "Intolerance Is Sweeping across Pakistan." *The Guardian*, 24 August 2009. http://www.theguardian.com/commentisfree/2009/aug/24/Islamization-intolerance-pakistan-christians.

Qizilbash, Talib. "Interview: I. A. Rehman, Director Hrcp." *Newsline*, July 2010, 24–26.

———. "No Room for the Other." *Newsline*, July 2010, 16–22.
Qureshi, Muhammad Ismail. *Muhammad: The Messenger of God and the Law of Blasphemy in Islam and the West*. Lahore: Nuqoosh Press, 2008.
———. *Nāmūs-Ē-Rasūl Aur Qānūn Tauhin-Ē-Risālat* [in Urdu] [Dignity of the Prophet and the Law of Blasphemy]. Lahore: Al-Faisal Kutab, 1994.
Rahim, I. A. "A Critique of Pakistan's Blasphemy Laws." In *Pakistan between Secularism and Islam*, edited by Tarik Jan. Islamabad: IPS, 1998.
Rahman, Fazlur. "Islam and the Consitutional Problem of Pakistan." *Studia Islamica* 32, no. 2 (1970): 275–287.
Rahman, S. A. *Punishment of Apostasy in Islam*. 2nd ed. Lahore: Institute of Islamic Culture, 1978.
———. *Punishment of Apostasy in Islam*. Lahore: IIC, 1972.
Raja, Mudassir. "Joseph Colony Case." *The Express Tribune*, 12 March 2013. http://tribune.com.pk/story/519502/joseph-colony-case-sc-suspects-land-occupation-as-motive-for-arson/.
Ramadan, Said. *Islamic Law: Its Scope and Equity*. London: Macmillan, 1961.
Rashid, Ahmed. *Descent into Chaos: The US and the Failure of Nation Building in Pakistan, Afghanistan, and Central Asia*. New York: Viking, 2008.
———. "In the Wake of Taseer's Murder." *The Guardian*, 9 January 2011. http://www.theguardian.com/commentisfree/2011/jan/08/ahmed-rashid-taseer-pakistan-precipice.
———. "Pakistan Is in the Grip of Chaos." *BBC News*, 25 January 2014. http://www.bbc.co.uk.
Rashid, Qasim. "Pakistan's Failed Committment." *RJGLB* 11, no. 1 (2011): 1-42.
Ratanlal, Ranchhoddas, Dhirajlal Keshavlal Thakore, D. A. Desai, Moti Lal Jain, and N. R. Madhava Menon. *Ratanlal & Dhirajlal's Law of Crimes: A Commentary on the Indian Penal Code, 1860*. 24th ed. 2 vols. Vol. 1. New Delhi: Bharat Law House, 1997.
Raza, M. Rafi. "The Continuous Process of Re-Writing the Constitution." In *Pakistan in the 80s*, edited by Wolfgang P. Zingel and Stephanie Z. Lallemant, 11–36. Lahore: Vanguard Books, 1985.
Raza, Mansoor. "Blasphemy Laws: A Fact Sheet." *Dawn*, 15 April 2010. http://archives.dawn.com/post?post_year=2010&post_month=4&post_day=15&monthname=April.
Razvi, Murtaza. "Murder Most Foul." *Dawn*, 4 January 2011. http://dawn.com/2011/01/04/murder-most-foul/comment-page-1/.
———. "Salaam Abdus Salam." *Dawn*, 21 November 2011. http://dawn.com/2011/11/21/salaam-abdus-salam/.
"Reforming the Judiciary in Pakistan: Asia Report No. 160." ICG, 2008.

Rehman, I. A. "The Blasphemy Law." *Dawn*, 25 November 2010. http://dawn.com.

———. "Blasphemy Law Revisted." Accessed 8 February 2013. http://archives.dawn.com/archives/19261.

———. "New Threats to Rights." *Dawn*, 9 December 2010. http://dawn.com/2010/12/09/new-threats-to-rights-by-i-a-rehman/.

———. "Recognising the UN." http://archives.dawn.com/archives/19239.

Rooney, John. *Into Deserts: A History of the Catholic Diocese of Lahore (1886–1986)*. Pakistan Christian History Rawalpindi: CSC, 1986.

———. *Shadows in the Dark: A History of Christianity in Pakistan up to the 10th Century*. Pakistan Christian History. Rawalpindi: CSC, 1984.

Sadaqat, Muhammad. "Girl Accused of Blasphemy for a Spelling Error." *The Express Tribune*, 25 September 2011. http://tribune.com.pk/story/259907/girl-accused-of-blasphemy-for-a-spelling-error/.

Saddiq, Nadeem Ahmad. "Enforced Apostasy: Zaheeruddin v. State and the Official Persecution of the Ahmadiyya Community in Pakistan." *Law and Inequility* 14 (1995).

Saeed, Abdullah. *Islamic Thought: An Introduction*. New York: Routledge, 2006.

———. "Rethinking Classical Muslim Law of Apostosy and the Death Penalty," ch. 15. In *Silenced: How Apostosy & Blasphemy Codes Are Choking Freedom Worldwide*, edited by Paul Marshall and Nina Shea. 295–303. Oxford: Oxford University Press, 2011.

Saeed, Abdullah, and Hassan Saeed. *Freedom of Religion, Apostasy and Islam*. Aldershot: Ashgate, 2004.

Sahi, Aoun. "Pakistani Christians Convert to Islam Because of Threats and Intimidations." *AsiaNews.it*, 16 March 2011. http://www.asianews.it/news-en/Pakistani-Christians-convert-to-Islam-because-of-threats-and-intimidations-21041.html.

Salahuddin, Ghazi. "Kingdom of Fear." *Newsline*, November 2012, 35–37.

Salim, Ahmed. "Religious Fundamentalism and Its Impact on Non-Muslims." Rawalpindi: Christian Study Centre, 2008.

Sarfraz, Emanuel. "Another Exodus of Refugees from Pakistan." *The Nation*, 19 March 2014. http://nation.com.pk/national/19-Mar-2014/another-exodus-of-refugees-from-pakistan.

Sarvaria, S. K. *R A Nelson's Indian Penal Code*. 9th ed., 4 vols. Vol. 1. New Delhi: LexisNexis Butterworths, 2003.

———. *R a Nelson's Indian Penal Code*. 9th ed. 4 vols. Vol. 2, New Delhi: LexisNexis Butterworths, 2003.

Sarwar, Beena. "Malicious Intent – Pakistan's Blasphemy Laws " (accessed 20 January 2013) http://newhumanist.org.uk/2887/beena-sarwar.

———. "Sherry Rehman Proposed Bill to Amend Offences Relating to Relgion." http://beenasarwar.wordpress.com/2010/12/16/sherry-rehman%e2%80%99s-proposed-bill-to-amend-offences-relating-to-religion/.

Schacht, Joseph. *An Introduction to Islamic Law*. Oxford: Clarendon Press, 1964.

Sethi, Ali. "Pakistan's Tyranny of Blasphemy." *The New York Times*, 21 May 2014.

Shackle, Samira. "Pakistan's Non-Citizens." *The Australian Financial Review*, September 23, 2011.

Shah, Mansoor Ahmed. "1974: Anti-Ahmadi Hostilities." *The Review of Religions* 103, no. 3 (2008): 53–60.

Shah, Nasim H. *Essays & Addresses on Constitution, Law and Pakistan Legal System*. Lahore: University of the Punjab, 1999.

Shah, Sabir. "Minorities Including Christians at Receiving End in Pakistan." *The News*, 15 March 2013. http://www.thenews.com.pk/Todays-News-2-165422-Minorities-including-Christians-at-receiving-end-in-Pakistan.

Shakir, Naeem. *The Blasphemy Law in Pakistan and Its Impact*. Edited by Mathews G. Chunakara. Hong Kong: CCA, 1998.

———. "Fundamentalism, Enforcement of Shariah and the Law on Blasphemy in Pakistan." *Al-Mushir* 34, no. 4 (1992): 113–129.

Sharaf, Samson S. "Pakistan's Unsung Hero." *The Nation*, 23 February 2013.

Sharma, Arvind. "Dr. B. R. Ambedkar on the Aryan Invasion and the Emergence of the Caste System in India." *JAAR* 73, no. 3 (2005): 843–870.

Shea, Nina. "Testimony before the Tom Lantos Human Rights Commission of the Committee on Foreign Affairs of the Us House of Representatives: Pakistan's Anti-Blasphemy Laws." Hudson Institute. Accessed 6 March 2013. http://www.hudson.org/files/documents/SheaPakistan108.pdf.

Shea, Nina, and Paul Marshall. "Blasphemy in Pakistan." *The Weekly Standard*, 24–31 January 2011. http://www.weeklystandard.com/archive/articles.

Shehzad, Mohammad. "Interview: Allama Tahir Ashrafi on Blasphemy Laws." *Newsline*, April 2013, 47–48.

———. "Murder by Law." *Newsline*, April 2013, 39–45.

Siddiqi, Muhammad I. *The Penal Law of Islam*. Delhi: International Islamic Publications, 1991.

Siddique, Osama, and Zahra Hayat. "Unholy Speech and Holy Laws: Blasphemy Laws in Pakistan – Controversial Origins, Design Defects, and Free Speech Implications." *MJIL* 17, no. 2 (2008): 303–385.

Singh, Jaswant. *Jinnah: India – Partition – Independence*. New York: Oxford University Press, 2010.

Sookhdeo, Patrick. *A People Betrayed: The Impact of Islamization on the Christian Community in Pakistan*. England: CFP, 2002.

Sourdel, D. "The History of the Institution of the Caliphate." In *The Encyclopedia of Islam*, edited by B. Lewis, 937–947. Leiden: E. J. Brill, 1990.

Staff Reporter. "120 Graves of Ahmadis Desecrated." *Dawn*, 4 December 2012.

———. "CII Suggests Amends to Blasphemy Laws." *The Nation*, 19 September 2013. http://www.nation.com.pk.

———. "Civil Society, Media Asked to Help Repeal Blasphemy Law." *Dawn*, 10 December 2009. http://www.dawn.com/news/507763/civil-society-media-asked-to-help-repeal-blasphemy-law.

———. "Clerics to Launch Campaign If Blasphemy Laws Amended." *Daily Times*, 13 December 2010. http://www.dailytimes.com.pk/default.asp?page=2010%5C12%5C13%5Cstory_13-12-10_pg7_13.

———. "Hate Compaign against Ahmadis Reaches New Height " *Daily Times*, 5 May 2012.

———. "International Human Rights Day." *Daily Times*, 10 December 2010. http://www.dailytimes.com.pk/default.asp?page=2010%5C12%5C10%5Cstory_10-12-10_pg7_13.

———. "Khatm-E-Nubuwat Moot Calls for Restrictions on Ahmadis." *Pakistan Today*, 11 September 2012.

———. "Minorities to Be Unsafe If Blasphemy Law Amended: CII." *The News*, 30 May 2013. http://www.thenews.com.pk/Todays-News-13-23178-Minorities-to-be-unsafe-if-blasphemy.

———. "Muneeb Says Blasphemy Accused Should Be Tried by FSC." *Dawn*, 18 March 2013. http://dawn.com/2013/03/18/muneeb-says-blasphemy-accused-should-be-tried-by-fsc/.

———. "Pakistan's Only Christian Minister Assassinated over Blasphemy Row." *The Telegraph*, 2 March 2011. http:www.telegraph.co.uk/news/worldnews/asia/pakistan/8356278/pakistans-only-C.

———. "Plea for Highlighting Christians' Role." *Dawn*, 23 August 2011.

———. "PTA Bans Ahmadi Website." *The Nation*, 6 July 2012, 22.

———. "Religious Minorities in Elections: Equal in Law, Not in Practice." Lahore: HRCP, 2013.

———. "Seperate Electorate Urged for Minorities." *Dawn*, 12 August 2014. http://www.dawn.com/news/1124718/separate-electorate-urged-for-minorities.

———. "Taliban Claim Responsibility for Lahore Attacks." *Daily Times*, 30 May 2010.

———. "Timeline: Accused under the Blasphemy Law." *Dawn*, 19 September 2012. http://dawn.com/2012/09/19/timeline-accused-under-the-blasphemy-law/.

———. "World Report 2014: Pakistan." Human Rights Watch, 2014. http://www.hrw.org/world-report/2014/country-chapters/pakistan.

Stewart, John. *Nestorian Missionary Enterprise: The Story of a Church on Fire.* Edinburgh: T&T Clark, 1928.
Stock, Frederick and Margaret Stock. *People Movements in the Punjab.* Pasadena, CA: William Carey Library, 1975.
Stott, John. *Acts.* BST. Edited by John Stott. Leicester: IVP, 1991.
Streefland, Pieter H. *The Christian Punjabi Sweepers.* Rawalpindi: CSC, 1974.
Streeter, B. H. and A. J. Appasamy. *The Sadhu: A Study in Mysticism & Practical Religion.* Delhi: Mittal Publications, 1987.
Strohmer, Charles. "Taliban Neighbors: Christian Witness in Pakistan." *Christian Century* 126, no. 1 (2009): 10–12.
Sultan, Pervaiz. "History of the Development of the Church of Pakistan." In *The Christian Church in Pakistan: A Vision for the 21st Century*, edited by Dominic Mughal and Jennifer Jivan. 13–26. Rawalpindi: CSC, 1997.
Taha, Mahmoud M. *The Second Message of Islam.* Translated by Abdullahi Ahmed An-Na'im. 1st ed. New York: Syracuse University Press, 1987.
Tahir, Zulqernain. "Qadri Case Judge Sent Abroad." *Dawn*, 24 October 2011. http://www.dawn.com/news/668688/qadri-case-judge-sent-abroad.
Talbi, Mohamed. "Religious Liberty: A Muslim Perspective." In *The New Voices of Islam*, edited by Mehran Kamrava. 105–117. London: I. B. Tauris, 2006.
Talbot, Ian. *Pakistan: A Modern History.* London: Hurst, 1998.
Tanveer, Rana. "Gujranwala Blasphemy Case: Ahmadis Point Fingers at Silent Spectators." *The Express Tribune*, 28 July 2014. http://tribune.com.pk/story/742273/gujranwala-blasphemy-case-ahmadis-point-fingers-at-silent-spectators/.
———. "Lahore High Court Stalls Pardon Moves for Aasia Bibi." *The Express Tribune*, 30 November 2010. http://tribune.com.pk/story/83404/lhc-issues-stay-order-against-aasia-death-sentence/.
Taseer, Shehrbano. "Pakistan Has Abdicated Its Responsibilities." *The Guardian*, 3 March 2011. http://www.theguardian.com/commentisfree/2011/mar/02/salmaan-bhatti-blasphemy-assassination.
Taymiyyah, Ibn. *Al-Sarim Al-Maslul Ala Shatim Al-Rasul* [in Urdu] [The Isssue of Blasphemy against the Prophet]. Translated by Ghulam Ahmed Harari. Lahore: Maktaba Qadusia, 2011.
Team, HRCP. "Report of HRCP Fact-Finding Mission." HRCP, 2009.
Tebbe, James A. "Freedom Movement Revisited." *Al-Mushir* 28, no. 1 (1986): 1–14.
———. "Interviews with Christian Members of National Assembly." *Al-Mushir* 27, no. 2 (1985): 93–103.
Tebbe, Robert F. "Education in Pakistan: A Minority Perspective." *Al-Mushir* 25, no. 3&4 (1983): 183–190.

Telegram. "Political Situation in Punjab (June 17, 1974)." Public Library of US Diplomacy (Plus D). Accessed 10 May 2013). http://www.wikileaks.org/plusd/cables.

———. "Reimposition of Section 144 in Lahore (May 11, 1973)." Public Library of US Diplomacy (Plus D), http://www.wikileaks.org/plusd/cables.

Titus, Murray T. *Islam in India and Pakistan*. Madras: CLS, 1959.

Tosatti, Marco. "Blasphemy: A Law of Blood." *Vatican Insider*, 16 June 2011. http://vaticaninsider.lastampa.it/en/the-vatican/detail/articolo/blasfemia-musulmani-pakistan-corano-129/.

"UK: Statement of His Holiness Mirza Masroor Ahmad Following Attacks on Ahmadis in Gujranwala, Pakistan." *Ahamdiyya Times*, 28 July 2014. http://ahmadiyyatimes.blogspot.com.au/2014/07/uk-statement-of-his-holiness-mirza.html.

Ullah, Barkat. *Saleeb Key Harawal* [in Urdu] [Guardians of the Cross]. 4 vols. Vol. 2, Lahore: NCCP, 2010.

United Nations. "Universal Declaration of Human Rights, 10 December 1948." http:www.un.org/en/documents/udhr/index.stm#a18.

"Use and Abuse of the Blasphemy Laws." Amnesty International, 1994. http://www.unhcr.org.

Voll, John O. "Renewal and Reform in Islamic History: *Tajdid and Islah*." In *Voices of Resurgent Islam*, edited by John L. Esposito. 32–47. New York: Oxford University Press, 1983.

Wahid, Abdurrahman. "God Needs No Defence." In *Silence: How Apostasy and Blasphemy Codes Are Choking Freedom Worldwide*, edited by Paul Marshall and Nina Shea. xvii–xxii. Oxford: Oxford University Press, 2011.

Walbridge, Linda S. *The Christians of Pakistan: The Passion of Bishop John Joseph*. Richmond: RoutledgeCurzon, 2003.

Walker, Martin. "The Revenge of the Shia." *The Wilson Quarterly* 30, no. 4 (2006): 16–20.

Walsh, Declan. "Islamic Scholar Attacks Pakistan's Blasphemy Laws." *The Guardian*, 21 January 2011. http://www.theguardian.com/world/2011/jan/20/islam-ghamidi-pakistan-blasphemy-laws.

Walter, H. A. *The Ahmadiya Movement*. Calcutta: Association Press, 1918.

Waqar, Ali. "Hate Mongering Worries Minorities." *Daily Times*, 25 April 2006. http://www.dailytimes.com.pk/default.asp?page=2006%5C04%5C25%5Cstory_25-4-06_pg7_26.

Waseem, Amir. "Sherry Submits Bill for Amending Blasphemy Laws." *Dawn*, 30 November 2010. http://dawn.com/2010/11/30/sherry-submits-bill-for-amending-blasphemy-laws-2/.

Wasim, Amir. "Shahbaz Bhatti, a Fearless Rights Crusader." *Dawn*. 3 March 2011. http://dawn.com/2011/03/03/shahbaz-bhatti-a-fearless-rights-crusader/.

Watson, Paul. "A Deadly Place for Blasphemy." *Los Angeles Times*, 5 August 2002. http://articles.latimes.com/2002/aug/05/world/fg-blasphemy5/4.

Web Desk. "Joseph Colony Backlash: Enraged Protesters Smash Metro Bus Office." *The Express Tribune*, 10 March 2013. http://tribune.com.pk/story/518645/joseph-town-backlash-enraged-protesters-smash-metro-bus-office/.

———. "Threatened in Pakistan, Rimsha Masih Escapes to Canada." *The Express Tribune*, 30 June 2013. http://tribune.com.pk/story/570264/threatened-in-pakistan-rimsha-masih-escapes-to-canada/.

Weber, Max. *The Sociology of Religion*. Boston: Beacon, 1993.

Webster, John C. B. *The Christian Community and Change in Ninteenth Century India*. Delhi: Macmillan, 1976.

———. "Dalits and Christianity in Colonial Punjab: Cultural Interactions." In *Christians, Cultural Interactions, and India's Religious Traditions*, edited by Judith M. Brown and Robert Eric Frykenberg. London: Routledge Curzon, 2002.

———. "The Legacy of John Charles Heinrich." *IBMR* 37, no. 1 (2013): 34–37.

Webster, Richard. *A Brief History of Blasphemy – Liberalism, Censorship and the Satanic Verses*. Southwold, UK: Orwell Press, 1990.

Wiederhold, Lutz. "Blasphemy against the Prophet Muhammad and His Companions." *JSS* 42, no. 1 (1997): 39–70.

Wilcox, Wayne A. "The Wellsprings of Pakistan." In *Pakistan: The Long View*, edited by Lawrence Ziring, Ralph Braibanti and W. Howard Wriggins. 25–39. Durham: Duke University Press, 1977.

Wolpert, Stanley. *Gandhi's Passion: The Life and Legacy of Mahatma Gandhi*. New York: Oxford University Press, 2001.

———. *Zulfi Bhutto of Pakistan: His Life and Times*. New York: Oxford University Press, 1993.

Wright, N. T. *The Climax of the Covenant*. London: T&T Clark, 1991.

Yancey, Philip. *Where Is God When It Hurts*. Grand Rapids, MI: Zondervan, 1997.

Young, William G. *Patriarch, Shah and Caliph*. Rawalpindi: CSC, 1974.

Youngson, J. W. *The Chuhras*. Bombay: Education Society's Press, 1907.

Yung, Hwa. "The Church in China Today." *Transformation* 21, no. 2 (2004): 126–128.

Yusuf, Huma. "No Room to Breathe." *Dawn*, 9 July 2012. http://www.dawn.com/news/732831/no-room-to-breathe.

Yusufzai, Rahimullah. "Ahmadis Were Target for the Militants since Long." *The News*, 30 May 2010.

Zafar, Emmanuel. *A Concise History of Pakistani Christians*. Lahore: Humsookhan, 2007.

Zafar, S. M. "Constitutional Development." In *Pakistan: Founder's Aspirations and Today's Realities*, edited by Hafeez Malik. Karachi: Oxford University Press, 2001.

Zaheer, Khalid. "The Real Blasphemers." *The Express Tribune*, 2 January 2011. http://tribune.com.pk.

Zaheer, Syed A. "Letter to Quaid-E-Azam by Syed Ali Zaheer July 1944 and Quaid's Reply." In *Pakistan Movement: Historic Documents*, edited by G. Allana. 375–379. Lahore: IBS, 1977.

Zahid, Luavut. "Youhanabad Incident." *Pakistan Today*, 21 March 2015. http://www.pakistantoday.com.pk/2015/03/21/featured/youhanabad-incident/.

Zehra, Nasim. "Time to Repeal the Blasphemy Law." *The Express Tribune*, 16 November 2010. http://tribune.com.pk/story/78368/time-to-repeal-the-blasphemy-law/.

Zia-ul-Haq. *President of Pakistan, General Muhmmad Zia-Ul-Haq, Interviews to Foreign Media*. Vol. 1. Islamabad: Government of Pakistan, 1980.

Zia, Asad. "Revised Curriculum: JI Pushes through Its Agenda on Textbooks in KP." *The Express Tribune*, 27 October 2014. http://tribune.com.pk/story/781717/revised-curriculum-ji-pushes-through-its-agenda-on-textbooks-in-k-p/.

Ziring, Lawrence. "Government and Politics." In *Pakistan, a Country Study*, edited by Richard F. Nyrop. 181–256. Washington: US Government Printing Office, 1984.

———. *Pakistan: At the Crosscurrent of History*. Oxford: Oneworld, 2003.

———. "The Phases of Pakistan's Political History." In *Iqbal, Jinnah, and Pakistan: The Vision and the Reality*, edited by C. M. Naim. 145–176. New York: Syracuse University, 1979.

Zwemer, Samuel M. *The Law of Apostasy in Islam*. New York: Marshall Brothers, 1924.

Court Cases

Abdul Karim v. State, 15 PLD 669 (1963).

Ayub Masih v. State, 54 PLD 1048 (2002).

Begum Nusrat Bhutto v. Chief of Army Staff and Federation of Pakistan, 29 PLD 657 (1977).

Devi Sharan Sharma and Another v. Emperor, AIR 594 (1927).

Emperor v. Raj Pal, AIR 195 (1926).
Fazal-I-Raziq v. Riaz Ahmad, 30 PLD 1082 (1978).
Federation of Pakistan v. Hazoor Bakhsh, 35 PLD 255 (1983).
Federation of Pakistan v. Moulvi Tamizuddin Khan, 7 PLD 240 (1955).
Hazoor Bakhsh v. Federation of Pakistan, 33 PLD 145 (1981).
Ilam Din v. Emperor, AIR 157 (1930).
Jagdesh Kumar v. State, 61 PLD 1 (2009).
Jaswant Rai v. King, 10 P.R (1907).
Kali Charan Sharma v. King-Emperor, AIR 649 (1927).
Khawaja Nazir Ahmad v. State, PLD 724 (1954).
Majibur Rehman and 3 Others v. Federal Government of Pakistan, 37 PLD 8 (1985).
Mirza Mubarak Ahmad v. State, 7 MLD 896 (1989).
Moulvi Tamizuddin Khan v. Federation of Pakistan, 7 PLD 96 (1955).
Muhammad Ashraf v. Niamat Bibi, 33 PLD 520 (1981).
Muhammad Ismail Qureshi v. Pakistan 43 PLD 10 (1991).
Muhammad Khalil v. State, 14 PLD 850 (1962).
Muhammad Mahboob v. State, 54 PLD 587 (2002).
Nasir Ahmad v. State, 26 SCMR 153 (1993).
Okil Ali and Others v. Behari Lal Paul, 14 PLD 487 (1962).
The Punjab Religious Book Society v. State, 12 PLD 629 (1960).
Qaiser Raza v. State, PCr.LJ 758 (1979).
Ranjah Masih v. State, 9 YLR 336 (2007).
Riaz Ahmad and 3 Others v. State, 46 PLD 485 (1994).
Rimsha Masih v. Police Station Ramna, APP (2012).
Saifullah Khan v. State, 54 PLD 140 (2006).
Salamat Masih v. State, 28 PCr.LJ 811 (1995).
Shafiqur Rehman v. State, PCr.LJ 1456 (1976).
State v. Anwar Masih, Session Court Samundri (1998).
State v. Muhammad Arshad Javed, 13 MLD 667 (1993).
State v. Younis Masih, Session Court Lahore (2007).
Zaheeruddin v. State, 26 SCMR 1718 (1993).

(The All) Pakistan Legal Decisions

Act 3 of 1986: Criminal Law (Amendment) Act. 5 October 1986, 38 PLD Central Statutes (1986).
Act 10 of 1991: Enforcement of Shariah Act. 5 June 1991, 43 PLD Central Statutes (1991).

Act 16 of 1991: Criminal Law (Second Amendment) Act. 25 November 1991, 44 PLD Central Statutes (1992).

Act 24 of 1977: Prohibition Act. 17 May 1977, 29 PLD Central Statutes (1977).

Act 28 of 1977: Prevention of Gambling Act. 21 May 1977, 29 PLD Central Statutes (1977).

Act 49 of 1974: Constitution (Second Amendment) Act. 17 September 1974, 26 PLD Central Statutes (1974).

CMLA Order 2 of 1981: Provisional Constitution (Amendment) Order. 7 April 1981, 33 PLD Central Statutes (1981).

Chief Executive's Order 7 of 2002: Conduct of General Elections Order. 27 February 2002, 54 PLD Central Statutes (2002).

Chief Executive's Order 15 of 2002: Conduct of General Elections (Second Amendment) Order. 17 June 2002, 54 PLD Central Statutes (2002).

Ordinance 1 of 1982: Pakistan Penal Code (Amendment) Ordinance. 17 March 1982, 34 PLD Central Statutes (1982).

Ordinance 1 of 1988: Enforcement of Shariah Ordinace. 15 June 1988, 40 PLD Central Statutes (1988).

Ordinance 3 of 1953: Punjab Disturbances (Public Inquiry) Ordinance. 19 June 1953, 5 PLD Central and Provincial Statutes (1953).

Ordinance 6 of 1979: Offences against Property (Enforcement of Hudood) Ordinance. 9 February 1979, 31 PLD (1979).

Ordinance 7 of 1979: Offence of Zina (Enforcement of Hudood) Ordinance. 9 February 1979, 31 PLD Central Statutes (1979).

Ordinance 8 of 1979: Offence of Qazf (Enforcement of Hudood) Ordinance. 9 February 1979, 31 PLD (1979).

Ordinance 8 of 2001: Mental Health Ordinance 20 February 2001, 54 PLD Central Statutes (2002).

Ordinance 9 of 1979: Execution of the Punishment of Whipping (Enforcement of Hudood) Ordinance. 9 February 1979, 31 PLD (1979).

Ordinance 20 of 1984: Anti-Islamic Activities of Quadiani Group, Lahori Group and Ahmadis (Prohibition and Punishment) Ordinance. 26 April 1984, 36 PLD Central Statutes (1984).

Ordinance 28 of 1980: Zakat and Ushr Ordinance. 20 June 1980, 32 PLD Central Statutes (1980).

Ordinance 44 of 1980: Pakistan Penal Code (Second Amendment) Ordinance. 17 September 1980, 33 PLD Central Statutes (1981).

President's Order 5 of 1981: Constitution (Amendment) Order. 13 April 1981, 33 PLD Central Statutes (1981).

President's Order 1 of 1980: Constitution (Amendment) Order. 26 May 1980, 32 PLD Central Statutes (1980).

President's Order 3 of 1979: Constitution (Amendment) Order. 7 February 1979, 31 PLD Central Statutes (1979).

President's Order 5 of 1982: Constitution (Second Amendment) Order. 22 March 1982, 34 PLD Central Statutes (1982).

President's Order 8 of 1982: Amendment of the Constitution (Declaration) Order. 12 April 1982, 34 PLD Central Statutes (1982).

President's Order 10 of 1984: Qanun-E-Shahadat (Law of Evidence). 26 October 1984, 37 PLD Central Statutes (1985).

President's Order 22 of 1978: Shariat Benches of Superior Courts Order. 2 December 1978, 31 PLD Central Statutes (1979).

President's Order No. 7 of 1981: Consitution (Second Amendment) Order. 27 May 1981, 33 PLD Central Statutes (1981).

President's Order No. 12 of 1982: Constitution (Third Amendment) Order 15 August 1982, 34 PLD Central Statutes (1982).

President Order No. 1 of 1961: Central Laws (Adoptation) Order. 21 January 1961, 13 PLD (1961).

President Order No. 4 of 1979: Prohibition (Enforcement of Hadd) Order. 9 February 1979, 31 PLD (1979).

Langham Literature and its imprints are a ministry of Langham Partnership.

Langham Partnership is a global fellowship working in pursuit of the vision God entrusted to its founder John Stott –

> *to facilitate the growth of the church in maturity and Christ-likeness through raising the standards of biblical preaching and teaching.*

Our vision is to see churches in the majority world equipped for mission and growing to maturity in Christ through the ministry of pastors and leaders who believe, teach and live by the Word of God.

Our mission is to strengthen the ministry of the Word of God through:
- nurturing national movements for biblical preaching
- fostering the creation and distribution of evangelical literature
- enhancing evangelical theological education

especially in countries where churches are under-resourced.

Our ministry

Langham Preaching partners with national leaders to nurture indigenous biblical preaching movements for pastors and lay preachers all around the world. With the support of a team of trainers from many countries, a multi-level programme of seminars provides practical training, and is followed by a programme for training local facilitators. Local preachers' groups and national and regional networks ensure continuity and ongoing development, seeking to build vigorous movements committed to Bible exposition.

Langham Literature provides majority world preachers, scholars and seminary libraries with evangelical books and electronic resources through publishing and distribution, grants and discounts. The programme also fosters the creation of indigenous evangelical books in many languages, through writer's grants, strengthening local evangelical publishing houses, and investment in major regional literature projects, such as one volume Bible commentaries like *The Africa Bible Commentary* and *The South Asia Bible Commentary*.

Langham Scholars provides financial support for evangelical doctoral students from the majority world so that, when they return home, they may train pastors and other Christian leaders with sound, biblical and theological teaching. This programme equips those who equip others. Langham Scholars also works in partnership with majority world seminaries in strengthening evangelical theological education. A growing number of Langham Scholars study in high quality doctoral programmes in the majority world itself. As well as teaching the next generation of pastors, graduated Langham Scholars exercise significant influence through their writing and leadership.

To learn more about Langham Partnership and the work we do visit **langham.org**

www.ingramcontent.com/pod-product-compliance
Lightning Source LLC
Chambersburg PA
CBHW052011290426
44112CB00014B/2196